THE STUDIA PHILONICA ANNUAL
Studies in Hellenistic Judaism

Program in Judaic Studies
Brown University
BROWN JUDAIC STUDIES
Edited by

Shaye J. D. Cohen and Calvin Goldscheider

Editor for Studia Philonica: Shaye J. D. Cohen

Number 309
THE STUDIA PHILONICA ANNUAL
Studies in Hellenistic Judaism

edited by
David T. Runia

THE STUDIA PHILONICA ANNUAL
Studies in Hellenistic Judaism

Volume VIII

1996

EDITOR:
David T. Runia

ASSOCIATE EDITORS:
Alan Mendelson
David Winston

BOOK REVIEW EDITOR:
Gregory E. Sterling

Scholars Press
Atlanta, Georgia

THE STUDIA PHILONICA ANNUAL
Studies in Hellenistic Judaism

The financial support of
C. J. de Vogel Foundation, Amsterdam
Leiden University
Coe College, Cedar Rapids, Iowa
University of Notre Dame
is gratefully acknowledged

Copyright © 1996 by Brown University
Copyright © 2007 by the Society of Biblical Literature

All rights reserved. No part of this work may be reproduced or transmitted in any form or by any means, electronic or mechanical, including photocopying and recording, or by means of any information storage or retrieval system, except as may be expressly permitted by the 1976 Copyright Act or in writing from the publisher. Requests for permission should be addressed in writing to the Rights and Permissions Office, Society of Biblical Literature, 825 Houston Mill Road, Atlanta, GA 30329, USA.

ISBN: 0-7885-0311-1 (cloth binding : alk. paper)
ISBN: 978-1-58983-503-0 (paper binding : alk. paper)

Printed in the United States of America
on acid-free paper

THE STUDIA PHILONICA ANNUAL
STUDIES IN HELLENISTIC JUDAISM

EDITORIAL BOARD

EDITOR: David T. Runia, *Universities of Leiden and Utrecht*

ASSOCIATE EDITORS: Alan Mendelson, *McMaster University*
David Winston, *Graduate Theological Union, Berkeley*

BOOK REVIEW EDITOR: Gregory E. Sterling, *University of Notre Dame*

ADVISORY BOARD

David M. Hay, *Coe College, Cedar Rapids* (chair)
Hans Dieter Betz, *University of Chicago*
Peder Borgen, *University of Trondheim*
Jacques Cazeaux, *CNRS, University of Lyon*
Lester Grabbe, *University of Hull*
Robert G. Hamerton-Kelly, *Stanford University*
Richard D. Hecht, *University of California at Santa Barbara*
Annewies van den Hoek, *Harvard Divinity School*
Pieter W. van der Horst, *Utrecht University*
Jean Laporte, *Paris*
Burton L. Mack, *Claremont Graduate School, Claremont*
Birger A. Pearson, *University of California at Santa Barbara*
Robert Radice, *Sacred Heart University, Milan*
Jean Riaud, *Catholic University, Angers*
James R. Royse, *San Francisco*
Dorothy Sly, *University of Windsor*
Abraham Terian, *Sterling College*
Thomas H. Tobin S.J., *Loyola University, Chicago*
Herold D. Weiss, *St. Mary's College, Notre Dame*

The Studia Philonica Annual accepts articles for publication in the area of Hellenistic Judaism, with special emphasis on Philo and his *Umwelt*.

Contributions should be sent to the Editor, Prof. D. T. Runia, Rijnsburgerweg 116, 2333 AE Leiden, The Netherlands. Please send books for review to the Book Review Editor, Prof. G. E. Sterling, Dept. of Theology, University of Notre Dame, Notre Dame, IN 46556, U.S.A.

Contributors are requested to observe the 'Instructions to Contributors' located at the end of the volume. Articles which do not conform to these instructions cannot be accepted for inclusion.

CONTENTS

ARTICLES

J. WHITTAKER, The Terminology of the Rational Soul in the Writings of Philo of Alexandria 1

K. L. GACA, Philo's Principles of Sexual Conduct and their Influence on Christian Platonist Sexual Principles 21

F. STRICKERT, Philo on the Cherubim 40

C. CARLIER, Sur un Titre Latin du *De Vita Contemplativa* 58

SPECIAL SECTION: PHILO AND MYSTICISM

G. E. STERLING, Introductory Notice 73

D. WINSTON, Philo's Mysticism 74

B. E. DALEY S. J., 'Bright Darkness' and Christian Transformation: Gregory of Nyssa on the Dynamics of Mystical Union 83

E. R. WOLFSON, Traces of Philonic Doctrine in Medieval Jewish Mysticism: A Preliminary Note 99

INSTRUMENTA

J. R. ROYSE, Yonge's Collection of Fragments of Philo 107

BIBLIOGRAPHY SECTION

D. T. RUNIA, A. C. GELJON, J. P. MARTÍN, R. RADICE, K.-G. SANDELIN, D. SATRAN, D. ZELLER, Philo of Alexandria: an Annotated Bibliography 1993 122

SUPPLEMENT: Provisional Bibliography 1994–96 143

REVIEW ARTICLE

D. WINSTON, Aristobulus: From Walter to Holladay 155

BOOK REVIEW SECTION

G. DORIVAL et al., *La Bible d'Alexandrie. Les Nombres.* Reviewed by Annewies van den HOEK 167

C. DOGNIEZ, *Bibliography of the Septuagint (1970–1993).* Reviewed by David T. RUNIA 172

J. W. VAN HENTEN and P. W. VAN DER HORST (edd.), *Studies in Early Jewish Epigraphy.* Reviewed by Gregory E. STERLING 174

C. RIEDWEG, *Jüdisch-hellenistische Imitation eines orphischen Hieros Logos.* R. RADICE, *La filosofia di Aristobulo e suoi nessi con il «De mundo» attribuito ad Aristotele.* Reviewed by Nikolaus WALTER 177

D. I. BREWER, *Techniques and Assumptions in Jewish Exegesis before 70 CE.* Reviewed by Francesca CALABI 185

J. COHEN, *The Origins and Evolution of the Moses Nativity Story.* Reviewed by Gregory E. STERLING 187

N. G. COHEN, *Philo Judaeus: His Universe of Discourse.* Reviewed by Ellen BIRNBAUM 189

J. LAPORTE, *Théologie Liturgique de Philon d'Alexandrie et d'Origène.* Reviewed by Michael S. DRISCOLL 196

B. DECHARNEUX, *L'ange, le devin et le prophète: chemins de la parole.* Reviewed by David T. RUNIA 199

D. T. RUNIA, *Philo and the Church Fathers: a Collection of Papers.* Reviewed by John C. CAVADINI 201

R. SGARBI, *Analisi linguistico-filologica dell'interpretazione armena della trattazione greca filoniana intorno all'altare*, *Problemi linguistici e di critica del testo nel* De vita contemplativa *di Filone alla luce della versione armena.* Reviewed by Abraham TERIAN 204

G. J. WARNE, *Hebrew Perspectives on the Human Person in the Hellenistic Era.* Reviewed by David M. HAY 205

T. SELAND, *Establishment Violence in Philo and Luke.* Reviewed by Richard I. PERVO 208

P. BORGEN and S. GIVERSEN (edd.), *The New Testament and Hellenistic Judaism.* Reviewed by David T. RUNIA 210

M. HADAS-LEBEL, *Flavius Josephus.* Reviewed by Gregory E. STERLING 212

NEWS AND NOTES 215

NOTES ON CONTRIBUTORS 219

INSTRUCTIONS TO CONTRIBUTORS 222

THE TERMINOLOGY OF THE RATIONAL SOUL IN THE WRITINGS OF PHILO OF ALEXANDRIA

John Whittaker

Philo identifies from time to time the rational element in the soul as 'intelligence and reason,' employing to this end sometimes the formula νοῦς καὶ λογισμός, at other times the formula νοῦς καὶ λόγος. In the case of the latter couplet, Philo makes mention in *Det.* 83, according to L. Cohn and other modern editors, of 'the highest form of soul, which has been termed intelligence and reason' (τὸ τῆς ψυχῆς ἄριστον εἶδος, ὃ νοῦς καὶ λόγος κέκληται). In the case of the couplet νοῦς καὶ λογισμός Philo speaks in *Praem.* 26, again according to his modern editors, of 'setting aside the irrational part of the soul, and employing only the part that has been called intelligence and reason' (ὅσον μὲν τῆς ψυχῆς ἄλογον μεθιέμενον, τῷ δ' ὃ κέκληται νοῦς καὶ λογισμὸς μόνῳ προσχρώμενον). In each of these texts, according to his modern editors, Philo appears to suggest by means of the identical perfect verb-form κέκληται that the terms νοῦς καὶ λόγος or νοῦς καὶ λογισμός had been commonly utilized by other writers to designate the rational element in the soul. In practice, however, neither of these designations, neither νοῦς καὶ λόγος nor νοῦς καὶ λογισμός, belongs to the usual Middle Platonic repertoire of terms upon which one would expect Philo to have drawn in speaking of the rational element in the human soul.[1]

My own conclusion is that in both these Philonic passages the accepted reading κέκληται is corrupt. That the text should read, in both instances, not κέκληται but κεκλήρωται is made probable, in my opinion certain, by two parallel passages elsewhere in Philo. In *Conf.* 21 Philo states that 'the human soul is tripartite, and that intelligence and reason (νοῦς καὶ λόγος) is said to have possession (κεκληρῶσθαι λέγεται) of one part of it, the spirited element of another, and the appetites of the third' (τριμεροῦς ἡμῶν τῆς ψυχῆς ὑπαρχούσης τὸ μὲν νοῦς καὶ λόγος, τὸ δὲ θυμός, τὸ δὲ ἐπιθυμία κεκληρῶσθαι λέγεται). The combination κεκληρῶσθαι λέγεται makes it apparent that in this instance κεκληρῶσθαι ('has been allotted') could not be a corruption of κεκλῆσθαι ('has been termed'). The second parallel occurs in *Spec.* 1.201 where Philo reports that 'the rational which is the province of intelligence and reason is of the masculine gender,

---

[1] For the appropriate Middle Platonic repertoire see Alcinoos, *Didask.* 5, p. 156.35-37 Whittaker with my note 73 *ad loc.*

whilst the province of sense-perception is feminine' (τὸ μὲν λογικὸν τῆς ἄρρενος γενεᾶς ἐστιν, ὅπερ νοῦς καὶ λογισμὸς κεκλήρωται, τὸ δ' ἄλογον τῆς πρὸς γυναικῶν, ὅπερ ἔλαχεν αἴσθησις). I shall return at the close of this paper to the triad of terms νοῦς/λογισμός/αἴσθησις introduced here by Philo.[2] In the meantime let us note that also in this instance that κεκλήρωται is indeed the correct reading is established beyond question by the parallel verb ἔλαχεν in the second portion of the sentence. Moreover, according to Cohn's *apparatus,* the reading κεκλήρωται does in fact occur at *Det.* 83 in the not unimportant family of manuscripts comprising U [= *Vaticanus gr.* 381] and F [= *Laurentianus,* plut. 85.10]. I propose therefore that the reading κεκλήρωται be introduced into the text of *Det.* 83, which will now read *post emendationem* as follows: ... ἀρχέτυπον μὲν φύσεως λογικῆς ὁ θεός ἐστι, μίμημα δὲ καὶ ἀπεικόνισμα ἄνθρωπος, οὐ τὸ διφυὲς ζῷον, ἀλλὰ τὸ τῆς ψυχῆς ἄριστον εἶδος, ὃ νοῦς καὶ λόγος κεκλήρωται. I likewise recommend that the parallel passage in *Praem.* 26 be emended, for the reasons stated above, to read as follows: ... ὅσον μὲν τῆς ψυχῆς ἄλογον μεθιέμενον, τῷ δ' ὃ κεκλήρωται νοῦς καὶ λογισμὸς μόνῳ προσχρώμενον.[3]

Notice how in all these four Philonic passages the couplets νοῦς καὶ λογισμός and νοῦς καὶ λόγος form grammatical units governing singular verbs, a circumstance suggesting that these couplets have their individual identities and associations. What is the provenance of these couplets, and what did Philo read into them? I shall attempt, if not to answer fully these questions, at least to show that these couplets do indeed have histories and ramifications of their own, in the light of which their presence in the writings of Philo finds its explanation. With this objective in mind we shall now consider, each in their turn, the backgrounds of the Philonic couplets νοῦς καὶ λογισμός and νοῦς καὶ λόγος.

For this purpose we shall first of all set our sights upon Plutarch of Chaeronea. For Plutarch, too, in speaking of the rational soul resorts from time to time to the formula νοῦς καὶ λογισμός. One such instance occurs in his *De exilio.* 'A man needs intelligence and reason (νοῦς καὶ λογισμός),' Plutarch writes, 'in the same way that a skipper needs an anchor in order to moor his ship in any harbour' (*De exil.* 601E-F: μόνον ἔχειν δεῖ πρὸς τούτοις νοῦν καὶ λογισμόν, ὥσπερ ἄγκυραν κυβερνήτην ἵνα

---

[2] See pages 17–20 below.
[3] For instances of the reverse confusion κέκληται›κεκλήρωται in the manuscript tradition of Philo see Cohn's *apparatus criticus* to *Opif.* 57 and *Spec.* 2.113. The *Thesaurus Linguae Graecae* lists 17 instances of κεκλήρωται in Philo, and 15 instances of κέκληται (including *Det.* 83 and *Praem.* 26). Note in particular *Somn.* 1.32 (ποῦ δ' ἐμπεφώλευκεν ὁ νοῦς [αὐτῷ]; ἆρα οἶκον κεκλήρωται; οἱ μὲν γὰρ τὴν ἀκρόπολιν ἐν ἡμῖν ἀνιέρωσαν αὐτῷ κεφαλήν, κτλ.).

παντὶ χρῆσθαι λιμένι προσορμισθεὶς δύνηται).⁴ But such casual occurrences of the formula νοῦς καὶ λογισμός hardly tell us more than that this locution was indeed employed in cultivated parlance, and that Plutarch, like Philo, considered its two components to constitute a unit. More to the point are Plutarch's remarks in his more specifically philosophical treatises. 'The soul,' Plutarch claims in the second of his *Plat. quaest.*, 'when it has partaken of intelligence and reason and harmony, is not merely a work but also a part of god and has come to be not by his agency but both from him as a source and out of his substance' (*Plat. quaest.* 1001C: ἡ δὲ ψυχή, νοῦ μετασχοῦσα καὶ λογισμοῦ καὶ ἁρμονίας, οὐκ ἔργον ἐστὶ τοῦ θεοῦ μόνον ἀλλὰ καὶ μέρος, οὐδὲ ὑπ' αὐτοῦ ἀλλὰ καὶ ἀπ' αὐτοῦ καὶ ἐξ αὐτοῦ γέγονεν).⁵ Plutarch presents here a characteristic Middle Platonic amalgam of obvious Platonic and Stoic elements. In particular the phrase 'partaken of reason and harmony' (μετασχοῦσα καὶ λογισμοῦ καὶ ἁρμονίας) is borrowed *verbatim* by Plutarch from Plato, *Tim.* 36e6f. (λογισμοῦ δὲ μετέχουσα καὶ ἁρμονίας ψυχή), and recurs in a similar context in Plutarch's *De an. procr. in Tim.* 1014E where Plutarch maintains that the irrational soul inherent in matter partook of intelligence and reason and rational harmony in order that it might become the soul of the universe (νοῦ δὲ καὶ λογισμοῦ καὶ ἁρμονίας ἔμφρονος⁶ μετέσχεν, ἵνα κόσμου ψυχὴ γένηται). To provide a context for Plutarch's pronouncements as to

---

⁴ For a further trivial instance see Plutarch, *Amat.* 765D (ὀλίγα δ' εἴρηται μετὰ σπουδῆς αὐτοῖς [sc. poets], εἴτε κατὰ νοῦν καὶ λογισμὸν εἴτε σὺν θεῷ τῆς ἀληθείας ἀψαμένοις).
⁵ For the rationale behind this statement cf. Plutarch, *Plat. quaest.* 1001A (καὶ ποιητοῦ μέν, οἷος οἰκοδόμος ἢ ὑφάντης ἢ λύρας δημιουργὸς ἢ ἀνδριάντος, ἀπήλλακται γενόμενον τὸ ἔργον· ἡ δ' ἀπὸ τοῦ γεννήσαντος ἀρχὴ καὶ δύναμις ἐγκέκραται τῷ τεκνωθέντι καὶ συνέχει τὴν φύσιν, ἀπόσπασμα καὶ μόριον οὖσαν τοῦ τεκνώσαντος) and the literature mentioned in H. Cherniss' notes *ad loc.*, in particular Plutarch, *De sera num. vind.* 559D-E (καὶ τὸ γεννηθὲν οὐχ ὥς τι δημιούργημα πεποιημένον ἀπήλλακται τοῦ γεννήσαντος· ἐξ αὐτοῦ γάρ, οὐχ ὑπ' αὐτοῦ, γέγονεν ὥστ' ἔχει τι καὶ φέρεται τῶν ἐκείνου μέρος ἐν ἑαυτῷ, καὶ κολαζόμενον προσηκόντως καὶ τιμώμενον. ... τῷ μὲν γὰρ ἀνδριάντι τῆς Κασάνδρου φύσεως οὐθὲν ἔνεστιν, κτλ.). See also Basil, *De orig. hominis hom.* 2.14.5-14 Smets-van Esbroeck (ἀλλὰ ἀνδριάντος μὲν πλάσις καὶ γύψου διάπλασις μέχρις ἐπιφανείας τὴν μίμησιν ἔχει ... Θεοῦ δὲ πλάσις οὐ τοιαύτη, ἀλλ' ἔπλασε τὸν ἄνθρωπον καὶ ἡ δημιουργικὴ αὐτοῦ ἐνέργεια πάντα διωργάνωσεν ἐπὶ τὸ βάθος χωρήσασα ἔνδοθεν). For the Stoic position see Epictetus, *Diss.* 1.14.6 (ἀλλ' αἱ ψυχαὶ μὲν οὕτως εἰσὶν ἐνδεδεμέναι καὶ συναφεῖς τῷ θεῷ ἅτε αὐτοῦ μόρια οὖσαι καὶ ἀποσπάσματα, οὐ παντὸς δ' αὐτῶν κινήματος ἅτε οἰκείου καὶ συμφυοῦς ὁ θεὸς αἰσθάνεται;). Plato, *Tim.* 73c7 (τὸ θεῖον σπέρμα) could be cited in justification of the appropriation of the Stoic term ἀπόσπασμα by Middle Platonists such as Plutarch, *Plat. quaest.* 1001A (cited above). The doctrine that human νοῦς is a part of god is attributed already to Diogenes of Apollonia by Theophrastus, *De sens.* 42, p. 511.12-14 Diels = 64 A 19 Diels-Kranz (ὅτι δὲ ὁ ἐντὸς ἀὴρ αἰσθάνεται μικρὸν ὢν μόριον τοῦ θεοῦ, σημεῖον εἶναι, διότι πολλάκις πρὸς ἄλλα τὸν νοῦν ἔχοντες οὔθ' ὁρῶμεν οὔτ' ἀκούομεν). Cf. also Menander, fr. 417 Koerte.
⁶ The term ἔμφρονος is borrowed from *Tim.* 36e4 (θείαν ἀρχὴν ἤρξατο ἀπαύστου καὶ ἔμφρονος βίου).

the origin of intelligence in the world-soul we may note that his statements have their counterpart in the similar claim of Plutarch's fellow Middle Platonist Alcinoos that the First God, by rousing the world-soul and turning it towards himself, is himself the cause of intelligence in the world-soul (*Didask.* 10, p. 165.1-3 Whittaker: ... τὴν ψυχὴν τοῦ κόσμου ἐπεγείρας [sc. ὁ πρῶτος θεός] καὶ εἰς αὑτὸν ἐπιστρέψας, τοῦ νοῦ αὐτῆς αἴτιος ὑπάρχων).[7] In support of their respective positions Plutarch, Alcinoos and others of similar conviction might have cited Plato, *Tim.* 30b4f. (νοῦν μὲν ἐν ψυχῇ, ψυχὴν δ' ἐν σώματι συνιστὰς τὸ πᾶν συνεκταίνετο) as well as Plato's account of the relationship between ἁρμονία and νοῦς in the human soul at *Tim.* 47d2-7.[8]

But why in the above passages has Plutarch thought fit to expand the Platonic couplet 'reason and harmony' (*Tim.* 36e6f.: λογισμοῦ δὲ μετέχουσα καὶ ἁρμονίας) into the triad νοῦς/λογισμός/ἁρμονία? The answer to this question lies, I believe, in Plato's own statements in the *Timaeus* itself and elsewhere. In the *Timaeus* Plato repeatedly emphasizes that the mental activity of the Demiurge is characterized by 'deliberation' (λογισμός) and that such, too, was the mental mode of the world-soul.[9] Similarly at *Laws* 897c4-7 Plato's Athenian Stranger maintains that the whole course and motion of the universe and of everything within it has a nature similar to the movement and revolution and calculations (λογισμοί) of intelligence (νοῦς) and progresses in a related manner (ἡ σύμπασα οὐρανοῦ ὁδὸς ἅμα καὶ φορὰ καὶ τῶν ἐν αὐτῷ ὄντων ἁπάντων νοῦ κινήσει καὶ περιφορᾷ καὶ λογισμοῖς ὁμοίαν φύσιν ἔχει καὶ συγγενῶς ἔρχεται).[10] The mental deliberation posited by Plato was attacked already by Aristotle, and was out of step with Middle Platonic and later notions of the immobility of god and of the absence of progression from his

---

[7] But see also Philo, *Leg.* 2.22 where νοῦς is there from the start!

[8] Cf. also *Tim.* 30b3 (νοῦν δ' αὖ χωρὶς ψυχῆς ἀδύνατον παραγενέσθαι τῳ) and 46d5f. (τῶν γὰρ ὄντων ᾧ νοῦν μόνῳ κτᾶσθαι προσήκει, λεκτέον ψυχήν), *Phileb.* 30c9f. (σοφία μὴν καὶ νοῦς ἄνευ ψυχῆς οὐκ ἄν ποτε γενοίσθην), and *Soph.* 248e7–249a10, as well as the discussion in Proclus, *Plat. theol.* 5.23, pp. 85.4–87.13 Saffrey-Westerink.

[9] Cf. *Tim.* 30b1 (λογισάμενος), *Tim.* 30b4 (διὰ δὴ τὸν λογισμὸν τόνδε), *Tim.* 33a6 (διὰ δὴ τὴν αἰτίαν καὶ τὸν λογισμὸν τόνδε), *Tim.* 34a8–b1 (οὗτος δὴ πᾶς ὄντος ἀεὶ λογισμὸς θεοῦ περὶ τὸν ποτὲ ἐσόμενον θεὸν λογισθείς), *Tim.* 36e6–37a1 (λογισμοῦ δὲ μετέχουσα καὶ ἁρμονίας ψυχή), *Tim.* 72e2f. (ἐκ δὴ λογισμοῦ τοιοῦδε συνίστασθαι μάλιστ' ἂν αὐτὸ πάντων πρέποι). Proclus, *In Tim.* has remarkably little to say regarding the term λογισμός in these texts. According to Hermeias, *In Phaedr.* p. 153.1-3 Couvreur, Plato's references to divine λογισμός are to be understood καταχρηστικῶς as is his mention of θεοῦ διάνοια at *Phaedr.* 247d1.

[10] The context is as follows (*Laws* 897c4-9): εἰ μέν, ὦ θαυμάσιε, φῶμεν, ἡ σύμπασα οὐρανοῦ ὁδὸς ἅμα καὶ φορὰ καὶ τῶν ἐν αὐτῷ ὄντων ἁπάντων νοῦ κινήσει καὶ περιφορᾷ καὶ λογισμοῖς ὁμοίαν φύσιν ἔχει καὶ συγγενῶς ἔρχεται, δῆλον ὡς τὴν ἀρίστην ψυχὴν φατέον ἐπιμελεῖσθαι τοῦ κόσμου παντὸς καὶ ἄγειν αὐτὸν τὴν τοιαύτην ὁδὸν ἐκείνην.

mental life.¹¹ God has no need to deliberate in order to create.¹² Nor does the activity of the world-soul presuppose deliberation. To render Plato's statements in the *Timaeus* more palatable to Middle and Neoplatonic temperaments minor reinterpretation was unavoidable. Thus, Plotinus says of the world-soul that it maintains without effort the beauty and order of the whole because it does not do so by means of deliberation, after the manner of us humans, but by intelligence (*Enn.* 4.8.8.13-16 Henry-Schwyzer: Καὶ ἡ μὲν ὅλη καὶ ὅλου τῷ αὑτῆς μέρει τῷ πρὸς τὸ σῶμα τὸ ὅλον κοσμεῖ ὑπερέχουσα ἀπόνως, ὅτι μηδ᾽ ἐκ λογισμοῦ, ὡς ἡμεῖς, ἀλλὰ νῷ, ὡς ἡ τέχνη οὐ βουλεύεται [= Aristotle, *Phys.* 2.8, 199b28]). Both here and elsewhere Plotinus appears to take sides with the Aristotelians in targeting the language of the *Timaeus*.¹³ Other Platonists were prepared to stand by the written word of Plato. Such was the case with the Middle Platonist Atticus, a dedicated literalist, who attacks Epicurus for claiming that human affairs are controlled not by the reasoning power of god but by some natural cause (Atticus, fr. 3.85 des Places: φύσει τινὶ καὶ οὐ θεοῦ λογισμῷ διοικούμενα). Atticus, it appears, identifies the λογισμός of the Platonic demiurge with the divine providence (πρόνοια) rejected by Epicurus.¹⁴

Without entering into the morass of problems surrounding the use of the term λογισμός in Hellenistic literature in general and in Philo in particular,¹⁵ I would conclude that when Philo designates the rational portion of the soul as νοῦς καὶ λογισμός he is under the influence of the same sort of Platonic considerations as were Plutarch and fellow Platonists in the above-mentioned texts. The association of νοῦς with

---

¹¹ Accepted with relish by Philo; cf., e.g., *Conf.* 134 (... συνόλως τὰς αὐτὰς τοῖς κατὰ μέρος ζῴοις σχέσεις καὶ κινήσεις ἴσχεσθαι καὶ κινεῖσθαι τὸ θεῖον ὑπολαμβάνειν ὑπερωκεάνιος καὶ μετακόσμιος, ὡς ἔπος εἰπεῖν, ἐστὶν ἀσέβεια). For the essentially discursive character of λογισμός cf., e.g., Proclus, *In Tim.* 1.399.18-28 Diehl (ἔστι γὰρ ὁ λογισμὸς τῶν μερῶν διῃρημένη διέξοδος καὶ ἡ διακεκριμένη τῶν πραγμάτων αἰτία. κτλ.).
¹² See the comments of R.T. Wallis, *Neoplatonism* (London 1972) 52f. and 79-81.
¹³ Cf. *Enn.* 6.2.21.32-38 Henry-Schwyzer (ὅλως γὰρ πανταχοῦ, ὅσα ἄν τις ἐκ λογισμοῦ λάβοι ἐν τῇ φύσει ὄντα, ταῦτα εὑρήσει ἐν νῷ ἄνευ λογισμοῦ ὄντα, κτλ.). For similar critique of the calculating Demiurge see D.J. O'Meara, *Plotinus: An Introduction to the Enneads* (Oxford 1993) 70-76 and 124. Plotinus takes the same view of the movements of the stars; cf. *Enn.* 2.2.2.23-27 H.-S. (καὶ Πλάτων δὲ τοῖς ἄστροις οὐ μόνον τὴν μετὰ τοῦ ὅλου σφαιρικὴν κίνησιν, ἀλλὰ καὶ ἑκάστῳ δίδωσι τὴν περὶ τὸ κέντρον αὐτῶν· ἕκαστον γάρ, οὗ ἐστι, περιειληφὸς τὸν θεὸν ἀγάλλεται οὐ λογισμῷ ἀλλὰ φυσικαῖς ἀνάγκαις). For the couplet λογισμός/νοῦς see also Plotinus, *Enn.* 1.4.4.6-8 H.-S. (ὅτι μὲν οὖν ἔχει τελείαν ζωὴν ἄνθρωπος οὐ τὴν αἰσθητικὴν μόνον ἔχων, ἀλλὰ καὶ λογισμὸν καὶ νοῦν ἀληθινόν, δῆλον καὶ ἐξ ἄλλων), *Enn.* 4.3.19.24 H.-S. (λογισμὸς καὶ νοῦς).
¹⁴ For the role assigned to hypostatized λογισμός in the cosmology of Simon the Mage see Hippolytus, *Ref.* 4.51.9; 6.12-13; 6.20.4; 10.12.2.
¹⁵ Cf. the remarks of A.-J. Festugière, *Hermès Trismégiste*, t. 3 *Fragments extraits de Stobée I-XXII* (Paris 1954) pp. LXXVI, XCIX n. 1, and pp. CI-CIII.

λογισμός in the context of the interpretation of *Tim.* 36e6f. would have been facilitated by Plato's attribution to the sphere of the universe of the movement which most properly belongs to intelligence and reason (*Tim.* 34a1-3: κίνησιν γὰρ ἀπένειμεν αὐτῷ τὴν τοῦ σώματος οἰκείαν, τῶν ἑπτὰ τὴν περὶ νοῦν καὶ φρόνησιν μάλιστα οὖσαν), as well as by the Athenian Stranger's declaration at *Laws* 897c4-7, to which we have already referred, regarding the movement of the universe in accordance with the motion, revolution and calculations of intelligence (νοῦ κινήσει καὶ περιφορᾷ καὶ λογισμοῖς). Moreover, at a later stage in the *Timaeus* Plato describes the appetitive element in the human soul as having no share in belief, reason and intelligence (*Tim.* 77b5: ᾧ δόξης μὲν λογισμοῦ τε καὶ νοῦ μέτεστιν τὸ μηδέν)[16] thereby implying, without actually saying so, that the rational portion of the soul possesses λογισμός τε καὶ νοῦς, the couplet used by Philo and Plutarch but in reverse order. Similarly at *Rep.* 586d1f. (πλησμονὴν τιμῆς τε καὶ νίκης καὶ θυμοῦ διώκων [sc. he who surrenders himself to the spirited element] ἄνευ λογισμοῦ τε καὶ νοῦ)[17] Plato permits the conclusion that also the spirited element of the soul lacks λογισμός τε καὶ νοῦς.[18] Aristotle maintains a similar stance in a well-known passage of his *Politics,* phrased in what could be considered Platonic terminology. 'Just as the body comes into being before the soul,' says Aristotle, 'so also is the irrational prior to the rational. This is shown by the fact that whilst passion and will and also desire are found in children right from birth, reason and intelligence (ὁ λογισμὸς καὶ ὁ νοῦς) come into their possession as they grow older'(*Pol.* 1334b22-25: θυμὸς γὰρ καὶ βούλησις, ἔτι δὲ ἐπιθυμία, καὶ γενομένοις εὐθὺς ὑπάρχει τοῖς παιδίοις, ὁ δὲ λογισμὸς καὶ ὁ νοῦς προιοῦσιν ἐγγίγνεσθαι πέφυκεν).

So much, then, for the Platonic background of the couplet νοῦς καὶ λογισμός as we have seen it employed by Philo with reference to the rational element in the soul. What conception Philo entertained of the relationship between the two terms νοῦς and λογισμός is a question to which there may be no satisfactory answer. I say no more than that in some Philonic instances of the couplet λογισμός is clearly subordinate to, or a faculty of νοῦς,[19] whilst in other contexts Philo gives the impression

---

[16] Cf. *Rep.* 431c5f. (αἱ δὴ [sc. moderate desires, pleasures and griefs] μετὰ νοῦ τε καὶ δόξης ὀρθῆς λογισμῷ ἄγονται). For the opposition ἐπιθυμίαι/λογισμός see also *Rep.* 440a8–b4.
[17] Cf. also *Rep.* 441a7–b1 where θυμός is opposed to λογισμός. See further below.
[18] Cf. *Rep.* 524b4 (λογισμόν τε καὶ νόησιν ψυχὴ παρακαλοῦσα).
[19] Cf. *Leg.* 1.42 (ὁ μὲν οὖν κατὰ τὴν εἰκόνα γεγονὼς καὶ τὴν ἰδέαν νοῦς πνεύματος ἂν λέγοιτο κεκοινωνηκέναι - ῥώμην γὰρ ἔχει ὁ λογισμὸς αὐτοῦ), *Mut.* 21 ("καὶ σύ", ὁ ἀγαλματοφορούμενος νοῦς, "καὶ οἱ θεράποντές σου [Exod. 9:30]," οἱ κατὰ μέρος δορυφοροῦντες λογισμοί), *Abr.* 88.

of exploiting the two terms interchangeably.[20] Other examples of this sort of terminological vacillation are not difficult to find. The Stoic Balbus in Book 2 of Cicero's *De natura deorum* speaks of 'that part of us which surpasses all others, I mean our reason, or, if you like to employ several terms to denote it, our intelligence, deliberation, thought, wisdom' (*ND* 2.7.18: *Illud autem quod vincit haec omnia, rationem dico et, si placet pluribus verbis, mentem consilium cogitationem prudentiam, ubi invenimus, unde sustulimus?*). A weakness for accumulations of this sort seems to have been a Stoic failing.[21] Galen is fond of emphasizing, not without signs of impatience, that it makes no difference whether you say διάνοια, νοῦς or λογισμός as long as the meaning is clear.[22]

In their exploitation of the term λογισμός Philo and other writers were surely influenced by Plato's use of that term in situations in which it could be construed by exegetes as referring to the rational element in the tripartite soul.[23] The term λογισμός was certainly so utilized by later writers, both within and outside the Platonic tradition, such as *Timaeus Locrus*,[24] Alcinoos,[25] Galen (for whom λογισμός is the normal designation of the rational faculty),[26] the Aristotelian commentator

---

[20] Cf. *Sacr.* 105 (ἀτίθασον μὲν [sc. τὸ αἰσθήσεων γένος] ὅταν ἀφηνιάσαν ὥσπερ βουκόλου τοῦ νοῦ φέρηται πρὸς τὰ ἐκτὸς ἀλόγως αἰσθητά, ἥμερον δὲ ὅταν ὑπείξαν πειθηνίως τῷ τοῦ συγκρίματος ἡγεμόνι λογισμῷ κυβερνᾶταί τε καὶ ἡνιοχῆται πρὸς αὐτοῦ), *Det.* 85, *Her.* 263 and 265, *Mos.* 2. 6, *QG* 2, fr. 59 (περὶ δὲ σάρκα ἡ αἴσθησις καὶ τὸ πάθος, οὐχ ὁ νοῦς καὶ ὁ λογισμός).
[21] Cf. my 'Platonic philosophy in the early centuries of the Empire' in W. Haase (ed.), *ANRW* II. 36.1 (Berlin–New York 1987) 92.
[22] Cf. *De plac. Hipp. et Plat.* pp. 542.30–544.1 De Lacy (καλεῖν δ' ἔξεστί σοι, ὡς πολλάκις εἴρηταί μοι πολλαχόθι, καὶ διάνοιαν καὶ νοῦν καὶ λογισμὸν ἢ ὅπως ἄν τις ἐθέλῃ φυλάττων τὴν ἔννοιαν ὡς Ἱπποκράτης βούλεται) with De Lacy's Commentary *ad loc.* (p. 698). Cf., e.g., Aspasius, *In Eth. Nic.* p. 37.5f. Heylbut (διάνοια γὰρ καὶ νοῦς καλεῖται τὸ λόγον ἔχον τῆς ψυχῆς).
[23] Cf., e.g., *Phaed.* 84a8 (ἑπομένη τῷ λογισμῷ καὶ ἀεὶ ἐν τούτῳ οὖσα [sc. ἡ ψυχή]), *Rep.* 496d5f., *Rep.* 603a4f. (τὸ μέτρῳ γε καὶ λογισμῷ πιστεῦον βέλτιστον ἂν εἴη τῆς ψυχῆς), *Rep.* 604d5-10, *Soph.* 248a10f., *Phil.* 21c4-8 and 52b2f.
[24] *Timaeus Locrus* 224.3-6 Marg (... τὸ μὲν λογικόν [codd. ἄλογον] τῷ λογισμῷ πείθεσθαι, τῷ δ' ἀλόγῳ θυμὸν μὲν πρᾶον εἶμεν, ἐπιθυμίαν δὲ ἐν ἀρεμήσει, ὡς μὴ δίχα λόγω κινέεσθαι, μηδὲ μὰν ἀτρεμίζειν τῷ νῷ ἐκκαλεομένῳ ἢ ποτὶ ἔργα ἢ ποτὶ ἀπολαυσίας). The author appears to treat νοῦς and λογισμός as equivalent.
[25] Cf. *Didask.* 7, p. 162.1f. Wh. (... ἐκεῖνα ἅ ἐστιν ἰδεῖν μόνῳ τῷ τῆς ψυχῆς λογισμῷ), *ibid.* 24, p. 177.4-9 Wh. and in particular *ibid.* 29, pp. 182.43–183.3 Wh. With the first of these texts compare [Ps.Arist.], *De mundo* 399a30f. (ὁ πάντων ἡγεμών τε καὶ γενέτωρ, ἀόρατος ὢν ἄλλῳ πλὴν λογισμῷ).
[26] Cf., e.g., *De plac. Hipp. et Plat.* p. 176.19-21 De L. (Πλάτωνος μὲν γὰρ λέγοντος οὐκ ἐκ ταὐτοῦ μέρους ὁρμᾶσθαι λογισμόν τε καὶ θυμὸν καὶ ἐπιθυμίαν, Ζήνωνος δὲ ἐν καρδίᾳ καθιδρύοντος ἅπαντα, κτλ.), *ibid.* p. 214.12f. De L. (λογισμῷ μὲν ἥκιστα χρῶνται [sc. οἱ παῖδες], θυμοῖς δὲ καὶ ἐπιθυμίαις ἰσχυροτάταις, ὥσπερ τὰ θηρία, δουλεύουσι), *ibid.* pp. 244.35–246.12 De L., etc.

Aspasius,[27] Aristides Quintilianus,[28] and Clement of Alexandria,[29] as well as Philo of Alexandria by whom the term is frequently so employed.[30] Moreover, since the term λογισμός was also utilized by Stoics to designate the ἡγεμονικόν,[31] it represents a convenient meeting-ground of Platonists and Stoics. I would go so far as to affirm that the Middle Platonic use of the term is, above all, the consequence of Stoic influence. Also to be taken into account is a long-standing pre-Platonic Greek tradition that identified as λογισμός the faculty of the human soul that controlled, or failed to control, the emotions and passions. Already Thucydides represents λογισμός in conflict with θυμός.[32] The theme became a regular feature of Stoic moralizing literature and spread out thence in all directions,[33] including that of Philo.[34]

I turn now to Philo's alternative designation of the rational element in the soul by means of the couplet νοῦς καὶ λόγος conceived as a unit. 'The highest form of soul,' we have seen Philo say (Det. 83),'is the province of intelligence and reason' (τὸ τῆς ψυχῆς ἄριστον εἶδος, ὃ νοῦς καὶ λόγος κεκλήρωται). The terms νοῦς and λόγος are, of course, loaded with an immensity of ramifications which it would take a lifetime to explore.

---

[27] According to Aspasius, In Eth. Nic. p. 66.28-32 H. the parts of the soul are λογισμός and τὸ θυμοειδὲς καὶ ἐπιθυμητικόν. Cf. ibid. 66.7f. H. (κατὰ γὰρ ἐπιθυμίαν πράττουσι [sc. οἱ παῖδες] καὶ διὰ θυμόν, οὐ κατὰ λογισμόν [cf. Aristotle, Pol. 1334b22-25, quoted page 6 above]).

[28] De mus. 3.8, p. 106.30-32 Winnington-Ingram (εἰ δέ γε καὶ τὰς ἐν ψυχῇ μεσότητας θεωρεῖν ἐθέλοις, εὑρήσεις λογισμοῦ καὶ ἐπιθυμίας μέσην τὴν κατὰ τὸ θυμικὸν ἀμφοῖν ἀναλογίαν).

[29] Str. 3.10.68.5 (εἶεν δ' ἂν καὶ ἄλλως οἱ μὲν τρεῖς θυμός τε καὶ ἐπιθυμία καὶ λογισμός, σάρξ δὲ καὶ ψυχὴ καὶ πνεῦμα κατ' ἄλλον λόγον).

[30] Cf. the many examples in H. Leisegang, Indices ad Philonis Alexandrini opera, pars 2 (Berlin 1930) 486-490.

[31] Cf. Aetius, Plac. 4.21.1 [Doxogr. 410.25-29] = SVF 2.836 (οἱ Στωικοί φασιν εἶναι τῆς ψυχῆς ἀνώτατον μέρος τὸ ἡγεμονικόν, τὸ ποιοῦν τὰς φαντασίας καὶ συγκαταθέσεις καὶ αἰσθήσεις καὶ ὁρμάς· καὶ τοῦτο λογισμὸν καλοῦσιν), and SVF 4 s.v. λογισμός. For νοῦς similarly employed see SVF 4 s.v.

[32] Thucydides, Hist. 2.11.7 (καὶ οἱ λογισμῷ ἐλάχιστα χρώμενοι θυμῷ πλεῖστα ἐς ἔργον καθίστανται), quoted by Galen, De plac. Hipp. et Plat. p. 358.8f. De L.

[33] For λογισμός doing combat with θυμός see Cleanthes ap. Galen, De plac. Hipp. et Plat. p. 332.20-31 De Lacy = SVF 1.570 = Posidonius, fr. 166 E.-K. = fr. 417 Theiler; Galen, ibid. pp. 184.11–190.15 passim; Alcinoos, Didask. 24, p. 177.4f. Wh. (ὁρᾶται δέ γε ἐπὶ μὲν τῆς Μηδείας ὁ θυμὸς λογισμῷ μαχόμενος); Basil, De orig. hominis hom. 1.19.20-26 Smets-van Esbroeck. For λογισμός in combat with ἐπιθυμία see Plutarch, De virt. mor. 447C (τὸν ἀντιταττόμενον τῇ ἐπιθυμίᾳ λογισμόν); Alcinoos, Didask. 24, p. 177.8f. Wh. (ἐπιθυμία λογισμῷ μαχομένη); Galen, ibid. p. 332.10-15, ibid. p. 350.13-352.16 De L.; Corpus Herm., fr. 17.2 with Festugière's note ad loc. and his Introduction pp. XCIX-CIII.

[34] Cf. Spec. 3.92 (ἐκ ταὐτομάτου διακινηθέντες καὶ θυμῷ δυνατωτέρῳ χρησάμενοι λογισμοῦ) and ibid. 4.10 (θυμὸν λογισμοῦ προτιμήσας καὶ τοὺς νόμους τῆς ἰδίας ἐπιθυμίας ἐν ὑστέρῳ θείς).

All that presently concerns us is the use of the couplet νοῦς καὶ λόγος to designate the rational element of the soul. For this purpose I take as my starting-point the claim of Alcinoos that the only elements in our make-up that can achieve likeness with god are intelligence and reason (*Didask.* 27, p. 180. 5-7 Whit.: μόνα δὲ τῶν ἐν ἡμῖν ἐφικνεῖσθαι αὐτοῦ τῆς ὁμοιότητος νοῦν καὶ λόγον). Only the rational soul, identified as νοῦς καὶ λόγος, can achieve ὁμοίωσις θεῷ, a distinction it obtains by separating itself from the lower, irrational parts of the soul, which, according to Plato, *Tim.* 69c5–e4, are inextricably tied to the body, and therefore mortal.[35] There is a noteworthy counterpart to Alcinoos' statement of ὁμοίωσις θεῷ in Gregory of Nyssa's equation of divinity (ἡ θειότης) with νοῦς καὶ λόγος in his disquisition *On the creation of man.* 'The λόγος καὶ διάνοια that we find in ourselves,' Gregory claims, 'are simply an imitation of the veritable νοῦς καὶ λόγος which is god himself' (*De hom. opif.* 5, PG 44.137B-C: νοῦς καὶ λόγος ἡ θειότης ἐστίν ... ὁρᾷς ἐν σεαυτῷ καὶ τὸν λόγον καὶ διάνοιαν, μίμημα τοῦ ὄντως νοῦ τε καὶ λόγου).[36]

The doctrine of ὁμοίωσις θεῷ may have been commonly formulated in similar terms already in Philo's day. A comparable statement of the perfectibility of the rational soul, consisting in the realisation of *perfecta mens* [= νοῦς], *id est absoluta ratio* [= λόγος/λογισμός], occurs in Cicero, *Tusc.* 5.13.38f. (*Humanus autem animus decerptus ex mente divina cum alio nullo nisi cum ipso deo, si hoc fas est dictu, comparari potest. Hic igitur, si est excultus et si eius acies ita curata est ut ne caecaretur erroribus, fit perfecta mens, id est absoluta ratio, quod est idem virtus*). The same goal is expressed in Aristotle's *Protrepticus* fr. 28 Düring [= Iamblichus, *Protrept.* p. 35.14-18 Pistelli] (αἰσθήσεως μὲν οὖν καὶ νοῦ ἀφαιρεθεὶς ἄνθρωπος φυτῷ γίγνεται παραπλήσιος, νοῦ δὲ μόνου ἀφῃρημένος ἐκθηριοῦται, ἀλογίας δ' ἀφαιρεθεὶς μένων δ' ἐν τῷ νῷ ὁμοιοῦται θεῷ), and reappears, without theological overtones, in an influential passage of Aristotle's *Politics*. 'Reason and intelligence (ὁ λόγος καὶ ὁ νοῦς),' says Aristotle, 'are the end to which our nature directs itself. It is to these that our birth and the training of our habits must tend' (*Pol.* 1334b12-17: φανερὸν δὴ τοῦτό γε πρῶτον μέν, καθάπερ ἐν τοῖς ἄλλοις, ὡς ἡ γένεσις ἀπ' ἀρχῆς ἐστι, καὶ τὸ τέλος ἀπό τινος ἀρχῆς ‹ἀρχὴ›

---

[35] The *Timaeus* passage is echoed by Philo, *Fug.* 69, as noted by D.T. Runia, *Philo of Alexandria and the Timaeus of Plato* (Leiden 1986) 244. Cf. Maximus of Tyre, *Diss.* 7.42-45 Trapp (δῆμος χρῆμα ὀξὺ ἐν ὀργαῖς, ἰσχυρὸν ἐν ἐπιθυμίαις, ὑγρὸν ἐν ἡδοναῖς, δύσθυμον ἐν λύπαις, χαλεπὸν ἐν θυμοῖς· ταῦτα [vel ταῦτα] καὶ σώματος πάθη, καὶ γὰρ ἐπιθυμητικὸν καὶ ἰτητικὸν καὶ φιλήδονον καὶ ὁρμητικόν); Galen, *De plac. Hipp. et Plat.* p. 600.4-18 De Lacy with De Lacy's commentary (p. 707).

[36] This text is discussed by H. Merki, ʽΟΜΟΙΩΣΙΣ ΘΕΩΙ: *Von der platonischen Angleichung an Gott zur Gottähnlichkeit bei Gregor von Nyssa* (Freiburg 1952) 144f., but without mention of the couplet νοῦς καὶ λόγος.

ἄλλου τέλους, ὁ δὲ λόγος ἡμῖν καὶ ὁ νοῦς τῆς φύσεως τέλος, ὥστε πρὸς τούτους τὴν γένεσιν καὶ τὴν τῶν ἐθῶν δεῖ παρασκευάζειν μελέτην). According to Plotinus, soul is by nature disposed toward intelligence and reason, which in their turn shape the soul and bring it to a better form (*Enn.* 2.4.3.4f. H.-S.: ψυχὴ πρὸς νοῦν καὶ λόγον πέφυκε μορφουμένη παρὰ τούτων καὶ εἰς εἶδος βέλτιον ἀγομένη). The same trend of thought regarding the perfectibility of the rational element in the human soul is apparent in Philo, *Praem.* 62 (φύσει γε μὴν πάντες οἱ ἄνθρωποι, πρὶν τελειωθῆναι τὸν ἐν αὐτοῖς λόγον, κείμεθα ἐν μεθορίῳ κακίας καὶ ἀρετῆς πρὸς μηδέτερά πω ταλαντεύοντες· ἐπειδὰν δὲ πτερυξάμενος ὁ νοῦς ὅλῃ τῇ ψυχῇ διὰ πάντων αὐτῆς τῶν μερῶν φαντασιωθῇ τὸ ἀγαθόν, ἄφετος πρὸς αὐτὸ καὶ πτηνὸς ὁρμᾷ τὸ συγγεγεννημένον ἀδελφὸν κακὸν ὀπίσω καταλιπών) and in other Philonic texts.[37]

According to Calcidius, *Comm. in Tim.* p. 210.3f. Waszink, the perfection of reason and intelligence pertains to god and man alone (*rationis autem perfectio et intellectus propria dei et hominis tantum*).[38] But, Calcidius adds, in the case of mortals the purity of reason and intelligence is polluted by the presence of anger and passion, the lower parts of the soul (*Comm. in Tim.* p. 180.13-15 Wasz.: ... *in his animis, quae vivificant morti obnoxia genera animalium, non pura ratio intellectusve sincerus sed aliquantum tam iracundiae quam libidinis invenitur*). This contamination of the rational faculties in man, Calcidius explains at some length,[39] is a consequence of the inferior mixture employed by the Platonic Demiurge in the composition of the human soul (*Tim.* 41d4-7: καὶ πάλιν ἐπὶ τὸν πρότερον κρατῆρα, ἐν ᾧ τὴν τοῦ παντὸς ψυχὴν κεραννὺς ἔμισγεν, τὰ τῶν πρόσθεν ὑπόλοιπα κατεχεῖτο μίσγων τρόπον μέν τινα τὸν αὐτόν, ἀκήρατα δὲ οὐκέτι κατὰ ταὐτὰ ὡσαύτως, ἀλλὰ δεύτερα καὶ τρίτα).

With Calcidius' exposition of *Tim.* 41d4-7 we may compare Philo's claim that although the human mind may indeed be qualified as divine (θεῖος or θεοειδής),[40] it falls nonetheless far short of equality with god.

---

[37] Cf., e.g., *Opif.* 103 (τῇ δὲ ἑβδόμῃ [sc. ἑπταετίᾳ] βελτίωσις ἀμφοῖν καὶ συναύξησις νοῦ καὶ λόγου· ὀγδόη δὲ ἡ ἐν ἑκατέρῳ τελείωσις), *De sacr.* 15f. and *Her.* 294-299.
[38] The context reads (*Comm. in Tim.* pp. 209.20–210.4 Waszink) *Cupiditas porro atque iracundia vel agrestium vel mansuetorum appetitus inrationabilis est, hominis vero, cuius est proprium rationi mentem applicare, rationabilis. Ratiocinandi tamen atque intellegendi sciendique verum appetitus proprius est hominis, qui a cupiditate atque iracundia plurimum distat; illa quippe etiam in mutis animalibus, et multo quidem acriora, cernuntur, rationis autem perfectio et intellectus propria dei et hominis tantum.* For god as the perfect νοῦς cf. [Justin], *De res.*, PG 6.1573B (ἔστι δὲ ἀλήθεια ὁ θεός, ὁ πατὴρ τῶν ὅλων, ὅς ἐστι νοῦς τέλειος. οὗ γενόμενος υἱὸς ὁ λόγος ἦλθεν εἰς ἡμᾶς, κτλ.).
[39] Cf. Calcidius, *ibid.* pp. 180.3–181.5 Wasz.
[40] Cf. *Det.* 84f., *Deus.* 105, *Decal.* 134, *Spec.* 3.207 (ψυχὴ γὰρ ἀνθρώπου τίμιον, ἧς μετανισταμένης καὶ μετοικιζομένης τὰ ἀπολειφθησόμενα πάντα μιαίνεται στερόμενα θείας εἰκόνος, ἐπειδὴ θεοειδὴς ὁ ἀνθρώπινος νοῦς πρὸς ἀρχέτυπον ἰδέαν, τὸν ἀνωτάτω λόγον, τυπωθείς). For the similarity of man and god see Runia, *op. cit.* (n. 35) 332-334, and F. Trisoglio,

More precisely put, man's intellectual capacity (i.e., the rational element in his soul) is, according to Philo, at thrice remove from the mind of god (*Her.* 231: τὸν καθ' ἕκαστον ἡμῶν νοῦν, ὃς δὴ κυρίως καὶ πρὸς ἀλήθειαν ἄνθρωπός ἐστι, τρίτον εἶναι τύπον ἀπὸ τοῦ πεποιηκότος).[41] The rational soul stands thrice removed from the creator, according to Philo, since it is no more than the copy of a copy. Philo was no doubt influenced here by Plato's attack on art, on similar grounds, in *Rep.* 597b2-15. But Philo's claim that the human soul is thrice removed from god is also, like that of Calcidius, in keeping with *Tim.* 41d6f. where human souls are fabricated from much the same mixture as the world-soul but in a second or third degree (ἀκήρατα[42] δὲ οὐκέτι κατὰ ταὐτὰ ὡσαύτως, ἀλλὰ δεύτερα καὶ τρίτα). Philo must have been thoroughly acquainted with this well-known text, to which Platonists made frequent appeal.[43] It is unlikely that Philo's reflections upon the relationship between god and soul could have remained uninfluenced by interpretations, current in his day, of the generation of the soul in the *Timaeus*.

That the application to god of the couplet νοῦς καὶ λόγος was already a Stoic practice is obvious from Cicero's statement that some philosophers, namely the Stoics, believed, in contrast to the atheists, that the universe is regulated and administered by the intelligence and reason of the gods (*ND* 1.2.4: *Sunt autem alii philosophi* [sc. Stoics], *et hi quidem magni atque nobiles, qui deorum mente atque ratione omnem mundum administrari et regi censeant*).[44] Here the couplet *mens et ratio* manifestly corresponds to νοῦς καὶ λόγος. Many parallels might be cited.[45] An important Stoic

---

'Filone Alessandrino e l'esegesi cristiana' in W. Haase (ed.), *ANRW* II. 21.1 (Berlin/New York 1984) 609f.
[41] See also *QG* 2.62 with the comments of Runia, *op. cit.* 343.
[42] That Philo had paid due attention to this text is suggested by the occurrence of the term ἀκήρατος in discussions of superhuman souls at *Gig.* 8 (καὶ γὰρ οὗτοι [sc. οἱ ἀστέρες] ψυχαὶ ὅλαι δι' ὅλων ἀκήρατοί τε καὶ θεῖαι) and *Conf.* 177 (κακίας δὲ ἀμέτοχοι μέν εἰσιν αὗται [sc. αἱ ψυχαὶ ἀσώματοι], τὸν ἀκήρατον καὶ εὐδαίμονα κλῆρον ἐξ ἀρχῆς λαχοῦσαι). Cf. similarly Plotinus, *Enn.* 3.5.2.19-21 and 3.5.3.27 H.-S.
[43] Cf., e.g., Plotinus, *Enn.* 3.3.4.45-48, *ibid.* 4.3.6.27-34, *ibid.* 4.3.7.8-12 H.-S.; Iamblichus *ap.* Stobaeus, *Anth.* 1.372.23–373.8 Wachsmuth (Οἱ δ' ἀσφαλέστερον τούτων [sc. Plotinus and Amelius] διατατόμενοι καὶ προόδους πρώτας καὶ δευτέρας καὶ τρίτας οὐσιῶν τῆς ψυχῆς διισχυριζόμενοι κτλ.); Proclus, *In Tim.* 1.111.14-28 D., *ibid.* 3.257.30-260.4 D., *In Parm.* 948.23-26 Cousin (οὔτε ὁμοούσιον τὴν ψυχὴν ὑποθετέον τοῖς θεοῖς· καὶ γὰρ τὴν ἐξ ἀρχῆς ἡμῶν ὑπόστασιν ἐκ δευτέρων καὶ τρίτων παρήγαγεν ὁ γεννήσας πατήρ). It should be noted that *Tim.* 41d4-7 is linked with the *Phaedrus* myth by Hermeias, *In Phaedr.* p. 123.12-14 C. and *ibid.* p. 153.3-6 C., and by Proclus, *In Alcib.* 227.9-19 Segonds, *In Tim.* 3.245.19–246.10 D. and *ibid.* 3.258.8-21 D.
[44] Cf. Epictetus, *Diss.* 2.8.2 (τίς οὖν οὐσία θεοῦ; ... νοῦς, ἐπιστήμη, λόγος ὀρθός).
[45] A.S. Pease's note *ad loc.* lists *ND* 1.35.98 (*His enim omnibus quae proposui adiunctis in homine rationem esse et mentem videbas*), *ND* 1.37.104 (*Quaero igitur vester deus ... quid appetat, ad quem denique rem motu mentis ac ratione utatur ...*), *ND* 2.14.38 (*Nihil autem*

instance occurs in the *Meditations* of Marcus Aurelius in a passage that borrows *verbatim* from the *Timaeus*. 'That man dwells with the gods,' according to the Emperor, 'who continuously demonstrates to them that his soul is satisfied with its lot and conforms itself to the wishes of the daemon whom god has given to each man, as a portion (an ἀπόσπασμα) of himself, to be his guardian and guide (προστάτης καὶ ἡγεμών). This daemon,' says the Emperor, 'is the intelligence and reason (νοῦς καὶ λόγος) of each individual' (*Med.* 5.27, pp. 40.29–41.2 Dalfen: συζῇ δὲ θεοῖς ὁ συνεχῶς δεικνὺς αὐτοῖς τὴν ἑαυτοῦ ψυχὴν ἀρεσκομένην μὲν τοῖς ἀπονεμομένοις, ποιοῦσαν δέ, ὅσα βούλεται ὁ δαίμων, ὃν ἑκάστῳ προστάτην καὶ ἡγεμόνα ὁ Ζεὺς ἔδωκεν[46] ἀπόσπασμα ἑαυτοῦ. οὗτος δέ ἐστιν ὁ ἑκάστου νοῦς καὶ λόγος). Here again the couplet νοῦς καὶ λόγος constitutes a grammatical unit: Zeus has given to each of us an ἀπόσπασμα of himself in the form of νοῦς καὶ λόγος. It follows from the Emperor's statement that Zeus himself, like the god of Gregory of Nyssa,[47] is to be identified with νοῦς καὶ λόγος. The couplet προστάτης καὶ ἡγεμών employed by Marcus Aurelius recurs, it should be noted, in a similar Platonic context in Proclus, *In Tim.* 3.166.14-16 Diehl (καὶ τί θαυμαστόν, ὅπου γε καὶ ψυχαὶ μερικαὶ τοὺς ἑαυτῶν προστάτας καὶ ἡγεμόνας ἐπιγνοῦσαι θεοὺς τοῖς ἐκείνων ὀνόμασιν ἑαυτὰς προσεῖπον;).[48] One may conclude that the couplet belongs to the terminology of Platonic commentary.

---

est mente et ratione melius; ergo haec mundo deesse non possunt), ND 2.17.46f. (see p. 19 below), *ND* 2.35.88 (*Hi autem dubitant de mundo, ex quo et oriuntur et fiunt omnia, casune ipse sit effectus aut necessitate aliqua an ratione ac mente divina), ND* 2.45.115 = *SVF* 2.549 (*Maxime autem corpora inter se iuncta permanent cum quasi quodam vinculo circumdato colligantur; quod facit ea natura quae per omnem mundum omnia mente et ratione conficiens funditur et ad medium rapit et convertit extrema*). Calcidius says the same: the world is endowed not merely with a soul but also with reason and intelligence (*Comm. in Tim.* p. 329.15f. Wasz.: ... *dicimus mundum non solum anima, sed etiam ratione atque intellegentia praeditum*). Other Ciceronian instances of the couplet are Cicero, *Orat.* 8 (*quod neque oculis neque auribus neque ullo sensu percipi potest cogitatione tantum et mente complectimur), De senect.* 19.67 (*mens et ratio et consilium in senibus est), Leg.* 1.6.19 = *SVF* 3.315 (*Ea* [sc. *lex*] *est enim naturae vis, ea mens ratioque prudentis, ea iuris atque iniuriae regula*) and *ibid.* 2.4.8 = *SVF.* 3.316 (*Ita principem legem illam et ultimam mentem esse dicebant omnia ratione aut cogentis aut vetantis dei. Ex quo illa lex quam di humano generi dederunt, recte est laudata : est enim ratio mensque sapientis ad iubendum et ad deterrendum idonea*).
[46] The phraseology is that of Plato, *Tim.* 90a3f. (δαίμονα θεὸς ἑκάστῳ δέδωκεν).
[47] See page 9 above.
[48] See also Proclus, *In Tim.* 3.260.15-17 D. (διαιρεῖ τε [sc. ὁ δημιουργός] κατὰ γένη τὰς πολλὰς ψυχὰς τοῖς προστάταις αὐτῶν θεοῖς καὶ κατὰ ἀγέλας ἄλλαις ἄλλους ἐφίστησιν ἡγεμόνας). For the couplet προστάτης καὶ ἡγεμών in other contexts see, e.g., Plutarch, *V. Mar.* 3.4.5f. (τίνα δὴ τοιοῦτον ἕξει μετ' ἐκεῖνον ἡγεμόνα κὰ προστάτην ὁ Ῥωμαίων δῆμος). Cf. Plato, *Phdr.* 241a2-4 (... μεταβαλὼν [sc. the ex-lover] ἄλλον ἄρχοντα ἐν αὑτῷ καὶ προστάτην, νοῦν καὶ σωφροσύνην ἀντ' ἔρωτος καὶ μανίας, ...).

Plutarch is under the same sort of Stoic influence as was Marcus Aurelius when he writes in his *De Iside et Osiride* that in the soul intelligence and reason (νοῦς καὶ λόγος), qualified by Plutarch as the guide and master of all that are best, is none other than the god Osiris (*De Iside* 371A: ἐν μὲν οὖν τῇ ψυχῇ νοῦς καὶ λόγος ὁ τῶν ἀρίστων πάντων ἡγεμὼν καὶ κύριος Ὄσιρίς ἐστιν, κτλ.). Here again the couplet νοῦς καὶ λόγος is treated as a unit, whilst the qualification 'guide and master' (ἡγεμὼν καὶ κύριος) provides a counterpart to the couplet 'guardian and guide' (προστάτης καὶ ἡγεμών) subsequently employed in the same connection, as we have just seen, by Marcus Aurelius and, later still, by Proclus. Plutarch goes on to report in the same treatise a remarkable story. The Egyptians relate, according to Plutarch, the following myth. Zeus was not able to walk because his legs had grown together, a circumstance of which the god was so ashamed that he lived in isolation. But Isis was able to separate his limbs and so provide Zeus with the means of mobility. The message of this myth, according to Plutarch's stoicizing interpretation, is that the intelligence and reason of the god (ὁ τοῦ θεοῦ νοῦς καὶ λόγος), which was established apart (καθ' ἑαυτόν) in the domain of the unseen and invisible, advanced to generation by means of motion —that is to say, Zeus took in hand the creation of the universe (*De Iside* 376C: αἰνίττεται δὲ καὶ διὰ τούτων ὁ μῦθος ὅτι καθ' ἑαυτὸν ὁ τοῦ θεοῦ νοῦς καὶ λόγος ἐν τῷ ἀοράτῳ καὶ ἀφανεῖ βεβηκὼς εἰς γένεσιν ὑπὸ κινήσεως προῆλθεν). Notice once again the grammatical singular! To Plutarch's words 'proceeded to generation' (βεβηκὼς εἰς γένεσιν) one could cite many Stoic equivalents.[49] The formula νοῦς καὶ λόγος reappears in a critique of a Stoic argument in Plutarch's essay *On the obsolescence of oracles*. 'Why if there were many worlds,' Plutarch asks, 'should it be necessary that there be many Zeuses? Surely it would suffice that there be in each world a governor and ruler of the whole in the form of a god endowed with intelligence and reason (νοῦν καὶ λόγον), like the one in our own world who is called lord and father of all' (*De def. orac.* 425F–426A: ἔπειτα τίς ἀνάγκη πολλοὺς εἶναι Δίας, ἂν πλείονες ὦσι κόσμοι, καὶ μὴ καθ' ἕκαστον ἄρχοντα πρῶτον καὶ ἡγεμόνα τοῦ ὅλου θεὸν ἔχοντα καὶ νοῦν καὶ λόγον, οἷος ὁ παρ' ἡμῖν κύριος ἁπάντων καὶ πατὴρ ἐπονομαζόμενος;). Here again the couplet νοῦς καὶ λόγος serves to characterize the divine. Intelligence and reason are, taken together, the supreme quality of both god and man.

---

[49] Aetius, *Plac.* 1.7.33 (*Doxogr.* 305.15–306.2) = *SVF* 2.1027 (οἱ Στωικοὶ νοερὸν θεὸν ἀποφαίνονται, πῦρ τεχνικόν, ὁδῷ βαδίζον ἐπὶ γένεσιν κόσμου, κτλ.) and the parallels listed in A.S. Pease's note on Cicero, *ND* 2.22.57 = *SVF* 1.171 (*Zeno igitur naturam ita definit ut eam dicat ignem esse artificiosum ad gignendum progredientem via*).

Although, as we have seen, the terms νοῦς καὶ λόγος are frequently treated as a unit, we must nonetheless ask how in the days of Philo and Plutarch the relationship between νοῦς and λόγος was conceived. Some guidance is afforded by the author of the treatise *On the Education of Children* attributed to Plutarch. 'Of the elements in us,' the unknown author writes, 'education alone is immortal and divine.[50] The most essential of the elements that compose human nature are two in number, namely νοῦς and λόγος, νοῦς being in command of λόγος, and λόγος being subservient to νοῦς' (*De lib. educ.* 5E: παιδεία δὲ τῶν ἐν ἡμῖν μόνον ἐστὶν ἀθάνατον καὶ θεῖον. καὶ δύο τὰ πάντων ἐστὶ κυριώτατα ἐν ἀνθρωπίνῃ φύσει, νοῦς καὶ λόγος. καὶ ὁ μὲν νοῦς ἀρχικός ἐστι τοῦ λόγου, ὁ δὲ λόγος ὑπηρετικὸς τοῦ νοῦ).[51] The passage is not as unequivocal as might at first sight appear, since it is not at all obvious what the author means by λόγος. Does he have in mind discursive reasoning or simply speech? Or both? That the couplet νοῦς καὶ λόγος can, and frequently does, refer to the combination of thought and speech is apparent from other texts. Consider, for example, Dio Chrysostom's remark that it is no easy matter to hold in check the thought or speech of the philosopher (*Or.* 12.38: τυχὸν γὰρ οὐ ῥᾴδιον τὸν τοῦ φιλοσόφου νοῦν καὶ λόγον ἐπισχεῖν, ἔνθ' ἂν ὁρμήσῃ, κτλ.), where the context and the continuation make it clear that λόγος refers, primarily, to speech whilst νοῦς denotes the process of thought which (in ideal circumstances) takes place before a speaker opens his mouth. The mode of progression from thought (διάνοια/ἐνθύμησις/νοῦς) to speech (λόγος) and thence to action (πρᾶξις) is neatly put as follows by Gregory of Nyssa, *De perf. Christ.*, vol. 8.1, p. 210.7-11 Jaeger (ἀρχὴ γὰρ γίνεται λόγου παντὸς ἡ διάνοια, δεύτερον δὲ μετὰ τὴν ἐνθύμησιν ὁ λόγος ἐστί, τὴν ἐντυπωθεῖσαν τῇ ψυχῇ διάνοιαν διὰ τῆς φωνῆς

---

[50] The notion is commonplace. Cf. Isocrates, *Ad Demon.* 19 (σοφία γὰρ μόνον τῶν κτημάτων ἀθάνατον); Aristotle, *Protrept.* fr. 108 Düring = Iamblichus, *Protrept.* p. 48.9-13 Pistelli, *PA* 686a29 (ἔργον δὲ τοῦ θειοτάτου τὸ νοεῖν καὶ φρονεῖν), *EN* 1178b20-32; Cicero, *De fin.* 5.4.11 = Theophrastus, fr. 482 FHS&G (*Vitae autem degendae ratio maxime quidem illis* [sc. Aristotle and Theophrastus] *placuit quieta, in contemplatione et cognitione posita rerum, quae quia deorum erat vitae simillima, sapiente visa est dignissima*); Plotinus, *Enn.* 4.7.10.16 H.-S. (φρόνησις γὰρ καὶ ἀρετὴ ἀληθὴς θεῖα ὄντα), etc.
[51] Other Plutarchean instances of the couplet νοῦς καὶ λόγος not mentioned elsewhere in this paper are *De virt. moral.* 444C-D (ἀλλ' ἡ μὲν ἀπροσδεὴς τοῦ ἀλόγου καὶ περὶ τὸν εἰλικρινῆ καὶ ἀπαθῆ νοῦν συνισταμένη [sc. ἀρετή], αὐτοτελής τίς ἐστιν ἀκρότης τοῦ λόγου καὶ δύναμις, κτλ.), *De gen. Socr.* 589B, *Quaest. conv.* 673E (... ὁ ἄνθρωπος, γεγονὼς φιλότεχνος καὶ φιλόκαλος, πᾶν ἀποτέλεσμα καὶ πρᾶγμα νοῦ καὶ λόγου μετέχον ἀσπάζεσθαι καὶ ἀγαπᾶν πέφυκεν), *Praec. ger. reipubl.* 801F (ὁ δὲ πολιτικὸς ἐν ἑαυτῷ μὲν ὀφείλει τὸν κυβερνῶντα νοῦν ἔχειν, ἐν ἑαυτῷ δὲ τὸν ἐγκελευόμενον λόγον, ὅπως μὴ δέηται φωνῆς ἀλλοτρίου, κτλ.), *De tuenda san. praec.* 124B (τὸ γὰρ ἀγροικίας φοβηθέντα δόξαν εἰς πλευρῖτιν ἢ φρενῖτιν ἐμβάλλειν ἑαυτὸν ἀγροίκου τινὸς ὡς ἀληθῶς ἐστι καὶ νοῦν οὐκ ἔχοντος οὐδὲ λόγον), *De Alexandri* 336B, *V. Cato. min.* 16.4.

ἐκκαλύπτων, τρίτην δὲ τάξιν ἐπέχει μετὰ τὸν νοῦν καὶ τὸν λόγον ἡ πρᾶξις, τὸ νοηθὲν εἰς ἐνέργειαν ἄγουσα).

In the case of Philo one might readily quote instances of the couplet νοῦς καὶ λόγος in which λόγος certainly refers to speech,[52] and others in which the term λόγος clearly refers to ratiocination.[53] The explanation of this terminological fluidity is not far to seek. The term λόγος was, in the nature of things, ambiguous and was recognized as such,[54] since it can denote both thought and speech—both λόγος ἐνδιάθετος and λόγος προφορικός to use the Stoic terminology—whether separately or simultaneously, the exact connotation being indicated, or left ambivalent, according to the requirements of the context.[55]

---

[52] Cf., e.g., *Congr.* 17 (ῥητορικὴ δὲ καὶ τὸν νοῦν πρὸς θεωρίαν ἀκονησαμένη καὶ πρὸς ἑρμηνείαν γυμνάσασα τὸν λόγον καὶ συγκροτήσασα λογικὸν ὄντως ἀποδείξει τὸν ἄνθρωπον ἐπιμεληθεῖσα τοῦ ἰδίου καὶ ἐξαιρέτου, ὃ μηδενὶ τῶν ἄλλων ζῴων ἡ φύσις δεδώρηται), *Fug.* 90 (ἀδελφὸν μὲν ψυχῆς τὸ σῶμα, τὸ δὲ λογικοῦ πλησίον τὸ ἄλογον, τὸν δὲ ἔγγιστα νοῦ τὸν προφορικὸν λόγον), *Mut.* 69 (φαμὲν δὴ τὴν μὲν ἠχὼ τὸν προφορικὸν εἶναι λόγον - τοῦ γὰρ ζῴου ἠχεῖον ὄργανόν ἐστι τὸ φωνητήριον -, τούτου δὲ πατέρα τὸν νοῦν - ἀπὸ γὰρ διανοίας ὥσπερ ἀπὸ πηγῆς φέρεται τὸ τοῦ λόγου νᾶμα), *ibid.* 208 (ἐπειδὴ γὰρ Μωυσῆς μέν ἐστι νοῦς ὁ καθαρώτατος, ᾿Ααρὼν δὲ λόγος αὐτοῦ, πεπαίδευται δὲ καὶ ὁ νοῦς θεοπρεπῶς ἐφάπτεσθαι καὶ ὁ λόγος ὁσίως ἑρμηνεύειν τὰ ὅσια, κτλ.), *Abr.* 83 (διὰ μὲν γὰρ τῆς ἠχοῦς τὸν προφορικὸν λόγον αἰνίττεται, διὰ τοῦ πατρὸς δὲ τὸν ἡγεμόνα νοῦν - πατὴρ γὰρ ὁ ἐνδιάθετος φύσει τοῦ γεγωνότος πρεσβύτερός γε ὢν καὶ τὰ λεκτέα ὑποσπείρων), *Mos.* 1.173 (καὶ διανείμας τὸν νοῦν καὶ τὸν λόγον κατὰ τὸν αὐτὸν χρόνον τῷ μὲν ἐνετύγχανεν ἀφανῶς τῷ θεῷ, ἵν᾿ ἐξ ἀμηχάνων ῥύσηται συμφορῶν, δι᾿ οὗ δ᾿ ἐθάρσυνε καὶ παρηγόρει τοὺς καταβοῶντας κτλ.), *Migr.* 3f. (πατρὸς δὲ οἶκος ὁ λόγος, ὅτι πατὴρ μὲν ἡμῶν ὁ νοῦς σπείρων εἰς ἕκαστον τῶν μερῶν τὰς ἀφ᾿ ἑαυτοῦ δυνάμεις καὶ διανέμων εἰς αὐτὰ τὰς ἐνεργείας κτλ.), *ibid.* 52 (δύο ταῦτα τῶν ἐν ἡμῖν ἀόρατα, νοῦς καὶ λόγος) and 80f., *Cher.* 7 (ἠχεῖ μὲν γὰρ ὁ γεγωνὼς λόγος, πατὴρ δὲ τούτου ὁ νοῦς ἐπειλημμένος τοῦ σπουδαίου), *Det.* 66,125-127 and 168, *Post.* 107, and *Spec.* 2.256. See also *Her.* 118 (καὶ εἴ τις καὶ συνόλως μήτραν διοιγνύειν ἀπὸ ἀνθρώπου, τοῦ λογισμοῦ καὶ λόγου, ἕως κτήνους, αἰσθήσεώς τε καὶ σώματος) where the distinction between λογισμός and λόγος is clearly that of ratiocination and speech.
[53] Cf., e.g., *Opif.* 73 (κακίας δὲ καὶ ἀρετῆς ὡς ἂν οἶκος νοῦς καὶ λόγος, ᾧ πεφύκασιν ἐνδιαιτᾶσθαι), *Aet.* 75 (ἀνθρώπων δὲ νοῦν καὶ λόγον), *Spec.* 1.260 (οὐ γὰρ ὑπὲρ ἀλόγων ὁ νόμος, ἀλλ᾿ ὑπὲρ τῶν νοῦν καὶ λόγον ἐχόντων), as well as *Det.* 83 (see page 1 above) and other Philonic texts cited in the course of this paper.
[54] Cf., e.g., Origen, *Cels.* 6.65 (ἐπεὶ δέ φησιν [sc. ὁ Κέλσος] ὅτι οὐδὲ λόγῳ ἐφικτός [sc. ὁ θεός], διαστέλλομαι τὸ σημαινόμενον, καί φημι, εἰ μὲν λόγῳ τῷ ἐν ἡμῖν, εἴτε ἐνδιαθέτῳ, εἴτε καὶ προφορικῷ, καὶ ἡμεῖς φήσομεν ὅτι οὐκ ἔστιν ἐφικτὸς λόγῳ ὁ θεός· κτλ.); [Gregory of Nyssa], *Imag.*, PG 44.1333D (γεννᾶται γὰρ ὁ λόγος ἐν τῇ καρδίᾳ γέννησίν τινα ἀκατάληπτον καὶ ἀσώματον, καὶ μένει ἔνδον ἀγνώριστος, καὶ γεννᾶται δευτέραν γέννησιν σωματικὴν διὰ χειλέων, καὶ τότε τοῖς πᾶσι γνωρίζεται), *ibid.*, PG 44.1344A (ἐπὰν γὰρ εἴπῃς ψυχὴν λογικὴν καὶ νοεράν, εὔδηλον ὅτι καὶ λόγον καὶ νοῦν ἐσήμανας· καὶ ἐπὰν ὀνομάσῃς λόγον, πάντως ὅτι καὶ τὴν λογικὴν ψυχὴν καὶ τὴν τούτου γεννητικὴν ἐδήλωσας. ὡσαύτως καὶ ἐπὰν εἴπῃς νοῦν, ἐκ παντὸς τρόπου ὅτι καὶ τὴν ψυχὴν καὶ τὸν λόγον ἐδήλωσας. τίνος γὰρ καὶ ἔσται νοῦς εἰ μὴ ψυχῆς καὶ λόγου; διὰ δὴ τοῦτο ὥσπερ φεράλληλον καὶ ἀλληλένδετον ἔχουσι τὴν προσηγορίαν, οὕτω κοινὴν καὶ ἀδιαίρετον ἔχουσι καὶ τὴν οὐσιώδη ἐνέργειαν).
[55] Some other noteworthy instances, more or less ambivalent, of the couplet νοῦς καὶ λόγος are Ps.-Onatas, fr. 1, p. 139.8-10 Thesleff = Stobaeus, *Anth.* 1.48.12f. W. (ὁ μὲν ὢν

As to the origins of the formula νοῦς καὶ λόγος in its application to souls human or divine, there is no obvious likelihood that the formula has been borrowed or adapted directly from the Platonic corpus. True enough, the Platonic Timaeus takes it upon himself to criticize those thinkers who ascribe too much influence to subordinate accessory causes which, according to Timaeus, are completely incapable of reason and intelligence (*Tim.* 46d4: λόγον δὲ οὐδένα οὐδὲ νοῦν εἰς οὐδὲν δυνατὰ ἔχειν ἐστίν), whilst the Athenian Stranger at the close of Plato's *Laws* affirms that without reason (ἄνευ λόγου) there never was nor will there be a soul that is both wise and in possession of intelligence (*Laws* 963e5-8: ἄνευ γὰρ λόγου καὶ φύσει γίγνεται ἀνδρεία ψυχή, ἄνευ δὲ αὖ λόγου φρόνιμός τε καὶ νοῦν ἔχουσα οὔτ᾽ ἐγένετο πώποτε οὔτ᾽ ἔστιν οὐδ᾽ αὖθίς ποτε γενήσεται, ὡς ὄντος ἑτέρου). These are the sort of texts that exegetes might find it opportune to quote as evidence that Plato did indeed hold a particular doctrine regarding the rational soul, but of themselves such Platonic statements can hardly have given rise to that doctrine. The same is true of Timaeus' familiar pronouncement that reality can be grasped only by intelligence with the aid of reason (*Tim.* 28a1f.: νοήσει μετὰ λόγου περιληπτόν).[56] And the same may well be said of the few relevant instances of the couplet νοῦς καὶ λόγος in the Aristotelian *corpus*.[57] The true source of the prevalence of the formula νοῦς καὶ λόγος lies rather, I believe, in the Stoic tradition as exemplified in many of the Stoic-inspired texts that I have already mentioned.

θεὸς αὐτὸς οὔτε ὁρατὸς οὔτε αἰσθητός, ἀλλὰ λόγῳ μόνον καὶ νόῳ θεωρατός); Athenagoras *Leg.* 10.1 (νῷ μόνῳ καὶ λόγῳ καταλαμβανόμενον [sc. god]) and *Res.* 15.5 (εἰ δὲ καὶ νοῦς καὶ λόγος δέδοται τοῖς ἀνθρώποις πρὸς διάκρισιν νοητῶν, κτλ.); Sextus Empiricus, *Adv. math.* 9.65 (οὕτω σκεπτόμενοι περί τινος τῶν λόγῳ θεωρουμένων οὐκ ἄλλοις τισὶ πιστεύειν ὀφείλομεν ἢ τοῖς τὸν νοῦν καὶ τὸν λόγον ὀξυωποῦσιν, ὁποῖοί τινες ἦσαν οἱ φιλόσοφοι); Plotinus, *Enn.* 6.8.18.1-7 H.-S.; Porphyry, *Sent.* 32, p. 25.5f. Lamberz (ἡγουμένου δὲ λόγου καὶ νοῦ καὶ μηδενὸς ἀντιτείνοντος), echoed by Marinus, *V. Procli* 21.523-525 Masullo and by Psellus, *De virt.* p. 110.29f. O'Meara.

[56] For the meaning of this phrase, analysed at length by Proclus, *In Tim.* 1.240.12-248.6 D., see F.M. Cornford, *Plato's Cosmology* (London 1937) 24.

[57] In addition to texts to which I have already made reference see *Protrept.* fr. 23 Düring = Iamblichus, *Protrept.* p. 34.13-16 P. (τῆς ψυχῆς δὲ τὸ μὲν ἦν ἔχον λόγον, τὸ δ᾽ οὐκ ἔχον, ὅπερ καὶ χεῖρον· ὥστε τὸ ἄλογον ἕνεκα τοῦ λόγον ἔχοντος. ἐν δὲ τῷ λόγον ἔχοντι ὁ νοῦς· ὥστε τοῦ νοῦ ἕνεκα πάντ᾽ εἶναι ἀναγκάζει ἡ ἀπόδειξις), and *Pol.* 1254 b6-9 (ἐν οἷς φανερόν ἐστιν ὅτι κατὰ φύσιν καὶ συμφέρον τὸ ἄρχεσθαι τῷ σώματι ὑπὸ τῆς ψυχῆς, καὶ τῷ παθητικῷ μορίῳ ὑπὸ τοῦ νοῦ καὶ τοῦ μορίου τοῦ λόγον ἔχοντος, τὸ δ᾽ ἐξ ἴσου ἢ ἀνάπαλιν βλαβερὸν πᾶσιν). Other more or less relevant Aristotelian instances of the couplet are *Protrept.* fr. 65 D. = Iamblichus, *Protrept.* p. 42.13-23 P. (εἰ μὲν οὖν ἁπλοῦν τι ζῷόν ἐστιν ὁ ἄνθρωπος καὶ κατὰ λόγον καὶ νοῦν τέτακται αὐτοῦ ἡ οὐσία, κτλ.), *EN* 1143a36–b1 (καὶ γὰρ τῶν πρώτων ὅρων καὶ τῶν ἐσχάτων νοῦς ἐστι καὶ οὐ λόγος), *MM* 2.8.2, 1207a1-5 and *ibid.* 2.8.4, 1207a13f.

A further related Philonic phenomenon demands our attention. Philo expands frequently the couplet νοῦς καὶ λόγος or νοῦς καὶ λογισμός into a triad of terms by the addition of sense-perception (αἴσθησις). A good example of this recurring phenomenon is *Spec.* 1.201 (τὸ μὲν λογικὸν τῆς ἄρρενος γενεᾶς ἐστιν, ὅπερ νοῦς καὶ λογισμὸς κεκλήρωται, τὸ δ' ἄλογον τῆς πρὸς γυναικῶν, ὅπερ ἔλαχεν αἴσθησις. κτλ.) to which I made reference at the outset of this paper.[58] Another important instance is Philo's statement à propos of Exod. 16:36 in *Congr.* 100 that we humans seem to contain three measures, namely sense, speech and intelligence (ἐν ἡμῖν γὰρ αὐτοῖς τρία μέτρα εἶναι δοκεῖ, αἴσθησις, λόγος, νοῦς· αἰσθητῶν μὲν αἴσθησις, ὀνομάτων δὲ καὶ ῥημάτων καὶ τῶν λεγομένων ὁ λόγος, νοητῶν δὲ νοῦς), a passage quoted and commented with approval by Clement of Alexandria, *Str.* 2.11.50. In this passage the context makes it clear that λόγος refers to the spoken word, as it normally does in Philonic instances of the triad.[59] Αἴσθησις provides the raw material to which νοῦς directs its attention before expressing its conclusions in speech (λόγος).

In yet other Philonic instances the triad νοῦς/λόγος/αἴσθησις is expanded into a tetrad of terms by the addition of σῶμα, the medium through which αἴσθησις operates. This is the case, for example at *Somn.* 1.25 (οὐκοῦν τέτταρα τὰ ἀνωτάτω τῶν περὶ ἡμᾶς ἐστι, σῶμα, αἴσθησις, λόγος, νοῦς), and *ibid.* 1.33 (ἀεὶ δὴ τὸ τέταρτον ἀκατάληπτον, οὐρανὸς μὲν ἐν κόσμῳ παρὰ τὴν ἀέρος καὶ γῆς καὶ ὕδατος φύσιν, νοῦς δὲ ἐν ἀνθρώπῳ παρὰ σῶμα καὶ αἴσθησιν καὶ τὸν ἑρμηνέα λόγον).[60] In other Philonic instances, however,

---

[58] See pages 1f. above.
[59] Further Philonic instances of the triad are *Post.* 55 (αὗται δὲ [sc. αἱ τρεῖς πόλεις] τροπικώτερον νοῦν, αἴσθησιν, λόγον, τὰ περὶ ἡμᾶς ὄντα, δηλοῦσιν), *Migr.* 3f., *Her.* 108 (τοῦ νοῦ τὰς διανοήσεις, τοῦ λόγου τὰς ἑρμηνείας, τῆς αἰσθήσεως τὰς φαντασίας), *Mut.* 56 (ἐπὶ πρόσωπον πεσεῖν λέγεται, ἐπὶ τὰς αἰσθήσεις, ἐπὶ τὸν λόγον, ἐπὶ τὸν νοῦν), *Somn.* 1.77, *Spec.* 4.92f.; *QG* 2, fr. 59 (περὶ δὲ σάρκα ἡ αἴσθησις καὶ τὸ πάθος, οὐχ ὁ νοῦς καὶ ὁ λογισμός).
[60] Further examples of the tetrad are *Leg.* 1.103f. (εἰς δὲ ἀπόλαυσιν κακίας οὐ μόνον δεῖ πως ἔχειν τὸν νοῦν, ἀλλὰ καὶ τὴν αἴσθησιν καὶ τὸν λόγον καὶ τὸ σῶμα· κτλ.), *Sacr.* 97 (μὴ δόντος γὰρ [sc. θεοῦ] οὐχ ἕξεις, ἐπεὶ πάντα αὐτοῦ κτήματα, καὶ τὰ ἐκτὸς καὶ τὸ σῶμα καὶ ἡ αἴσθησις καὶ ὁ λόγος καὶ ὁ νοῦς καὶ αἱ πάντων ἐνέργειαι καὶ οὐ σὺ μόνος ἀλλὰ καὶ ὅδε ὁ κόσμος), *Migr.* 192 (εἰ μὴ νομίζετε τὸν μὲν ὑμέτερον νοῦν ἀποδυσάμενον σῶμα, αἴσθησιν, λόγον, δίχα τούτων γυμνὰ δύνασθαι τὰ ὄντα ὁρᾶν, τὸν δὲ τῶν ὅλων νοῦν, τὸν θεόν, κτλ.) and *ibid.* 219, *Ebr.* 71, *Her.* 119 (ὁ γὰρ διοιγνὺς τὴν μήτραν ἑκάστων, τοῦ μὲν νοῦ πρὸς τὰς νοητὰς καταλήψεις, τοῦ δὲ λόγου πρὸς τὰς διὰ φωνῆς ἐνεργείας, τῶν δὲ αἰσθήσεων πρὸς τὰς ἀπὸ τῶν ὑποκειμένων ἐγγιγνομένας φαντασίας, τοῦ δὲ σώματος πρὸς τοὺς οἰκείους αὐτῷ σχέσεις τε καὶ κινήσεις κτλ.), *Spec.* 1.211 (κἂν περὶ ἑνὸς ἀνδρός, τέμε τῷ λόγῳ τὴν εὐχαριστίαν, μὴ εἰς τὰ λεπτότατα μέχρι τῶν ἐσχάτων, ἀλλὰ εἰς τὰ συνεκτικώτατα, σῶμα καὶ ψυχὴν τὸ πρῶτον, ἐξ ὧν συνέστηκεν, εἶτα εἰς λόγον καὶ νοῦν καὶ αἴσθησιν). See also *Sacr.* 73 (τὰ μὲν οὖν τῇ τάξει πρῶτα τοιαῦτά ἐστιν, οἷς κατὰ τὴν πρώτην γένεσιν εὐθὺς ἐκοινωνήσαμεν, τροφὴ αὔξησις ὅρασις ἀκοὴ γεῦσις ὄσφρησις ἁφή λόγος νοῦς, μέρη ψυχῆς, μέρη σώματος, αἱ τούτων ἐνέργειαι, συνόλως κινήσεις αὐτῶν καὶ σχέσεις αἱ κατὰ φύσιν).

the triad νοῦς/λόγος/αἴσθησις is reduced to two members, namely νοῦς and αἴσθησις. Examples of this reduction are *Somn*. 1.118 where Philo refers to sensation and intelligence as 'our own accepted criteria of judgment' (... αἴσθησίν τε καὶ νοῦν, τὰ νενομισμένα καθ' ἡμᾶς αὐτοὺς εἶναι κριτήρια) and *Conf*. 127 (καὶ μὴν σφαλλομένων γε τῶν καθ' ἡμᾶς αὐτοὺς περί τε νοῦν καὶ αἴσθησιν κριτηρίων ἀνάγκη τἀκόλουθον ὁμολογεῖν, κτλ.).[61] Here we are on familiar ground represented by, for example, Sextus Empiricus' affirmation that 'the primary criteria of the knowledge of things are sensation and intelligence' (*Adv. math*. 7.226: πρῶτα κριτήρια τῆς τῶν πραγμάτων γνώσεως ἥ τε αἴσθησις καὶ ὁ νοῦς).[62] But in other, more frequent, Philonic instances the couplet νοῦς/αἴσθησις represents mind and sensation not in co-operation but at variance with each other, as for example in *Opif*. 165 (ἐν ἡμῖν γὰρ ἀνδρὸς μὲν ἔχει λόγον ὁ νοῦς, γυναικὸς δ' αἴσθησις· ἡδονὴ δὲ προτέραις ἐντυγχάνει καὶ ἐνομιλεῖ ταῖς αἰσθήσεσι, δι' ὧν καὶ τὸν ἡγεμόνα νοῦν φενακίζει).[63]

---

[61] See also *Leg*. 2.24 (μετὰ γὰρ νοῦν εὐθὺς ἔδει δημιουργηθῆναι αἴσθησιν βοηθὸν αὐτῷ καὶ σύμμαχον. τελεσιουργήσας οὖν ἐκεῖνο τὸ δεύτερον καὶ τῇ τάξει καὶ τῇ δυνάμει πλάττει δημιούργημα, τὴν κατ' ἐνέργειαν αἴσθησιν, πρὸς συμπλήρωσιν τῆς ὅλης ψυχῆς καὶ πρὸς τὴν τῶν ὑποκειμένων ἀντίληψιν), *Det*. 52-54 (ἐάν τε γὰρ τὸν νοῦν ὡς πατέρα τοῦ συγκρίματος ἐάν τε τὴν αἴσθησιν ὡς μητέρα διὰ τιμῆς ἔχωμεν, εὖ πρὸς ἐκείνων αὐτοὶ πεισόμεθα. κτλ.).
[62] The context reads as follows: Sextus Empiricus, *Adv. math*. 7.226 (φαίνεται οὖν ἐκ τῶν εἰρημένων πρῶτα κριτήρια τῆς τῶν πραγμάτων γνώσεως ἥ τε αἴσθησις καὶ ὁ νοῦς, ἡ μὲν ὀργάνου τρόπον ἔχουσα ὁ δὲ τεχνίτου. ὥσπερ γὰρ ἡμεῖς οὐ δυνάμεθα χωρὶς ζυγοῦ τὴν τῶν βαρέων καὶ κούφων ἐξέτασιν ποιεῖσθαι, οὐδὲ ἄτερ κανόνος τὴν τῶν εὐθέων καὶ στρεβλῶν διαφορὰν λαβεῖν, οὕτως οὐδὲ ὁ νοῦς χωρὶς αἰσθήσεως δοκιμάσαι πέφυκε τὰ πράγματα). See further Sextus Empiricus, *Adv. math*. 7.217f. [= Theophrastus, fr. 301A Fort.; cf. also fr. 301B Fort.], 307-309, 370, 445, *ibid*. 8.63 [= Epicurus, fr. 253 Us.]; Ptolemy, *De judic*. passim (cf. Lammert's *Index verb*. s.v. αἴσθησις); Plotinus, *Enn*. 3.2.1.2f. H.-S. (ἀνδρὸς οὔτε νοῦν οὔτε αἴσθησιν κεκτημένου), as well as R.W. Sharples, 'The criterion of truth in Philo Judaeus, Alcinous and Alexander of Aphrodisias' in P. Huby and G. Neal (ed.), *The Criterion of Truth* (Liverpool 1989) 231-256.
[63] See further *Leg*. 2.25 (τῷ γὰρ ὄντι ὑπνώσαντος νοῦ γίνεται αἴσθησις, καὶ γὰρ ἔμπαλιν ἐγρηγορότος νοῦ σβέννυται) and *ibid*. 46, *Leg*. 3.222 (ἀλυσιτελέστατόν ἐστιν ἀκούειν αἰσθήσεως νοῦν, ἀλλὰ μὴ αἴσθησιν νοῦ· ἀεὶ γὰρ τὸ κρεῖττον ἄρχειν, τὸ δὲ χεῖρον ἄρχεσθαι δεῖ· νοῦς δὲ κρεῖττον αἰσθήσεως), *Det*. 53f. (τιμῇ δὲ τοῦ μὲν νοῦ ‹τὸ› διὰ τῶν συμφερόντων ἀλλὰ μὴ διὰ ἡδέων θεραπεύεσθαι ... τῆς δὲ αἰσθήσεως τὸ μὴ ἀφεθῆναι ῥύμῃ μιᾷ φέρεσθαι πρὸς τὰ ἐκτὸς αἰσθητά, ἐγχαλινωθῆναι δὲ ὑπὸ νοῦ κυβερνᾶν καὶ ἡνιοχεῖν τὰς ἀλόγους ἐν ἡμῖν δυνάμεις ἐπισταμένου. κτλ.), *Conf*. 133 (οἱ δὲ ταῦτα τολμῶντες αἴσθησιν μὲν διανοίας προκρίνουσιν, ἀξιοῦσι δὲ καὶ διὰ τῶν αἰσθητῶν τὰ νοητὰ πάντα ἑλεῖν ἀνὰ κράτος, εἰς μὲν δούλων τάξιν τὰ δεσπόζοντα, εἰς δὲ ἡγεμόνων τὰ φύσει δοῦλα μεθαρμόσασθαι βιαζόμενοι), *Spec*. 1.219 (... ἐπειδὰν τῶν ἡμερινῶν φροντίδων ἀναχωρήσας ὁ νοῦς, ὕπνῳ μὲν παρειμένου τοῦ σώματος, μηδεμιᾶς δὲ τῶν αἰσθήσεων ἱσταμένης ἐμποδών, ἀνακυκλεῖν αὐτὸν ἄρξηται καὶ τὰ νοήματα καθαρῶς ἐφ' αὑτοῦ σκοπεῖν). With the latter text one may compare *Leg*. 2.25 (cited above) and Cicero, *De div*. 1.57.129f. = Posidonius, fr. 110 Edelstein-Kidd = fr. 378 Theiler (*A natura autem alia quaedam ratio est, quae docet quanta sit animi vis seiuncta a corporis sensibus, quod maxime contingit aut dormientibus aut mente permotis.* etc); for the continuation see note 66 below. See also PGL s.v. αἴσθησις A.3.

The full triad νοῦς/λόγος/αἴσθησις, although a Philonic speciality, is not unique to him. The same triad appears, for example, in Cicero, *ND* 2.17.46f. (*Mundo autem certe nihil est melius; nec dubium quin quod animans sit habeatque sensum et rationem et mentem id sit melius quam id quod iis careat. Ita efficitur animantem, sensus, mentis, rationis mundum esse compotem*),[64] in Plutarch' essay *De fortuna* 98C (... ἕνεκα τῶν αἰσθήσεων, εἰ μὴ νοῦν μηδὲ λόγον ὁ ἄνθρωπος ἔσχεν, οὐδὲν ἂν διέφερε τῷ βίῳ τῶν θηρίων),[65] in a Plutarchean fragment preserved by Porphyry, *De abst.* III. 19.3 = Plutarch, fr. 193 Sandbach (πῶς δ' οὐκ ἄλογον πολλοὺς τῶν ἀνθρώπων ἐπ' αἰσθήσει μόνον ζῶντας ὁρῶντας, νοῦν δὲ καὶ λόγον οὐκ ἔχοντας, ...;) and also, if editors have correctly restored the text, in Plutarch's treatise *De fac. in orbe lun.* 943A (ποιεῖ δ' ἡ μὲν ψυχῆς ‹καὶ σώματος μῖξις αἴσθησιν ἡ δε νοῦ καὶ ψυχῆς› σύνοδος λόγον· ὧν τὸ μὲν ἡδονῆς ἀρχὴ καὶ πόνου τὸ δ' ἀρετῆς καὶ κακίας). According to Ps.-Justin not only god but also his works are beyond the reach of human νοῦς, αἴσθησις and λόγος (*Quaest. Graec. ad Christ.* 17, PG 6.1484B: Οὐ χρὴ δὲ τοῖς ἡμετέροις ἐνθυμήμασι μετρεῖν τοῦ θεοῦ τὰ ἔργα· ὑπὲρ νοῦν γὰρ καὶ αἴσθησιν καὶ λόγον τοῦ θεοῦ τὰ ἔργα), whilst Plotinus claims that the One is greater than λόγος, νοῦς and αἴσθησις. Being their author, the One is not to be identified with them (*Enn.* 5.3.14.18f. H.-S.: αὐτὸς κρείττων λόγου καὶ νοῦ καὶ αἰσθήσεως, παρασχὼν ταῦτα, οὐκ αὐτὸς ὢν ταῦτα). The context makes it clear that in this instance the term λόγος certainly refers to 'speech.' But elsewhere Plotinus maintains that perfect life involves not only sense-perception but also reason and true intelligence (*Enn.* 1.4.4.6-8 H.-S.: ὅτι μὲν οὖν ἔχει τελείαν ζωὴν ἄνθρωπος οὐ τὴν αἰσθητικὴν μόνον ἔχων, ἀλλὰ καὶ λογισμὸν καὶ νοῦν ἀληθινόν, δῆλον καὶ ἐξ ἄλλων). A similar doctrine appears in Lactantius, *De opif. dei* 2.1 (*Dedit enim homini artifex ille noster ac parens deus sensum atque rationem, ut ex eo appareret nos ab eo esse generatos, qui ipse intelligentia, ipse sensus ac ratio est*). According to Lactantius, god gave to man *sensum atque rationem* (i.e., the shortened version of the Philonic triad), whilst god himself is *ipse intelligentia, ipse sensus ac ratio* (i.e., the full Philonic triad). I decline to enter into the interpretation of the term *sensus* in this remarkable parallel to Philo's triad νοῦς/λόγος/αἴσθησις.

---

[64] Cf. *ND* 2.8.22 = *SVF* 1.114 (*Nullius sensu carentis pars aliqua potest esse sentiens; mundi autem partes sentientes sunt; non igitur caret sensu mundus*).
[65] The continuation reads (*De fortuna* 98C): νῦν δ' οὐκ ἀπὸ τύχης οὐδ' αὐτομάτως περίεσμεν αὐτῶν καὶ κρατοῦμεν [sc. τῶν αἰσθήσεων], ἀλλ' ὁ Προμηθεύς, τουτέστιν ὁ λογισμός, αἴτιος

ἵππων ὄνων τ' ὀχεῖα καὶ ταύρων γονὰς
δοὺς ἀντίδουλα καὶ πόνων ἐκδέκτορα

κατ' Αἰσχύλον [fr. 194 Nauck, quoted by Plutarch also in *De soll. animal.* 964F and fr. 193 Sandbach = Porphyry, *De abst.* 3.18.6, p. 208.13-18 Nauck].

That god has no need of sense-perception was a commonplace theme with which Lactantius must have been familiar,[66] and modern commentators have in consequence not been slow to conclude, whether correctly or not, that Lactantius can hardly have intended to attribute to god some transcendent counterpart of sense-perception.[67] The similarity, however, between Lactantius' statement and Philo's triadic thinking is overwhelming. I resist the temptation to distract attention from Philo by dilating at length upon such real or apparent contradictions. The limited purpose of my discussion has been no more than that of illustrating with the aid of examples the affiliations and nuances of some minor, but far from insignificant, items of Philonic terminology.

Memorial University, St. Johns
Newfoundland

---

[66] Cf., e.g., Cicero, De div. 1.57.129 = Posidonius, fr. 378 Theiler (Ut enim deorum animi sine oculis, sine auribus, sine lingua sentiunt inter se quid quisque sentiat (ex quo fit ut homines, etiam taciti optent quid aut voveant, non dubitent quin di illud exaudiant), sic animi hominum, cum aut somno soluti vacant corpore aut mente permoti per se ipsi liberi incitati moventur, cernunt ea quae permixti cum corpore animi videre non possunt) with the notes of A.S. Pease (citing in particular Clement of Alexandria, Str. 7.7.37.1-3 = SVF 2.1058: οὔκουν ἀνθρωποειδὴς ὁ θεὸς τοῦδ' ἕνεκα, [καὶ] ἵνα ἀκούσῃ, οὐδὲ αἰσθήσεων αὐτῷ δεῖ) and Theiler (citing in particular Plutarch, De gen. Socr. 589 B-C). Cf. further PGL s.v. αἴσθησις Β.4.

[67] On the transcendental counterpart of sense-perception (αἴσθησις) enjoyed by divinities and their mode of communication amongst themselves and with mankind see Hermeias, In Phdr. pp. 68.2–69.18 C. à propos of Plato, Phdr. 242c1f. (καί τινα φωνὴν ἔδοξα αὐτόθεν ἀκοῦσαι) and Proclus, In Crat. 77-79, pp. 36.20–37.21 Pasquali. The extent to which the visible gods enjoyed sense-perception was debated; cf. Olympiodorus, In Phaed. 4.9f. West. with Westerink's note ad loc. listing further relevant texts. See also the account of the perceptive capacity of the world-soul in Proclus, In Tim. 2.83.3–85.31 D. On the mode of communication between disembodied souls see Plotinus, Enn. 4.3.18.13-22 H.-S. (οὐδὲ δὴ φωναῖς, οἶμαι, χρῆσθαι νομιστέον ἐν μὲν τῷ νοητῷ οὔσας [sc. ψυχάς], ... γινώσκοιεν δ' ἂν καὶ τὰ παρ' ἀλλήλων ἐν συνέσει. ἐπεὶ καὶ ἐνταῦθα πολλὰ σιωπώντων γινώσκοιμεν δι' ὀμμάτων· ἐκεῖ δὲ καθαρὸν πᾶν τὸ σῶμα καὶ οἷον ὀφθαλμὸς ἕκαστος καὶ οὐδὲν δὲ κρυπτὸν οὐδὲ πεπλασμένον, ἀλλὰ πρὶν εἰπεῖν ἄλλῳ ἰδὼν ἐκεῖνος ἔγνω), Enn. 6.7.1.11-15 H.-S. (... ὅπως μὴ φθείροιτο ῥᾳδίως τῶν ζῴων τὰ σώματα, τὸ αἰσθάνεσθαι ἔδωκε, καὶ δι' ὧν ἐνεργήσουσιν αἱ αἰσθήσεις ὀργάνων. ἀλλ' ἤτοι ἐχούσαις τὰς δυνάμεις ἔδωκε τὰ ὄργανα ἢ ἄμφω. ἀλλ' εἰ μὲν ἔδωκε καὶ τὰς αἰσθήσεις, οὐκ ἦσαν αἰσθητικαὶ πρότερον ψυχαὶ οὖσαι), Enn. 2.9.14.8f. H.-S. (εἰ δὲ μὴ βούλονται τοῦτο λέγειν [sc. οἱ ἐπαοιδὰς γράφοντες], ἀλλὰ πῶς φωναῖς τὰ ἀσώματα [sc. ὑπακούουσι];); Philoponus, De aetern. 4.9, p. 77.15-20 Rabe (ὥσπερ οὖν ἐπὶ τῶν λογικῶν ἐπιστημῶν εἴ τις γυμνὰς αὐτὰς καθ' αὑτὰς σωμάτων τὰς ἡμετέρας ψυχὰς ἐπινοήσειεν, εἶδεν ἂν αὐτὰς οὐδενὸς οὐκέτι δεομένας ὀργάνου εἰς τὸ ἐκφαίνειν ἀλλήλοις τὰς οἰκείας ἐννοίας ἀλλὰ γυμνοῖς τοῖς ἀλλήλων προσβαλλούσας νοήμασιν, κτλ.); Elias, In Porph. Isag. p. 95.29f. Busse (ὁ μέντοι ἄγγελος λόγῳ οὐ χρῆται ὡς ἐνδιάθετον μόνον ἔχων λόγον, οὐ μὴν καὶ προφορικόν), ibid. p. 191.14f. B. (ὁ λόγος διάφορα σημαίνει· λέγεται γὰρ λόγος καὶ ὁ ἐνδιάθετος, καθὸ καὶ τοὺς ἀγγέλους φαμὲν λογικούς, καὶ ὁ προφορικός). Disembodied souls, like angels, have λόγος ἐνδιάθετος but not προφορικός! See further PGL s.v. αἴσθησις Α.4 (souls after death) and 5 (angels and daemons).

PHILO'S PRINCIPLES OF SEXUAL CONDUCT AND THEIR INFLUENCE ON CHRISTIAN PLATONIST SEXUAL PRINCIPLES[*]

Kathy L. Gaca

Philo of Alexandria, though not a Christian himself, is a figure of major importance in the development of early Christian sexual morality. His reinterpretation of the LXX sexual regulations, I will argue, forms one of the bases of Christian Platonist sexual values.[1] Philo's reinterpretation is important because he combines some of the Pythagorean and Platonic principles of sexual conduct with the LXX regulations. His selective use of Pythagorean and Platonic thought is a characteristic feature of Middle Platonism.[2] Philo extends Middle Platonism further by melding its sexual norms with those of the Pentateuch. In so doing he constructs an innovative conception of the sexual rules that the LXX has bequeathed to the Lord's Greek-speaking people,[3] and particularly to the Christian Platonist church fathers. Philo is important because the sexual principles of Christian Platonism develop from his synthesis of Middle Platonism and the Pentateuch and are not understandable without it.

Previous scholars on Philo's sexual ethics, however, have studied the Jewish and pagan philosophical roots of Philo's sexual ethics,[4] not the innovative synthesis that he constructs from Middle Platonist and Pentateuchal sexual principles. Consequently neither Philo's synthesis

---

[*] I would like to thank Jonathan E. Bremer, Howard Jacobson, John M. Rist, an anonymous referee and the editors of this Annual for their many valuable comments and suggestions.

[1] On Philo's predominantly Septuagintal Pentateuch see *SHJP* 3.1.479–80 and for the relatively few exceptions that P. Katz argues indicate a different LXX recension, see his *Philo's Bible* (Cambridge 1950), esp. 96-7, which supersedes earlier scholarship on the textual basis of Philo's Pentateuch, 125-38.

[2] For the Middle Platonist aspect of Philo's thought and its Pythagorean elements see D. T. Runia, *Philo and the Timaeus of Plato* (Leiden 1986) 20-22, 46-57 and J. Dillon, *The Middle Platonists* (New York 1977) 139-83.

[3] Except where greater specificity is warranted I generically refer to the people who worshipped the OT God in some form in antiquity as 'the Lord's people,' because more specific proper names (e.g. Israelites, Jews, Samaritans, God-fearers, Christians) do not include all groups who identified themselves as members of the Lord's people. I refer to God of the OT both as 'the Lord' and as 'God'.

[4] I. Heinemann, *Philons griechische und jüdische Bildung* (Leiden 1932, reprint Darmstadt 1962) 261-92, S. Belkin, *Philo and the Oral Law* (Cambridge, Mass. 1940) 219-70.

nor the formative role it plays in the making of Christian Platonist sexual values have received the attention they deserve. In this study I will explicate Philo's synthesis of Middle Platonist and LXX sexual principles. I will also indicate, by exploring Philo's influence on Clement of Alexandria, how the Christian Platonist interpretation of the biblical sexual principles develops from Philo's synthesis.

Philo's sexual principles

Philo has two criteria by which he distinguishes impermissible from permissible sexual activity: First, is the sex act practiced 'for pleasure' rather than 'for procreation'? The Pythagoreans, as we will see, are Philo's source for this 'procreationist' criterion. Second, does the sex act entail apostasy from the Lord? The LXX Pentateuch is Philo's source for his conception of sexual apostasy from the Lord.

Philo maintains that human sexual activity should be motivated only by the purpose of procreation, that reproductive sexual relations should occur within the marriage bond, and that all other sexual relations are overly hedonistic and hence blameworthy.[5] For example, in his biographies of Abraham, Joseph, and Moses, Philo portrays the biblical patriarchs as exemplars of the strictly reproductive sexual behavior that he thinks his readers should emulate. Abraham's sexual relations with Hagar are strictly for reproduction, not for pleasure (*Abr.* 249).[6] Abraham further believes that Isaac should make love to Rebecca only for the procreation of children, not for pleasure (*QG* 4.86). Joseph similarly supports the procreationist principle when he resists the advances of Potiphar's wife: 'Before acts of legitimate marital intercourse, we do not know other women, but come as chaste males to chaste females, not with pleasure as the end, but for the production of legitimate children' (*Ios.* 43). Moses too remains oblivious of sexual pleasures except insofar as they are necessary for 'the sowing of legitimate children' (*Mos.* 1.28). The biblical patriarchs thus teach, according to Philo, that sexual relations should be for procreation and otherwise reveal an excessive indulgence in sexual pleasure.

Philo, insofar as he supports the procreationist position, believes that it is unjustifiable to engage in marital sexual intercourse for the purpose

---

[5] Philo is a strict adherent of the position that procreation within marriage is the sole justifiable purpose for engaging in sexual activity, as has already been observed by Heinemann, *Philons Bildung* 267-8, Belkin, *Philo* 219-20, A.C. van Geytenbeek, *Musonius Rufus and Greek Diatribe* (Assen 1963) 73, and J. Cohen, '*Be Fertile and Increase, Fill the Earth and Master It*': *The Ancient and Medieval Career of a Biblical Text* (Ithaca 1989) 139.
[6] Philo allows for the polygamy of the patriarchs, such as Abraham's sexual relations with his concubine Hagar, but otherwise he assumes the norm of the married couple.

of sating one's erotic drive. He observes that some husbands engage in this sexual practice with their wives (*Spec.* 3.9, *Virt.* 109), but he does not approve of it himself. Such husbands, Philo thinks, are so sexually undisciplined that they are 'maddened by eros.' They make love 'licentiously, not with other women, but with their own wives' (*Spec.* 3.9). Hence Philo disagrees with the idea that one may justifiably engage in marital sexual relations for the non-reproductive purpose of erotic fulfillment.[7]

The procreationist principle supported by Philo is a Pythagorean teaching. Pythagoreans who lived at least as early as Aristoxenus maintained that men should ejaculate only for the purpose of reproduction within the marriage bond. They supported this sexual restriction on the principle that 'there should be as many impediments as possible to the exercise of human sexual activity' (*Vit. Pyth.* 209-10).[8] The Pythagoreans further specified that men, while reaching an orgasm, should be as temperate and attentive to the reproductive goal as possible: 'One must leave as admissible only those [reproductive sex acts] that are for the purpose of temperate and lawful reproduction of children' (*Vit. Pyth.* 210). Later Pythagoreans strongly supported this teaching. For example, the Neopythagorean *Preambles to the Laws*, under the pseudonym

---

[7] On Philo's strongly negative evaluation of human sexual desire, see also Cohen, *Be Fertile and Increase*, 74, 239-40 and Runia, *Philo and the Timaeus*, 346. *Spec.* 3.35, in which Philo allows a husband to remain married to a wife who proves barren after years of marriage, does not show that Philo considers the fulfillment of sexual desire to be a justifiable purpose of marital sexual relations. In this passage he states only that he allows the barren marriage to continue, not that he permits barren marital sexual relations to continue. Further, Philo justifies the continuation of the barren marriage by appealing to a non-sexual purpose of marriage that was well recognized by ancient moralists: the husband and wife have habitual bonds of affection for each other etched into their hearts. On the marital purpose of sharing of one's heart, mind, and life with a spouse, see Antipater 508.11-19, Hierocles, 503.24-505.7 in Stobaeus, ed. C. Wachsmuth and O. Hense (Berlin 1884-1909, reprint Berlin 1974), vol. 4 and Musonius 90.24-92.6, in *Musonius Rufus*, ed. and tr. C. Lutz, *Yale Classical Studies* 10 (1947). The husband and wife therefore have strong non-sexual reasons to stay together despite their inability to have children. Philo might presume, on the one hand, that the couple would proceed to have a continent marriage. On this custom see P. Brown, *The Body and Society* (New York 1988) 96, 101, 403-4. On the other hand, Philo would not be inconsistent as a procreationist if he were to allow the couple to remain sexually active so long as they persevere with their seemingly hopeless goal of reproducing. The biblical example of Sarah giving birth to Isaac despite her barrenness would indicate to someone as religious as Philo that the couple's procreative intent may, God willing, come to fruition someday.
[8] Aristoxenus was born between 375 and 360 BC and the date of his death is unknown. References to Aristoxenus are to excerpts of his *Pythagorean Declarations*, which are in Iamblichus, *De vita pythagorica liber*, ed. L. Deubner 1937 (reprint Leipzig 1975). See also J. Dillon and J. Hershbell, *Iamblichus: On the Pythagorean Way of Life; Text, Translation, and Notes* (Atlanta 1991) 211, n. 18.

'Charondas', normatively defines semen as 'the seed of a man's children,' urges that 'nature made [this] seed for the sake of children, not for pleasure,' and asserts that a man should ejaculate for no other reason than to reproduce (62.30-33).[9] Similarly, the Neopythagorean *On the Nature of the Universe*, under the pseudonym 'Ocellus', asserts that 'we [Pythagoreans] do not engage in sexual relations for pleasure, but for the procreation of children' (135.11-12). He also quotes extensively and advocates the Pythagorean regimen of temperate procreationism as described by Aristoxenus (137.6-138.12). Philo learned the procreationist principle at least in part from the Neopythagorean treatise of 'Ocellus', as Heinemann has already observed.[10] His reputation as 'the Pythagorean Philo' among the early church fathers is thus supported by his conception of justifiable sexual conduct.[11]

The procreationist principle is a Pythagorean doctrine because it is motivated by a theory of the human birth process that presupposes and builds from the following Pythagorean ideas: the existence of the immortal soul, soul-body dualism, and the claim that the soul is ordered by harmonic intervals. The Pythagoreans according to Aristoxenus interpret conception and birth to be an act of 'leading someone into birth and existence' (*Vit. Pyth.* 212), that is, of leading an immortal soul into embodiment.[12] If the prospective parents reproduce 'randomly and brutishly,' then they lead souls carelessly into embodiment and consequently have offspring with bad moral character: 'Wretched offspring come from the bad, discordant, and disturbing blending in reproduction' that fails to be temperate and purposeful (*Vit. Pyth.* 211). The blending is discordant and bad for the child's moral character because the immortal soul, when embodied by non-purposeful and unrestrained

---

[9] All references to 'Charondas' and 'Ocellus' are to the edition of H. Thesleff, *The Pythagorean Texts of the Hellenistic Period,* Acta Academiae Aboensis 30 (Åbo 1965) 1-266. *The Preambles to the Laws* was written before the mid-first century BC, for it is mentioned by Cicero (*Leg.* 2.5.14), and it has an uncertain *terminus post quem*. *On the Nature of the Universe* was written before the mid-first century BC and was certainly written after Aristotle and probably after Critolaus. The likely approximate date of this treatise is 150 BC, for which see F. Sandbach, *Aristotle and the Stoics* (Cambridge 1985), 63-4. See also W. Burkert, 'Zur geistesgeschichtlichen Einordnung einiger pseudopythagorica' and H. Thesleff, 'On the Problem of the Doric Pseudo-Pythagorica,' *Pseudepigrapha I* (Geneva 1971) 42 and 73.

[10] *Philons Bildung,* 267-9. Philo refers to 'Ocellus' at *Aet.* 10.

[11] Clement of Alexandria, for example, refers to Philo as 'the Pythagorean Philo' at *Str.* 2.100. On Philo's reputation as a Pythagorean and other affinities of his thought with Pythagoreanism, see D. T. Runia, 'Why Does Clement of Alexandria call Philo 'The Pythagorean'? *VC* 49 (1995), 1–22.

[12] For this Pythagorean notion of human conception and birth see Plato, *Tim.* 43c7-d2 and F. M. Cornford, *Plato's Cosmology* (New York 1937) 147.

acts of reproduction, is subjected to having its harmonic intervals thrown badly out of tune, which registers as bad moral character in the offspring's personality.[13] If, by contrast, prospective parents act as good leaders of souls into embodiment, as the Pythagoreans urge them to do, then they conceive carefully and deliberately and thereby produce offspring who will have harmonious souls and hence a good moral character. The procreationist principle is therefore a Pythagorean teaching.[14] It is motivated by a cluster of tenets that are distinctive features of this thought system and is advocated by Pythagoreans or Pythagorean-influenced writers.[15]

Though procreationism is a Pythagorean teaching, it has hitherto not been recognized as Pythagorean by scholars, with the exception of De Vogel in her discussion of Pythagorean sexual mores.[16] Other scholars, such as Yarborough, Meeks, and Harder, have not distinguished the procreationist principle, which maintains that reproduction is the sole justifiable purpose of marital sexual relations, from the other more widespread sexual norm in the Hellenistic moral tradition, that reproduction is a central duty but not the only justifiable purpose of marital sexual relations. As a result, they have attributed the pre-Christian

---

[13] On the discordance with which the soul's harmonic intervals are afflicted during embodiment, see Plato *Tim.* 43c7-d2.

[14] Plato in the *Laws* similarly supports aspects of procreationism on Pythagorean grounds, 774c4-e2, 838e4-39a6. By the time of the early Roman empire the Pythagorean sexual principle gained a somewhat wider currency under the influence of Roman Pythagoreanism, on which see Seneca, *Ad Helv.* 13.3 and Musonius 86.4-12, ed. Lutz. Stoics other than Seneca and Musonius do not support the procreationist position. The Stoics Zeno, Chrysippus, Antipater, and Hierocles, for example, argue that sexual relations are in accordance with nature and hence justifiable provided that they occur for the purpose of fostering friendship, SVF 3.650, 652, 716-18, 721-2 and Stobaeus 508.2-3 (Antipater) and 503.24-505.7 (Hierocles). See also M. Foucault, *The Care of the Self* (New York 1986) 159-62, originally published as *Le souci de soi* (Paris 1984). The procreationist principle, by contrast, maintains that sexual relations are justifiable only if they are motivated by the purpose of reproduction.

[15] Van Geytenbeek (*Musonius Rufus*, 73) is mistaken to claim that absolute sexual renunciation is a Pythagorean principle of sexual conduct. He asserts, largely on the basis of Porphyry (AD 232/3-ca 305), that the Neopythagorean sexual principle was 'complete sexual abstention,' and not, as I have argued, the practice of strictly reproductive sexual relations within marriage. Porphyry, however, supports complete sexual abstention for reasons unrelated to Pythagoreanism. His principle of sexual renunciation is inspired by non-Pythagorean practitioners of sexual asceticism, such as the Gymnosophists of India and prophets of Zeus on the island of Crete (who practiced temporary periods of sexual abstention), *De abstinentia* 4.17, 19-20. Porphyry thus does not argue as a Pythagorean in favor of sexual renunciation.

[16] My argument in favor of the Pythagorean provenance of procreationism supports C. J. de Vogel's claim to the same effect, *Pythagoras and Pythagoreanism: An Interpretation of the Neglected Evidence on the Philosopher Pythagoras* (Assen 1966) 179-80.

origins of procreationism erroneously to the Hellenistic moral tradition at large merely because this tradition supports the position that reproduction is a central duty of marriage.[17] Van Geytenbeek, by contrast, recognizes the philosophical difference between procreationism and the less restrictive Hellenistic sexual norm. Partly under the influence of Geurts, however, he misinterprets the unambiguously procreationist passages by Aristoxenus and 'Charondas' to be expressions of the latter and he does not mention 'Ocellus'. Hence he mistakenly contends that procreationism is an exceptionally anomalous position shared only by Musonius, Philo, and Clement.[18] For these reasons the distinctively Pythagorean roots and motives for advocating procreationism have largely been overlooked by scholars in the modern day.

Philo extends the normative force of the procreationist principle by contending that Pentateuchal Law mandates it. He maintains that God's law as written in the LXX Pentateuch is identical with the pagan philosophical conception of natural law. For Philo, as previous scholars have shown, God's law and natural law 'are in mutual accord' and the person who adheres to God's law lives 'according to nature's intent' (*Opif.* 1-3).[19] Philo further believes that natural law mandates that human sexual conduct should be strictly procreationist (*Abr.* 249, *Her.* 163-4). Proper sexual obedience to God's law and procreationist sexual conduct are therefore one and the same for Philo: 'Servants of God fulfill the law of nature' by practicing strictly reproductive sexual relations in marriage (*Decal.* 119, *Praem.* 109-10). Philo accordingly interprets the LXX Pentateuch in support of his claim that Mosaic Law mandates procreationism. For example, he interprets Leviticus 18:19, which prohibits a man from having sexual relations with a menstruating woman, to mean that a husband should not have sexual intercourse with his wife during her period because the field of her womb is flooded during that time (*Spec.*

---

[17] O. Yarborough, *Not Like the Gentiles* (Atlanta 1985), 11; W. Meeks, *The First Urban Christians* (New Haven 1983), 101; and R. Harder, *Ocellus Lucanus* (Berlin 1926, reprint Dublin 1966) 122.

[18] Van Geytenbeek, *Musonius Rufus*, 72-3; N. Geurts, *Het Huwelijk bij de griekse en romeinse Moralisten* (Amsterdam 1928) 152-56.

[19] See D. Winston, 'Philo's Ethical Theory' *ANRW* 21.1 (1984) 381-88 and D.T. Runia, *Philo and the Timaeus*, 535-38; and on the Stoic notion of natural law, which Philo identifies with Pentateuchal Law, see P. Vander Waerdt, 'Zeno's *Republic* and the Origins of Natural Law,' in *The Socratic Movement* ed. Vander Waerdt (Ithaca, New York 1994) 272-7; G. Striker, 'Following Nature: A Study in Stoic Ethics,' *Oxford Studies in Ancient Philosophy* 9 (1991) 2-13, 35-50; G. Watson, 'The Natural Law and Stoicism' in *Problems in Stoicism*, ed. A.A. Long (Berkeley 1971) 216-38, and for earlier scholarship on Stoic natural law see M. Colish, *The Stoic Tradition from Antiquity to the Early Middle Ages* (Leiden 1990) 31-32, n. 62.

3.32-3). The husband is to be strictly a 'good farmer' of his wife's womb, and as any farmer knows, flooded fields cannot be successfully planted with productive seed.[20] Philo similarly attributes a procreationist motive to the prohibition of male homoerotic sex acts at Leviticus 18:22. Agents of male homoerotic sex acts reveal themselves to be bad farmers, for they labor over fields known to be sterile at the expense of fruitful ones (*Spec.* 3.39-40). Philo's patriarchs Abraham, Joseph, and Moses, further, show exemplary obedience to his conception of God's law by being dutifully procreationist, as we have previously seen. Philo thus attributes the procreationist doctrine to the Pentateuch and in so doing teaches that procreationism is part of God's mandate for his people.

Philo reinterprets the LXX Pentateuch in terms of the Pythagorean sexual principle by claiming that the Pentateuch is procreationist. The Pentateuch does not advocate the procreationist position by any strict interpretation of the text. For example, it claims that a man should refrain from sexual relations with a menstruating woman or with another man because such relations are, respectively, unclean and an abomination, not because God intends that sexually active men must be strictly procreative farmers, as Philo claims (Lev 18:19, 22). The Pentateuch does promote reproduction as a central and honorable reason for the Lord's people to engage in sexual activity.[21] This position is not procreationist, however, because it does not restrict religiously acceptable marital sexual behavior to the motive of reproduction only, which is what Pythagorean and Pythagorean-influenced advocates of the procreationist principle—including Philo—seek to do. Philo's conception of God's procreationist mandate for his people is therefore distinct from the biblical sexual principles. It is also distinct from the conceptions of permissible sexual conduct in other major sectors of Judaism and in pre-Platonist Christianity, which remain closer to the biblical background.[22]

---

[20] On the more general ancient Greek idea that female sexuality is like a fertile field to be sown, see P. DuBois, *Sowing the Body: Psychoanalysis and Ancient Representations of Women* (Chicago 1988) 39-85.

[21] For example, the honor owed mothers and fathers by their children is second only to the honor owed to the Lord, Exod 20:12, Deut 5:16. Further, the primordial man and woman and Noah's family are commanded to 'grow and multiply' by the voice of the Lord, Gen 1:28, 9:1. Finally, extensive genealogical lists show an interest in maintaining social continuity through the reproduction of offspring, Gen 4:25-31. On the importance of procreation in Judaism and the priority assigned to it in Jewish marital sexual regulations, see also Cohen, *Be Fertile and Increase*, 13, 27-35, 76-82, 125-40, 167-80; A. Mattioli, *La realtà sessuali nella Bibbia: Storia e dottrina* (Casale Monferrato 1987) 77-171; and L. Epstein, *Sex Laws and Customs in Judaism* (New York 1948) 138-47, and *Marriage Laws in the Bible and the Talmud* (Cambridge, Mass. 1942) 293-4.

[22] The procreationist principle is foreign to and incompatible with the thought of the rabbinic tradition, Paul, and Hellenistic Jewish and Christian sects that practice

Philo's second criterion for distinguishing impermissible from permissible sexual activity is largely consistent with and motivated by the LXX. If, in his estimation, a sex act constitutes sexual apostasy from the Lord, it is absolutely forbidden and its agents must be put to death either by human or divine agency, depending on the circumstances (*Spec.* 3.11, 31, 49-51). The notion of apostasy in the LXX refers to sexual and other kinds of activity that break the old covenant rules so thoroughly that transgressors must be put to death according to the Pentateuch and Prophets.[23] The LXX forbids the Lord's people from engaging in such acts

---

absolute sexual renunciation. The rabbinic tradition is not procreationist because of its position that a husband is not freed from the conjugal duty of marital sexual relations simply because he and his wife have produced all the children that they plan to have. A husband owes his wife conjugal rights to sexual relations on at least a weekly or bimonthly basis. The only time he *must* abstain from marital sexual relations with her occurs during his wife's menstrual period, on which see Belkin, *Philo and the Oral Law*, 219; O. Yarborough, *Not Like the Gentiles* (Atlanta 1985) 27. See also D. Boyarin, *Carnal Israel: Reading Sex in Talmudic Culture* (Berkeley 1993) 109-13 for further indications that rabbinic sexual principles are not procreationist. Paul is not a procreationist because he argues that the need to avoid sexual fornication (viz. extra-marital sexual activity) provides sufficient justification for Christians to engage in marital sexual relations, 1 Cor 7:1-3. Hellenistic Jewish and early Christian practitioners of absolute sexual renunciation, moreover, maintain that one should reject all sexual activity, not that one should limit sexual activity to procreation within marriage, on which see, for instance, Josephus, *BJ* 2.120-21, Matt 19:9-12, 1 Tim 4:1-5, Rev 14:4. The only other Hellenistic Jews besides Philo who are said to have advocated procreationism are the married Essenes (but not the sexually renunciatory Essenes) as described by Josephus, *BJ* 2.160-61. Josephus' Essenes too were possibly influenced by Pythagoreanism, for which see P. Gorman, 'Pythagoras Palestinus', *Philologus* 127 (1983) 30-42, who has revived and strengthened I. Lévy's argument to the same effect in *Le légende de Pythagore de Grèce en Palestine* (Paris 1927). Dillon and Hershbell (*Iamblichus*, 15), however, remain skeptical about this question of Pythagorean influence. In any event, regardless whether the historical Essenes were influenced by Pythagoreanism, Josephus's description of the Essenes, including their procreationism, clearly reveals such influence.

[23] Moses rewards Phineas with a hereditary priesthood for averting the Lord's wrath by killing a sexual apostate and his female lover, Num 25:1-9, 13. Negative reactions to apostasy lead also to mob violence and battles for purity. For example, the usurper Jehu, anointed king of Israel by the prophet Elisha, kills Jezebel's son Jehoram on the battlefield because of the apostasy instigated by his mother's 'fornications and magical potions,' that is, her religiously apostate ways, 4 Kgs 9:20-26. Jezebel too is killed for this reason in a manner that fulfills Elisha's grim prophecy, 9:10, 9:30-37. Because of sexual and other apostasy Hosea condemns Ephraim and its princes and vows to kill their offspring, 9:16; Amos warns the house of Jacob that its men and women will fall by the sword in Israel, 7:17; Isaiah warns the women of Zion that their acts of apostasy will cause their sons and husbands to be killed, 3:16-25, esp. 3:16, 24-25, cf 1:21; and Ezekiel says in the voice of the Lord, about apostates in Samaria and Jerusalem, 'Lead a mob against them, hand them over to uproar and plunder. Stone them with the stones of mobs and hollow them out with their swords. They shall kill their sons and daughters and burn down their houses,' 23:46-47. Biblical defilements that are less dangerous than apostasy, by contrast, have comparatively unproblematic purifications, such as washing

and further specifies that the Lord will disinherit and destroy them if sexual apostates remain alive, because their apostasy defiles the Lord's people to an intolerable degree.[24] Sexual apostates among the Lord's people are thus like agents of sexual treason, for they break the covenant and thereby threaten the monolatrous standard and security of their religious community. They must be put to death as sexually defiled renegades from the Lord in order to protect obedient members of the community from retaliation by the Lord. Consequently sexual apostasy is dangerous and sexual purity is beneficial because of the biblical position that sexual defilement threatens the hegemony of the Lord's people, while sexual purity helps the people attain and preserve their hegemony. The LXX therefore provides the basis for Philo's conception of sexual apostasy as well as for his claim that sexual apostates must be put to death.

The biblical rule that sexual and other apostates must be put to death seems harsh, rigid, and archaic. Numerous members of the Lord's people have understandably dissented from the rule in favor of the principle that God is merciful and that his people must be merciful as well, even toward sexual apostates.[25] Philo, however, is not one of them. We can understand his sexual values only by recognizing that he agrees with the biblical rule and hence would think that clemency

---

and temporary periods of isolation. For example, menstruating women and women in childbirth rejoin daily life after a set time of isolation that purifies their defilement, see J. Neusner, *Purity in Judaism* (Leiden 1973) 16-17, 21-23, 108, 110.

[24] The tribes whose lands the Lord claims as patrimony for his people are described as being defiled through certain sexual and other acts that are apostasy for the Lord's people to practice. Because of these pollutions they are said to be doomed by the Lord to be driven out, exterminated, and their sacred places destroyed. Provided that the Lord's people refrain from such acts and from marrying these religious aliens the Lord deems them pure and guarantees them his invincible protection. Should they fail, they are defiled and likewise subject to the Lord's wrath, Exod 23:23-33, 34:11-16, Lev 20:11-26, Num 25:1-9, Deut 4:25-28, 7:1-9:29, esp. 7:4, 9:4-5, 13-14, Hos 5:3-7, Ezek 20:30, 23:17, cf 1 Esdr 8:80, 9:7-10. *Jub.* 16.6, 20.6, 30.14-15, and 33.10-20 show the continuation of this biblical teaching in the second century BC. My thanks to Peter Brown for drawing my attention to *Jubilees*. On the work's approximate date between 170 and 150 BC, see James C. Vanderkam, *The Book of Jubilees* in *CSCO: Scriptores Aethiopici* 88 (Louvain 1989) v-vi.

[25] There is, for example, a strong and admirable humanitarian tendency in the rabbinic tradition. Though this tradition grants in theory that apostasy is to be punished by death, it requires, for example, that adultery meet extremely unlikely conditions to warrant killing adulterers and is tolerant of intermarriages, see Belkin, *Philo and the Oral Law*, 111-16, Epstein, *Sex Laws*, 324-5, 170-171. See also the didactic tale against stoning adulterous women at John 7:53-8:11. This tale is probably not part of John as first composed (see, however, J. P. Heil, 'The Story of Jesus and the Adulteress [John 7,53-8,11] Reconsidered,' *Bib* 72 [1991], 182-91), but nonetheless it is an early Christian teaching known to Papias, *PCB* 759d.

toward sexual apostates poses too much of a threat to the purity and attendant safety of the Lord's people.

Philo, in accordance with the LXX Pentateuch, urges that sexual apostates within his religious community be put to death. He maintains, for example, that '[Adulterers]... must be punished with death' because they defile the purity of family lines (*Spec.* 3.11, 58, 65). Similarly, men who make love to other men are 'worth killing by those who obey the Law' (*Spec.* 3.38). Men and women who have sexual intercourse with animals also 'must die' along with their four-footed sexual partners (*Spec.* 3.49-50).[26] These kinds of sexual activity are unambiguously marked as apostasy in the LXX Pentateuch and the penalty of death is their purification.[27] For Philo, therefore, if members of the Lord's people commit the kinds of sexual activity that are unambiguously apostasy according to the LXX, then they must be put to death in order to preserve the purity and safety of the community as a whole.[28]

Philo extends the death penalty to kinds of sexual activity that are classified as an abomination but do not explicitly warrant a death penalty in the LXX.[29] For example, the LXX Deuteronomy states that it is an abomination for female members of the Lord's people to become prostitutes (23:18-19), but it does not state how the Lord's people should react to prostitution within their community.[30] Philo interprets this prohibition to mean that the female members who become prostitutes are 'a pest, a bane,' and a source of 'communal defilement' and hence

---

[26] Leviticus (18:22-23, 29, 20:13) classifies male homoerotic and bestial sexual activity as abominations and prescribes violent death as the required purification.

[27] For adultery see Lev 20:10 and Deut 22:13-23, and for male homoerotic and bestial sexual activity see Lev 18:22-23, 29, and 20:13.

[28] Philo also claims that transgressions of the incest prohibitions in Leviticus 18 have led to the death and destruction of many by divine retribution, but he does not expressly urge the preventive measure of putting incestuous persons to death by human agency, as he does for other kinds of sexual apostasy, *Spec.* 3.14-19, 26-8.

[29] Prohibited sexual activity is occasionally described as an abomination in the eyes of the Lord. The OT, by means of this normative description, encourages members of the Lord's people to view such sexual activity with aversion, just as the Lord is said to view them, and thereby to refrain from them. Some sexual abominations explicitly warrant a death penalty, such as male homoerotic and bestial sexual relations (Lev 18:22-23), whereas other sexual abominations are not said to merit a death penalty and hence are not explicitly marked as apostasy according to the strict letter of the Law. Prostitution and the reconciliation of a woman with her first husband are LXX examples of the latter, Deut 23:18, 24:4, cf Jer 3:1.

[30] On the LXX interpretation that Deut 23:18-19 is a generic prohibition against female members of the Lord's people becoming prostitutes (as opposed to the Hebrew original, which prohibits the women from becoming cult functionaries whose religious duties may have been partly sexual in nature), see M. Gruber, *The Motherhood of God and other Studies* (Atlanta 1992) 22-24, n. 9.

that they must be stoned to death (*Spec.* 3.51, cf. *Ios.* 43).[31] As another example, the LXX Deuteronomy states that a woman becomes defiled by having a second husband and that she and her first husband commit an abomination if they reconcile (24:4, cf Jer 3:1). Deuteronomy does not state, however, what the community should do, if anything, in response to this abomination. Philo, however, explains that a divorcee transgresses 'ancient and divine sanctions' by cohabiting with a man other than her first husband. If the first husband takes the woman back upon her return, Philo thinks that he commits 'two of the worst transgressions, adultery and pandering.' Because their reconciliation is adultery according to Philo, the couple must be put to death (3.31). Philo thus classifies some of the more ambiguous kinds of biblically forbidden sexual activity as apostasy and extends the death penalty to those who engage in such sexual conduct.[32]

Philo's conception of sexual apostasy is thoroughly grounded in his exegesis of the LXX Pentateuch, not in his Middle Platonist learning. In some respects he adheres to the strict letter of the Law and in other respects he is stricter than the letter. Despite Philo's greater stringency, the Pentateuch nonetheless provides the basis from which Philo develops his notion of sexual apostasy, the religious dangers that he associates with it, and the kinds of sexual activity that he considers to be apostasy. Philo's second principle of impermissible sexual conduct is therefore part of his biblical and not of his philosophical training.

Philo assimilates the biblical principle of sexual apostasy to the Pythagorean principle of procreationism in an important but limited way. He believes that acts of sexual apostasy are motivated by the sexual appetite being driven to exceed the procreationist limit in its insatiable lust for the erotic pleasures of physical sexual activity. Philo supports the Pythagorean and Platonic conception and distrust of the sexual appetite: The sexual appetite, along with the other physical appetites, 'dwells farthest from the royal abode of reason [near the navel and diaphragm], for it is the most insatiable and unrestrained of beasts and is fed in those regions where food, digestion, and copulation are located' (*Spec.* 4.92-4).[33] Philo

---

[31] Previous scholars have argued that Philo's strong hostility toward female prostitutes should not be taken as a representative Jewish view. Epstein (*Sex Laws*, 152-7, 164-67), for example, notes that 'rabbinic law agrees that there is no death penalty for prostitution, no matter what kind,' and see also Belkin, *Philo and the Oral Law*, 256-61.

[32] Philo, I would suggest, views the LXX term 'abomination (βδέλυγμα)' to signify apostasy and he accordingly interprets as apostasy the LXX abominations of female prostitution and the reconciliation of married couples.

[33] Philo explicitly agrees with Plato and the Pythagoreans, who 'researched the nature of the soul and found that its nature is tripartite: reason, spirit, and the irrational appetite,' *Spec.* 4.92-4. The sexual appetite belongs to the irrationally appetitive part of

further agrees with Plato and the Pythagoreans that the appetite for sexual pleasure needs to be put on a short leash because otherwise its inherently unrestrained proclivity leads to sexual and social depravity (*Spec.* 4.84-91). He extends this claim in a revolutionary way, however, by maintaining that the incidents of sexual apostasy in biblical history were caused by the unrestrained appetite for sexual pleasure as interpreted by Plato and the Pythagoreans. For instance, Philo thinks that the Sodomites were motivated by their unrestrained sexual appetite for pleasure when they committed acts of sexual apostasy (*Abr.* 134-46).[34] The Israelites, further, committed sexual apostasy for the same motive of appetitive sexual licentiousness when they fornicated with the Moabite women (*Mos.* 1.295, 297). Philo therefore believes that the human sexual appetite, as interpreted in the Platonic and Pythagorean tradition, has a proclivity to disobey the LXX sexual regulations. This is a completely different proposition from Plato's claim that the sexual appetite has a proclivity to act contrary to reason in the rational part of the human soul.[35] Philo considers the sexual appetite to be prone toward acts of sexual apostasy unless it abides by the procreationist limit. He thus offers the procreationist principle as the way to cure the Lord's people of succumbing to sexual apostasy and its religious dangers: The Lord's people must heed God's procreationist law, as the Philonic Abraham, Joseph, and Moses did, for otherwise the sexually appetitive beast in their souls will likely lead them, as it led the Sodomites and Israelites, into sexual apostasy and then into suffering God's wrath.

---

the soul, Plato, *Rep.* 580e2-4 and Aristoxenus in Iamblichus, *Vit. Pyth.* 207-10. Plato in the *Phaedrus* sharply distinguishes the sexual appetite from Platonic eros. The former is 'the physical appetite for sexual pleasures,' whereas Platonic eros is 'an acquired belief' from Platonic philosophy that stimulates the rational part of the soul to desire the form of the Good or Beauty, *Phdr.* 237d3-9, cf 238b7-c4, 242d11-43a2, 246b1-3, 253d2-e5. On Plato's negative evaluation of the physical sexual appetite, see *Tim.* 91a1-d5, *Rep.* 329c3-4, 403a4-6, 458d5-e1, 573b6-7, 573d5, *Phdr.* 256c1-5, *Phlb.* 47b2-7, 65c1-e1, and *Laws* 734b4-6, 836a6-b4. For Philo's frequent repetition of this Platonic theme, see Runia, *Philo and the* Timaeus, 309-11.

[34] Philo states that the Sodomites committed sexual apostasy because they 'threw off the yoke' of sexual restraint, *Abr.* 134-46. In other words, they wrongly gave their sexual appetite free rein and for this reason, according to Philo, they committed sexual apostasy.

[35] On Plato's claim that the sexual appetite is prone to acting contrary to human reason see *Rep.* 439a1-40a2, 444b1-8, 573b6-d5, *Phdr.* 237e1-38a2, *Tim.* 70e4. Philo, however, contends that the sexual appetite has an innate proclivity to act contrary to Pentateuchal Law. From his perspective, to be sure, sexual conduct in accordance with Pentateuchal Law is also in accordance with reason, for reason is the basis of natural law and Philo identifies natural law with Pentateuchal Law. Unlike Philo, however, Plato's conception of sexual conduct in accordance with reason does not involve identifying the originally Stoic notion of natural law with a religious code of conduct.

Philo does not think, however, that sexual activity is an act of apostasy simply by virtue of occurring 'for pleasure' rather than 'for procreation'. Non-procreationist sexual activity within marriage is not apostasy according to Philo even though he argues that non-procreationist sexual activity transgresses God's law. If husbands make love for non-reproductive pleasure with their wives, as I have previously discussed, Philo censures them for being love-mad and behaving in an overly licentious manner (*Spec.* 3.10).[36] He recommends, however, the regimen of Moses' dietary laws, not death, for this class of sexual offenders (*Spec.* 4.96-7).[37] Further, Philo maintains that if men seek out women who are already known to be barren as wives, they willingly 'destroy their procreative semen' contrary to the law of nature.[38] He castigates such men severely in order to deter them from destroying their reproductive semen in the interest of sexual pleasure: They are 'adversaries of God' (*Spec.* 3.36). Despite the severity of this castigation, Philo neither claims nor suggests that such husbands are destined for divine retribution or should be put to death by human agency. Transgressors of procreationism are consequently unrestrained but not necessarily apostates in Philo's estimation. Husbands who make love for the purpose of erotic pleasure with their wives are in this group. They are sexually unrestrained, which Philo deplores, but they are not renegades from the Lord.

Philo refrains from identifying non-reproductive acts of sexual pleasure with sexual apostasy because he does not consider God's procreationist law to be as inflexible as the bona fide Pentateuch sexual regulations. Despite his claim that God's law is strictly procreationist, Philo distinguishes 'the great evils' of acting on the unrestrained appetite for sexual pleasure from an 'even greater evil,' namely, of engaging in a kind of sexual activity that is on Philo's largely Pentateuchal list of sexually apostate acts, such as adultery (*Mos.* 1.295-6). Philo's assimilation of the procreationist principle to the LXX sexual regulations is therefore incomplete: acts of sexual apostasy are also motivated by the unrestrained sexual appetite, but acts of unrestrained sexual appetition

---

[36] Philo finds non-procreationist sexual relations to be overly licentious because they show that the irrational sexual appetite is exceeding its strictly reproductive function as ordained by the law of nature as represented by the LXX Pentateuch.

[37] Philo recommends this dietary regimen because he believes the Pythagorean claim that a well-regulated diet is conducive to sexual restraint, whereas excessive eating habits lead to sexual licentiousness, *Spec.* 3.9-10, cf 'Ocellus' (quoting Aristoxenus) 137.26-138.3. Philo further maintains that Moses' dietary regulations are particularly conducive to sexual restraint, *Spec.* 4.92-97.

[38] Philo's position here is to be distinguished from the tolerance he shows toward the husband who remains with a wife who proves to be barren after years of marriage. See note 7 above.

are apostasy only if the Pentateuch explicitly outlaws or stigmatizes them.

There are nonetheless some aspects of Philo's conception of impermissible sexual activity that can be used to argue that the Lord's people commit apostasy if they engage in non-procreationist sexual activity within marriage. First, though Philo himself is relatively lenient toward non-procreationist sexual intercourse within marriage, such practices nonetheless transgress his conception of God's procreationist law. Consequently, if Philo's Christian patristic readers were to accept Philo's conception as the letter of the Law, then they would have reason to argue that the Lord's people commit apostasy by engaging in non-procreationist sexual activity within marriage. Second, Philo uses strongly negative imagery to depict the irrational sexual appetite: Nothing escapes the sexual appetite just as no fuel escapes being consumed by fire (*Decal.* 173-4). The sexual passions function like poison and poisonous animals (*Spec.* 4.86). They also have the capacity to be a 'city-destroyer of the soul' (*Spec.* 4.95). If the irrational sexual appetite is, as Philo claims, a fiery, poisonous, and snake-like destroyer of the soul, which Moses himself 'cast off with loathing' except for the purpose of reproduction (*Spec.* 4.95, *Mos.* 1.28), then Philo's patristic readers have reason to fear and abhor the practice of non-procreationist sexual activity within Christian marriage as much as Philo fears the sexual abominations. Clement of Alexandria, I will now argue, follows through on these implications of Philo's thought.

Clement's sexual principles

Clement of Alexandria, like Philo, supports the procreationist principle. He defines marriage as 'the union of husband and wife for the sowing of legitimate children' (*Str.* 2.137). If a husband engages in sex acts strictly for procreation with his wife, he does so with 'an earnest and temperate will' and his marriage is temperate (*Str.* 3.58, 86). If, however, a husband makes love to his wife for reasons other than procreation, Clement thinks his sexual conduct is blameworthy and not even fit to be considered marital because it fails to be strictly reproductive (*Paed.* 2.92, 95). Clement learned the procreationist position partly from the Pythagorean tradition: The Pythagoreans, he states, make love only for procreation, not for pleasure with their wives (*Str.* 3.24). He thus supports procreationism and shows some awareness of its Pythagorean provenance.

Clement, who was very familiar with Philo's writings,[39] draws upon

---

[39] See D. T. Runia, *Philo in Early Christian Literature: A Survey* (Minneapolis 1993), 132-

Philo's biblical exegesis to support and extend the claim that the LXX supports procreationism. For example, Clement refers to and agrees with Philo's distinctive claim that the Pentateuch has a procreationist motive in forbidding a man from making love to a menstruating woman (*Paed.* 2.92). Clement also draws some procreationist conclusions from other passages of Philo's biblical exegesis. For instance, Philo claims that the biblical ritual of circumcision signifies partly that the Lord's people must 'circumcise', that is, curtail their excessive appetite for sexual pleasure lest they commit sexual apostasy.[40] Clement assumes Philo's notion of 'circumcising' the sexual appetite in order to give a procreationist twist to Ezekiel's outcry, 'Circumcise the fornication among you!' Clement interprets Ezekiel to mean that Christians must 'circumcise' sexually appetitive transgressions of procreationism from their marriages because non-procreationist sexual activity is 'a violent outrage to nature' (*Paed.* 2.95). For another instance, Clement supplements Philo's claim that male biblical role models such Abraham, Joseph, and Moses obeyed God's procreationist law: 'You could not show any instance of any of the elders in the scriptures approaching a pregnant woman in order to have sexual relations with her. Rather, you would find men engaging in sexual relations with women only after their pregnancy and lactation' lest the men waste their strictly reproductive seed in defiance of God's procreationist law (*Str.* 3.72, *Paed.* 2.92).[41] Clement thus accepts Philo's arguments that the patriarchs heed procreationism and that the biblical taboo on making love to a menstruating woman has a procreationist motive. He also explicates and supports the procreationist implication of Philo's notion of circumcision.

For the final example of Philo's influence of Clement's procreationism, let us consider how Clement interprets Deuteronomy 21:10-13 in terms of Philo.[42] Deuteronomy prescribes that when a man takes a female prisoner of war as his wife, he must allow her thirty days of mourning prior to 'consummating' his marriage. During this period the woman's head must be shaved and her nails clipped. Philo maintains that this passage in Deuteronomy aims to prevent the man from

---

156; A. van den Hoek, *Clement of Alexandria and his Use of Philo in the Stromateis* (Leiden 1988) 23-230 passim, with earlier scholarship cited therein.

[40] On the allegorical interpretation of circumcision in Philo, see P. Borgen, *Philo, John and Paul* (Atlanta 1987) 62-65.

[41] Clement adds that Jeremiah 5:8 calls adulterers 'female-mad stallions' because they exercised the 'bad horse' in their souls, that is, the irrational sexual appetite, which Plato portrays as the bad horse in his chariot metaphor of the soul, *Paed.* 2.89, cf Plato *Phdr.* 246a6-b4.

[42] For Clement's verbal borrowings from Philo's *Virt.* 110-14 in his exegesis of Deut 21:10-13, see van den Hoek, *Clement and his Use of Philo*, 88-90.

behaving with such sexual unrestraint that he rapes his female prisoner of war immediately. The woman's thirty-day mourning period gives the man time to restrain such licentious urges. Philo allows the man to engage in sexual relations with him once her time of mourning is over, but only provided that he marries her first (*Virt.* 110-14). The husband has one of two conceivable reasons for copulating with his captive wife according to Philo. The first is the reproductive purpose that Philo strongly supports. The second is to sate the husband's erotic drive, that is, his licentious sexual appetite according to Philo's largely Platonic conception of male sexual arousal. Even though Philo criticizes this purpose for being overly licentious (*Spec.* 3.9), he nonetheless finds it the lesser of two evils if a husband sates his sexual appetite with his captive wife than if he rapes her without marrying her and then casts her aside.[43] Clement, however, thinks that even the lesser of the two evils is unjustifiable. He maintains that the head-shaving and mourning period are meant to ensure that the man will have sexual relations with his captive wife only in order to procreate. The husband finds his bald prisoner sexually unappealing and his thirty-day period of sexual abstinence from her gives him time to regain his sense of procreationist discipline and act accordingly (*Str.* 3.71). Clement therefore agrees with and further emphasizes Philo's Pythagorean-inspired claim that the LXX mandates procreationism.

Clement intensifies Philo's procreationist interpretation of the LXX by arguing that the LXX is inflexibly procreationist. He classifies non-procreationist sexual relations within Christian marriage as apostasy, and more specifically as adultery. Clement teaches married Christians that they commit adultery simply by virtue of engaging in acts of sexual unrestraint: 'By the unrestrained sexual appetite alone you commit adultery.'[44] He considers any non-procreationist sexual activity to be unrestrained, as we have seen. Clement consequently maintains that God will punish as adultery any non-reproductive sexual activity that a married Christian couple practices within marriage. He supports this claim by citing Ecclesiasticus 23:18-19, which warns that God is watching

---

[43] Philo asserts that the husband treats his captive wife with greater respect and sexual decorum than he would have shown if he raped her without marrying her, *Virt.* 112-13.

[44] *Protr.* 10.108, cf *Str.* 3.71, 94, *Paed.* 3.82. Clement's phrase 'by the unrestrained sexual appetite alone you commit adultery' is an allusion to Matt 5:27-8, but his allusion is mediated through his Platonic and Pythagorean conception of the irrational sexual appetite. Clement's sense of *epithumia* is Middle Platonist and refers to the irrational appetite in the third part of the tripartite soul, whereas the Matthean sense of *epithumia* as lust is not indebted to the Platonic position that the soul is tripartite and has an irrational sexual appetite in its physically appetitive part.

and will punish men who commit adultery by making love to other men's wives (*Paed.* 2.99). Clement recognizes the difference between his innovative notion of adultery and adultery in the biblical sense presumed in Ecclesiasticus: Non-procreationist sex acts within Christian marriage are not transgressions 'against neighbors' but of the married couple 'against themselves' (*Paed.* 2.100). Clement nonetheless thinks that biblical warnings about God's wrath against adulterers apply to non-reproductive sexual relations within Christian marriage because he interprets Philo's conception of God's procreationist law as the inflexible word of the Lord.[45]

Philo, by contrast with Clement, argues the more lenient position that marital sexual relations motivated by the purpose of pleasure are blameworthy but not apostasy, as I have previously shown. He is lenient toward non-reproductive marital sexual pleasure because his conception of apostate sexual activity is restricted to the kinds of sexual activity that the Pentateuch genuinely outlaws or at least stigmatizes. Clement, however, presumes that the anti-hedonistic principle of Philo's procreationism has the force of a Mosaic sexual regulation. For this reason he emphasizes the claim that non-reproductive sexual pleasure is a very serious religious danger to Christians. First, he makes the sensation of sexual pleasure seem the opposite of God: Pleasure is the very opposite of God's goodness (*Str.* 3.43). Clement accordingly transmutes Matthew's statement that Christians cannot serve both God and Mammon to mean that Christians cannot serve both 'God and pleasure' (*Str.* 3.26). Second, Clement bases his soteriology on the claim that the experience of sexual and other physical pleasures is the essence of the sinful human condition: Christ came into the world in order to save us from 'enjoying pleasures' (*Str.* 3.94). For Clement, consequently, God is the light and pleasure, including non-reproductive sexual pleasure within marriage, is the darkness. Even though Philo does not argue this position and Clement does, Clement does so because Philo's procreationist interpretation of the LXX Pentateuch makes Clement's line of reasoning possible.

Clement reinterprets the biblical distinction between sacred and defiled sexual activity in light of his position that the Pythagorean principle of procreationism is God's inflexible law. In biblical terms sexual intercourse is sacred provided that it is performed in keeping

---

[45] Clement, like Philo, supports the death penalty for adulterers in the traditional biblical sense, *Str.* 2.147. He does not go so far as to argue that Christian agents of non-reproductive sexual relations within marriage should be put to death, however, even though he classifies these acts as adultery and claims that adulterers 'against themselves' will be subject to God's wrath.

with God's sexual regulations. Sexual intercourse that deviates from these regulations is, by biblical definition, defiled.[46] Clement accordingly maintains that Christian sexual conduct is sacred provided that Christians obey the Pentateuchal sexual regulations: 'Given that the Law is sacred, marriage in accordance with the Law is sacred' (*Str.* 3.84). If, as Clement claims, the Law mandates the procreationist principle, then marital sexual relations that transgress the principle are defiled. Clement for this reason expands the biblical notion of defiled sexual activity to include transgressions of the procreationist dictate. He interprets Baruch's statement 'You were defiled in an alien land' (1 Bar 3:10-11) to mean that Christians who engage in sexual activity for pleasure rather than for procreation are defiled in the alien land of appetitive sexual pleasure (*Str.* 3.89). Christian marital sexual relations that deviate from the procreationist principle are thus a 'stained and defiled practice' that Christians need to cleanse from their marriages in order to keep the marriages sacred (*Str.* 2.143). Clement further suggests that married Christians face grave religious consequences if they fail to adhere to the procreationist standard of sexual purity. Angels fell from heaven, he claims, because they failed to restrain their sexual appetite (*Str.* 3.59, *Paed.* 3.14). Similarly, Christian spouses will fall from God's grace if they commit non-reproductive 'adultery' within marriage. Clement thus believes that Christian agents of non-reproductive sexual activity within marriage will incur the wrath of God for the sexual defilement that they bring upon themselves and the Christian community.

Clement is motivated to argue that non-procreationist sexual activity within Christian marriage is apostasy for at least two reasons relevant here.[47] First, Philo's various exegetical arguments supporting the notion of God's procreationist law gain the stature of God's law in Clement's mind. Hence Philo's procreationist exegesis of the Pentateuch seems to him like an implicit eleventh commandment that Christians must not transgress. Second, Philo's negative descriptions of non-procreationist sexual activity contribute to this impression. Since, according to Philo, the unrestrained human sexual appetite is poisonous, snakelike, and loathed as apostasy-prone by God's preeminent spokesman Moses,

---

[46] The adjective *hagios*, for example, denotes 'sacred' in the sense of 'separate from the profane and consecrated to God', cf. BAGD and Lampe, s.v. ἅγιος. Sexual activity is thus sacred if it occurs in proper devotion and obedience to God. By contrast, sexual activity that transgresses God's Law is defiled, on which see, for example, Gen 34:5, 27.

[47] These two reasons do not exhaust Clement's motives for arguing that Christian transgressions of procreationism are apostasy. His other motives for supporting this position are indebted to his interpretation of the apostle Paul's sexual principles and hence are beyond the scope of this article.

Clement has reason to argue that any non-reproductive sexual activity is apostasy, even within marriage.

Conclusion

Philo, I have argued, combines the Pythagorean principle of procreationism and the LXX sexual regulations together to a limited degree. He maintains that God's law is procreationist and that members of the Lord's people should therefore engage in strictly reproductive relations within marriage. Otherwise they are at risk of being led by the apostasy-prone nature of their sexual appetite to transgress the sexual regulations of the Pentateuch. Even though Philo himself does not believe that agents of non-procreationist sexual activity within marriage commit sexual apostasy, he makes such a position feasible given his arguments that God's law is procreationist and that the unrestrained human sexual appetite is religiously abhorrent. Clement, I have also shown, argues this position under the influence of Philo and in so doing takes the step that Philo himself refrains from taking: Christians commit sexual apostasy if their marital sexual relations fail to be strictly reproductive. Philo's limited synthesis of Pythagorean procreationism and the LXX sexual regulations is therefore important in the making of Christian Platonist sexual values. By casting the LXX Pentateuch into a procreationist mode, Philo enables Christian Platonist writers such as Clement to argue the latter-day Pythagorean view that the procreationist sexual principle is the inflexible mandate of God.[48]

Princeton University

---

[48] Other Christian patristic writers, such as Augustine, are sympathetic to Christian procreationism. Augustine, however, is not as inflexible as Clement. He, with Paul, recognizes that marital sexual activity is justifiable in order to prevent the married Christian couple from engaging in sexual activity outside of the marital bond, *De bono coniugali* 5-6. The procreationist doctrine continues in a mitigated form today in Roman Catholicism, due in large part to the influence of Augustine, and especially his *De bono coniugali*. See, for instance, R. Lawler, J. Boyle and W.E. May, *Catholic Sexual Ethics* (Huntington, Indiana 1985) 38-41.

PHILO ON THE CHERUBIM

Fred Strickert

The topic of the Cherubim is of great interest to Philo. Not only does he write a treatise which refers to the Cherubim in the title, but he discusses them in five other works as well. In *On the Cherubim,* his starting point is the mention of the Cherubim in the Garden of Eden in Gen. 3:24. This same text is treated again in *Questions and Answers on Genesis* 1.57. In the *Life of Moses* 2.97-100, Philo treats the Cherubim found on the ark of the covenant as described in Exodus 25. This material is likewise covered in *Questions and Answers on Exodus* 2.62–68. In the treatises *On Flight and Finding* 100-101 and *Who is the Heir* 166, these latter Cherubim are treated in passing with Ex. 25: 22 quoted in both cases.

All six passages are linked by a common interpretation in which the Cherubim symbolize the two powers of God, the kingly and creative powers, which correspond to the names κύριος and θεός. As far as I can ascertain, Philo is unique in making such an interpretation of the Cherubim. Philo himself goes so far as to state that he arrived at this interpretation by divine inspiration (*Cher.* 27):

> But there is a higher thought than these. It comes from a voice in my own soul, who oftentimes is god-possessed and divines where it does not know.

This statement led me to search out the origins of Philo's interpretation.[1] Did he create it totally anew or did he make use of elements already present combining them into a new interpretation? Philo gives us some assistance by also presenting several alternate interpretations and an etymology of the name Cherubim. By studying this material one would hope to find a few clues why Philo was so attracted to the Cherubim and how he arrived at this interpretation. Thus I will proceed in the following order: First, I will analyze Philo's etymology for the name Cherubim. Then I will look at alternate interpretations. Finally, I will direct myself to Philo's 'higher' interpretation of the Cherubim as

---

[1] According to the study of David M. Hay, this is one of four passages in Philo which connect the theme of inspiration to his exegetical activity (*Somn.* 2.252; *Cher.* 48; *Spec.* 3.1-6). Philo does not merely cite his 'inspired' insights, but demonstrates them in terms of exegetical argumentation. David M. Hay, 'Philo's View of Himself as an Exegete: Inspired, but not Authoritative,' *SPhA* 3 (1991) 40-52. See also Ronald Williamson, *Jews in the Hellenistic World: Philo* (Cambridge 1989) 169; S.-K. Wan, 'Charismatic Exegesis: Philo and Paul Compared', *SPhA* 6 (1994) 54–82, esp. 56 ff.

powers of God. My conclusion will be that various pieces of evidence point to the hypothesis that Philo drew his inspiration from the mention of the Cherubim in the archaic hymn preserved in the prophet Habakkuk.

The Name Cherubim

In *Mos.* 2.97, Philo presents an etymology for the name Cherubim. The ones who are called Cherubim in the Hebrew tongue are called 'Recognition and Much Knowledge' (ἐπίγνωσις καὶ ἐπιστήμη πολλή). As scholars have pointed out,[2] this interpretation is derived through division of the Hebrew word הַכְּרֻבִים into two parts: הַכָּרָה which means 'knowledge' or 'recognition', and בִּינָה which means 'insight'. Likewise the adjective πολλή can be found in the word רַב . Philo does not say clearly whether he was drawing upon traditional material or whether he arrived at this interpretation himself. However, a closer analysis of the texts may be helpful in determining the origins of this etymology.

There are several problems which are immediately raised by this etymology of 'Recognition and Much Knowledge'. First, such an interpretation is conspicuously absent from rabbinic literature. Rabbi Abbahu, for example, claimed that the name Cherubim derived from the preposition כְּ added to the noun רוּבֶה . Thus the Cherubim were described as being 'like a youth'.[3] Secondly, it is not perfectly clear how Philo's etymology relates to the description of the Cherubim in the Hebrew Bible. Thirdly, Philo's 'Recognition and Much Knowledge' requires the repetition of a number of letters. One might expect either 'Much Knowledge' (ἐπίγνωσις πολλή) or 'Recognition and Knowledge' (ἐπίγνωσις καὶ ἐπιστήμη). However, Philo's etymology seems to have added something.

The Church Fathers, unlike the rabbis, appear to have been very interested in this etymology. However, there is no case where Philo's definition 'Recognition and Much Knowledge' is repeated *in toto*. Clement of Alexandria says that Cherubim meant ἐπίγνωσις πολλή.[4] This occurs in a context which shows knowledge of *Mos.* 2.97ff., but which

---

[2] Lester L. Grabbe, *Etymology in Early Jewish Interpretation: The Hebrew Names in Philo*, Brown Judaic Studies 115 (Atlanta 1988) 219; Edmund Stein, *Die Allegorische Exegese des Philo Alexandria*, Beihefte zur Zeitschrift für die Altestamentliche Wissenschaft, 51 (Giessen 1929) 52; Hermann L. Strack und Paul Billerbeck, *Kommentar zum Neuen Testament aus Talmud und Midrasch* (München 1926) 3.168.
[3] *Chag* 13b; *Sukka* 5b.
[4] Clement, *Stromata* 5.35.6.

includes other traditional material as well.⁵ It would appear that Clement has either reduced Philo's two terms for knowledge into one or relied on an etymology in his other sources. Likewise Origen, following Clement, uses *multitudo scientiae*⁶ and Augustine uses *plenitudo scientiae*.⁷

Jerome offers an exception. In his book on the *Interpretation of Hebrew Names*, he offers the following interpretation concerning Ex. 25:18: *Cherubin scientiae multitudo aut scientia et intellectus*.⁸ What is significant about these two alternatives is that both fit the number of letters in the Hebrew word הַכְּרֻבִים. It is striking that Jerome does not also allow a parallel to Philo, such as *scientiae multitudo et intellecti*. Here it is clear that Jerome is not making use of the *Life of Moses*, but rather Philo's *Questions and Answers on Exodus*. In QE 2.62, Philo does refer to a translation of Cherubim as ἐπίγνωσις πολλή. In §67, he speaks of γνῶσιν καὶ ἐπιστήμην specifically with reference to the Cherubim, though not in the form of a definition. In this case, the Philo reading fits Jerome. Yet throughout the remainder of Jerome's *Interpretation of Hebrew Names* and throughout the rest of his corpus of writing, Jerome prefers the alternate etymology: *multitudo scientiae*.⁹ Unfortunately, Jerome never explains his choice.

This short survey of the Church Fathers on the topic of the Cherubim demonstrates that there was clear interest in the etymology presented in Philo's *Life of Moses*. However, it was never repeated quite in that form. One can conclude either that the Fathers rejected Philo's etymology as awkward, or that they had a better alternative available in another source.

Jerome noted that he employed an onomasticon which had been composed by Philo himself and expanded by Origen.¹⁰ However, recent study of Philo's etymologies shows that Jerome was actually mistaken and that Philo himself was likely using onomastica already common in his day.¹¹ A careful examination of Philo's QE 2.62, in fact, supports this

---

[5] For a detailed study of Clement's use of Philo, whom he mentions four times by name, see Annewies van den Hoek, *Clement of Alexandria and his Use of Philo in the Stomateis: An Early Christian Reshaping of a Jewish Mode*, Supplements to Vigiliae Christianae 3 (Leiden 1988), and David T. Runia, *Philo in Early Christian Literature: A Survey*, CRINT 3.3 (Minneapolis 1993) 132–156.
[6] Origen, *Num. Hom.* 5.3.
[7] Augustine, *Expositions on the Book of Psalms*, LXXX.2.
[8] Jerome, *Liber Interpr. Hebr. Nom.* 12.20.
[9] Jerome, *Liber Interpr. Hebr. Nom.* 4.11; 17.15-17; 35.7; *Letter* 53.9; *Homily on the Psalms* 7 and 26; *Commentariorum in Hiezenchielem* I, i.6-8; III, x.18-22; IX, xxviii.11-19; XII, xli.22-26.
[10] Jerome, *Liber Interpr. Hebr. Nom.* 72.1; 59.1-60.3.
[11] Grabbe (n. 2) 102-7; D. Rokeah, 'A New Onomasticon Fragment from Oxyrhynchus and Philo's Etymologies,' *JTS* 19 (1968) 70-82; Runia (n. 2) 318.

view that Philo himself employed onomastica. Here Philo seems to be offering a choice of two traditional interpretations:

τὰ χερουβὶμ ἑρμηνεύεται μὲν ἐπίγνωσις πολλή
ἢ ἐν ἑτέροις ὄνομα
ἐπιστήμη πλουσία καὶ κεχυμένη.

The introductory formula ἑρμηνεύεται in fact is quite typical of Philo and signals that he is relying on such a source.[12] It is thus significant that the etymology which follows, ἐπίγνωσις πολλή, is that employed by the Church Fathers. They are relying on a common source (this is more likely than that they all took it direct from this Philonic text).

Philo's further explanation ἐπιστήμη πλουσία καὶ κεχυμένη is introduced by ἢ ἐν ἑτέροις ὄνομα. In this case Marcus' translation may be misleading. He translates the words ἐν ἑτέροις as 'in other words' suggesting that Philo is simply expanding on his previous statement.[13] Rather it is also possible to read this as 'the name [is translated] among others...' which suggests that what follows is an already proposed alternate interpretation. Thus it is proper to separate the definitions in order to arrive at their origin.

From QE 2.62, it appears that Philo, in fact, does favor the interpretation ἐπίγνωσις πολλή. It is striking that these words are related only to the texts which deal with Exodus 25. Philo does not introduce this etymology in his two works on Genesis or in the two general works mentioning the Cherubim. It only occurs in Mos. and QE. Thus a careful analysis of Exodus 25 may be helpful in arriving at the origin of this etymology. QE 2.67 helps to clarify the matter. Here the words γνῶσιν καὶ ἐπιστήμην in the answer are related to the question: 'What is the meaning of the words, 'I shall be known to thee from there?'' Philo makes a definite connection between the verb 'be known' in the text of Ex. 25:22 and the etymology of the word for Cherubim. It becomes apparent that this etymology developed in a setting where the Septuagint was used—characteristic of the onomastica[14]—because the reading in the Hebrew Bible differs on this important point.

The word in the MT here is נוֹעַדְתִּי which is usually translated 'I will meet' or 'I will appoint'. However, the LXX reads γνωσθήσομαι. The obvious explanation is that the translator transposed letters so that he understood the verb ידע in place of יעד. The same words occur in MT Ex. 29:42 where the LXX reads τάξομαι.[15] Unlike the LXX, the Targums

---

[12] It is used in 175 of the 250 etymological pericopae of Philo: Grabbe 41-3.
[13] Philo PLCL, Supplement 2.108.
[14] Grabbe (n. 2) 105.
[15] Rudolf Bultmann refers to this as evidence of the LXX's anthropocentric view.

support the MT reading: 'And I will appoint my Word with Thee....'[16] We can conclude then that the etymology for Cherubim developed from the LXX reading of Ex. 25:22. Thus it is not surprising that there is no evidence for it in rabbinic literature while it is common both in Philo and in the Church Fathers.

The reading of LXX Ex. 25:22, of course, is γνωσθήσομαι not ἐπιγνωσθήσομαι and Philo writes in QE 2.67 γνῶσιν not ἐπίγνωσιν. How then does the next step in development take place? Again the Church Fathers provide a clue. This time it comes from an obscure third century writing, sometimes attributed to Methodius, called 'An Oration Concerning Simeon and Anna.'[17] The author first describes the presence of Anna in the temple in terms of the Seraphim of Is. 6:3 and then goes on to speak of the Cherubim:

> As also the blessed prophet Habakkuk has charmingly sung, saying, 'In the midst of two living creatures thou shalt be known: as the years draw nigh, thou shalt be recognized—when the time is come thou shalt be shown forth.' See, I pray you, the exceeding accuracy of the Spirit. He speaks of knowledge, recognition, showing forth. As to the first of these: 'In the midst of two living creatures thou shalt be known,' he refers to that overshadowing of the divine glory which, in the time of the law, rested in the Holy of Holies upon the covering of the ark, between the typical Cherubim, as He says to Moses, 'There will I be known to thee.'

This oration, while making a totally different application, is important because it focuses on the verb 'to make known' with regard to the Cherubim and because it draws attention to another text which otherwise might have been overlooked, Hab. 3:2.

At first glance, Hab. 3:2 would appear to have nothing to do with the Cherubim. This verse reads:

> O Lord, I have heard the report of thee and your work.
> O Lord, do I fear.
> In the midst of the years renew it.
> In the midst of the years make it known.

This is simply a general recalling of the great deeds of the Lord in the past and a call for him to continue to make himself known in the future. A very unusual thing, however, has happened in the process of translation. The LXX text is significantly expanded:

'Gnosis,' TDNT, 1.699.

[16] Jerusalem Targum and Palestinian Targum Ex. 25:22.

[17] This work is dated to the third century because of interest in the Theotokos question and because of similarity in style to Methodius; see ANF, 6.385ff. See also CPG 1.1827, where it is noted that some scholars prefer a 5th or 6th cent. date.

Κύριε, εἰσακήκοα τὴν ἀκοήν σου καὶ ἐφοβήθην
κατενόησα τὰ ἔργα σου καὶ ἐξέστην.
ἐν μέσῳ δύο ζῴων γνωσθήσῃ·
ἐν τῷ ἐγγίζειν τὰ ἔτη ἐπιγνωσθήσῃ·
ἐν τῷ παρεῖναι τὸν καιρὸν ἀναδειχθήσῃ·
ἐν τῷ ταραχθῆναι τὴν ψυχήν μου
ἐν ὀργῇ ἐλέους μνησθήσῃ.

Lord, I have listened to the report of thee and I was afraid,
I have considered thy works and was amazed.
In the middle of two living creatures thou shalt be known,
In the drawing near of the years thou shalt be recognized.
In the coming of the right time thou shalt be revealed,
In the troubling of my soul in anger thou shalt remember mercy.

LXX Hab. 3:2 thus calls for God to reveal himself on the mercy seat of the ark between the two Cherubim.

How this change took place is relatively simple to explain. The critical lines of Hebrew text are:

בְּקֶרֶב שָׁנִים חַיֵּיהוּ
בְּקֶרֶב שָׁנִים תּוֹדִיעַ

In the first line, it is not difficult to see how the words שָׁנִים חַיֵּיהוּ meaning '[in the midst of] years, make alive' have been misread as שְׁנַיִם חַיִּים '[in the midst of] two living creatures.' The translator has just read in the previous verses (2:20):

The Lord is in His holy temple.
Let all the earth give praise before him.

With the translator's attention directed to the thought of the Lord on the Cherubim throne in the temple,[18] it is not surprising that he wrote ἐν μέσῳ δύο ζῴων in Hab. 3:2. At this point, however, he would have noticed that he was left without a verb and thus borrowed from the parallel line below writing γνωσθήσῃ. This, of course, made perfectly good sense because of the LXX Ex. 25:22 reading. The translator apparently saw his mistake because he then went on to create a new set of parallel lines which include the omitted material. However, he was clever enough not to draw the parallel lines too closely to his errant line. Thus he made a bold new beginning by reading not בְּקֶרֶב, a prepositional phrase which he had translated ἐν μέσῳ above, but rather

---

[18] One must take into consideration the unusual connection between these verses with the originally independent and ancient Psalm in chapter 3 attached to the the words of the prophet Habakkuk. Musical and liturgical terms such as Shigionoth in verse 1 (see Psalm 7:1) and Selah in verses 3, 9, and 13 (see Psalm 3) suggest its use in Temple worship.

בְּקֶרֶב, a preposition with a *kal* infinitive construct which he translated first as ἐν τῷ ἐγγίζειν and then as ἐν τῷ παρεῖναι. He then completed these two parallel lines with words for time and two parallel verbs. The result is a sentence which now refers to the Cherubim and presents three parallel verbs to describe God's appearance in their midst: γνωσθήσῃ, ἐπιγνωσθήσῃ, and ἀναδειχθήσῃ.

What is important for this discussion is that this reading of Hab. 3:2 became scripture for the Diaspora and thus new source material arose for understanding the Cherubim. The verb ἐπιγνωσθήσῃ thus became part of the vocabulary associated with the Cherubim and resulted in the etymology for Cherubim: ἐπίγνωσις πολλή. I would suggest therefore that this part of Philo's etymology developed in a context where LXX Ex. 25:22 and LXX Hab. 3:2 were studied together. It is significant that Philo was free to make use of both γνῶσιν (*QE* 2.67) and ἐπίγνωσις (*QE* 2.62). Thus his interpretation was fairly recent and had not yet achieved a fixed form.

The other key word ἐπιστήμη is somewhat more difficult to pin down since it is a common term in Philo. In fact, it occurs no less than ten times in *Cher*.[19] Notably in his discussion of the soul, 'the love of knowledge' is the bridle (*Cher.* 19). It is striking, however, that the words which follow ἐπιστήμη in *QE* 2.62 are πλουσία καὶ κεχυμένη. What this refers to is not totally clear although the idea of richness may suggest a context in the Eden story. *QG* 1.57, in fact, may offer a clue in this regard. Here the Cherubim are described as the overseers of wisdom (Marcus retroverts as ἐπιστάται τῆς σοφίας) who are like a mirror. Again in Ezekiel 28, where the guardian Cherubim are located in Eden, the theme of knowledge and wisdom is prominent.[20] As in the case of the first etymology, it would appear that this alternate second tradition arose where a number of texts were studied together.

Our analysis of *QE* 2.62 shows that Philo had before him two separate traditions for the name Cherubim. The first, ἐπίγνωσις πολλή, was a common etymology which derived from the LXX Ex. 25:22 and Hab. 3:2 and which understood the Hebrew word הַכְּרֻבִים to be divided into two parts: הַכָּרָה and רַב. The second tradition, ἐπιστήμη πλουσία καὶ κεχυμένη, was probably a freer explanation based on the Eden story. The contribution of Philo was to combine these two traditions and thus in *Mos.* he gives the etymology: ἐπίγνωσις καὶ ἐπιστήμη πολλή. This combination thus supports the view that Philo did not know Hebrew.[21] The Hebrew

---

[19] *Cher.* 9, 19, 32, 41, 48, 52, 68, 71, 105, 127.
[20] ἐπιστήμη occurs several times in verses 3-7.
[21] S. Sandmel, 'Philo's Knowledge of Hebrew,' *SPh* 5 (1978-79) 107-112; V. Nikipro-

word הַכְּרֻבִים can be divided into הַכָּרָה (knowledge, recognition) and בִּינָה (insight) or it can be divided into הַכָּרָה (knowledge) and רַב (much). However, the combination of both does not correlate with the number of Hebrew letters. Philo himself seems to have sensed an awkwardness about this new etymology since his introduction is somewhat tentative: 'as (some) Greeks would say' (ὡς δ' ἂν Ἕλληνες εἴποιεν – Mos. 2.97). It is striking that in the following line he changes from optative to indicative mood in order to introduce the commonly-held allegory of the two hemispheres: ταῦτα δέ τινες μέν φασιν (Mos. 2.98). Then he returns to the optative once again when he introduces his own 'inspired' allegory: ἐγὼ δ' ἂν εἴποιμι (Mos. 2.99).

Philo thus is not presenting here the 'accepted' etymology, but rather an altered version of it. The important question to be faced is the reason why he made this change. It does not seem to be that Philo intended to offer the reader a complete summary of existing etymologies. Rather, coming at the beginning of a section on the Cherubim, the etymology is used to set the theme for the allegory which follows. Yet it is striking that the concept of knowledge does not recur in the discussion. Thus in the etymology it is not so important that the Cherubim are related to the concept of knowledge, but that this concept is expressed in parallel terms. For Philo it is important that the Cherubim are associated with duality.[22] This suggests, I submit, that two names are needed to describe them. The 'twoness' of the Cherubim is a point that Philo emphasizes every time he brings them under discussion. His two 'physical' allegories are built on the idea of twoness: two hemispheres and two heavenly realms. The same is the case in his 'higher' interpretation of the two powers. Thus Philo chooses an etymology which expresses duality: 'Recognition and Much Knowledge.' This is not at all the case in the Church Fathers where the focus is often on the variegated makeup of the Cherubim as described in Ezekiel. However, Philo is concerned entirely with two texts which emphasize the duality of the Cherubim: Gen. 3:24 and Ex. 25. Thus it may not be insignificant that one term ἐπίγνωσις derives from Ex. 25 while the other ἐπιστήμη derives from the

---

wetzky, Le commentaire de l'Ecriture chez Philon d'Alexandrie (Leiden 1977) 50-51; Grabbe, 63; Yehoshua Amir, 'The Interpretation of Hebrew Names according to Philo,' [Hebrew] Tarbiz 31 (1961), 297 [translated and published in Grabbe, 233-5]. This is contrary to H.A. Wolfson, Philo (Cambridge 1947) 1.89; A.T. Hanson, 'Philo's Etymologies,' JTS 18 (1967) 128-39.

[22] Cf. Irmgard Christiansen, Die Technik der allegorischen Auslegungswissenschaft bei Philon von Alexandrien (Tübingen 1969) 93. David Winston points out to me a similar preoccupation in Maimonides, Guide to the Perplexed 3.45, p. 577 Pines. See also E. R. Goodenough, Jewish Symbols in the Greco-Roman Period (New York 1953–68) 4.131–133.

Genesis account. Philo's intention in presenting this etymology, therefore, is to draw attention to the 'twoness' of the Cherubim.

Philo's 'Physical' Allegories

In *Cher.*, before he presents his 'inspired' interpretation, Philo offers the reader two physical interpretations of the Cherubim. In the first, one Cherub represents the outermost sphere of the fixed stars while the other represents the inner sphere in which the planets travel through seven zones (*Cher.* 23-24). Since Philo has used Gen. 3:24 as his springboard in this discussion, the flaming sword is said to stand for the revolution of the whole heaven (§25). In the second interpretation, the two Cherubim represent the two hemispheres. This interpretation seems to have originated, not from the Eden story, but from the reference in the description of the ark that the two Cherubim are standing face to face (Ex. 25:19). However, the sword also is given a role, representing the sun (§25-26). This second interpretation is repeated in *Mos.* 2.98 in a context in which the ark of Ex. 25 is described. The reference to the sword is missing, as would be expected. Two details have been added. The two hemispheres are described as 'one above the earth and one under it.' Secondly, the detail is added that 'the whole heaven has wings.' In the other four works of Philo which treat the Cherubim, nothing is said about such interpretations.

I have chosen to discuss these interpretations in reverse order because Philo makes it quite clear that he is making use of other sources. In one account, he begins with the words 'Some say...' (τινες μέν φασιν – *Mos.* 2.98). Unfortunately, Philo does not reveal his sources. Here too, however, the Church Fathers are of some help. Jerome refers to those who accept the interpretation of the two hemispheres as those 'who follow the foolish wisdom of philosophers.'[23]

Clement of Alexandria, however, seems to hold this interpretation in a higher regard. Although Clement knows Philo,[24] here he employs other sources (*Str.* 5.35.5–36.2):

> And those golden figures, each of them with six wings, signify either the two bears, as some will have it, or rather the two hemispheres. And the name Cherubim meant 'Much knowledge.' But both together have twelve wings, and by the zodiac and time, which moves on it, point out the world of sense. It is of them, I think, that tragedy, discoursing on nature, says:
> Unwearied time circles full in perennial flow,
> Producing itself. And the twin-bears

---

[23] Jerome, *Commentariorum in Hiezenchielem*, I, i.6-8.
[24] Van den Hoek (n. 5) 132-3.

> On the swift wandering motions of their wings,
> Keep the Atlantean pole.
>
> And Atlas, the unsuffering pole, may mean the fixed sphere, or better perhaps, motionless eternity.

Here the Cherubim are described as symbolizing the two hemispheres, not because of their position facing one another on the ark, but because they each have six wings (a conflation with the Seraphim of Isaiah 6) and thus the total of twelve fits nicely into the zodiac. That Clement here is drawing on a pre-Philonic tradition is suggested by Philo's seemingly unimportant comment: 'For the whole heaven has wings' (*Mos.* 2.98). The wings in this interpretation are constellations, yet in a second interpretation they represent only two of those constellations, the two bears. This is especially interesting because the bears are described in Homer as carriages (ἅμαξα),[25] and this is the common Biblical description of the Cherubim as the chariot of God. Thus Clement also includes a quotation attributed to Critias, uncle of Plato, which describes the motion of the twin bears via their wings.[26]

From this description by Clement it is possible to understand what Jerome meant by the 'foolish wisdom of philosophers.' What we have here is not so much an allegorical interpretation based on the description of the Cherubim. Rather it seems that Clement's source (or perhaps even Clement himself) has simply drawn an identification of the Cherubim conflated with already existing symbolism of mythology and popular religion.

Would Philo also fall under Jerome's rebuke? He, of course, does not allude to the twin bears. However, he does something quite similar. In his treatise *On the Decalogue*, in a context in which the Cherubim are never mentioned, he refers to the idea of 'a deluded mankind' (§52) which divides heaven into two hemispheres, 'one above the earth and one below it' (§56).[27] Their delusion is that 'they called them the Dioscuri and invented a further miraculous story of their living on alternate days.' This, of course, refers to the myth that the twins, Castor and Pollux, one the son of Zeus and the other the son of the mortal Tyndareus, shared their immortality by living half the time below the earth and half the time above the earth.[28] Though not a wagon or chariot, they are frequently portrayed as riding on white steeds. They are also related to the stars as the constellation Gemini and are regarded as the

---

[25] Homer, *Il.* 18.487; *Od.* 5.273.
[26] Critias, Pirithous, fr. 594 = fr. B18 Diels-Kranz.
[27] The wording is very similar to *Mos.* 2.98.
[28] Pindar, *Nem.* 10.80.

patron deities of sailors. Because of this, one should not overlook the importance of the Dioscuri in Alexandria.[29] With this in mind, one can easily understand Philo's need to present a 'higher thought.'

As was noted earlier, in his work *Cher.* Philo offers a another physical interpretation, one that is not repeated in other works. Again the Cherubim are described in terms of the stars. However, the source does not come from popular religion or mythology, but from philosophy. The Cherubim symbolize the outermost sphere of fixed stars and the innermost sphere of seven planetary zones. The description Philo offers here is taken directly from Plato's *Timaeus* 36c–d and 38d.[30]

Unlike the previously discussed interpretation, it would seem that it was Philo himself who made the connection between Plato's system and the Cherubim. This can be seen from the way he handles the symbolism of the flaming sword. It would seem that the sword itself is the starting point for this allegory since the sword is described as revolving and since motion is an important element in this description of the heavens.[31] Yet Philo only mentions the sword as an afterthought in §25, after he has already drawn his concluding sentence: 'This then is one interpretation of the allegory of the Cherubim.' Thus it would seem that Philo is not drawing on an already existing allegory, but rather he is composing it as he is writing. It is also worth noting that he does not repeat this allegory in the *Life of Moses* where the sword is not part of the Biblical text.

The description of God in Plato's *Timaeus* is significant. He is the one who 'makes' and 'places' bodies into their orbits (ποιήσας ὁ θεὸς ἔθηκεν – 38c). He is 'the engendering Father' (ὁ γεννήσας πατήρ – 37c). Philo picks up this latter designation in *Cher.* to describe how God ordered the sphere of the stars (§23). These descriptions of God also become important later in Philo's 'higher allegory'. There is one element which is new to this interpretation. Philo adds the imagery of the charioteer to describe God as still holding the reins in the orderly movement of the planets across their proper zones.[32] God not only is the one who sets the planets in their positions, he is also one who continues to guide them (§24). It is interesting that Philo concludes this allegory with a doxology:

---

[29] This was the name of Paul's Alexandrian ship to Rome (Acts 28:11).
[30] On the use of the *Timaeus* in this entire passage, see David T. Runia, *Philo of Alexandria and the Timaeus of Plato*, Philosophia Antiqua 44 (Leiden 1986²), esp. 208–209.
[31] See Runia 209, who suggests that the participle στρεφομένην played a decisive role in the exegesis.
[32] On the influence of Plato's *Phaedrus* myth here see below n. 35.

> For when God is with us, all we do is worthy of praise;
> all that is done without Him merits blame (§24).

The focus therefore is on the role of God.

This leads then to an important connection with Philo's treatise *On the Decalogue*. His understanding of the first commandment seems to play an important role in his evaluation of both 'physical' allegories. In that discussion, Philo clearly shows a disdain for those who see God as part of the created universe. As already seen, Philo describes as 'deluded' those who consider the two hemispheres as deity (*Decal.* 56). Likewise, he includes in that category one who makes the planets gods. In fact, he mentions in *Decal.* 54 those very planets mentioned as part of the innermost sphere in *Cher.* 22. What makes these two allegories 'lesser' to Philo is that some who use them may see God as 'many'. Thus, Philo is careful to show that God is one, creating and ruling. He made them all dependent upon himself (*Cher.* 22). This is the picture of the one God in *Decal.* 53. He is 'the highest and the most august, the Begetter, the Ruler' (τὸν δ' ἀνωτάτω καὶ πρεσβύτατον, τὸν γεννητήν, τὸν ἄρχοντα – §53). Not only is he the one who sets things in place, he is 'the invisible Charioteer who guides in safety the whole universe' (§60). God is one.

Philo's Higher Thought

From the previous section, it is evident that Philo's concern in the two physical allegories was to emphasize the oneness of God. From the etymology of the Cherubim in the first section, it is evident that Philo wished to stress the duality of the Cherubim. In Philo's 'higher allegory,' which he said he received by inspiration, his purpose is to show that (*Cher.* 27):

> While God is indeed one, His highest and chiefest powers are two, even goodness and sovereignty.

Thus in six different works, Philo shows that the Cherubim represent these two 'highest and chiefest powers' of the one God. It is not difficult to see how the Cherubim fit into this symbolism.

In the description of the ark in Exodus 25, God declares that he will make himself known in the midst of the two Cherubim. In the Targums this is expressed:[33]

> And I will appoint My Word with thee there, and will speak with thee from above the mercy seat, between the two Kerubaia that are over the ark of the testament.

---

[33] Jerusalem Targum, Ex. 25:22.

The two Cherubim symbolize the presence of the one God. Likewise in the Eden Story, the two Cherubim have a uniting force in the turning flaming sword. That God is also represented here is reflected in the tradition of the Jerusalem Targum:[34]

> And He cast out Adam and made the glory of His Shekina to dwell at the front of the east of the garden of Eden, *above* the two Kerubaia.

In *Cher.*, this presence is expressed in terms of the Logos who brings the powers together. In the other five works, Philo presents a number of variations on this theme. In *Fug.* 100–101, the Logos is represented as the image of God. In *Her.* 166, it is God himself who is present, not bringing together, but dividing.

Behind this symbolism one must look to Plato's image of the charioteer guiding the two horses.[35] Such a picture is obvious when one considers the role of the Cherubim in the Bible as God's chariot. Jerome, in fact, explicitly cites Plato as he makes use of the charioteer imagery, though for him it is a four-horse team, with each of the faces of the Cherubim representing a horse.[36] Philo likewise appears interested in the charioteer imagery throughout his works. As already noted, this occurs in his discussion of the first commandment in *Decal.* 60 and in Philo's allegory of the outer and inner spheres. In *Fug.* 100-101, Philo makes it quite clear that there is a charioteer of the powers who obey the directions of the seated speaker. Thus it is certain that this imagery of the charioteer helped to shape Philo's description of the Logos between the two powers.

A number of terms are used to describe the powers. One is termed as creating and begetting, and is marked by goodness and beneficence. The other is termed as kingly and sovereign, and is marked by punishment and legislation. As numerous writers have pointed out, this division corresponds somewhat with old rabbinic traditions which speak, not of powers, but of measures.[37]

Also an important element in this division (as also in rabbinic literature) is the presence of two divine names.[38] Philo links the name θεός with the creative power because in Greek thought θεός is said to derive

---

[34] Jerusalem Targum, Gen. 3:24.
[35] Plato, *Phaedrus* 246-49 and see above n. 33. Here we encounter influence of Plato's *Phaedrus* myth; cf. A. Méasson, *Du char ailé de Zeus à l'Arche d'Alliance: Images et mythes platoniciens chez Philon d'Alexandrie* (Paris 1986) 29–34 and *passim*.
[36] Jerome, *Commentariorum in Hiezenchielem*, I, i.6-8; cf. *Homily on the Psalms* 7.
[37] N.A. Dahl and Alan F. Segal, 'Philo and the Rabbis on the Names of God,' *JSJ* 9 (1978), 1-28. Williamson (n. 1) 50-51.
[38] Williamson 97-99.

from the verb τίθημι.³⁹ Likewise, he links κύριος with kingly power because the term κύριος was closely tied to the political realm of that day. Philo clearly pays close attention to the names of God as they occur in the Biblical text. He recognizes that in the creation account of Genesis 1, the name θεός stands alone because this is the creative name.⁴⁰ In Gen. 2:15, he shows that both names κύριος ὁ θεός are used in giving commandments and exhortations to Adam because the command involves both the bestowal of good things and the exercise of authority.⁴¹ At that point, Philo prepares the reader for the Cherubim episode at the end of Genesis 3 by stating that the terms κύριος ὁ θεός will occur once again when Adam is sent forth from the garden, since 'the Lord' as Master and 'God' as Benefactor had issued the commands, so in both capacities He inflicts punishment on him who had disobeyed them.⁴² Thus the occurrence of both terms κύριος and θεός in the Cherubim allegory is related to the fact that both are present in Gen. 3:23-24.

As noted, Philo is not unique in drawing this distinction between benevolence and sovereignty and in applying the two names of God. This apparently was part of the tradition both in Alexandria and Palestine. However, Philo is unique on a number of points. He alone uses the term 'powers' here. He alone combines the concept of Logos. He alone ties this all to the symbol of the Cherubim. What then was Philo's inspiration which brought this all about? I would suggest as a possibility a text from the first section of this paper, the third chapter of Habakkuk. As noted above, LXX Hab. 3:2 has undergone an extreme change so that it clearly speaks of God's self-revelation in the midst of the two Cherubim. I demonstrated earlier on that this text is directly related to the etymology of the term Cherubim as used in Alexandria and presented by Philo. Thus it is reasonable to assume that it was in fact an important source of material for study on the Cherubim in Philo's community.

The issue of Philo's use of Habakkuk, however, is not without problems. Nowhere else does he quote Habakkuk. It is quite clear that Philo's primary interest is in the Pentateuch and that the remainder of Scripture is only a supplement.⁴³ However, that is not to say that the

---

³⁹ Cf. Herodotus, 2.52.
⁴⁰ *Plant.* 86.
⁴¹ *Leg.* 1.95.
⁴² *Leg.* 1.96.
⁴³ E.R. Goodenough, *By Light, Light* (New Haven 1935) 75-80; David M. Hay (n. 1), 45f.; Ronald Williamson, *Philo and the Epistle to the Hebrews* (Leiden 1970) 498-501; Sidney G. Sowers, *The Hermeneutics of Philo and Hebrews: a Comparison of the Interpretation of the Old Testament in Philo Judaeus and the Epistle to the Hebrews* (Zurich 1965) 136. For a list of Philo's citations of the LXX outside the Pentateuch see *Biblia Patristica Supplément Philon d'Alexandrie* (Paris 1982) 88–91. Nikiprowetzky (n. 21) 236, 246 has argued that

prophets are totally neglected. In *Cher.* 49 he speaks of the exegetical process in terms of mystery religions where he has been initiated to the 'greater mysteries' through Moses, while the prophet Jeremiah is 'a worthy minister of the holy secrets.' He makes similar references to Isaiah (*Her.* 25) and Hosea (*Mut.* 139). It must be said, however, that references to the prophets are slight.

The case of Habakkuk 3, however, is somewhat more complicated. As W.F. Albright noted long ago, this chapter is likely a very archaic hymn which demonstrates the origins of the Yahweh cult in the southern regions and which recounts his triumphant activities in language highly dependent upon the mythical traditions of the ancient Near East. Although these words were later attached to the book of the prophet Habakkuk, liturgical language suggests that they had an independent use in the temple cult. That this independent status continued long after the association with Habakkuk is demonstrated by the existence of five Greek manuscripts which contain only Habakkuk chapter 3.[44] These manuscripts, known as the Barberini version of Habakkuk 3, present a non-LXX translation whose provenance is most likely Alexandria.[45] At some point the Barberini version and the Septuagint version were studied together since one verse is virtually identical in both versions. What is striking is that this is verse 2, precisely the one which is radically different from the Hebrew and which is related closely with the etymology of the name Cherubim. It is possible then that this is evidence of early lectionary use in Alexandria.[46] Philonic dependence upon Habakkuk 3, therefore, may be indirect rather than a direct reference to the LXX version.[47]

As was demonstrated earlier, the Greek translation of Hab. 3:2 (in both LXX and Barberini versions) describes the Cherubim throne where Yahweh makes himself known.[48] This is consistent with the reference of Yahweh going forth to battle with his horse and chariot in verse 8. Although the Hebrew is plural מַרְכְּבֹתֶיךָ , it is rendered in Greek with the singular ἡ ἱππασία σου. In view of this image, an analysis of verses 3b-5 is significant:

---

there are many more allusions to the rest of the LXX in Philo than appear on the surface.
[44] Edwin M. Good, 'The Barberini Greek Version of Habakkuk III,' *VT* 9 (1959) 11-30.
[45] Good 28-30.
[46] H. St. J. Thackeray, 'Primitive Lectionary Notes in the Psalm of Habakkuk,' *JTS* 12 (1911) 191-213.
[47] See also Peter Katz, *Philo's Bible: The Aberrant Text of Bible Quotations in some Philonic Writings and its Place in the Textual History of the Greek Bible* (Cambridge 1950).
[48] See further Theodore Hiebert, *God of My Victory: The Ancient Hymn in Habakkuk 3* (Atlanta 1986) 145-146.

His glory covered the heavens,
and the earth was full of his praise.
The brightness was like the sun;
rays came forth from his hand,
where his power lay hidden.
Before him went pestilence,
and plague followed close behind (NRSV).

Hiebert[49] has chosen to translate the final two lines as follows:

Before him marched Deber.
Resheph advanced at his feet.

Here the Hebrew terms דֶּבֶר and רֶשֶׁף , translated as pestilence and plague, are personified. Resheph[50] is a deity known throughout the ancient Near East and associated with Syrian and Egyptian kings as a military patron.[51] Deber[52] as a figure mentioned in the Ebla texts also is characterized as a deity.[53] Together they serve as Yahweh's military entourage.

The Greek versions of verse five provide several significant readings. The Barberini version reads:

πρὸ προσώπου αὐτοῦ προελεύσεται πτῶσις
καὶ κατὰ πόδας αὐτοῦ ἀκολουθήσει τὰ μέγιστα τῶν πετεινῶν.

Here the Resheph figure is described as 'the great winged ones' at his feet.[54] Good notes that Resheph was associated in some traditions with Apollo the charioteer of the sun and that the sun was portrayed in Egypt as a winged disk.[55] It may be that several images are conflated here, but for the reader the picture is clearly that of the winged Cherubim chariot throne. Thus it is significant that this is a plural reading. The LXX version is quite different:

πρὸ προσώπου αὐτοῦ πορεύσεται λόγος
καὶ ἐξελεύσεται, ἐν πεδίλοις οἱ πόδες αὐτοῦ.

Here the reading ἐν πεδίλοις may seem at first altogether different although Good suggests that the image here is of the winged sandals of

---

[49] Hiebert 4.
[50] See also Deut. 32:24; Ps. 78:48; Job 5:7.
[51] Albright 14; Hiebert 92; Frank Moore Cross, *Canaanite myth and Hebrew Epic* (Cambridge 1973), 50, 70-1, 102; William J. Fulco, *The Canaanite God Resep* (New Haven 1976).
[52] See also Ps. 78:48; 91:5-6; Deut. 28:21.
[53] Hiebert 93.
[54] Likewise Aquila reads πτῆνον and Symmachus and Theodotion read ὄρνεον. Good 13 notes that similar readings occur in Latin, Syriac, and Coptic.
[55] Good 14.

Perseus.[56] The point is no longer that Resheph is following along in the retinue of Yahweh, but that Yahweh has a standing place.

The parallelism between Deber and Resheph is lost in the Greek versions since this latter figure is rendered in the plural. The former figure therefore is rendered as λόγος, positioned not at Yahweh's feet, but before his face. This results in the picture of Yahweh in control through the λόγος which guides the winged Cherubim under his feet. This is precisely the image portrayed by Philo in *On the Cherubim*. The ideas of unity and duality have been brought together by the translator of Hab. 3:5.

There is another underlining duality which comes forth in Habakkuk 3. As in Philo, it is suggested through the names for God. While verse 2 employs κύριε, verse 3 uses ὁ θεός. This distinction in names is brought out again at the chapter's end. Verse 18 draws out that distinction is poetic parallelism:

ἐγὼ δὲ ἐν τῷ κυρίῳ ἀγαλλιάσομαι,
χαρήσομαι ἐπὶ τῷ θεῷ τῷ σωτῆρι.

In the following verse 19, the names are brought back together again:

κύριος ὁ θεὸς δύναμίς μου (LXX).

While the translations here are from the LXX, the Barberini version is in complete agreement on the use of names for God.

It is also significant, in view of Philo's discussion of the 'powers,' that the LXX version concludes with a reference to the Lord God's δύναμις. The Barberini version mentions δύναμις at the beginning. In verse 4c, just prior to the mention of the winged chariot throne in verse 5, the reader is told that the power of God's glory is established there (ἐκεῖ ἐπεστήρικται ἡ δύναμις τῆς δόξης αὐτοῦ). There is no explicit discussion of the creating and ruling powers of God in this section. However, there is no question that the numerous references to waters conquered by God in verses 8-15 recall the creation imagery of the Baal Myth and the E'numa E'lish creation accounts and that the references to God's judgment point to the establishment of his rule. Therefore the sun and moon stand in awe of God (verse 10-11). Beneficence and sovereignty are two sides of the power of the Lord God. Therefore, the Psalmist's prayer in verse 2 is that 'in wrath may you remember mercy' (ἐν ὀργῇ ἐλέους μνησθήσῃ). For Philo, the mixed potencies show the goodness of God when 'the glory of His sovereignty is seen amid the beneficence' (*Cher.* 29). As a result those pondering the nature of God acquire the

---

[56] Good 13 cites Thackery for that observation.

virtues of courage and reverence (εὐλάβεια θεοῦ). In the same way, the Psalmist in Hab. 3:2 hears the report about the victorious God and stands in awe (εὐλαβήθην – Barberini version).

Just as Philo reminds the reader of the fiery sword in Eden (*Cher.* 28), the hymn of victory in Hab. 3 also includes numerous allusions to weaponry and to light. John Day, in fact, has noted seven different instances of the imagery of lightning and thunder as his weaponry in Habakkuk 3 (and also Psalm 29) which again echo the Baal myth.[57] He goes on to suggest that the Seraphim in fact are personifications of lightning and therefore this text has important parallels with Isaiah 6.[58] Thus an appropriate parallel to Is. 6:3 is provided by Hab. 3:3:

> His glory covered the heavens,
> and the earth was full of his praise.

This is significant since the Church Fathers connect the Seraphim and Cherubim in their discussions and show knowledge of an exegetical process which weaves together a number of Biblical texts—a connection and a process which appears to be prior to Philo.

The case of Methodius, mentioned above, is noteworthy. His quotation of Hab. 3:2 follows directly a reference to Isaiah 6:3 and continues with Exodus 25:22. The fact that he quotes Hab. 2:20 shortly thereafter, points to his dependence upon the LXX version of Habakkuk. Philo also is dependent upon a large number of passages which allude to the Cherubim and, as I have attempted to show, Habakkuk 3 may well stand behind his 'inspired' allegory. It is not so easy, however, to demonstrate a direct dependence upon the LXX version. Rather his allegory points to readings in both the Barberini and LXX versions, which may betray a source where these two versions had already come together.

Wartburg College, Waverly, Iowa

---

[57] John Day, 'Echoes of Baal's Seven Thunders and Lightnings in Psalm XXIX and Habakkuk III 9 and the Identity of the Seraphim in Isaiah VI,' *VT* 29 (1979) 143-51.
[58] Day 149.

SUR UN TITRE LATIN DU *DE VITA CONTEMPLATIVA*

Caroline Carlier

Introduction

Les œuvres de Philon, philosophe juif d'Alexandrie, ont été conservées grâce à des chrétiens. En 233, Origène fit venir d'Alexandrie à Césarée sa bibliothèque personnelle dans laquelle se trouvaient des textes de Philon. Eusèbe, évêque de Césarée en établit un catalogue. Plus tard, un autre évêque de Césarée, Euzoius, découvrit la bibliothèque d'Origène entre 376 et 379 et fit des copies sur parchemins des textes de Philon. Ces codices constituent le fonds de la tradition byzantine dont sont issus soixante cinq manuscrits datés du IXe au XVIIe siècle.[1] Dès le IVe siècle, des textes de Philon furent disponibles en Italie. C'est le début de la tradition occidentale avec notamment les traductions latines de *Quaestiones in Genesim* 4.154–245 et du *De vita contemplativa* 1–41. Le texte original dont sont issues ces traductions semble être le même que celui de la tradition manuscrite de Césarée.[2]

Il est, donc, possible de reconstituer les jalons de la transmission de l'œuvre de Philon depuis le premier siècle jusqu'à la fin de l'époque byzantine. Malheureusement, il est difficile, comme on le verra dans cette étude, de suivre le cheminement des textes de Philon en Occident surtout entre le IXe et le XVIe siècle, époque des *editio princeps* en grec (Turnebius 1552)[3] et en latin (Justinianus 1520).[4] Il est émouvant de constater avec quel intérêt Philon a été édité et commenté depuis le XVIe jusqu'à nos jours. Mais tout spécialiste de Philon reste interloqué devant le matériel à sa disposition. Le passage de l'original grec aux traductions latines, en particulier, constitue un problème difficile pour la recherche philonienne.

Notre attention a été attirée par F. C. Conybeare[5] sur une version

---

[1] Runia (1993) 21–22.
[2] *Ibid.* 25–26.
[3] Φίλωνος Ἰουδαίου εἰς τὰ τοῦ Μωσέως, κοσμοποιητικά, ἱστορικά, νομοθετικά. Τοῦ αὐτοῦ Μονόβιβλα. *Philonis Iudaei in libros Mosis, de mundi opificio, historicos, de legibus. Eiusdem libri singulares*, edidit Adr. Turnebus, Paris, 1552 = G-G n° 391.
[4] *Philonis Judaei quaestiones centum et duae, et totidem responsiones morales super Genesin*, latine ex editione Aug. Justiniani, Paris, 1520 = G-G n° 444.
[5] Conybeare (1895).

latine du *De vita contemplativa*, publiée par Jean Sichard à Bâle en 1527.[6] L'édition de J. Sichard est la deuxième édition de Philon après *l'editio princeps* des *Quaestiones in Genesin* à Paris en 1520. Le texte que propose Jean Sichard est très intéressant car il diffère de toutes les autres éditions latines du *De vita contemplativa*; il comporte un titre et un sous-titre tout à fait originaux: *De Essaeis* et *Philonis Iudaei liber de statu Essaeorum, id est Monachorum qui temporibus Agrippae regis monasteria sibi fecerunt* (Des Esséniens; livre de Philon le Juif au sujet du mode de vie des Esséniens, c'est-à-dire des moines qui se sont faits construire des monastères au temps du roi Agrippa).[7] Je me propose d'enquêter ce sous-titre. J'essaierai de rassembler les données connues: éditions et manuscrits du *De vita contemplativa* (lui-même) ou d'autres œuvres de Philon susceptibles de nous renseigner sur le texte latin édité par Jean Sichard. Puis, je comparerai la version latine à la version grecque pour en faire ressortir les différences. Finalement, je tenterai d'expliquer pourquoi un tel sous-titre et qui pourrait en être l'auteur ou l'inspirateur. On constatera que dans la chaîne de transmission de l'œuvre de Philon, les intervenants connus ne sont pas toujours 'honnêtes' et que les inconnus sont d'hypothétiques coupables.

L'édition de Conybeare

L'édition polyglotte et critique de F. C. Conybeare présente le texte latin du *De Vita Contemplativa*.[8] Ce texte est celui de l'édition de Jean Sichard.[9] Conybeare, dans ses 'introductory remarks',[10] explique pourquoi il a préféré ce texte du *De Vita Contemplativa* de Bâle (1527) à celui de l'édition de Paris (1520) dont il donne un descriptif.

L'édition de Paris dépend du seul manuscrit de Fulda. Comme l'explique Conybeare: 'In this volume [c'est-à-dire l'édition de Paris], the last lines of *Quaestio* 102 and the first twenty or so of the *Contempl.* are absent, and the two run into one section as if they belonged together'.[11] F. Petit commente cette même édition dans son étude sur *Quaestiones et Solutiones in Genesin*.[12] En recensant les manuscrits de *Quaestiones in*

---

[6] *Philonis Judaei, libri antiquitatum. Quaestionum et solutionum in Genesin. De Essaeis. De nominibus Hebraicis. De Mundo.* Johannes Sichardus et Adamus Petrus, Basileae, 1527 = G-G n° 445.
[7] La comparaison avec des éditions latines postérieures permet aussi de conclure que ce titre et ce sous-titre apparaissent uniquement dans l'édition de Bâle de 1527.
[8] Conybeare (1895) 146–153.
[9] Que j'ai moi-même consultée à la Bibliothèque Nationale de Jérusalem.
[10] *Ibid.* 139–145.
[11] Conybeare (1895) 142.
[12] Petit (1973) 43 sqq.

Genesin, elle a constaté la même particularité que celle trouvée dans l'édition de Paris. Ayant examiné cette même édition à la Bibliothèque Nationale de Paris, j'ai pu constater qu'elle ne comporte que le texte des *Quaestiones in Genesin* auquel est 'ajouté un morceau de *Contempl.*'

L'édition de Jean Sichard, en revanche, recense cinq textes: *(Libri) Antiquitatum, Quaestionum et Solutionum in Genesin, De Essaeis, De Nominibus Hebraicis, De Mundo.* Dans l'édition de Sichard, *Quaestionum... in Genesin* et *De Essaeis* sont deux traités séparés. *Contempl.* est intitulé *De Essaeis*[13] et au début du texte lui même se trouve le sous-titre: *Philonis Iudaei liber de statu Essaeorum, id est Monachorum qui temporibus Agrippae regis monasteria sibi fecerunt*. Ce sous-titre latin, pour un lecteur familier de Philon et connaisseur du traité du *Contempl.* dans son original grec, a lieu de surprendre: quel en est l'auteur? Pourquoi une telle description du sujet? Je commencerai par un examen détaillé de l'édition de Jean Sichard, texte et préface.

L'édition de Jean Sichard

Dans sa préface, Jean Sichard explique qu'il a travaillé sur deux manuscrits: le manuscrit de Fulda et le manuscrit de Lorsch. Il s'avère que le manuscrit de Fulda, daté du Xe siècle, est son manuscrit de base[14] et que l'édition de Bâle est l'unique témoin d'un emploi du manuscrit de Lorsch. J. Sichard dit que les deux manuscrits se ressemblent (... *quae tamen ita erant inter se similia, ut nec ovum diceres ovo magis*...). Si les manuscrits de Fulda et de Lorsch étaient si semblables et dépendants l'un de l'autre, comment se fait-il qu'il y ait une si grande différence de textes entre l'édition de Paris de 1520 (d'après le manuscrit de Fulda) et celle de Bâle de 1527 (combinaison des deux manuscrits de Fulda et de Lorsch avec prépondérance du manuscrit de Fulda)? Dans son édition, Jean Sichard a écrit en marge du texte des *Quaestiones* onze lignes avant la fin du traité la note suivante: *Variabant hic exemplaria, secuti tamen sumus Laurissanum ut vetustius* (Ici les exemplaires étaient différents l'un de l'autre, nous avons, alors, suivi le manuscrit de Lorsch qui était le plus ancien). Autrement dit, la fin de *Quaestiones* et le début du *Contempl.*, absents du manuscrit de Fulda dépendent du manuscrit de Lorsch. La note de Jean Sichard est elle crédible? ou est-il lui-même responsable de corrections et d'ajouts personnels?

---

[13] A ma connaissance, c'est l'exemple unique d'un tel titre comme il résulte d'une comparaison avec d'autres éditions latines postérieures. Les autres éditions comportent généralement le titre traduit du grec soit: *De Vita Contemplativa, sive supplicum virtutibus*.

[14] Cf. Petit (1973) 32: 'il (le manuscrit de Fulda) est annoté de sa main et corrigé par lui d'après Lorsch. Sichard l'a transmis à son imprimeur qui y a porté des indications de mise en page conformes à l'édition de 1527.'

Il est impossible de comparer les deux manuscrits; en effet, tous les chercheurs qui ont travaillé sur *Contempl.*[15] ou sur les *Quaestiones*[16] ou sur *Liber Antiquitatum Biblicarum* (ci-après *L.A.B.*)[17] ou même sur Jean Sichard lui-même[18] n'ont pu retrouver la trace du manuscrit de Lorsch. Ce manuscrit, daté de la fin du Xe au début du XIe siècle, provient du monastère bénédictin du même nom situé à Mayence. Dom Dekkers, cité par F. Petit, fait remarquer que le fonds de livres du monastère correspond à celui du monastère de St Riquier dont le catalogue daté de 831 mentionne 'Liber Philonis Judaei I Vol.' Selon F. Petit, il s'agit de l'exemplaire unique de la tradition latine groupant *Liber Antiquitatum Biblicarum, Quaestiones et Contempl.*[19]

P. Lehmann dans son livre[20] a étudié l'édition de Bâle de 1527 et la méthode de travail de Jean Sichard de manière générale. L'observation du texte latin, l'étude des manuscrits utilisés et l'analyse des remarques de Jean Sichard lui font conclure que toute la lacune du manuscrit de Fulda comblée par le manuscrit de Lorsch n'est pas une interpolation de Jean Sichard ni du scribe de Lorsch.[21]

Donc, si la remarque de Dom Dekkers est exacte, on peut supposer que le texte fondé sur le manuscrit de Lorsch et transmis par l'édition de J. Sichard, est sous la forme que nous lui connaissons depuis 831. Il faut alors enquêter ce qui s'est passé pendant le laps de temps entre la traduction latine et l'année 831, date du catalogue de St Riquier.

Le traducteur latin

Que savons-nous du traducteur latin de *Contempl.* et que penser de sa traduction? L'identité du traducteur latin est inconnue. Dans mon observation de l'édition de Jean Sichard, j'ai constaté que *Quaestiones in Genesin* et *De Essaeis* n'ont pas de traducteur mentionné. Ils sont recensés simplement sous leur titre alors que le premier texte *L.A.B.* possède la mention 'incerto interprete' et que les autres textes sont cités avec comme traducteurs Jérôme d'une part, et Guillaume Budé d'autre part. Cette différence entre 'incerto interprete' et l'absence de toute mention a-t-elle un sens? 'Incerto interprete' est-elle une remarque de copiste au sujet d'un nom obscur ou difficile à déchiffrer?

---

[15] Cf. Conybeare (1895).
[16] Cf. Petit (1973).
[17] *Liber Antiquitatum Biblicarum*, est le premier des cinq textes édités dans l'édition de Sichard. L'édition de Bâle de 1520 constitue *l'editio princeps* de ce traité attribué à Philon; voir Kisch (1949).
[18] Sur Jean Sichard, voir Lehmann (1911).
[19] Petit (1973) 14–15, 30–31, 39.
[20] Lehmann (1911).
[21] *Ibid.* 78–82.

F. C. Conybeare et F. Petit ont fait un travail remarquable d'étude de la langue et ont établi qu'une seule et même personne a traduit *Quaestiones* et *Contempl.* Ainsi, F. Petit explique: 'Bien que le caractère des traités soit très différent, les rencontres de vocabulaire sont tellement nombreuses qu'aucun doute n'est possible'. Mais F. Petit ne suit pas l'opinion de Pitra pour attribuer le même traducteur à *L.A.B.*[22] A cause de la familiarité du traducteur avec la vie monastique, les chercheurs ont daté la traduction du IVe siècle et l'ont localisée en Italie; ils ont mis l'accent sur une mauvaise traduction latine d'un traducteur qui connaissait mal le grec.[23] Si le travail de traduction a été confié à un piètre latiniste, peut-être les copistes ont-ils préféré ne pas transmettre son nom et ainsi le nom du traducteur n'est mentionné dans aucune des deux éditions (Paris 1520 et Bâle 1527).

Ces premières lignes ont résumé quelles étaient les données connues au sujet de la traduction latine de *Contempl.* A partir de ces données, se pose la question suivante: qui peut être l'auteur d'un tel sous-titre ? Dans l'édition de Jean Sichard, notre sous-titre s'intercale dans la lacune comblée par le manuscrit de Lorsch. Mais faute de manuscrit, il n'est pas possible de savoir si le sous-titre est une interpolation postérieure ou s'il se trouvait réellement dans le manuscrit. P. Lehmann a montré que le traitement de la lacune de Fulda par le manuscrit de Lorsch n'est pas dû à Jean Sichard, ni au scribe de Lorsch. Si l'on considère que le sous-titre est une partie de la lacune, ni Jean Sichard, ni le scribe de Lorsch ne sont responsables du sous-titre. En revanche, si l'on considère que le sous-titre est un titre supplémentaire, il est susceptible d'avoir été interpolé à tout moment, depuis le IVe siècle jusqu'à l'édition de J Sichard au XVIe siècle. J. Sichard ne semble pas être l'auteur de ce sous-titre, car P. Lehman a remarqué, dans son observation des différentes éditions de Sichard, que lorsque le philologue allemand ajoutait un titre de son propre cru, il le précisait lui-même[24]. Il apparait aussi que J. Sichard a travaillé sur le manuscrit original de Lorsch; s'il avait remarqué une interpolation postérieure au texte du manuscrit, il l'aurait, sans doute, signalée. L'auteur du sous-titre peut être aussi bien le traducteur lui-même qu'un copiste ultérieur, scribe de Lorsch compris. Le sous-titre semble exister, au moins, depuis le Xe/ XIe siècle, voire depuis 831, date du catalogue de St Riquier.

Pour tenter de répondre à la question—quel est l'auteur d'un tel sous-

---

[22] Petit (1973) 7 n. 6.
[23] Cf. Conybeare (1895) 143–145 qui conclut d'après l'étude de la langue à une date entre 300 et 400; de même Petit (1973) 8–9.
[24] Lehmann (1911) 119.

titre?—il convient maintenant d'adopter comme méthode l'examen du titre du point de vue de sa logique interne. En effet, ce titre comporte quatre problèmes à savoir la mention: *de statu Essaeorum*; leur caractérisation: *id est Monachorum* et la précision: *qui ... monasteria sibi fecerunt* avec comme indication de temps: *temporibus regis Agripae*. La recherche de la fin du XIXe siècle (L. Massebiau, L. Cohn, P. Wendland et F. C. Conybeare) a résolu les trois premiers problèmes en expliquant la confusion faite entre le monachisme chrétien et la communauté des ascètes du lac de Maréotis décrite par Philon dans *Contempl*. Le dernier problème, passé inaperçu, que j'espère éclaircir est la mention du roi Agrippa. La méthode de la logique interne tiendra compte des différents problèmes dans leur relation l'un à l'autre.

Pourquoi une allusion aux Esséniens?

Ainsi, le titre du *Contempl*. est *De Essaeis* dans le sommaire de Jean Sichard et le sous-titre commence par *De statu Essaeorum* en tête du texte. Pourquoi un tel début quand il s'agit de parler de la communauté des Thérapeutes près du lac Maréotis? Il faut, à mon avis, traiter différemment la question du titre *De Essaeis* et celle du sous-titre.

Commençons par le sous-titre: *de statu Essaeorum*; une première explication vient d'une compréhension interne du texte latin en comparaison avec la version grecque. En effet, le texte grec comporte comme début: Ἐσσαίων περὶ διαλεχθείς .... Cela signifie que le sujet des Esséniens *a déjà été traité*.[25] Le traducteur latin, au lieu de rendre littéralement le texte, traduit: *de statu Essaeorum disputaturus*; c'est-à-dire que le sujet des Esséniens *va être traité*. Le sous-titre: *de statu Essaeorum ...* est, donc, en harmonie avec la traduction latine que le traducteur a donnée de la première phrase. Aucun élément dans la suite du texte n'invite à penser le contraire; la communauté des Thérapeutes peut s'apparenter à celle des Esséniens par similitude de vie;[26] ou alors si le traducteur a laissé le texte sans sous-titre, un copiste ultérieur au vu du début du texte comprend que le traité va parler des Esséniens et propose ce sous-titre.

---

[25] A la lecture de ce début du texte grec, s'est posée la question d'une division des œuvres de Philon. C'est la théorie de L. Massebieau, qui utilisant le fragment d'Eusèbe sur les Esséniens (*Prep. Evang.*, VIII, 10.19–12.20), c'est-à-dire le fragment sur les Esséniens dans les *Hypoth*. 11.1–18, voit une division des œuvres de Philon dans un recueil appelé l' Ἀπολογία ὑπερ Ἰουδαίων avec d'une part, un traité sur les Esséniens et d'autre part, le *Contempl*. Cf. L. Massebieau (1888) 59–65.
[26] Sur la question Thérapeutes-Esséniens, voir Schürer–Vermes (1973–87) 2.595–6, 597 n. 20 et Runia (1993) 227–231.

Que penser du titre De Essaeis?

Il y a une 'harmonie' entre le titre *De Essaeis* et le sous-titre commençant par *De statu Essaeorum*; l'un a pu influencer l'autre et vice-versa. Je serais tentée de penser que le titre est une proposition de Jean Sichard. En effet, lorsque le philologue allemand cite le catalogue des écrits de Philon établi par Jérôme, il écrit dans la marge à la hauteur du traité *De Iudaeis* (cité après *De Providentia* et avant *De Conversatione Vitae*), 'forte legendum est Essaeis'. Cette remarque est, selon moi, à la fois une suggestion d'interprétation de la part de Jean Sichard comme un aveu de 'proposition' de titre.[27] On peut, donc, supposer que Jean Sichard a été aussi influencé par le sous-titre et que, pour cette raison, il a opté pour le titre *De Essaeis* dans son sommaire.

Cette première tentative d'explication au sujet du sous-titre: *de statu Essaeorum* et du titre: *de Essaeis* m'a été suggérée par l'observation du texte latin. Mais l'on verra que titre et sous-titre peuvent aussi se comprendre à l'aide d'une autre méthode. Cette nouvelle méthode que j'adopterai maintenant pour le traitement des autres problèmes est celle de l'utilisation des 'témoins indirects', à savoir tous les écrivains postérieurs à Philon qui le mentionnent, le paraphrasent, le commentent. Dans la majorité des cas, il s'agit de Pères de l'Eglise. Ce terme de 'témoins indirects' se justifie car toute édition d'humaniste telle celle étudiée ici de Jean Sichard comporte en préambule ou même dans la préface de l'éditeur lui-même les opinions de ces Pères de l'Eglise. Or, le témoignage des Pères sur Philon comporte des inexactitudes et des incompréhensions. Toute ressemblance avec des thèmes chrétiens est interprétée comme un signe que Philon était chrétien ou qu'il a fréquenté des chrétiens. Le degré de fidélité aux Pères a engendré de nombreux problèmes historiques jusqu'à la fin du XIXe siècle.

La 'lecture' de Philon et sa 'transmission'

La mention de la communauté des Esséniens constitue, donc, le premier problème du sous-titre de *Contempl.*; les deux autres problèmes sont liés à cette appellation. Il est écrit: *id est Monachorum qui temporibus Agrippae regis monasteria sibi fecerunt*. L'utilisation de *id est* en latin donne un ton d'explication au sujet de cette communauté dite des Esséniens mais en fait, accentue les problèmes historiques. Ainsi, les deux emplois de 'moines' et 'monastères' donnent un caractère institutionalisé de vie

---

[27] Voir ci-dessus les conclusions de Lehmann sur la méthode de travail de Jean Sichard; note 20.

cénobitique en ce qui concerne les Thérapeutes-'Esséniens' de *Contempl.* Pour les expliquer, il faut avoir recours aux témoins indirects.

Dans l'ordre chronologique, le premier témoin indirect mentionné par Jean Sichard, dans sa préface, est Eusèbe de Césarée (260-339).[28] L'évêque de Césarée parle assez longuement des Thérapeutes et cite des passages du *Contempl.* dans son *Histoire Ecclésiastique*; il conserve le nom original de Thérapeutes et explique que ce sont des chrétiens mais que le nom n'était pas utilisé à cette époque.[29] Il argumente dans ce sens en faisant un parallèle entre le genre de vie des Thérapeutes et celui des disciples des apôtres tel qu'il est décrit dans les *Actes*.[30] Dans sa préface, Sichard reprend l'argument d'Eusèbe sur les Thérapeutes, chrétiens avant la lettre et ajoute d'autre part, qu'il est confirmé dans son idée par Jérôme. En effet, à la fin de son catalogue, Jérôme écrit: *et de vita nostrorum liber de quo supra diximus, id est de apostolicis viris quam et inscripsit* περὶ βίου θεωρετικοῦ ἢ ἱκετῶν, *quod videlicet caelestia contemplentur et semper orent Deum, id est de hac vita contemplativa* (un livre au sujet de la vie des nôtres dont nous avons parlé plus haut, c'est-à-dire au sujet de ceux qui vivent la vie apostolique; livre auquel [Philon] a donné comme titre 'de la vie contemplative ou des suppliants', apparemment parce qu'ils contemplent les choses célestes et qu'ils prient Dieu perpétuellement; c'est-à-dire au sujet de la vie contemplative).[31] Comment comprendre *supra*? Est-il question du début de la notice de Jérôme où il est dit que Philon le Juif a écrit un livre sur la première Eglise d'Alexandrie fondée par l'apôtre Marc et que ces premiers chrétiens vivaient dans des monastères? S'il en est ainsi, Jérôme fait clairement, par fidélité à Eusèbe, le lien entre Thérapeutes et chrétiens[32] car il cite le *Contempl.* selon le titre original grec mais curieusement, il ne donne pas la traduction latine du titre dans son catalogue.[33]

Un autre témoin indirect, cité par Jean Sichard, est Epiphane de Salamine (315-403), contemporain de Jérôme (347-420). Il dit que les ascètes du lac Maréotis sont des chrétiens mais il ajoute qu'ils sont

---

[28] *H.E.* 2, 16, 2–18, 8.
[29] *H.E.* 2, 17, 4.
[30] *H.E.* 2, 17, 6.
[31] Hieronymus, *De Vir. inl.* 11 (et aussi 8 *ad init.*).
[32] Cette histoire de la première église d'Alexandrie se trouve chez Eusèbe, *H.E.*, 2, 16, 1, 2 et 17, 1, 3.
[33] Or, le catalogue de Jérôme, comme le fait remarquer D.T. Runia: 'makes for rather strange reading because many of the latin titles do not match these to which we have been accustomed'; voir Runia (1993) 313. Une comparaison du catalogue de Jérôme avec celui d'Eusèbe est un défi qui renvoie à la question difficile du classement des œuvres de Philon.

décrits par Philon dans son ouvrage ὑπὲρ Ἰεσσαίων (sic).³⁴ Le terme d'Epiphane de Salamine propose une légère variante linguistique au terme habituel 'Essaioi'.

Lorsque Jean Sichard comprend 'De Essaeis' en lisant 'De Judaeis' dans le catalogue de Jérôme, il semble accepter les différentes lectures de Philon par Eusèbe, Jérôme et Epiphane et accorder du crédit à l'idée suivante: les contemplatifs du *Contempl.* sont des chrétiens appelés, au temps de Philon, Esséniens. Or, la problématique qui considère les Thérapeutes comme Esséniens existe déjà au IVᵉ siècle, date aussi de notre traduction latine du *Contempl.* Cette problématique Thérapeutes-Esséniens-chrétiens est étroitement liée à celle de la vie cénobitique où les ascètes sont des 'moines' et se font construire des 'monastères'.

'La vie monastique' dans le De vita contemplativa

S'il est vrai que le terme μοναστήριον³⁵ employé par Philon en doublet avec σεμνεῖον ³⁶ a le sens de résidence solitaire, une pièce à part propice à la prière et à la méditation, il n'est nullement question, dans le traité grec de Philon, d'établissements monastiques. En revanche, la translittération des termes dans le texte latin donne une impression différente.³⁷ En effet, au IVᵉ siècle, les deux mots latins *monasterium* et *semneium* décrivent une réalité de la vie cénobitique chrétienne. D'ailleurs, Jean Sichard les mentionne dans sa préface comme preuves de la vie chrétienne des contemplatifs du *Contempl.*: ... *de Zemnio, monasteriis, hymnis veterum cultorum.*³⁸ Or, l'idée d'un monachisme chrétien du temps de Philon résulte de l'incompréhension par Eusèbe de Césarée du témoignage de Philon; l'erreur d'Eusèbe, non seulement, se transmet mais aussi se développe chez les écrivains postérieurs.³⁹ Un humaniste comme Jean Sichard accorde du crédit à ces idées par respect de la tradition chrétienne.

---

³⁴ Epiphanius, *Haer* 29, 51–3.
³⁵ μοναστήριον: *Contempl.* 25, 30; ce néologisme de Philon n'apparait pas ailleurs avant le IIIᵉ siècle dans les textes chrétiens concernant le monachisme, voir Daumas–Miquel (1963) 94 n. 1.
³⁶ σεμνεῖον: *Contempl.* 25, 32, 89.
³⁷ Le texte latin en *Contempl.* est (cf. Conybeare (1895) 150): *Singulis ergo habitaculum est religiosum, quod semnium vocant, sive monasterium in quo desolati modestissimae vitae sacramentis occupantur* (A chacun d'entre eux est une habitation religieuse qu'ils appellent *semnium* ou monastère dans lequel, isolés, ils passent leur temps dans les sacrements d'une vie très humble).
³⁸ *Ibid.* 141.
³⁹ Voir Runia (1993), 227–231, 'The subsequent history of the 'Eusebian' Therapeutae.

Pourquoi une mention du roi Agrippa ?

Le recensement des trois problèmes historiques du titre était nécessaire pour montrer quel est le degré de manipulation de la pensée et de l'œuvre de Philon par la transmission chrétienne. En effet, les problèmes liés à la mention du roi Agrippa dans le sous-titre sont de plusieurs sortes: en premier lieu, y a-t-il une corrélation significative entre la problématique chrétienne du début du monachisme et le temps du roi Agrippa ? Ensuite, s'il n'y en a pas, examinons cette mention du roi Agrippa au moyen de la même méthode: nouvelle observation de l'édition de Jean Sichard et étude des témoins indirects cités par lui au sujet du roi Agrippa. A cela, il faudra ajouter une observation d'éditions postérieures à celle de 1527 et bien sûr, un examen des témoins indirects cités par ces éditions.

Il n'y a aucune relation entre les Thérapeutes 'Esséniens', précurseurs du monachisme chrétien et le roi Agrippa. En effet, tous les témoins indirects cités pour expliquer la problématique chrétienne d'une telle description des Thérapeutes de *Contempl.* n'ont jamais fait mention du roi Agrippa, ni comme repère chronologique, ni comme ayant influencé directement ou indirectement la mise en place de l'institution monacale. *Qui temporibus Agrippae regis monastaria sibi fecerunt* dit le sous-titre mais il n'y a pas d'explication textuelle interne en ce qui concerne l'indication du temps du roi Agrippa, c'est-à-dire de 37 à 44 ap. J.C. ou plus particulièrement de 41 à 44 comme roi de l'ancien royaume d'Hérode.

La prépondérance du témoignage d'Eusèbe

Pour tenter de comprendre l'allusion au roi Agrippa, il est donc nécessaire d'avoir recours aux témoins indirects cités par Jean Sichard. Celui-ci a lu Eusèbe de Césarée à la fois dans la traduction de Rufin, et dans son original grec. Il n'a pas seulement lu ce qui concerne les Thérapeutes mais aussi toutes les indications sur Philon. Or, il est question de Philon au livre II, ch. 4 de *l'Histoire Ecclésiastique*. Au début du chapitre, Eusèbe écrit:

> (§ 1) Tibère, ayant régné environ vingt-deux ans, mourut et après lui Gaius reçut le pouvoir. Aussitôt, il accorda à Agrippa le diadème du pouvoir sur les Juifs et l'établit roi des tétrarchies de Philippe et de Lysanias, auxquelles, peu de temps après, il ajouta la tétrarchie d'Hérode qu'il condamna à l'exil perpétuel (cet Hérode était celui qui régnait au temps de la passion du Sauveur) avec sa femme Hérodiade, à cause de ses très nombreux crimes. Josèphe est aussi témoin de ces choses.
> (§ 2) Ce fut sous Gaius que devint célèbre auprès d'un très grand nombre, Philon, homme très remarquable non seulement parmi les nôtres, mais aussi parmi ceux qui ont

été formés par les disciplines étrangères. Par sa famille très ancienne, il était hébreu ...

Le contexte historique dans lequel Eusèbe place Philon est très caractéristique. Après la succession des empereurs Tibère, Gaius, est rapporté le pouvoir concédé à Agrippa par Gaius. Le début du § 2 rappelle comme indication de temps le règne de l'empereur Gaius mais la façon dont le § 1 est écrit montre l'extrême concomitance entre l'ascension au trône de Gaius et le couronnement d'Agrippa: Γάϊος τὴν ἡγεμονίαν παραλαβὼν, αὐτίκα τῆς Ἰουδαίων ἀρχῆς Ἀγρίππᾳ τὸ διάδημα περιτίθησιν, βασιλέα καταστήσας αὐτὸν ...

La présentation de Philon dans le contexte historique des dirigeants romains et un dirigeant juif a sans doute influencé plus d'un lecteur postérieur à Eusèbe. L'influence s'exprime surtout dans le rapprochement entre l'identité juive de Philon et celle du roi Agrippa.

Qui mentionne le roi Agrippa?

Eusèbe, qui vécut à la fin du IIIe siècle peut avoir influencé aussi bien le traducteur du IVe siècle que tous ceux qui respectent son témoignage, J. Sichard y compris. Si la mention *temporibus Agrippae regis* est une interpolation postérieure au reste du sous-titre, il ne faut probablement pas l'attribuer à Jean Sichard. Rappelons que lorsque Jean Sichard propose un titre qui lui est propre, il le précise. (voir ci-dessus p. 62). On pourrait arguer d'un oubli volontaire ou involontaire dans le cas du *Contempl.* On notera surtout l'influence prépondérante d'Eusèbe sur les éditions latines postérieures à celle de 1527. Ainsi, dans une traduction latine de 1614[40] où le *Contempl.* est cité sous le titre *De Vita contemplativa, sive supplicum virtutibus*, Philon est présenté dans l'introduction, de la manière suivante: *Philonis Hebraei scriptoris ecclesiastici qui floruit circa annum ab orbe condito quater millesimum et vigesimum quartum, regnante in Judaea Agrippa a Christo vero nato quinquagesimum, sub Impp Tiberio, Gaio et Claudio*, ([livre] de Philon l'Hébreu, écrivain écclésiastique qui fut actif environ quatre mille vingt-quatre ans après la création du monde, pendant le règne d'Agrippa en Judée, cinquante ans après la naissance du Christ, sous les empereurs Tibère, Caius et Claude).[41] Cette présentation comporte des similitudes avec le passage d'Eusèbe (*H.E.* 2, 4, 1-2) expliqué ci-dessus. De plus, dans la même édition sont donnés les

---

[40] *Opera Philonis Judaei exegetica in libros Mosis, de mundi opificio, historicos et legales, quae partim ab Adriano Turnebo partim a Davide Hoschelio, Johannes Keerbergius, Antverpiae,* 1614 = G-G n° 460.
[41] D.T. Runia m'a indiqué dans un entretien du 31 mai 1994 à Jérusalem qu'il s'agit d'un titre caractéristique d'humaniste du XVIIe siècle.

illustrium et praecellentium scriptorum de Philone testimonia: Flavius Josèphe, *Antiquités judaïques*, livre XVIII; Eusèbe, *Histoire Ecclésiastique*, livre II; le catalogue de Jérôme; Photius, *Bibliothèque*, cod. CIII, CIV, CV; et l'auteur de *la Souda*.[42] Ce sont les témoins indirects que l'éditeur cite en avant-propos des textes de Philon.

Dans cette édition de 1614, sont mentionnés deux témoins indirects qui ne se trouvent pas chez Jean Sichard: Photius, patriarche de Constantinople (820-895), auteur de *la Bibliothèque* et un lexicographe byzantin, auteur d'un lexicon au Xe siècle, appelé *la Souda*.[43] Dans la liste des *Testimonia*, est cité ce passage de Photius en latin: *Floruit (Philon) Caii Caesaris temporibus, ad quem pro sua gente (hebraea) legationem se suscepisse scribit, regnante in Judaea Agrippa* (Philon fut actif sous le règne de l'empereur Caius; il écrit s'être rendu en ambassade auprès de l'empereur pour défendre sa nation [celle des Hébreux] alors qu'Agrippa était roi de Judée).

Notons aussi que ce qu'ils écrivent tous deux concernant Philon est très proche de ce que dit Eusèbe. La notice de Photius est plus intéressante car plus précise que celle de *la Souda*.[44] On y retrouve, dans le *Cod*. 104 de *la Bibliothèque*, les problématiques et les formulations qui nous intéressent: Ἀνεγνώσθησαν δὲ καὶ τῶν παρὰ Ἰουδαίοις φιλοσοφησάντων τήν τε θεωρητικὴν καὶ πρακτικὴν φιλοσοφίαν βίοι· ὧν οἱ μὲν Ἐσσηνοί, οἱ δὲ Θεραπευταὶ ἐκαλοῦντο, οἳ καὶ μοναστήρια καὶ σεμνεῖα, ὡς αὐταῖς λέξεσιν λέγει, ἐπήγνυντο καὶ τῶν νῦν μοναζόντων τὴν πολιτείαν προϋπέγραφον (ont été lues des vies de Juifs, adeptes de la philosophie contemplative et pratique; les uns sont appelés Esséniens, les autres Thérapeutes; ils ont construits des monastères et des *semneia*, selon les propres mots de Philon, et ils ont esquissé d'avance le mode de vie des moines de maintenant). Dans le *Cod*. 105 parmi les 'événements cités', apparaissent: la conduite de Flaccus, l'ambassade auprès de Caligula, l'initiation de Philon au christianisme[45], la rencontre avec Pierre à Rome et l'évangélisation d'Alexandrie par Marc. Les indications de temps sont les règnes des empereurs Caius et Claude ainsi que la mention: Ἀγρίππα τῆς Ἰουδαίας βασιλεύοντος.

---

42 Pour une mise à jour récente de tous les 'testimonia' voir Runia (1994b).
43 Sur Photius, voir Schamps (1987), spéc. 460–469.
44 Textes cités par C-W 1, cix–cxii. L'auteur de *la Souda* est sans doute très dépendant de Photius ou tous deux ont une source commune; dans le catalogue de *la Souda*, le *Contempl*. est cité sous le titre : περὶ τῆς διαγωγῆς τῶν χριστιάνων (ἢ) περὶ ἱκετῶν.
45 Ce thème d'une initiation de Philon au Christianisme est un ajout de Photius (cf. Runia (1993) 6). L'affirmation de Photius est si outrée que la précision de l'abandon par Philon de sa foi chrétienne quelque temps après est un soulagement pour nous lecteurs modernes!

Ces témoignages ont-ils influencé à leur suite les copistes du texte latin du *Contempl.*? Il faudrait pour l'affirmer pouvoir préciser le *terminus post quem* de leur diffusion en Occident. J'ai tenté de trouver quelques indices de la diffusion de Photius en Occident avant la fin du X⁰ ou le début du X⁰ siècle afin de voir si la notice de Photius sur Philon était connue du scribe de Lorsch. Malgré l'existence d'un manuscrit de Photius de la deuxième moitié du X⁰ siècle, il n'y a aucune trace d'une diffusion d'un manuscrit de Photius vers l'Occident avant le XV⁰ siècle.[46]

En y réfléchissant bien, l'analyse ci-dessus du livre II chapitre IV de l'*Histoire Ecclésiastique* d'Eusèbe est suffisante pour suggérer, encourager et inciter à mentionner le roi Agrippa. Est-il question du roi Agrippa à cause de Philon lui-même, devenu célèbre au temps du roi Agrippa? En effet, l'ambassade auprès de Caligula au temps du roi Agrippa semble avoir contribué au renom de Philon. Il s'est, donc, maintenu dans les esprits une association de temps. Il est possible alors que le traducteur lui-même localisé en Italie ait écrit ce sous-titre en mentionnant le roi Agrippa.

Il faut ajouter, cependant, que la mention *Philonis Judaei*[47] a un lien avec la mention du roi Agrippa. En effet, le roi Agrippa est le roi des Juifs. Dans les *Actes des Apôtres*, ch. 12, il est le persécuteur de l'Eglise. La lecture du *Thesaurus temporum* d'Eusèbe témoigne non seulement de la mention d'Agrippa comme *rex Judaeorum*, mais aussi présente un tableau chronologique du premier siècle divisé en années romaines, juives et chrétiennes.[48] Le sous-titre présente donc le contraste d'un auteur juif qui, à l'époque d'un roi juif, décrit les premières communautés de moines chrétiens.

Conclusion

L'édition polyglotte du *Contempl.* par F.C. Conybeare, publiée en 1895, a attiré notre attention, sur un sous-titre latin peu commun d'une œuvre de Philon: *De statu Essaeorum, id est Monachorum qui temporibus Agrippae regis monasteria sibi fecerunt*. La méthode de recherche traditionnelle (enquête des éditions et des manuscrits) n'a pas permis d'identifier l'auteur du titre ni de dater le titre lui-même. L'édition de Bâle de 1527 par Jean Sichard est l'unique témoin de ce sous-titre et le philologue allemand a utilisé un manuscrit perdu, le manuscrit de Lorsch, daté de la fin du X⁰, début du XI⁰. Il apparaissait impossible de dire quand et par

---

[46] Martini (1911) 6–15.
[47] Si l'expression Philon le Juif est extrêmement répandue au moyen-âge, le premier témoignage est chez Théodore de Mopsueste (350–428). Cf. Runia (1994a) 17.
[48] *Eusebius Werke* (Leipzig 1913) VII 160–161.

qui avait été écrit un tel sous-titre. Seule la manière de travailler de Jean Sichard permettait de conclure que ce titre se trouvait déjà dans le manuscrit de Lorsch.

Faute de données connues, j'ai tenté par le biais de la méthode des 'témoins indirects' d'expliquer ce titre et surtout la mention du roi Agrippa. A la lecture de ce sous-titre, les spécialistes reconnaissent aussitôt l'amalgame fait entre Esséniens et moines qui établissent des monastères; cela est dû à l'incompréhension de l'œuvre et de la personnalité de Philon: les parallèles avec d'autres traités philoniens sont inexacts; les conclusions d'Eusèbe de Césarée sont adoptées, les néologismes philoniens du Ier siècle σεμνεῖον, μοναστήριον ne sont pas compris dans leur spécificité, mais en termes d'institutions d'Eglise comme ils le sont devenus au IVe siècle, époque de la traduction la traduction latine. La recherche moderne depuis la fin du XIXe siècle a éclairci cette confusion entre 'Esséniens et chrétiens, fondateurs de la vie cénobitique'. En revanche, l'indication *temporibus regis Agrippae* était passée inaperçue et j'ai donc essentiellement enquêté ce détail après rappel et éclaircissement des précédents problèmes.

Il en ressort qu'Eusèbe a eu une influence prépondérante; l'analyse textuelle du livre II chapitre IV de *l'Histoire Ecclésiastique* a mis en lumière l'idée que l'on se faisait de Philon dans les cercles chrétiens à la fin du IIIe siècle. L'évêque de Césarée a transmis sa propre perception de l'œuvre et du personnage[49] de Philon. Son témoignage dans *l'Histoire ecclésiastique* est connu dans l'original grec et surtout en Occident, dans la traduction latine de Rufin.[50] Eusèbe peut, donc, déjà avoir influencé le traducteur latin du IVe siècle.

Si le traducteur n'a pas écrit, lui-même, le sous-titre que nous avons enquêté, tout intervenant postérieur au IVe siècle dans la chaîne de la transmission de l'oeuvre de Philon respecte le témoignage d'Eusèbe. Le rôle de Jérome est à signaler. Il est le traducteur latin du *Thesaurus Temporum* d'Eusèbe où le traitement de la chronologie de l'époque philonienne invite encore à des confusions entre problématiques chrétiennes et histoire juive. En conclusion, on signalera que les différents 'témoins indirects' (*testimonia*) reprennent, tous, le témoignage de l'évêque de Césarée, quitte à l'enrichir et l'amplifier dans une perspective chrétienne.

Jerusalem

---

[49] Voir les termes de la présentation de Philon dans *H.E.* 2, 4, 2: 'homme très remarquable non seulement *parmi les nôtres*, mais parmi ceux qui ont été formés par les disciplines étrangères.'
[50] Voir les extraits cités par Conybeare (1895) 187–191.

Bibliographie

G. Bardy, *Eusèbe de Césarée Histoire Ecclésiastique*, livres I-IV (Paris 1952, 1978).

L. Cohn & P. Wendland, *Philonis Alexandrini opera quae supersunt*, 6 vols. (Berlin 1896-1915).

F. H. Colson, G. H. Whitaker, R. Marcus, *Philo of Alexandria in Ten Volumes (and Two Supplementary Volumes)*, LCL (Cambridge Mass. 1929-62).

F. C. Conybeare, *Philo About the Contemplative Life* (Oxford 1895).

F. Daumas – P. Miquel, *Philon De vita contemplativa*, Les Oeuvres de Philon d'Alexandrie 29 (Paris 1963).

Eusebius Werke VII, Die Chronik des Hieronymus, Hieronymi Chronicon, GCS 1 (Leipzig 1913).

H. L. Goodhart & E. R. Goodenough, 'A General Bibliography of Philo Judaeus' in E. R. Goodenough, *The Politics of Philo Judaeus: Practice and Theory* (New Haven 1938; réimpréssion Hildesheim 1967).

G. Kisch, *Pseudo-Philo's Liber Antiquitatum Biblicarum* (Notre-Dame 1949).

P. Lehmann, *Johanes Sichardus und die von ihm benutzten Bibliotheken und Handschriften*, Quellen und Untersuchungen zur lateinische Philologie des Mittelalten IV/I (München 1911).

L. Massebieau, *Le classement des œuvres de Philon*, extrait du tome I de la Bibliothèque de l'Ecole des Hautes Etudes. Section des Sciences Religieuses (Paris 1888).

E. Martini, *Textgeschichte der Bibliotheke des Patriarchen Photius von Konstantinopel*, (Teubner 1911).

F. Petit, *L'ancienne version latine des* Questions sur la Genèse *de Philon d'Alexandrie*, 2 vol.,Texte und Untersuchungen 113-14 (Berlin 1973).

D. T. Runia, *Philo in Early Christian Literature, a Survey*, CRINT III 3 (Assen-Minneapolis 1993).

—— 'Philonic Nomenclature', *SPhA* 6 (1994a) 1-27.

—— 'References to Philo from Josephus up to 1000 A.D.', *SPhA* 6 (1994b) 111-121.

J. Schamps, *Photios historien des lettres:* la Bibliothèque *et ses notices biographiques*, Bibliothèque de la faculté de Philosophie et Lettres de l'université de Liège 248 (Paris 1987).

E. Schürer – G. Vermes et al., *The History of the Jewish people in the Age of Jesus Christ*, 3 vols. in 4 (Edinburgh 1973-87).

SPECIAL SECTION

PHILO AND MYSTICISM

GREGORY E. STERLING

Recent work in hermeneutics has taught us to treat the reception of texts with the same seriousness we do their sources and predecessors. The publication of David Runia's *Philo in Early Christian Literature* provided the Philo of Alexandria Seminar of the Society of Biblical Literature an ideal opportunity to review Philo's reception among Christians. The reviews of the panelists were published as a Special Section of *The Studia Philonica Annual* (6 (1994) 90–110). Several scholars pointed out that while we owe the preservation of Philo's works to Christians, intriguing questions about his career in the worlds of pagan Greek, later Jewish, and even Islamic thought and discourse remain unanswered.

At last year's meeting of the Philo of Alexandria Seminar, the organizers felt it would be a good idea to pursue this aspect of Philo's *Nachleben* further. But this time the speakers would leave behind more general issues and concentrate on a particular theme. It was decided to concentrate on a subject where the phenomenological similarities between Philo's thought and later pagan, Christian and Jewish traditions are evident, the theme of mysticism. Three papers were presented. David Winston summarized his research into Philo's mysticism so that we would have a basis for comparison. Brian Daley explored Gregory of Nyssa's debt to Philo so that we would have a case where Philonic influence is demonstrable and widely accepted. It is also important to bear in mind that later Jewish thinkers might have been influenced by Philo indirectly through Christian sources. Elliott Wolfson sketched the history of scholarship on the possible use of Philo by medieval Jewish mystics and gave a tentative answer to the question whether we can accept Philonic influence in this area. Bernard McGinn served as a respondent to all presenters. The session was so well attended and received that the editors of *The Studia Philonica Annual* decided to publish the three papers. We offer revised versions here in the hope that they will encourage future exploration in what remains a *quaestio difficillima*.

PHILO'S MYSTICISM

David Winston

In view of the lack of a consensus on the nature of mysticism, I shall preface my discussion of Philo's mysticism by indicating very briefly how I intend to employ that term in this article. By mysticism I understand the claim that a direct experience of the Ultimate Reality is possible through a profound awakening that takes place, however briefly, within the soul's interior. This experience is neither envisaged as essentially conceptual nor is it perceived as a psychic invasion from without. Moreover, although persistent efforts of continuous searching and meditation are required, its consummation is by no means guaranteed and cannot be artificially manipulated.

In light of the above, I shall argue that Philo can indeed lay claim to being a mystic, albeit within certain restricted parameters. We shall find that Philo had no notion of the possibility of achieving a state of undifferentiated union with God, and that he probably conceived of a mystical contact that was limited only to an aspect of the Deity, namely, his manifestation as Logos. If this should be the case, it could be seen as somewhat similar to the later mystical notion of the contact or conjunction (*ittiṣāl*) of one's acquired intellect with the so-called 'Active Intellect' associated with such philosophers as Ibn Bajjah and Ibn Rushd in the twelfth century, and derived from Aristotle's famous commentator Alexander of Aphrodisias, who flourished in the early third century CE. This is obviously quite different from the Plotinian notion of the human capacity to 'become' Intellect and even to be absorbed into the ineffable One itself (4.8.1; 5.3.17; 6.9.9; 6.9.11).

It will be useful to begin with a review of some of the key elements, as conveniently outlined by Margaret Smith, that appear to characterize most forms of mysticism, and note the correspondences in the writings of Philo. To do so, however, is no easy task, since Philo's scattered mystical and quasi-mystical pronouncements are more often than not fragmentary and vague and the interpreter is at times constrained to resort to patchwork and conjecture. It is nonetheless clear that some of the most well-known motifs of mystical experience are consistently echoed in many of his writings. It is with these non-controversial motifs that I shall open my discussion, leaving the most important but controversial component for last.

(1) Mystics often speak of a state of God-intoxication, in which the self and the world are alike forgotten.¹ Rumi, for example, says that the lover is so intoxicated by the presence of his beloved that he knows neither time nor place in his ritual prayers. He also addresses his own restless and loving heart as follows: 'I shouted, 'Where does my intoxicated heart go?'/ The King said, 'Quiet! It goes towards me!''² Philo similarly speaks of a mind that, having transcended all sensible substance, goes on to behold beauties beyond measure in the Intelligible Realm and is then possessed by a sober intoxication, like those seized with a Corybantic frenzy (*Opif*. 70–71).³ Although similar to a state of frenzy, its sober character is an indication of its fundamentally intellectual character.⁴ In *Fug*. 166–68, the Isaac-type soul, which is self-taught, is similarly described as sucking in wisdom ready-made, showered down from heaven above, and being continually drunk with the sober drunkenness that comes with right reason. It is nonetheless described as superior to [discursive] reasoning (κρεῖττον λόγου), and taking shape not through human design but through God-inspired frenzy (ἐνθέῳ μανίᾳ; cf. Plato *Phaedrus* 244d4). In *Leg*. 3.82, Philo takes pains to emphasize that the 'divine intoxication is more sober than sobriety itself' (νηφαλεωτέρα νήψεως αὐτῆς).⁵

(2) Mysticism further 'assumes that man must be a partner of the Divine nature, if he is to know the Divine. The mystics throughout the ages have contended that God Himself is 'the ground of the soul' and that all men in the depths of their being have a share in one central, Divine life'.⁶ For Philo, too, the soul can conceive of God because He has breathed into it from above of His own Deity and mightily laid hold of it. 'The invisible Deity stamped on the invisible soul the impress of itself, to the end that not even the terrestrial region should be without a share in the image of God' (*Leg*. 1.38; *Det*. 86).

---

¹ M. Smith, 'The Nature and Meaning of Mysticism', in R. Woods (ed.), *Understanding Mysticism* (Garden City, NY 1980) 20.
² A. Schimmel, *The Triumphal Sun* (Albany 1993) 278, 356–57. Ibn al-Farid gives the name of 'sobriety' (ṣaḥw) to normal experience; to ecstatic experience the name of intoxication (sukr), and to supernormal experience the name of 'the sobriety of union' (ṣaḥw'l-jam) or 'the second sobriety' (al-ṣaḥw al-thānī), in which the seer regards himself as united with God. This is the supreme degree of oneness (ittiḥād) and al-Farid claims to possess it permanently. See R. A. Nicholson, *The Idea of Personality in Sufism* (Cambridge 1923).
³ Cf. *Leg*. 1.84; *Prob*. 13; *Ebr*. 146–49; Plotinus 6.7.22.1–11.
⁴ Cf. *Mut*. 39; *Ebr*. 47; *Her*. 68–70.
⁵ Cf. Plotinus 6.7.35.24, where he speaks of 'Intellect in love (νοῦς ἐρῶν), when it goes out of its mind 'drunk with the nectar'', and then goes on to say that 'it is better for it to be drunk with a drunkenness like this than to be more respectably sober' (3.5.9.17).
⁶ Smith, *art. cit*. (n. 1) 21.

(3) 'Mystics, both East and West, have maintained that the stripping of the soul of selfishness and sensuality is essential for the beholding of the Vision of God. Self-loss, withdrawal from self, self-annihilation, these are essential to those who would approach the Absolute. Only when all images of earth are hushed and the clamor of the senses is stilled and the soul has passed beyond thought of itself can the Eternal Wisdom be revealed to the mystic who seeks that high communion with the Unseen'.[7] Philo similarly writes in *Leg.* 3.41 'that it behoves the mind that would be led forth and let go free to withdraw itself from the influence of everything, the needs of the body, the organs of sense, specious arguments, the plausibilities of rhetoric, last of all itself'. Again, in *Migr.* 191 he writes:[8]

> For when the mind is mastered by some philosophical speculation and is drawn to it, it follows this, but remains oblivious to all that concerns the bodily mass. And if the senses thwart the contemplation of the intelligible, those fond of such contemplation are concerned to eliminate their onset. They shut their eyes, plug their ears, and restrain the impulses derived from the other senses, and deem it right to spend their time in solitude and darkness, so that the eye of the soul, to whom God has given the power to perceive things intelligible, may not be obscured by any object of sense.

(4) 'The guide on the upward path of the mystic is, and must be, Love. ... To the mystic, wherever he is found ... the object of his search is conceived of as the Beloved, and the mystic regards himself as the lover, yearning for the consummation of his love in union with the One he loves. ... The term Love as used by the mystics implies far more than a mere emotion: 'it is to be understood in its deepest, fullest sense; as the ultimate expression of the self's most vital tendencies ... the deep-seated tendency of the soul towards its source''.[9] For Philo, it is 'the mind that is filled with the Deity, and no longer in itself, but is agitated and maddened by a heavenly passion, drawn by the truly Existent and attracted upwards to it, preceded by truth ... that has the inheritance' (*Her.* 70). In a passage that finds an echo in Plotinus (6.9.11.18) he writes (*Somn.* 2.232):[10]

---

[7] Smith, *art. cit.* (n. 1) 21. For self-annihilation in Hasidism with Christian parallels, see R. Shatz-Uffenheimer, *Quietistic Elements in Eighteenth Century Hasidic Thought* (Jerusalem 1968) 21–31 (Hebrew) and the fine discussion in D. C. Matt, 'Ayin: The Concept of Nothingness in Jewish Mysticism', in R. K. C. Forman (ed.), *The Problem of Pure Consciousness* (New York 1990) 121–59.
[8] Cf. *Leg.* 3.44, 127; *Her.* 68–71; *Somn.* 2.232; *Migr.* 1–4, 7–12; *Det.* 158–59; *Fug.* 92; *Ebr.* 69–70; *Gig.* 14–15.
[9] Smith, *art. cit.* (n. 1) 21–22. Cf. Plotinus 5.3.17.17; 3.5.4.23; 6.7.31; 5.5.12.6–12.
[10] Cf. *Somn.* 1.165; *Leg.* 3.84; *QG* 4.140; *Praem.* 84; *Deus* 138; *Her.* 70; *Post.* 92; *Plant.* 22.

When the mind is possessed by divine love, when it exerts itself to reach the innermost shrine, when it moves forward with all effort and zeal, under the impact of the divine inspiration it forgets everything else, forgets itself, and retains memory and attachment for him alone whose attendant and servant it is. ...

(5) 'All the faculties, feeling, intellect and will must be cleansed and brought into harmony with the Eternal Will. This is the Sufi doctrine of unification: an old Persian writer says that it means the cessation of human volition and affirmation of the Divine Will, so as to exclude all personal initiative.'[11] According to Ibn al-Arabi, one of the several types of 'annihilation' (*fanā'*) the mystic may experience is the 'annihilation of acts'. 'The servant is annihilated from his acts through God's standing over them. ... Hence the servants see the act as belonging to God from behind the veil of the engendered things, which are the locus wherein the acts become manifest'.[12] Philo similarly speaks of the mind that ascribes all things to God: 'He that abandons his own mind grants that that which pertains to the human mind is nothing, and attributes all things to God' (*Leg.* 3.29).[13] In the fragment from the lost fourth book of his *Legum Allegoriae*, Philo writes: 'But when [Moses] affirms the first and better principle, namely, that God acts not as man, he ascribes the powers and causes of all things to God, leaving no work for a created being but showing it to be inactive and passive'. Those, however, who are uninitiated in the great mysteries about the sovereignty and authority of the Uncreated and the exceeding nothingness of the created, do not as yet recognize this truth (Harris, *Fragments* 8; cf. *Cher.* 77, 128).

(6) 'To know [the One] at first hand—not to guess, believe or accept, but to be certain—is the highest achievement of human consciousness, and the ultimate object of mysticism'.[14] Philo similarly writes (*Praem.* 46):

> They do but make a happy guess (στοχασταί, 'makers of inferences'), who strive to discern the Uncreated and Creator of all from his creation, acting similarly to those

---

[11] Smith, *art. cit.* (n. 1) 23.
[12] W. C. Chittick, *The Sufi Path of Knowledge* (Albany 1989) 207. 'The proper human attitude toward the acts adds another dimension to the question. Though one group may ascribe all acts to God, in fact 'courtesy' (*adab*) demands that only good and beautiful acts be ascribed to God, while evil and ugly acts must be ascribed to the servants' (*ibid*, 209–10). Philo similarly writes: 'The treasuries of evil things are in ourselves, with God are those of good things only. Whosoever, therefore, takes refuge, that is, whosoever blames not himself but God for his sins, let him be punished. ...' (*Fug.* 79–80). The Hasidic master R. Yosef Mordechai Leiner expresses the same thought: 'All the good that you do you may refer to God, but all the evil you must attribute to yourselves' (*Mei ha-Shiloah* (Jerusalem repr. 1976) 128a). For Philo's theory of relative free will, see D. Winston and J. Dillon (edd.), *Two Treatises of Philo of Alexandria* (Chico 1983) 181–95.
[13] Cf. *Leg.* 1.48–49; 1.82; 2.46; 3.44; *Her.* 74; *Cher.* 71; *Conf.* 125–27.
[14] E. Underhill, 'The Essentials of Mysticism', in *Understanding Mysticism* (cited n. 1) 30.

who search the nature of the monad from the dyad, whereas observation of the dyad should begin with the monad, which is the source. The pursuers of truth are they who form an image of God through God, light through light.

To the above motifs, I shall now add a number of others that I have already discussed elsewhere.[15] Like most mystics, Philo is convinced that the human goal and its ultimate bliss lie in the knowledge of God.[16] Indeed, the mere quest is sufficient of itself to give a foretaste of gladness (*Post.* 20). The first step leading to God is the recognition of one's own nothingness, which induces departure from self.[17] Having gone out of himself, the devotee is then asked to attach himself completely to God: 'Most vividly does he [Moses] invite us to honor Him who is much longed for and worthy of love, saying that we should cleave to Him, thereby indicating the continuity, closeness, and uninterruptedness of the harmony and union founded on affinity [with the Divine]' (*Post.* 12).[18] This is the only passage that speaks explicitly of union, yet even here it is by no means certain that the reference is to the soul's union with God rather than to its own inner state of harmony and union when cleaving to Deity. Moreover, in abandoning body and sense-perception, the mind becomes absorbed in a form of intellectual prayer that is wordless and unencumbered by petition (*Fug.* 92):[19]

> [The reasoning faculty must sever and banish from itself the word of utterance] so that the thought within the mind may be left behind alone, bereft of body, bereft of sense perception, bereft of the utterance of resonant speech [cf. Plotinus 5.1.6.10]. For thus left behind, it will live a life in accord with such solitude, and will cleave in purity and without distraction to the Alone Existent.

The human mind may also enjoy a timeless contact with the entire universe (*Det.* 90):[20]

---

[15] D. Winston, 'Was Philo a Mystic?' in J. Dan and F. Talmage (edd.), *Studies in Jewish Mysticism* (Cambridge, MA 1982) 15–39, esp. 29–35.
[16] *Decal.* 81; *Det.* 86; *Abr.* 58; *Praem.* 14; *Legat.* 4; *QG* 4.4.
[17] *Somn.* 1.60, 212; *Sacr.* 55; *b. Ḥul.* 89a.
[18] Cf. *Plant.* 64; *Congr.* 133–34. For the concept of *devekut*, cleaving to God, in Jewish mysticism, see G. Scholem, 'Devekut, or Communion with God', in *The Messianic Idea in Judaism* (New York 1971) 203–27; M. Idel, *Kabbalah: New Perspectives* (New Haven 1988) 35–38; idem, *Hasidism* (Albany 1995) 86–89; M. Pachter, 'The Concept of Devekut in the Homiletical Ethical Writings of Sixteenth Century Safed,' in I. Twersky, *Studies in Medieval Jewish History and Literature* (Cambridge, MA 1984) 2.171–230; M. Piekarz, 'Devekut as Reflecting the Socio-Religious Character of the Hasidic Movement', *Daat* 24 (1990) 127–44 (Hebrew).
[19] Cf. *Her.* 71; *Gig.* 52; *Plant.* 126; *Migr.* 12; *Spec.* 1. 272; *Ebr.* 94. For contemplative prayer in Hasidism, see Uffenheimer, *op. cit.* (n. 7) 22–31, 95–110.
[20] Cf. *Fug.* 169; Xenophon, *Mem.* 1.4.17; *Corp. Herm.* 11.19–20; Aristotle, *EN* 7,1178a; Lucretius 3.209; Plutarch, *Mor.* 1002B, 1048B; Plotinus 5.2; Manilius, *Astronom.* 2.115–29; 4.923–35.

> For how was it likely that the human mind being so tiny, hemmed in by such puny masses as brain and heart, should be able to contain such an immense magnitude of sky and universe, had it not been an inseparable portion of that divine and blessed soul? For nothing is severed or detached from the divine, but only extended. When the mind, therefore, that has received its share in the perfection of the whole conceives of the universe, it stretches out as widely as the bounds of the whole, for its force is susceptible of attraction.

The mystic state is further described as producing tranquillity and stability,[21] and it is sometimes indicated that it supervenes suddenly.[22] Finally, like most mystics, Philo is keenly aware of the human inability to maintain a steady, single-minded concentration on the Divine, and the consequent ebb and flow of such an experience:[23]

> The one who is begotten and brought into being is not wont to be God-possessed always, but when he has been divinely inspired for some time he then goes and returns to himself. ... And so, just as music is by its laws adapted not only to distinct and increased intensities but also to medium ones and to relaxations, so too it is with the mind. For when it is wholly intent upon pleasing the Father and becomes God-possessed, it is rightly said to be fortunate. And when it ceases to be inspired, after its enthusiasm it returns to itself and reflects upon its own affairs and what is proper to it. ... While God stays, the wise man remains there, and when He departs, he too departs. And the Father takes his departure because of His providential care and consideration for our race, knowing that it is by nature shackled and involved in its needs. Wherefore he [Abraham] saw fit to return and be alone, for not everything is to be done by sons in the sight of the Father.

We must now turn our attention to a key definition of mysticism that is referred to by Smith and see where Philo comes out with regard to it. 'Mysticism', she writes, 'is to be described as an attitude of mind; an innate tendency of the human soul, which seeks to transcend reason and to attain to a direct experience of God, and which believes that it is possible for the human soul to be united with Ultimate Reality, when 'God ceases to be an object and becomes an experience''.[24] The first point that needs to be made is that it is very striking that in all the passages in which Philo speaks of the vision of God, all references to experiential mystical language, such as sober intoxication, Bacchic frenzy, a body flushed and fiery, agitation by heavenly passion, being mastered by

---

[21] *Somn.* 2.226–29; *Gig.* 49; *Post.* 27–28; *Fug.* 174; *Deus* 12; *Conf.* 31–32. Cf. Wis 8:16; Plotinus 6.9.11.13–16; 6.9.8.43–45; 4.8.1.8. For the Gnostic notion of *anapausis* as the fruit and goal of gnosis, see P. Vielhauer, *Aufsätze zum Neuen Testament* (München 1965) 215–34; O. Hofius, *Katapausis* (Tübingen 1970) 75–90.

[22] *Praem.* 37; *Somn.* 1.71. Cf. Plato, *Symp.* 210e; *Ep.* 7.341c–d; Plotinus 5.3.17.29.

[23] *QG* 4.29; cf. *Somn.* 2.233; 1.115–16, 150. For the necessity of interruption in *devekut*, see Scholem, *art. cit.* (n. 18) 218–22.

[24] Smith, *art. cit.* (n. 1) 20.

divine love, forgetting of self, and the mind that is no longer in itself, are entirely absent.[25] These mystical motifs seem to be restricted to the psychic state of those who have succeeded momentarily in achieving a single-minded concentration on God to the exclusion of all earthly concerns. Moreover, the vision of God, according to Philo, appears to culminate in a state of tranquillity.

Let us now take a closer look at the passages dealing with the vision of God. The most extensive and interesting text is that which describes Israel's vision of the Divine (*Praem.* 36–46). The Man of Practice, we are told, receives as his special reward the vision of God. After much toil and effort he finds the physical domain to be enveloped in darkness, inasmuch as it possesses only a semblance of form, being in its essence indeterminate. In Platonism and Neopythagoreanism the dyad, the principle of matter, is described as ἀόριστος, 'undefined' or 'indeterminate'.[26] This seems to imply that he has at this stage already arrived at the understanding that material reality bears only a faint impress of the intelligible. Through unremitting struggles he laboriously begins to open the eye of his soul and succeeds in throwing off the obscuring mist. An incorporeal beam purer than ether now suddenly flashes over him disclosing the fact that the intelligible world is led by a charioteer (38–40):[27]

> That charioteer, irradiated by a circle of undiluted light, was difficult to discern or to divine, for the eye was enfeebled by the sparkling light (ταῖς μαρμαρυγαῖς). Yet is spite of the abundant light that flooded it, it held its own in its extraordinary yearning to behold the vision. The Father and Saviour, perceiving his genuine longing and desire, felt pity, and lending strength to the penetration of his sight did not grudge him a vision of himself, to the extent that it was possible for created and mortal nature to contain it. Yet it was not a vision showing what he is (ὅ ἐστιν), but only that he is (ὅτι ἔστιν).[28] For that being, which is better than the good, more venerable than the monad, and purer than the unit, cannot be discerned by anyone else; for to him alone is it allowed to comprehend himself.

As for God's existence, continues Philo, neither do all apprehend it, nor do they do so in the best manner. Some are outright atheists, others remain agnostic, while others still possess only a superstitious belief in God's existence, which they have acquired through inculcation rather

---

[25] A state of sober intoxication does accompany the mind's contemplation of the beauties of the Intelligible World, whereupon it is filled by a longing to see the Great King himself. At this point, however, a flood of concentrated light streams forth and causes the mind to spin with dizziness (*Opif.* 70–71).

[26] Diogenes Laertius 8.25. Cf. *Leg.* 1.3, where the 'two' is said to be an image of matter.

[27] The context, I think, requires this rendering of τὸν νοητὸν ἀνέφηνεν ἡνιοχούμενον, rather than simply 'disclosed the intelligible world led by its charioteer', as I had earlier rendered it (37). It is so rendered also by Beckaert in the French translation.

[28] Cf. *Fug.* 141; *Virt.* 215; *Post.* 16.

than through reasoning. But even of those who have the capacity to form an image or representation (φαντασιωθῆναι) of the Creator,²⁹ some have arrived at this, as the saying goes, by advancing from down to up, i.e. by employing the so-called cosmological and teleological arguments for God's existence.³⁰ By a sort of heavenly ladder (cf. Plato, *Symp.* 211c) they have inferred (στοχασάμενοι) the Creator from his works (cf. Wis 13:9).

There are others, however, who have succeeded in apprehending God through himself, without the cooperation of any reasoning process (λογισμός) to lead them to the sight (θέα), and these are the genuine worshipers and friends of God (44–45):

> Of their number is he who in the Hebrew is called Israel, but in Greek the God-seer, who sees not the nature of God (οἷός ἐστιν), for that, as I said, is impossible, but that he is. This knowledge he has gained from no other source, not from things terrestrial or celestial, nor from the elements or compounds mortal or immortal, but summoned by him alone who was pleased to reveal his own proper existence to the suppliants. How this means of approach has come about is worth looking at through the use of a similitude. Do we see the sense-perceptible sun by anything other than the sun, or the stars by any other than the stars, and in general is not light seen by light? Similarly, God too is his own splendor and is discerned through himself alone, without anything else assisting or being capable of assisting with a view to the perfect apprehension of his existence.

Philo clearly does not allow the perfected mind to deduce the existence of God from the concept of the Logos, since, as he puts it in *Leg.* 3.100, it is rather from God himself that the latter apprehends both God and his shadow, that is, the Logos and the physical universe. It is probably true nonetheless that the Practicer's sudden insight consisted in his realization that he had heretofore been misapplying his conception of the Primary Ἀρχή to that which could not properly be so conceived inasmuch as the self-thinking Logos implies a measure of duality, and thus fails to reach the standard of that which must be sheer Unity and utterly simplex. This would explain why Philo describes the Practicer's sudden vision as a vision of the Guide of the Intelligible World.³¹

---

²⁹ Philo is apparently employing Stoic terminology here. According to Diogenes Laertius 7.51, the Stoics said that 'some presentations (φαντασίαι) are data of sense (αἰσθητικαί) and others are not: the former are impressions conveyed through one or more sense-organs; while the latter are those received through the mind itself (διὰ τῆς διανοίας), as in the case with incorporeal things and all the other presentations that are received by reason (λόγῳ)'. Philo frequently uses the term φαντασία when referring to the vision of God (*Abr.* 122; *Sacr.* 59–60; *Virt.* 215; *Mut.* 3, 16–17; *Somn.* 1.70, 240; *Spec.* 1.40, 45; *Det.* 159; *Her.* 301; *Decal.* 105; *Cher.* 13).
³⁰ Cf. *Spec.* 3.187–89; Aristotle, *ap.* Cicero, *ND* 2.95.
³¹ Cf. Plotinus 5.3.10. For my interpretation of the intuitive intellectual nature of the

It has been suggested that the vision of God that Philo sometimes refers to as a vision of God's incorporeal or intelligible light[32] may simply serve as a metaphor for an ineffable experience of God's presence.[33] It seems to me, however, that it is rather unlikely that this could have been Philo's intention, since he tells us that the Practicer's vision of God is a permanent one (*Praem.* 27: ὁρᾶν ἀεὶ τὸ ὄν). Mystic experience is usually not conceived as an ongoing state, but rather as one of brief duration. There are, of course, exceptions, such as the Sufi mystic Ibn al-Farid, who wrote from the level of one who had attained a permanent oneness with God, but there is no indication in Philo's writings of the possibility of reaching such a permanent unitive state. Indeed, as we have already seen, he seems to insist strongly that such a powerful mystical focus cannot be maintained continuously, but is subject to an inevitable law of ebb and flow.[34] Consequently, Israel's permanent vision of God must be viewed as an intellectual vision of God's existence. Hence, the highest divine level with which mystical experience is associated by Philo is of the Intelligible World, or God qua Logos.[35]

The Graduate Theological Union
Berkeley

---

vision of God through God, see *Philo of Alexandria*, Classics of Western Spirituality (New York 1981) 26–30.

[32] *Praem.* 37–39; *QG* 4.4; *QE* 2.51. For other passages on the vision of God, see W. Michaelis, 'ὁράω', *TDNT* 5.334–38; and E. Birnbaum, *The Place of Judaism in Philo's Thought* (Atlanta 1996).

[33] B. McGinn, *The Foundations of Mysticism: Origins to the Fifth Century*, The Presence of God: A History of Western Mysticism 1 (New York 1991) 40. Cf. E. R. Wolfson, *Through a Speculum That Shines* (Princeton 1994) 59.

[34] The passage in *Fug.* 166, describing the Isaac-type soul that maintains a continuous state of sober intoxication, does not speak of the vision of God, but only of the contemplation of wisdom. As for the passage in *Somn.* 1.115 that describes the practicer's mind ascending and descending, this clearly refers to his early period, before he had arrived at the permanent vision of God. With regard to Plotinus, the consensus is that the hypernoetic unitive experiences of the One are brief and rare. Bussanich, however, has argued strongly for the view that union with either Intellect or the One results in a permanent state of being. One can become a permanent member of the Intelligible World, and the individual soul can ultimately be absorbed by the One. See John Bussanich, 'Mystical Elements in the Thought of Plotinus', *ANRW* 2.36.7 (Berlin 1994) 5300-5330; *idem, The One and its Relation to Intellect in Plotinus* (Leiden 1988) 180-93.

[35] My statement in *Philo of Alexandria* (n. 31) 30, that the unmediated intuitive vision of God's existence 'may at times culminate in an experience of mystical union accompanied by a Bacchic frenzy' is therefore incorrect. Moreover, the statement on p. 21 of the same volume that 'man's highest union with God, according to Philo, is limited to the Deity's manifestation as Logos', should read instead 'man's highest mystical contact with God ...'

'BRIGHT DARKNESS' AND CHRISTIAN TRANSFORMATION: GREGORY OF NYSSA ON THE DYNAMICS OF MYSTICAL UNION

Brian E. Daley, S.J.

'Mysticism', like 'hermeneutics' and perhaps 'democracy', is a word that suffers from overuse. It can be wielded with negative connotations of obscurantism and logorrhea, as in Ko-Ko's spectre of 'sermons by mystical Germans who preach from ten to four'; or it can be used with a reassuring hint of compassion and hipness, as in Matthew Fox's invitation to be a 'musical, mystical bear'. As the Olympic skater said when asked if she was happy with a silver medal, it all depends on what you mean.

So when one asks in what sense, if at all, Gregory of Nyssa can be considered a mystical theologian, one is likely to receive a variety of answers. Understanding mysticism as an interior union with the God who is beyond all conceiving, a matter not simply of ideas but of intensely personal experience, Jean Daniélou saw in Gregory's work the first comprehensive attempt to describe such a contact with God in Christian terms; so Daniélou boldly bestowed on Gregory the epithet, 'le fondateur de la théologie mystique'.[1] Other scholars in the past century have agreed that Gregory's writings delineate a 'mystical' knowledge of God, but are less convinced of the originality or experiential roots of his treatment, pointing out the continuities between his thought and the Platonic tradition,[2] or its similarity to mystical elements in the earlier Judaeo-Christian theology of Alexandria.[3] Still others—understanding

---

[1] J. Daniélou, *Platonisme et théologie mystique. Essai sur la doctrine spirituelle de saint Grégoire de Nysse* (Paris 1944) 6f. Daniélou is followed, if in somewhat less enthusiastic language, by L. Bouyer, *The Spirituality of the New Testament and the Fathers*, History of Christian Spirituality 1 (New York 1963), esp. 362–68; idem, *The Christian Mystery: from Pagan Myth to Christian Mysticism* (Petersham, MA 1989) 175–79, 210–16.

[2] So, for instance, H. Koch, 'Das mystische Schauen bei Gregor von Nyssa', *Theologische Quartalschrift* 80 (1898) 397–420 and E. von Ivánka, 'Vom Platonismus zur Theorie der Mystik', *Scholastik* 11 (1936) 163–95.

[3] The principal exponent of Gregory's mysticism as a link in the tradition reaching from Philo and Origen to Ps.-Dionysius and Maximus Confessor is W. Völker, *Gregor von Nyssa als Mystiker* (Wiesbaden 1955). Völker's approach was anticipated in the important articles of A. Lieske, 'Zur Theologie der Christusmystik Gregors von Nyssa', *Scholastik* 14 (1939) 485–514; idem, 'Die Theologie der Christusmystik Gregors von

mysticism essentially as non-cognitive identification, in which the human mind's sense of selfhood is simply swallowed up, at least for a brief moment, in blissful union with the absolute Being who is beyond both knowledge and sensation—have been more sceptical about Gregory's qualification as a mystical theologian,[4] or have even flatly denied it.[5]

What Gregory's own experience of God may have been seems, from this distance, impossible to know; biographical details about him are almost completely lacking. What his philosophical and theological sources were, how much originality his work reveals, remains a fascinating but complex question. But if we simply accept, as a working definition of mystical theology, the Pseudo-Dionysius's assertion that 'the most divine knowledge of God, received through ignorance, is obtained in virtue of an incomprehensible union',[6] it is hard to deny that Gregory of Nyssa not only does describe such knowledge of God in his works, at length and with great subtlety, but that he presents it as the fulfilment of every intellectual creature's natural dynamism, the crown of our well-being. This is not to say that Gregory would go so far as either Plotinus or the Ps.-Dionysius in denying cognitive content to such union with the transcendent Mystery, or that he suggests the mind ever loses all consciousness of the difference between itself and its creator—a consciousness that is the foundation of its relatedness to him. Nor does Gregory describe knowledge of God in the 'bright darkness' of ecstasy simply in affective terms, or as characteristically a transitory, passive state, followed by a relapse into a more ordinary, conceptually

---

Nyssa', *Zeitschrift für katholische Theologie* 70 (1948) 49–93, 129–68, 315–40. For a perceptive discussion of the issues in the debate between Daniélou and Völker, especially on the question of Gregory's debt to Origen and on Origen's 'intellectualism', see H. Crouzel, 'Grégoire de Nysse est-il le fondateur de la théologie mystique? Une controverse récente', *Revue d'ascétique et de mystique* 33 (1957) 189–202.

[4] F. Diekamp, *Die Gotteslehre des Hl. Gregor von Nyssa* (Münster 1896), was willing at most to acknowledge that Gregory did not exclude the possibility of a direct human experience of the essence of God (111).

[5] So H. Langerbeck, 'Zur Interpretation Gregors von Nyssa', *TLZ* 82 (1975) 82–90 (reviewing Völker's book); E. Mühlenberg, *Die Unendlichkeit Gottes bei Gregor von Nyssa* (Göttingen 1966); and M.-B. von Stritzky, *Zum Problem der Erkenntnis bei Gregor von Nyssa* (Münster 1973), esp. 67–104. These scholars insist that even Gregory's stress on the unknowability of the divine reality, in which we are nevertheless called to participate, is essentially a philosophical argument rather than a reference to ecstatic personal experience.

[6] Ps.-Dionysius, *On the Divine Names* 7.3; cf. *Mystical Theology* 2; *Ep.* 1 (PG 3.1065A). For a helpful discussion of the characteristics of mysticism and (as it is more traditionally called) 'mystical theology' in the Christian tradition, see B. McGinn, *The Foundations of Mysticism: Origins to the Fifth Century*, The Presence of God: A History of Western Christian Mysticism 1 (New York 1991) xiii–xx.

focussed kind of consciousness.[7] In Gregory's thought, our knowledge of God certainly has an ineradicably cognitive element, even if it is only the paradoxical realization, as we strain to conceive God, of the limitations of our positive concepts and the growing sense that God is always greater than our thoughts. Knowledge of God is also, for Gregory, developmental: it is part of a continuing process that begins in moral and intellectual conversion, includes the transformation of our behavior by virtue, and finds its perfection not in rest or static completion but precisely in continuous movement, in never coming to an end. Yet while these features may set his thought apart from some other ancient approaches to 'mystical theology', philosophic and Christian, it is undeniable that for him, as for the classical Christian mystics who followed, the fullest possible knowledge of God is realized in a growing consciousness of one's own ignorance, as well as in a growing awareness of being one with God in and through Christ—of genuinely sharing, through Christ, in the living characteristics of the divine being.

To see what is characteristic of Gregory's mystical theology, and what elements of it seem to be his personal contribution to the history of spirituality, it is important to glance briefly first at the mystical elements in the theology of the two authors in the tradition of biblical faith whose thought influenced his most strongly: Philo and Origen. In many passages of his writings, Philo expressed the conviction that knowledge of God, although beyond the natural powers of the mind itself, is the highest bliss the mind can enjoy. In *On Abraham*, for instance, he writes:[8]

> The one to whose lot it falls, not only by means of his or her knowledge to comprehend all the other things which exist in nature, but also to behold the Father and Creator of the universe, has advanced to the very summit of happiness. For there is nothing above God; and if anyone, directing towards God the eye of the soul, has reached up to him, let that person then pray for the ability to remain and to stand firm before him; for the roads which lead upwards to God are laborious and slow, but the descent down the declivity, being more like a rapid dragging down than a gradual descent, is swift and easy.

Because God does not belong to the perceptible world, the mind cannot

---

[7] For allusions to such occasional, ecstatic experiences of God, see, e.g., Plotinus, *Ennead* 4.8.1; Augustine, *Confessions* 9.10 (24f.); 10.40 (65).

[8] Philo, *Abr.* 57f. (tr. C. D. Yonge, *The Works of Philo* (Peabody, MA 1993) 417. Cf. *Decal.* 81; *Det.* 86; *Legat.* 4; *Praem.* 14; *Deus* 143f. For concise descriptions of Philo's mystical theology, see H. Chadwick, 'Philo and the Beginnings of Christian Thought', in A. H. Armstrong (ed.), *The Cambridge History of Later Greek and Early Medieval Philosophy* (Cambridge 1970) 148–52; D. Winston, 'Was Philo a Mystic?' in J. Dan and F. Talmage (edd.), *Studies in Jewish Mysticism* (Cambridge, MA 1982) 15–39; idem, *Logos and Mystical Theology in Philo of Alexandria* (Cincinnati 1985) 54f.

hope to comprehend anything more of him than the fact that he exists.⁹ One reaches such an understanding of the existence of 'the uncreated and divine being, the first good of all', in Philo's view, through a kind of inductive reasoning from the order and beauty of the world around us;¹⁰ the human *logos* or reasoning faculty must detach itself from its own uttered *logoi*, the words or concepts that limit and define its comprehension of created things, so that it can be left alone to seek 'that which alone is to be embraced with purity'.¹¹ This vision of the mind is, first of all, a vision of the Logos, the image of God, as 'the place ... on which the unchangeable and unalterable God stands'; on the other hand, it is a vision of the ordered universe, 'the world of the senses', which lies 'under the feet' of the Logos who created it.¹² Yet there is ultimately a quality of self-transcendence in the created mind's highest knowledge of God, for Philo, that moves even beyond such contemplative thinking and that can only be described in images of ecstasy, loss of self-awareness, even drunkenness or frenzy. So in a famous passage of his treatise *On the Creation*, Philo first describes the uniqueness of the human mind among terrestrial creatures, and its likeness to the universal mind that governs the world. By using its 'wings', the mind can rise to contemplate the highest structures of the universe,

> ... and being led on by love, which is the guide of wisdom, it proceeds onwards till, having surmounted all essence intelligible by the external senses, it comes to aspire to such as is perceptible only by the intellect; and perceiving in that the original models and ideas of those things intelligible by the external senses which it saw here full of surpassing beauty, it becomes siezed with a sort of sober intoxication like the zealots engaged in the Corybantian festivals, and yields to enthusiasm, becoming filled with another desire and a more excellent longing, by which it is conducted onwards to the very summit of such things as are perceptible only to the intellect, till it appears to be reaching the great King himself. And while it is eagerly longing to behold him pure and unmingled, rays of divine light are poured forth upon it like a torrent, so as to bewilder the eyes of its intelligence by their splendor.¹³

---

⁹ *Deus* 62; cf. *Leg*. 6; *Mut*. 7; *Praem*. 40. In *Spec*. 1.20, Philo takes a somewhat different position, suggesting that God can only be comprehended by the mind as it transcends the world of sense and 'visible essences'.
¹⁰ *Legat*. 5; cf. *Post*. 167; *Leg*. 3.97–99; *Praem*. 40–46.
¹¹ *Fug*. 92; cf. *Gig*. 52.
¹² *Conf*. 95f. (tr. Yonge 242). In his paper presented at the Philadelphia meeting before this one, D. Winston argues persuasively that Philo's writings suggest all knowledge of God which we might call 'mystical'—knowledge involving ecstasy, characterized by love and longing, and leading to a union with God beyond consciousness—is really knowledge of the Logos. The 'vision' of God himself, described in *Praem*. 36–46, is, in Winston's view, simply a clear intellectual grasp of God's existence. See above pp. 80–82.
¹³ *Opif*. 70f. (tr. Yonge 11); cf. a similar description in *Ebr*. 152; also *Somn*. 2.232. For a classic treatment of the background and later tradition of Philo's image of 'sober

In this powerful text one can hear already, by anticipation, many of the central themes and images of later Jewish and Christian mysticism.

Origen, the most influential Christian source of Gregory of Nyssa's thought, also stresses the crucial importance of knowledge of divine realities as the ultimate fulfilment of our natural human longing. Much has been written about whether, or in what sense, Origen is a 'mystical theologian'.[14] It is certainly true that he gladly uses the language of 'mystery', especially in his exegetical works, in speaking of the divine plan of salvation.[15] It is also true that he sometimes portrays the human quest for divine wisdom and knowledge as an unending journey towards a share in incomprehensible reality,[16] and emphasizes, in fact, that the goal of that quest is not simply intellectual knowledge but a joyful and loving personal contact with the God who has been revealed in Christ; it is to 'touch the hem of his garment', to 'take him in our arms' as Simeon did, and find in him our 'peace'.[17] Nevertheless, the most striking aspect of Origen's treatment of our relationship with God, for all its affective warmth, is its fundamentally cognitive character: the luminous union with the Logos that puts an end to human longing is for Origen ultimately 'the light of knowledge'.[18] So in his *De principiis*—a work apparently intended to sketch out a reasoned synthesis of the apostolic faith as the hermeneutical background for an authentically

---

drunkenness', see H. Lewy, *Sobria Ebrietas. Untersuchungen zur Geschichte der antiken Mystik*, BZNW 9 (Giessen 1929).

[14] The genuinely mystical direction of Origen's thought, in continuity with that of Philo and Clement of Alexandria, has been emphasized especially by W. Völker, *Das Vollkommenheitsideal des Origenes* (Tübingen 1931), esp. 91–144; see also Bouyer, *Spirituality* (*op. cit.* n. 1) 283–300. H. Crouzel, in his magisterial study, *Origène et la 'connaissance mystique'* (Paris 1961), takes a more cautious approach, emphasizing the spiritual and contemplative character of the knowledge of God that Origen seeks to mediate to his readers, yet acknowledging Origen's reticence in describing the 'ecstatic' or 'enthusiastic' aspects of such knowledge (see esp. 527–31). See also *idem, art. cit.* (n. 3) 200–02.

[15] On this theme, see especially H. U. von Balthasar, *Parole et mystère chez Origène* (Paris 1936).

[16] See, for example, the famous passage in *Hom. 17 in Num.* 4 (GCS 30.159–164).

[17] *Hom. 15 in Lc* 1 (GCS 49.93f.); for other allusions to 'touching' Jesus' garments or Jesus himself in order to be saved, see also *Hom. 17 in Jer.* 6 (SC 238.172.11–23); *Hom. 1 in Lev.* 4 (GCS 29.286.1–9); *Hom. 4 in Lev.* 8 (*ibid.* 327.4–13). For a discussion of how Origen conceives and emphasizes a personal relationship to Jesus, see especially F. Bertrand, *Mystique de Jésus chez Origène* (Paris 1951).

[18] So *Cant.* 3 (GCS 33.202.27–203.2), on the presence of the divine Spouse to the soul: 'Sic et animae, cum quaerit aliquem sensum et agnoscere obscura et arcana desiderat, donec invenire non potest, absens ei sine dubio est Verbum Dei. Ubi vero occurrerat et apparuerit quod requiritur, quis dubitat adesse Verbum Dei et illuminare mentem ac scientiae ei lumen praebere?' For a further discussion of this point, see Crouzel, *op. cit.* (n. 14); McGinn, *op. cit.* (n. 6) 124–26.

Christian spiritual exegesis of Scripture[19]—Origen emphasizes that the 'vision' of the incorporeal God promised to the 'pure of heart' is nothing else but 'to understand and to know him with the mind'.[20] And in his treatment, in the same work, of the eschatological fulfilment promised to rational creatures (*Princ.* 2.11.4–7), Origen presents union with God as the fulfilment of the mind's natural desire to know the causes of all things.[21] So he interprets our 'being with Christ' after death, which Paul refers to in Phil 1:23, as a chance finally to learn the secrets of the visible world and the meaning of Scripture that now tantalize us, in a heavenly 'school for souls'.[22] And since Jesus, the incarnate Logos, is for Origen always the chief revealer of God's mysteries, he will be the main object of contemplation for those in that school: 'but we will no longer understand him in that narrow form in which he has come to be for our sakes—that is, not in that circumscribed state which he had when placed on earth among men and women in our kind of body'.[23] The perfection of the rational creature, according to *De principiis*, is reached when 'the mind, having grown in mental and sensible power to perfect knowledge, is now made perfect, no longer impeded by these fleshly senses, but when increasing in its intellectual measure it attains perfection, gazing on what is pure and, so to speak, at the causes of things 'face to face' ... '[24] So, later in the same work, Origen explains the Pauline phrase, 'God will be all in all' (1 Cor 15:28), precisely as the perfection of human knowledge of God:[25]

> He will be 'all' in every individual in this way: that whatever the reasonable mind, purged from all stain of vice and thoroughly cleansed from the cloud of evil, can feel or understand or think, all will be God, nor will he then feel anything else but God, but he will think God, see God, hold God, and God will be the shape and measure of all his movements.

Just as God knows all things, so the perfected intellectual creature, made in God's image, will come to know all things in knowing him, and find in that knowledge its perfection and fulfilment.[26] If such knowledge can

---

[19] See my forthcoming article, 'Origen's *De principiis*: a Guide to the 'Principles' of Christian Scriptural Interpretation', in J. Petruccione (ed.), Καινὰ καὶ Παλαιά (Festschrift for Thomas J. Halton).
[20] *Princ.* 1.1.9.
[21] *Princ.* 2.11.4.
[22] *Ibid.* 6f.
[23] *Ibid.* 6. Cf. *Hom. 27 in Num.* 12 (GCS 30.273.21–25; 275.11–13), where Origen emphasizes that the main content of this eschatological knowledge will be the meaning of the divine economy itself.
[24] *Ibid.* 7.
[25] *Ibid.* 3.6.3.
[26] *Ibid.* 4.4.10.

be called 'mystical', it is certainly mysticism of a radiantly conscious kind.

When one turns to the passages in the works of Gregory of Nyssa that deal with human knowledge of God and human fulfilment, one finds both continuities with these two great Alexandrian theologians and new emphases. Like Philo and like his own Cappadocian contemporaries—but unlike Origen—Gregory emphasizes repeatedly that the created intellect can know nothing directly of the essence of God; all one can know of God is *that* God is, not *what* God is.[27] The reason, for Gregory, is that the nature of God is unlimited goodness, and 'what is unlimited is also infinite (τὸ δὲ ἀόριστον τῷ ἀπείρῳ ταὐτόν ἐστιν)'.[28] So he writes in his fifth homily on the Song of Songs:[29]

> The blessed, eternal nature surpassing all understanding contains all things in itself and is limited by nothing. For no name or concept, nothing associated with it in thought, can impose limits to it: not time, place, color, form, image, bulk, quantity, dimension, or anything else. Every good conceived as belonging to God's nature extends to the infinite and the unbounded. For evil has no place and the good is boundless.

So Gregory boldly asserts the radical unknowability of the divine nature:[30]

> This is the Being in which, to use the words of the Apostle, all things are formed. ... It is above beginning, and presents no marks of its inmost nature: it is to be known of only in the impossibility of perceiving it. That indeed is its most special characteristic (ἰδιαίτατον γνώρισμα), that its nature is too high for any distinctive attribute (παντὸς χαρακτηριστικοῦ νοήματος ὑψηλότεραν).

The result is that the created mind, which knows through perceiving and identifying defined form, can only come to inadequate concepts of God's essence: concepts that are either negative in character, denying to

---

[27] See, e.g., *Eun.* 2.67 (*Gregorii Nysseni Opera* [= GNO] 1.245.19-24); *Beat.* 6 (PG 44.1268B); *On the Inscriptions of the Psalms* 2.14 (GNO 5.155.25-156.4): all that human wisdom can attain to is the 'shadows of God's wings', not the 'wings' themselves. Cf. Gregory of Nazianzus, *Or.* 28.5, 15. On Gregory's differences from Origen concerning the intelligibility of God, see McGinn, *op. cit.* (n. 6) 141.
[28] *Eun.* 1.169 (GNO 1.77.17-20); cf. *Inscr. Psal.* 1 (GNO 5.46.8-10: 'the limit of what has no end is limitlessness (πέρας δὲ τοῦ ἀτελευτήτου ἡ ἀπειρία)'. E. Mühlenberg, in his celebrated study, *Die Unendlichkeit Gottes bei Gregor von Nyssa* (Göttingen 1966), has shown that Gregory is the first Christian theologian to conceive of the infinity and inconceivability of the divine nature as a positive characteristic of God, rather than simply as proof of the limitations of the created mind.
[29] GNO 6.157.14-158.1; tr. C. McCambley, *Saint Gregory of Nyssa, Commentary on the Song of Songs* (Brookline, MA 1987) 118 [altered].
[30] *Eun.* 1.373 (GNO 1.137.1-8; tr. H. Wace, NPNF 2.5 (1892) 70); cf. *V. Mos.* 2.234 (SC 1 bis, 266): 'The proper characteristic (γνώρισμα) of the divine nature is to lie beyond every characteristic'.

God some qualities found only in finite creatures, or else formed simply from our experience of God's 'operations' in the created world.[31] In contemplating the universe, one can gain at least some sense of the 'skill' of the artist who created it: his wisdom, his goodness, his freedom —all qualities that 'engrave on the soul the impress of a divine and transcendent Mind',[32] even though they do not provide adequate concepts of what the divine, creative nature in itself is.

So God is, in God's own self, simply unnameable, Gregory argues at the end of his first book against Eunomius,[33]

> ... incapable of being grasped by any term, or any idea, or any other device of our apprehension, remaining beyond the reach not only of the human but of the angelic and of all supramundane intelligence, unthinkable, unutterable, above all expression in words, having but one name that can represent his proper nature, the single name of being 'above every name' ...

The divine nature, he suggests somewhat earlier in the same work, can only be imagined fleetingly by a mind limited to categories of time and space, as something utterly beyond itself: 'Having traversed the ages and all that has been produced in them, our thought catches a glimpse of the divine nature, as of some immense ocean, but when the imagination stretches onward to grasp it, it gives no sign in its own case of any beginning. ...'[34]

Alongside this stress on the radical unknowability of God, however, Gregory emphasizes with equal insistence the created intellect's paradoxically insatiable drive to penetrate the mysteries of the divine being. This dynamism, rooted in the natural desire of every created consciousness for what is good and beautiful,[35] is most fully exemplified for Gregory in the story of Moses, whose 'ascent' to a direct experience of the mysterious reality of God becomes a model both for growth in moral virtue and for the achievement of human perfection.[36] So in the second, allegorically interpretative section of his *Life of Moses*, Gregory asserts

---

[31] See especially the important discussion of this subject in *Eun.* 2.142–158 (GNO 1.266–271); cf. *Ad Ablabium* (GNO 3/1.42–48).
[32] *Beat.* 6 (PG 44.1209A5f.; tr. H. Graef, ACW 18 (New York 1954) 147).
[33] *Eun.* 1.683 (GNO 1.222.19–25; tr. Wace, NPNF 2.5.99). For this notion that the nature of God is 'above every name', see also *Eun.* 2.587 (GNO 1.397.27–31); *Hom. 6 in Cant.* (GNO 6.182.1f.).
[34] *Eun* 1.364 (GNO 1.134.17–22; tr. Wace, NPNF 2.5.69).
[35] See, e.g., *Beat.* 5 (PG 44.1249C7f.); *Mort.* (GNO 9/1.29.9); *V. Mos.* 2.231–39.
[36] It seems likely that Gregory borrowed the idea of constructing a life of Moses out of the material in the Pentateuch, and of interpreting it allegorically as a model of human growth in virtue and knowledge of God, from Philo's two books *De vita Moysis*. However, the details of Gregory's work show surprisingly few echoes of that of Philo; see D. T. Runia, *Philo in Early Christian Literature*, CRINT 3.3 (Assen/Minneapolis 1993) 256–60.

that when Moses had progressed, by ascetical practice, to the higher levels of moral virtue, and had conquered his enemies both without and within, he was 'led on to the ineffable knowledge of God (τῇ ἀπορρήτῳ ἐκείνῃ θεογνωσίᾳ)'.[37] Such 'contemplation of God' (Θεοῦ θεωρία) involves no sense perception, Gregory assures us,[38] and continues to demand a steep and laborious 'climb';[39] more important, it is ultimately realized only in the paradoxical act of voluntarily entering the 'darkness' of complete ignorance, of moving beyond any ideas we may have of God, useful as they have been, into the deeper realization that God completely transcends our ideas. Gregory writes:[40]

> Scripture teaches ... that religious knowledge comes at first to those who receive it as light. Therefore what is perceived to be contrary to religion is darkness. ... But as the mind progresses and, through an ever greater and more perfect diligence, comes to apprehend reality, as it approaches more nearly to contemplation (θεωρία), it sees more clearly what of the divine nature is not to be contemplated. For leaving behind everything that is observed, not only what sense comprehends but also what the intelligence thinks it sees, it keeps on penetrating deeper, until, by the intelligence's busy activity (πολυπραγμοσύνη), it gains access to the invisible and the incomprehensible, and there it sees God. This is the true knowledge of what is sought; this is the seeing that consists in not seeing, because that which is sought transcends all knowledge, being separated on all sides by incomprehensibility as by a kind of darkness. Wherefore John the sublime, who penetrated into the luminous darkness (ἐν τῷ λαμπρῷ γνόφῳ), says, 'No one has ever seen God', thus asserting that knowledge of the divine essence is unattainable not only by human beings but also by every intelligent creature.

This entry into the 'bright darkness' of God's incomprehensibility, as the experience which both satisfies the highest desire of his nature and awakens in him a longing for a still greater conscious share in God's beauty and goodness, becomes for Moses—and for every human person, all of whom Moses represents—a process of eternal self-transcendence in knowledge and love: a process which Gregory, in an allusion to Phil 3:13, elsewhere labels ἐπέκτασις, 'moving beyond [oneself]'.[41] So Gregory

---

[37] *V. Mos.* 2.152 (SC 1bis, 202.5f.).
[38] Ibid. 157 (206.1).
[39] Ibid. 158.
[40] Ibid. 162f. (210.7–212.13; tr. A. J. Malherbe and E. Ferguson, *Gregory of Nyssa, The Life of Moses*, Classics of Western Spirituality (New York 1978) 95 [altered]). Gregory is describing here what St. Bonaventure, inspired by Ps.-Dionysius, would later call the movement from the 'illuminative' to the 'Unitive' or 'perfective' stage in a creature's conscious relationship to the Creator: see Ps.-Dionysius, *C. h.* 3.2; Bonaventure, *De triplici via* 13.17 (Quaracchi ed. 8 [1898] 7). For a discussion of the traditional conception of the 'triple way' of growth towards union with God, with bibliography, see the article of A. Solignac, *Dictionnaire de spiritualité* 16 (Paris 1994) 1200–15.
[41] *Hom. 6 in Cant.* (GNO 6.173f.). Daniélou popularized the idea that this process of

suggests, in a famous passage at the climax of his interpretation of Moses' 'vision', that the perfection of our knowledge of God is precisely a process of restless, endless growth beyond the knowledge we already possess:[42]

> This truly is the vision of God: never to reach satiety in the desire to see him. Rather, by looking at what one can see, one must always allow one's desire to see more be kindled anew. Thus no limit could interrupt growth in the ascent to God, since no limit to the Good can be found, nor is our increase of desire for the Good brought to an end because it is satisfied.

Gregory gives, in his other writings, various explanations for the basis in human nature on which this paradoxical relationship with God—this insatiable yet perfecting desire, this knowledge fulfilled in ignorance—is based. Being made in God's image, he argues in his *Great Catechetical Oration*, the human person has in his own nature 'something akin to the divine': a kind of participation by likeness in the divine perfection, which allows him 'to recognize the transcendent and have the desire for God's immortality',[43] on the presupposition—common to many ancient theories of knowledge—that 'like is known by like'.[44] In several works, Gregory develops the related idea that by purifying ourselves from the sinful, self-generated passions that distort the image of God in us, we enable ourselves to reflect God's archetypal reality as in a mirror, so that by looking within ourselves we can come, indirectly, to a vision of God. So he writes, interpreting the sixth Beatitude:[45]

ἐπέκτασις or self-transcendence is one of the most characteristic and central themes in Gregory's spiritual theology: see *Platonisme et théologie mystique (op. cit. n. 1)* 309–26. The word itself appears, however, only in this one passage; related verbal forms occur in several others (*Hom. 9 in Cant.* (GNO 6.291.17); *V. Gr. Thaum.* (PG 46.901C7); *Hex.* (PG 44.121A3), directly alluding to Phil 3:13; *V. Mos.* 2.225 (SC 1bis, 262.5)). For a description of the process in different words, also using Moses as its classical representative, see *Hom. 12 in Cant.* (GNO 6.354.1–357.2).

[42] *V. Mos.* 2.239 (SC 1bis, 270; tr. Malherbe and Ferguson 116 [altered]).

[43] *Or. catech.* (PG 45.21C8f.; D10–12; tr. C. C. Richardson, in E. R. Hardy (ed.), *Christology of the Later Fathers* (Philadelphia 1954) 276). For a discussion of Gregory's use of the Platonic concept of participation, see D. L. Balás, Μετουσία Θεοῦ. *Man's Participation in God's Perfections according to St. Gregory of Nyssa* (Rome 1966); cf. Von Stritzky, *op. cit.* (n. 5) 70–73. For his use of the notion of 'likeness to God', see H. Merki, Ὁμοίωσις Θεῷ. *Von der platonischen Angleichung an Gott zur Gottebenbildlichkeit bei Gregor von Nyssa* (Fribourg 1952).

[44] For early expressions of this theory of knowledge, see Empedocles, 31 A 86 D-K; Democritus, 68 A 135 D-K); Plato, *Tim.* 45 c–d. Gregory makes explicit use of the maxim in *Virg.* 11.5 (SC 119.392–394); see M. Aubineau's note *ad loc.*, with further references.

[45] *Beat.* 6 (PG 1272 B; tr. Graef, 148f. [altered]). Cf. *Hom. 3 in Cant.* (GNO 6.89ff.); *Anim. et res.* (PG 46.89BC); *Virg.* 11.5 (SC 119.392–396).

> The Lord does not say it is blessed to know something about God, but to have God present within oneself. 'Blessed are the clean of heart, for they shall see God'. ... By this we should learn that if a person's heart has been purified from every creature and all unruly affections, he will see the Image of the Divine Nature in his own beauty. ... Hence, if someone who is pure of heart sees himself, he sees in himself what he desires; and thus he becomes blessed, because when he looks at his own purity, he sees the archetype in the image.

The key to this ability of the soul to be for itself a reflection of the divine reality is clearly, in Gregory's view, moral purification: growth in virtue (ἀρετή), which reaches its summit in freedom from passion (ἀπάθεια). In the preface to the *Life of Moses*, Gregory makes the bold assertion that since the divine nature is goodness itself, 'God himself is perfect virtue'.[46] So the 'garment' of virtues we so laboriously weave for ourselves, he suggests in the ninth homily on the Song of Songs, 'imitates the divine blessedness and resembles the transcendent divine nature by [its] purity and freedom from passion'.[47] And the *way* by which the believer accomplishes this purification, the pattern for this growth in virtue and freedom, is for Gregory the way of Christ; for Christ is the embodiment and revealer of virtue, the 'founding source of passionlessness (ἀρχηγὸς τῆς ἀπαθείας)'. For every disciple, the key to restoring the inner beauty that reflects the divine reality is to imitate him.

It is here, I would argue, in his understanding of the person and role of Christ, that Gregory of Nyssa's approach to human experience of and union with God—his 'mystical theology', such as it is—takes on its most original and characteristic shape. It is not simply that Gregory, like Origen before him (if usually in somewhat cooler and more philosophical terms), stresses the central importance of personal love for Christ in the soul's growth to perfection. Certainly this is important for him; in the Song of Songs, for instance, as Gregory interprets it, the Bride cries out to Christ, the Bridegroom, 'How can I not love you who have loved me so much? Even though I am black, you laid down your life for the sheep that you shepherd. No greater love than this can be comprehended, that you exchanged your life for my salvation'.[48] But still more important, it seems, in Gregory's understanding, is the *person* of Christ, for it is there, in the transformation of a complete human individual by the Logos who has 'taken him up' and made his humanity God's own,

---

[46] *V. Mos. Praef.* 7 (SC 1bis, 50.1-8). For a discussion of this important connection, in Gregory's work, between growth in virtue and contemplation, see A. Meredith, *The Cappadocians* (New York 1995) 59-62.
[47] GNO 6.272 (tr. McCambley 175f. [altered]). Cf. *Hom. 11 in Cant.* (GNO 6.334).
[48] *Hom. 2 in Cant.* (GNO 6.61.17-21; tr. McCambley 67 [altered]).

that Gregory seems to be offering both the model and the explanation of the 'mystical' union of totally unequal realities that is the realization of human perfection.

Original, speculative, and somewhat puzzling by the standard of later Chalcedonian terminology, Gregory's Christology could perhaps best be called a 'Christology of transformation'.[49] The real news of the Gospel, according to Gregory's letter to Theophilus of Alexandria against the Apollinarians, is that the transcendent and unchanging Logos of God has, in the man Jesus, taken on human nature and made it his own; as a result, 'everything that was weak and perishable in our nature, mingled with the Godhead, has become that which the Godhead is'.[50] From this perspective, Gregory defends his own picture of Christ against the Apollinarian charge that it implies two distinct Sons, the eternal Son and the man Jesus:[51]

> He who is always in the Father, and who always has the Father in himself and is united with him, is and will be as he was for all ages. ... But the first fruits of the human nature which he has taken up, absorbed—as one might say figuratively—by the omnipotent divinity like a drop of vinegar mingled in the boundless sea, exists *in* the Godhead, but *not* in its own proper characteristics (ἰδιώμασιν). For a duality of Sons might consistently be presumed, if a nature of a different kind could be recognized by its own proper signs within the ineffable Godhead of the Son, so that the one element were weak or small or corruptible or transitory, while the other were powerful and great and incorruptible and eternal; but since all the traits we recognize in the mortal [Jesus] we see transformed by the characteristics of the Godhead, and no difference of any kind can be perceived—for whatever one sees in the Son is Godhead, wisdom, power, holiness, freedom from passivity—how could one divide what is one into double significance ...?

Gregory's conception of salvation in Christ, in fact, as presented throughout his works, is nothing less than a transformation of our own human characteristics (ἰδιώματα), damaged and distorted by passion through our history of sin, into the the characteristics of the God who is in himself virtue and transcendent beauty, through our union with Christ, in whom that transformation has first been fully realized. In Jesus, 'the divine being, changeless and unvarying in essence, has come to be in a changeable and alterable nature, so that by his own unchangeability he might heal our tendency to change for the worse'.[52] In the

---

[49] For a fuller discussion of Gregory's Christology, especially as a response to that of the Apollinarian school, and for further literature, see my article, 'Divine Transcendence and Human Transformation: Gregory of Nyssa's Anti-Apollinarian Christology', *Studia Patristica* (forthcoming; paper given at the Oxford Patristic Conference, 1995).
[50] GNO 3/1.126f.; translation mine.
[51] *Ibid.* 126f.
[52] *Apoll.* 2 (GNO 3/1.133.6–9; trans. mine); cf. 53 (222.25–223.10).

risen Christ, the believer can contemplate in faith, and can share both through natural kinship and through the sacraments,[53] a humanity now become divine by the substitution of divine for human characteristics. In him, the believer can recognize that although our human reality (τὸ ἀνθρώπινον) remains in some way unalterably itself, all its characteristics are now swallowed up in the infinite ocean of God's ineffable Mystery. In him, too, the believer can rejoice that God the Word, who is above all knowledge and naming in himself, and whose self-emptying in the Incarnation is expressed by having taken on the human name of Jesus, has now bestowed on that one ἄνθρωπος 'the name that is above every name', expressing the man Jesus' participation to a hitherto unguessed-at degree in the reality of God.[54]

For every Christian, Gregory argues in his treatise On Perfection, growth towards ἀρετή is made possible first of all through the reverent contemplation of the many names of Christ. Since the Savior has bestowed on believers 'a partnership in his name' (i.e., 'Christian') as 'the one authoritative name' for them, it is only through learning the significance of his various titles in Scripture that they can come to realize what they themselves are called to be.[55] In doing this, Gregory argues, one gradually becomes an imitator and even an 'image' of Christ, who is the 'image of the invisible God', and so acquires the virtues that conform one to the divine beauty itself.[56] By taking up an individual instance of our common humanity and turning it, in his own transformation, into the 'first fruits' of a renewed human nature, the risen Christ offers us both a model and an anchor within the divine Mystery:[57]

> Just as the first fruit of the dough was assimilated through purity and innocence— through the transformation, in other words, of the ἰδιώματα of fallen humanity—to the true Father and God, so we, also, as [the rest of the] dough, will cleave in similar

---

[53] For Gregory's development of the central role of baptism and the Eucharist in the involvement of the believer in the transformed life of Christ, see especially the Or. catech. 33–37; for his treatment of the role of faith, ibid. 38f.; for his sense of the 'physical' solidarity of the whole human race, ibid. 32. For a full treatment of Gregory's understanding of the connection between the community of believers and Christ, see R. M. Hübner, Die Einheit des Leibes Christi bei Gregor von Nyssa. Untersuchungen zum Ursprung der 'physischen' Erlösungslehre (Leiden 1974).
[54] See Apoll. 21 (GNO 3/1.161.13–26); Hom. 2 in Cant. (GNO 6.61).
[55] Perf. (GNO 8/1.173.15–174.20). Gregory's treatise seems clearly modelled on the first book of Origen's Commentary on John, which is also largely taken up with spiritual exegesis of the various titles or ἔννοιαι associated with Christ in the New Testament.
[56] Ibid. 194.4–196.15.
[57] Ibid. 206.9–14 (tr. V. Woods Callahan, Fathers of the Church 58 (Washington 1967) 117 [altered]).

ways to the Father of incorruptibility by imitating, as far as we can, the innocence and stability of the Mediator.

In becoming a disciple of Christ, one begins the process of transformation which, in Gregory's eyes, alone makes mystical union possible.

So it seems to be no accident that when Gregory takes up the Philonian metaphor of the 'sober drunkenness' of mystical knowledge, he does so—on two occasions out of three—in the context of an allusion to the transformation of the Christian believer by participation in Christ's glorified humanity through the Eucharist.[58] So, too, in the course of his explanation of Moses' vision of 'the back parts of God' from his hiding-place in a cleft of a rock on the top of Mount Sinai, Gregory does not fail to point out that according to Paul, 'the rock was Christ' (1 Cor 10:5): 'For, since Christ is understood by Paul as the rock, and since all hope for good things is believed to be in Christ, in whom, we have learned are 'all the treasures of good things' (Col 2:3), he who finds he shares any good must surely be in Christ, who contains all that is good'.[59]

Christ in his very person, then, is for Gregory the key to understanding the possibility of a mystical knowledge of God, as well the necessary way to its realization. So he speaks of Christ as himself a part the infinite, inconceivable Mystery of God, whose Incarnation in our world makes possible for us both a new understanding of God's goodness and a new participation in it. He writes in the treatise *On Perfection*:[60]

> He who is beyond all knowledge and understanding, the ineffable and unutterable and inexplicable one, has himself become an 'image of the invisible God' out of love for humanity, that he might make you once again into an image of God; his purpose was that he might be formed in you in his own form, which he has taken up, and that you might once again be shaped through him to correspond to that form of the archetypal beauty, and so become what you were from the beginning.

---

[58] *Hom. 10 in Cant.* (GNO 6.308); *Ascens.* (PG 46.692). For a discussion of Gregory's use of this image, see Lewy, *op. cit.* (n. 13) 132–37.

[59] *V. Mos.* 2.248 (SC 1bis, 276; tr. Malherbe and Ferguson 118 [altered]). See also another passage, just before this (*V. Mos.* 2.244: 274; trans. mine): 'Those who climb uphill in sand, even if they happen to take large steps with their feet, toil endlessly, since their steps always slip downwards in the sand, so that they undertake movement but no progress comes of the movement. But if someone, as the psalm says, has drawn up his feet from the miry pit and plants them on the rock–and 'the rock is Christ', who is perfect virtue–then as much as he is, according to the advice of Paul, 'firm and unshakeable in the good' (1 Cor 15:58), so much the more quickly will he complete the race, using the firm footing as a kind of wing and flying upwards on his way because of the firmness of good in his heart'.

[60] GNO 8/1.194.14–195.5 (translation mine). For a similar emphasis on the eternity and transcendence of Christ, contrasted with his entry into human history to remake our humanity, see *Apoll.* 53 (GNO 3/1.222.25–223.10).

The place of Christ, after his resurrection and glorification, is not only within the transcendent Mystery—his human characteristics now divinized, even as his divine characteristics were previously revealed in human terms; his place is also *within* the believer, who both carries Christ and is carried by him.[61] As a result, the believer himself gradually becomes divinized, too—not through total absorption into God but through a steady, endless process of 'ascent' that involves a transformation of our fallen human ἰδιώματα into the characteristics of God. So the Bride, in Gregory's reading of the Song of Songs, is not only 'wounded' by Christ, who is God's 'sweet arrow of love', penetrated by Christ's divine presence and touched by his revelation of the reality of God; she herself becomes, with Christ and in him, 'an arrow in the bowman's hands', sharing in his incorruptibility and aimed by him, in turn, deep into the Mystery of God.[62]

How one interprets the 'mystical theology' of Gregory of Nyssa depends largely, as I said at the beginning, on what one takes 'mysticism' to mean. Despite the enthusiasm of some of his twentieth-century interpreters, those who make a clear distinction between Gregory's 'mysticism' and that of Meister Eckhart or even of Ps.-Dionysius, let alone that of Eastern religions, seem to be closest to the truth. The 'darkness' of which Gregory speaks in describing the human mind's ultimate place of encounter with the infinite God does not seem to imply a loss of consciousness, let alone a merging of identity between creature and creator; the ἔκστασις to which Gregory occasionally refers is less the love-wounded swoon of Bernini's St. Teresa than the recognition of the limits of language by a great rhetorician who is also a man of deeply perceptive faith. Like John of the Cross, Gregory is always concerned with the moral foundation of union with God, with virtue and 'philosophical' praxis, and always takes pains to emphasize the cognitive implications of religious experience. Yet he does succeed, at the same time, in reviving and reshaping the Alexandrian insight that the human mind must ultimately move beyond its own cognitive categories in its quest for the fullness of truth and beauty, and must rest simply in a sense of graced union with the God who is both utterly near and fundamentally unknown. In the process, Gregory succeeds in combining Philo's emphases on God's radical inconceivability with Origen's Christocentrism. What is new in his approach to this unitive 'knowledge' of the transcendent Mystery is the clarity with which he

---

[61] So, e.g., *Hom. 7 in Cant.* (GNO 6.207); *Ep.* 3.1f (GNO 8/2, 20.3–23, suggesting that the 'holy places' of Christ's life are within us). Cf. Meredith, *op. cit.* (n. 46) 82f.
[62] *Hom. 4 in Cant.* (GNO 6.127ff.).

rests it on the paradox of Christ's own person, as the place where the Mystery has come palpably near, and where the absorption into God of all that is knowably human has already begun. As Gregory peers into the divine darkness, it is for him of paramount significance that his feet are firmly planted on the rock which is Christ.[63]

Weston Jesuit School of Theology

---

[63] Another version of this article will appear in M. J. Himes and S. Pope (edd.), *Finding God in All Things: Essays in Honor of Michael J. Buckley* (New York 1996).

TRACES OF PHILONIC DOCTRINE IN MEDIEVAL JEWISH MYSTICISM: A PRELIMINARY NOTE

Elliot R. Wolfson

The relation of Philo of Alexandria and mysticism can be viewed in two ways: the first involves the appropriateness or inappropriateness of using the term 'mystical' to characterize Philo's writings when judged in their own historical, philological, and conceptual terms.[1] The second is the question of the possible influence of Philo on various mystics in the three major monotheistic traditions: Judaism, Christianity, and Islam. Although the former is an issue of much interest to me, it is not at all the concern of my focus in this brief note. With respect to the latter, I am principally concerned with the traces of Philonic doctrine in medieval Jewish mysticism; thus I will not discuss the possible influence of Philo on some forms of ancient Jewish mystical speculation, most notably in *Sefer Yetzirah*.[2] I must note, however, that the least contested claim is the presumed influence of Philo on Christian mysticism insofar as we have clear evidence that the Philonic writings were read and used by several of the major Church fathers, such as Clement, Origen, and Eusebius.[3] It stands to reason, therefore, that if Philo had any discernible influence on Christian mystics, this can be explained in terms of the aforecited channels of textual transmission. With respect to the question of Philonic influence on Jewish and Islamic mysticism in the medieval period, the lines of transmission are far more difficult to draw. The impact of Philo on mystics in these two traditions is, of course, related to the larger problem concerning the fate of Philo's writings in Jewish and Islamic thought in the Middle Ages.

---

[1] See, for example, E. R. Goodenough, *By Light, Light: The Mystic Gospel of Hellenistic Judaism* (New Haven 1935); D. Winston, 'Was Philo a Mystic?', in J. Dan and F. Talmage (edd.), *Studies in Jewish Mysticism* (Cambridge, MA 1982) 15–39; *idem*, *Logos and the Mystical Theology in Philo of Alexandria* (Cincinatti 1985); and B. McGinn, *The Foundations of Mysticism: Origins to the Fifth Century*, The Presence of God: A History of Western Mysticism 1 (New York 1991) 35–41.
[2] See I. Gruenwald, 'Some Critical Notes on the First Part of Sefer Yeẓira', *REJ* 132 (1973) 503–04.
[3] For an extensive summary, see D. T. Runia, *Philo in Early Christian Literature: A Survey*, CRINT 3.3 (Assen/Minneapolis 1993).

A. Harkavy, H. Hirschfeld, and S. Poznanski, were of the opinion that Jewish sectarians in Persia and Babylonia as late as the ninth and tenth centuries utilized the writings of Philo.[4] Poznanski argued, for example, that the ninth-century Karaite author, Benjamin al-Nahawendi, may have reflected the Philonic doctrine of the Logos in his insistence that God created the world through the intermediacy of an angel.[5] The view of al-Nahawendi is cited in the *Kitâb al-anwâr* of the Karaite Ya'qub Qirqisani, which was composed in 937. In addition to its demiurgic role, this angel, which is created by God, also appears to the prophets and performs miracles. To support his opinion that al-Nahawendi reflects the Philonic doctrine of the Logos, Poznanski observes that in his description of the sectarian Maghâriya, Qirqisani mentions the 'Alexandrian', whom Poznanski thinks should be identified with Philo. In another fragment of Qirqisani's work, one can find other citations from the 'Alexandrian'. Moreover, in a passage from Saadiah Gaon's polemical treatise against the Karaites, *Kitâb al-tamyîz*, found in the Genizah, there is a reference to 'Judah the Alexandrian', which perhaps is a corrupt form of the 'Alexandrian Jew'. Poznanski acknowledged that no precise parallel to this text can be found in the extant corpus of Philo, but he is hesitant to conclude that it is definitely not a passage from an authentic Philonic composition. He suggests that Saadiah may have gained knowledge of this source from David al-Muqammis.[6]

With respect to the question regarding the precise transmission of the Philonic material, there are two possible explanations. Harkavy was of the opinion that the Maghâriya sect, to whom the 'Alexandrian' belonged according to Qirqisani, were the Essenes, whose material was miraculously found in a cave by an Arab in 790. These sources, in turn, were read by some of the Karaite authors from whom knowledge of Philo was transmitted to Rabbanite Jews. Poznanski, by contrast, was of the opinion that some of the Philonic material was translated into Syriac within a Christian community whence it became known to al-Muqammis and Qirqisani, both of whom were well versed in the Syriac

---

[4] A. Harkavy, 'Abu Yusuf Ya'qub al Qirqisani on the Jewish Sects', in B. Chiesa and W. Lockwood (edd.),*Ya'qub al Qirqisani on Jewish Sects and Chirstianity*, Judentum und Umwelt 10 (Frankfurt 1984) 49–90; H. Hirschfeld, 'The Arabic Portion of the Cairo Genizah at Cambridge VII', *JQR* 17 (1905) 65–68; and S. Poznanski, 'Philon dans l'ancienne littérature judéo-arabe', *REJ* 50 (1905) 10–31.

[5] For a critique of Poznanski's theory regarding the Philonic origin of the demiurgic angel of al-Nahawendi, see H. A. Wolfson, 'The Pre-Existent Angel of the Magharians and al-Nahawandi', *JQR* 51 (1960) 89–106.

[6] Relying on the work of Poznanski, A. Altmann, *Studies in Religious Philosophy and Mysticism* (Ithaca 1969) 154, posited an influence of the Philonic conception of the Logos, as mediated through Karaite sources, on Saadiah's theory of revelation.

Christian literature. It is less likely, according to Poznanski, that these texts were translated directly into Arabic.

A number of scholars have also noted the indirect influence of Philo on medieval Jewish philosophers. For example, Poznanski, building on the work of Wittman, suggested that Solomon ibn Gabirol's notion of the will (*voluntas*), which on occasion is characterized in terms that are associated with the divine speech (*verbum*), may reflect the Philonic doctrine of the Logos.[7] A similar identification of the will and speech is found in other medieval Jewish philosophers, for example, in Saadiah Gaon's *Kitâb al-Almânât wa'l-I'tiqâdât* when he comments on the delineation of the first *sefirah* in *Sefer Yetzirah* as the *ruaḥ* and in the description of the *amr ilahi* in Judah Halevi's *Sefer ha-Kuzari*. More recent scholarship has noted that an important source for medieval Jewish and Muslim philosophers was the long recension of the *Theology of Aristotle*, in reality a paraphrase of books 4, 5, and 6 of the *Enneads* of Plotinus, for in that version of the text the divine will, interposed between the One and *Nous*, is identified as the divine speech or word. However, one cannot rule out the possibility that Philonic material was utilized by those who redacted the Plotinian material in what we call the long recension of the *Theology of Aristotle*.

H. A. Wolfson noted a number of interesting conceptual and terminological similarities between Philo and Judah Halevi.[8] The passages analyzed by Wolfson deal with some critical features of the Sinaitic theophany as treated by the two thinkers. Wolfson acknowledged the possibility that Halevi derived his views independently of Philo on the basis of a similar exegesis of the relevant scriptural texts, but he does not rule out the possibility of a literary connection, and indeed, some of the philological parallels that he notes are striking. More recently, A. Wasserstein has noted parallels between Philo and Abraham ibn Ezra's *Commentary on Psalms*, although he admits that the Philonic influence may be due to Christian sources with which ibn Ezra was familiar.[9] I note, parenthetically, that I, too, have pointed out a striking parallel between ibn Ezra and Philo, related especially to the interpretation of

---

[7] For more recent discussions on the topic of the identification of the Will and the Logos in the thought of ibn Gabirol, see J. M. Dillon, 'Solomon Ibn Gabirol's Doctrine of Intelligible Matter', in L. E. Goodman (ed.), *Neoplatonism and Jewish Thought*, Studies in Neoplatonism 7 (Albany 1992) 51–52 and B. McGinn, 'Ibn Gabirol: The Sage Among the Schoolmen', *ibid.*, 90–92.

[8] H. A. Wolfson, *Studies in the History of Philosophy and Religion* (Cambridge, MA 1977) 2.104–06.

[9] A. Wasserstein, 'Greek (and Christian?) Sources in Ibn Ezra's *Commentary on Psalms*', *Scripta Classica Israelica* 7 (1983–84) 101–12. On the possible influence of Philo on ibn Ezra, see the passing comment of Altmann, *op. cit.* (n. 6) 206.

the biblical notion of the divine image in which Adam was created, understood as a reference to the demiurgic angel or the Intellect, the image of God in whose image the human being was created.[10]

On the basis of the same textual evidence, G. Scholem argued that the influence of the Philonic doctrine of the Logos is discernible in the mystical theosophy of the Rhineland Jewish Pietists, the Haside Ashkenaz, who were active in the twelfth and thirteenth centuries.[11] Scholem focused on a specific doctrine that has been attributed (based on the scholarly research of J. Dan) to a particular group known as the *ḥug ha-keruv ha-meyuḥad*, 'the circle of the special cherub'. The central idea expressed in the writings that stem from members of this circle is that from the invisible and incorporeal deity there emanates an angel (designated the 'special cherub', *keruv meyuḥad*), which is the enthroned form of the divine manifest in corporeal terms. Scholem argues that in this doctrine there is an 'echo of Philonic thought', for the enthroned cherub is none other than the Logos described by Philo. In response to the historical question regarding how these ideas could have penetrated the circles of German Pietists, Scholem provides two answers: (1) such speculation on the Logos may have become part of an 'orthodox Jewish Gnosticism' already present in some of the Merkavah treatises; (2) there is the possibility that some of the Pietists came into direct contact with heretical thoughts. It is even possible, according to Scholem, that some of the Pietists had personal encounters with Jewish sectarians or heretics.

The most extreme argument mounted to date to document the influence of Philo on medieval Jewish mysticism was offered by S. Belkin in his attempt to show that one of the literary strata of the *Zohar*, the *Midrash ha-Ne'elam* reflected an ancient Hellenistic-Jewish allegorical midrash.[12] I will not rehearse here all the details of Belkin's complex and convoluted argument, but suffice it to say that R. J. Zwi Werblowsky subjected Belkin's study to a pointed critique that revealed the historical shortcomings and methodological flaws in his attempt to trace the zoharic views to Philo.[13]

---

[10] E. R. Wolfson, 'God, the Intellect, and the Demiurge: On the Usage of the Word *Kol* in Abraham ibn Ezra', *REJ* 149 (1990) 77–111.
[11] G. Scholem, *Major Trends in Jewish Mysticism* (New York 1954) 114–15.
[12] S. Belkin, 'The *Midrash Ha-Ne'elam* of the *Zohar* and Its Sources in Ancient Alexandrian Literature', *Sura* 3 (1957–58) 25–92 (Hebrew).
[13] R. J. Zwi Werblowsky, 'Philo and the *Zohar*: a Note on the Methods of the 'scienza nouva' in Jewish Studies', *JJS* 10 (1959) 25–44, 113–35. See the rejoinder by J. Finkel, 'The Alexandrian Tradition and the Midrash ha-Ne'elam', in *The Leo Jung Jubilee* (New York 1962) 77–103.

The possibility that the views expressed by medieval kabbalists reflect earlier Platonic ideas, which informed either Philo or the Palestinian rabbis reflected in midrashic anthologies such as *Genesis Rabbah* or *Midrash Tadsche*, has been affirmed in a number of studies by Y. Baer and, to a lesser extent, by E. R. Goodenough.[14] The underlying claim of Baer's approach, as M. Idel noted,[15] is to affirm that a Platonic substratum was laid for later Jewish mysticism. Idel himself has taken a position that is similar to the orientation of Baer. Thus, in his discussion of the theosophic interpretation of the cherubim as representing the masculine and the feminine attributes of God reflected in one of the earliest kabbalistic documents of the Middle Ages, Idel analyzes the treatment of the cherubim found in a passage from Philo's *Quaestiones et Solutiones in Exodum*.[16] Idel approvingly cites Goodenough's assertion that Philo's symbolic understanding of the cherubim is in 'harmony with later cabbalistic speculation'. The specific text cited by Idel, which is an explication of the mystery of the androgyne (*du-partzufim*) attributed to Abraham ben David of Posquiéres, corroborates Goodenough's remark. According to Idel's own reconstructionist project, the use of Philo (as well as other texts from antiquity) supports the claim that there is a much older Jewish theosophy that was fully articulated in the medieval kabbalistic sources.[17]

From this brief and highly selective survey, it can be concluded that two sorts of argument have been offered in support of the claim that Philo had an instrumental role in the shaping of medieval Jewish mysticism: the textual-historical which presumes that there was a transmission of Philonic material through a chain of translations, and the phenomenological-typological which assumes minimally that there are striking resemblances between ideas and/or symbols embraced by Philo and later kabbalists. With respect to the former, it must be admitted that at present the information that has surfaced is not sufficient to make a convincing and incontestable case. David Runia has recently raised some important questions regarding the assumption that Philo was really known (directly or indirectly) by Jews and Arabs in the Middle Ages. He notes that the 'Alexandrian' mentioned in the Jewish sectarian

---

[14] Y. Baer, *Israel Among the Nations* (Jerusalem 1955 (Hebrew)); *idem*, 'On the Problem of the Eschatological Doctrine During the Period of the Second Temple', *Zion* 23–24 (1958–59) 3–34, 141–65 (Hebrew); *idem*, 'The Service of Sacrifice in Second Temple Times', *Zion* 40 (1975): 95–153 (Hebrew); and E. R. Goodenough, *Jewish Symbols in the Greco-Roman Period* (New York and Princeton 1953–68) 4:132.
[15] M. Idel, *Kabbalah: New Perspectives* (New Haven 1988) 13.
[16] *Ibid.*, 131–32.
[17] For another example, see *ibid.*, 190.

sources from the ninth and tenth centuries may not necessarily refer to Philo. Indeed, Runia even expresses doubt about translations of Philo's writings into Syriac or Arabic.[18] The cautionary remarks of Runia are, in my opinion, fully justified at the present stage of research. More textual work is needed before we have a solid foundation on which to build the larger claim that Philo had an impact on medieval Jewish and Islamic philosophers, theologians, and mystics.

I would like to conclude with the observation that the centrality of the doctrine of the Logos in a variety of mystical trends in the Jewish Middle Ages lends support to those who posit that the influence of Philo was significant.[19] As I have noted, we still cannot account for this influence in a fully convincing way. However, one cannot rule out the possibility that remarks concerning the Logos found in Jewish mystical sources reflect the influence of either Christian or Islamic sources, which in turn may be traced to Philo in one way or another. Another possibility is that other Hellenistic works in which the notion of the Logos was articulated, such as the Wisdom of Solomon, influenced medieval Jews. Indeed, there is strong textual evidence that this particular work circulated in elite rabbinic circles in the Middle Ages in Byzantium and Europe. It also reasonable to assume that occasional remarks concerning the divine word scattered throughout the rabbinic corpus were interpreted in a more systematic way by the medieval mystics. Nevertheless, my inclination is to pursue the Philonic influence above all other possible channels, for the descriptions of the Logos in the mystical sources are expressed in a mythical language, informed by an allegorical-symbolic reading of scriptural verses that is found in Philo as well. Perhaps the key to solving the textual riddle lies buried in manuscripts, especially in the Genizah fragments that may yet surface to allow us to complete the picture of the transmission of Philonic writings and their impact on Jewish intellectual history. But we cannot rule out the possibility that similar hermeneutical conditions led the medieval mystics to interpret Scripture in a manner congenial to Philo without necessitating any direct or indirect textual links. This is the position adopted by Scholem:[20]

---

[18] Runia, *op. cit.* (n. 3) 15–16, 28.

[19] The possibility that the Philonic doctrine of the Logos influenced a statement of Samuel ben Nahman recorded in *Genesis Rabbah*, which in turn had a great impact on the emanationist doctrines of the early kabbalists, was entertained by Altmann, *op. cit.* (n. 6) 128–39.

[20] *Kabbalah* (Jerusalem 1974) 9. See *ibid.*, 171, and *idem, On the Kabbalah and Its Symbolism* (New York 1965) 34–35, 45–46.

It should be noted that there is no definite proof that Philo's writings had an actual direct influence on rabbinic Judaism in the post-tannaitic period. ... However, the fact that the Karaite Kirkisani (tenth century) was familiar with certain quotations drawn from Philonic writings shows that some of his ideas found their way, perhaps through Christian-Arab channels, to members of Jewish sects in the Near East. But it should not be deduced from this that there was a continuous influence up to this time, let alone up to the time of the formulation of the Kabbalah in the Middle Ages. Specific parallels between Philonic and kabbalistic exegesis should be put down to the similarity of their exegetical method, which naturally produced identical results from time to time.

I noted earlier the observation of Scholem that the demiurgical angel in the German Pietistic literature suggested to him an echo of Philo whom he tellingly calls the 'Alexandrian theosophist'.[21] To the example provided by Scholem one could add many more, for the identification of the demiurgical aspect of God with the cherubic angel, portrayed as the anthropomorphic form upon the throne, is a central motif in a variety of medieval mystical texts, including the theosophic and the ecstatic kabbalah. In my opinion, this is one of the most essential symbolic complexes in medieval Jewish mystical literature.[22] It is particularly the figure of Metatron who plays a critical role in this dual aspect as divine and angelic.[23] Interestingly enough, several scholars have observed that Metatron is the counterpart in Jewish mysticism to the Logos in Philonic thought.[24] While one may challenge the historical accuracy of this comparison, on conceptual and terminological grounds one must agree that the similarities are striking. Consider, for example, the following remark of a late-thirteenth-century Castilian kabbalist, Jacob ben Jacob ha-Kohen, in his mystical diary, *Sefer ha-'Orah*:[25]

> 'God said, 'Let there be light'' (Gen 1:3). Metatron is the utterance (*'amirah*), the thought of the intellect (*maḥshevet ha-sekhel*), speech through the power of the utterance (*dibbur bekhoaḥ ha-'amirah*). ... This is the principle: speech speaks and communicates through the utterance of the intellect. When the Holy One, blessed be He, spoke to Moses the voice, spirit, and word were created from the power of the intellect.

---

[21] Scholem, *op. cit.* (n. 11) 114.
[22] See E. R. Wolfson, *Through a Speculum That Shines: Vision and Imagination in Medieval Jewish Mysticism* (Princeton 1994) 255–63.
[23] See E. R. Wolfson, 'Metatron and Shi'ur Qomah in the Writings of Haside Ashkenaz', in K. Grözinger and J. Dan (edd.), *Mysticism, Magic and Kabbalah in Ashkenazi Judaism* (Tübingen 1995) 60–92.
[24] See J. Abelson, *Jewish Mysticism* (London 1913) 67 and Goodenough, *op. cit.* (n. 1) 366.
[25] MS Jerusalem, Schocken Library 14, fol. 60a, cited in D. Abrams, 'The Book of Illumination of R. Jacob ben Jacob HaKohen: A Synoptic Edition From Various Manuscripts' (Ph.D. diss., New York University 1993) 88, 410.

To understand Jacob ha-Kohen's position properly, it would be necessary to explicate a host of medieval philosophic and mystical texts, a task that lies beyond my immediate concern.[26] What is important to emphasize for the purposes of this study is that the hypostatic theology articulated by this kabbalist relates not to the sefirotic *anthropos*, but to a conception of the Logos, designated by the Hebrew *'amirah*, and linked to the angelic Metatron. God creates by means of this power, which is the expression of the thought of the intellect. In other parts of this text, Jacob explicitly identifies Metatron as the intellect that is derived (or emanated) from the intellect. Moreover, Jacob upholds the possibility that Moses can become one with Metatron. Moses is granted a vision of God that is denied all other people, a unifying vision that results in his becoming one with the Logos.[27] It lies beyond the scope of human potential to become one with God, but it is within human potential to become one with the intellect that is derived from the One. The position assumed by Jacob ha-Kohen bears a strong phenomenological resemblance to the view of Philo, at least as it is articulated by some Philonic scholars, regarding the possibility of achieving a state of conjunction with the manifestation of God as Logos.

At this stage of my research I cannot say with certainty that the kabbalistic author was influenced by Philo. It is possible that other sources (Jewish, Christian, or Islamic) led to the formulation of his views. On the other hand, the possibility that there is a genuine trace of Philo here should not be rejected. The matter requires further study of the extant texts, most of which are still buried in manuscripts. In the final analysis, the problem of the influence of Philo on medieval Jewish mysticism cannot be treated in isolation from the larger question of the transmission of Philonic works into the Middle Ages.

New York University

---

[26] For an explication of Jacob ha-Kohen's views regarding Metatron, see Wolfson, *art. cit.* (n. 10) 92 n. 61 and 95–96 n. 71; *idem, art. cit.* (n. 23) 77 n. 87; and Abrams, *op. cit.* (n. 25) 65–89.

[27] See Wolfson, *op. cit.* (n. 22) 201 n. 48 and *idem, art. cit.* (n. 23) 74 n. 73.

INSTRUMENTA

YONGE'S COLLECTION OF FRAGMENTS OF PHILO

JAMES R. ROYSE

The recent one-volume edition of Philo's works presents a revised version of Yonge's English translation of much of Philo.[1] In particular, this edition also includes a collection of fragments (appendix 2, 880–97), deriving from Mangey's extensive collection of Greek fragments.[2] Yonge's edition further includes a translation of the Eusebian extracts from Philo's *Hypoth.* (and *Apol.*) and *Prov.*, as well as 'A Treatise Concerning the World' (867–879), which is a translation of the treatise *De mundo*, a collection of excerpts from Philo.[3]

Runia has the following comment on appendix 2: 'These will surely be a [of?] very little use to anyone because most fragments are insufficiently identified, and the references that are given are totally out of date.'[4] This is true, but it is regrettable, since we have here (I believe) the only English translation of many of these texts. Indeed, we have here the only translation into any modern language of what are likely to be some genuine fragments of Philo. Of course, this material must be isolated from the spurious fragments. And the translations of the texts that are found in Cohn-Wendland or the Armenian appear definitely inferior to the standard translations of these texts.[5] Nevertheless, one hesitates to consign all of this material to oblivion.

---

[1] *The Works of Philo Complete and Unabridged: New Updated Edition*, translated by C. D. Yonge, with a foreword by David M. Scholer (Peabody, MA 1993). For a general assessment of this volume, see David T. Runia, 'Philo in a Single Volume', *SPhA* 6 (1994) 171–82.
[2] Thomas Mangey, *Philonis Judaei opera*, 2 vols. (London 1742) 2:625–80.
[3] Mangey, 2:601–24. On this 'work' see my *The Spurious Texts of Philo of Alexandria* (Leiden 1991) 144.
[4] 'Philo in a Single Volume' 177 n. 23.
[5] There is a remarkable slip in the fragment of *QG* 1.77 at 885.5a, where the Greek ὁ μὲν Κάϊν κτλ. is translated as 'Gaius ... ' (Yonge, *The Works of Philo Judaeus* [London 1855] 4:254, has 'Caius.') Philo is, of course, speaking of Cain, as the mention of Lamech suggests. At yet other places the reprinted text has deteriorated from the text in Yonge's edition.

The Studia Philonica Annual 8 (1996) 107–121

Consequently, I have provided here an index to the Eusebian extracts and the fragments included in appendix 2. The following information is given: the page and order on the page of the text; the beginning and end of the text in English with the beginning and end of Mangey's Greek in parentheses; and the identification of the text with the location in Mangey in parentheses. Since the texts derive from Mangey, it has seemed convenient to include the reference to his collection of fragments. Further occurrences of these texts in other editions and collections may be found by consulting the information concerning Mangey in my *The Spurious Texts of Philo of Alexandria*, 170–79, and the cross-references in my 'Reverse Indexes.'[6] The fragments cited in *The Spurious Texts* simply as 'unidentified' are numbered here as in 'Reverse Indexes.'[7]

---

[6] 'Reverse Indexes to Philonic Texts in the Printed Florilegia and Collections of Fragments', *SPhA* 5 (1993) 156–79.
[7] *Ibid.*, 174–79, where the 124 unidentified fragments are listed.

YONGE'S COLLECTION OF FRAGMENTS OF PHILO 109

742-56: From Eusebius, *Praeparatio Evangelica* (= Mangey 625-647)

742 (6.1)	That their — this moment. (τὸν μὲν παλαιὸν — πολυανδρίαν)	= *Hypoth.* (= Mangey 626.1)
742-43 (6.2-6.9)	And they — he established. (ἀνήρ γε μὴν — πεισθῆναι)	= *Hypoth.* (= Mangey 627.1)
743-44 (7.1-7.9)	Now, is there — every place. (ἆρά τι τούτων — ἁπανταχοῦ)	= *Hypoth.* (= Mangey 628.1)
744-45 (7.10-7.20)	And if it — nature of man. (ὅλην δὲ ἡμέραν — λόγος)	= *Hypoth.* (= Mangey 630.1)
745-46 (11.1-11.18)	But our lawgiver — confer on them. (μυρίους δὲ τῶν — σεμνοποιοῦσι)	= *Hypoth. (Apol.)* (= Mangey 632.1)
747	Why, then, does — himself alone. (διὰ τί ὡς — ἐξομοιοῦσθαι)	= *QG* 2.62 (= Mangey 625.1)
747	But concerning — exists in nature. (περὶ δὲ τοῦ — φύσει)	= *Prov.* 2.50-51 (= Mangey 625.2)
748 (1)	Do you say — in a mean condition. (πρόνοιαν εἶναι — ταπεινοί)	= *Prov.* 2.3 (= Mangey 634.1)
748-52 (2-42)	God is not a tyrant — real truth is. (οὐ τύραννος — εἰσόμεθα)	= *Prov.* 2.15-33 (= Mangey 634.2)
752-56 (43-72)	God causes the — of human affairs. (ἀνέμων καὶ — πραγμάτων)	= *Prov.* 2.99-112 (= Mangey 642.1)

Appendix 2: Fragments

880-86: "Extracted from the Parallels of John of Damascus" (= Mangey 648-60: "Ex Johannis Damasceni Sacris Parallelis")

880.1	If one is to tell — existing things. (πάντων μὲν — κύριον)	= unidentified 68 (= Mangey 648.1)
880.2	If you wish to be — as your king? (εἰ βούλει — θεοῦ)	= unidentified 20 (= Mangey 648.2)
880.3	Some men, making — than before. (ἔνιοι — ἐναπέθετο)	= *QE* 1.7 (b) (= Mangey 648.3)
880.4	When a man — the abyss of hell. (ὅταν ἄνθρωπος — ᾅδου)	= Fr. sp. 49 (= Mangey 648.4)
880.5	It is not possible — and balance. (οὐκ ἔστι — θεόν)	= unidentified 65 (= Mangey 649.1)
880.6	The mind is — of all judges. (ὁ νοῦς — ἀψευδέστατος)	= *Post.* 59 (= Mangey 649.2)
880.7	He who has learnt — rule of others. (ὁ μαθὼν — ἄρχεσθαι)	= *QG* 3.30 (b) (= Mangey 649.3)
880.8	Alas, how many and — and death.	= *Legat.* 17 (= Mangey 649.4)

	(ὦ πόσα — φόβοι)	
880.9a	No wicked man — men are poor. (τῶν φαύλων — πένητες)	= unidentified 110 (= Mangey 649.5a)
880.9b	Every foolish man — of room. (στενοχωρεῖται — διάγειν)	= QG 4.33 (a) (= Mangey 649.5b)
880.10	There is no — and intellect. (μεῖζον — ζημιωθέντι)	= QG 4.179 (= Mangey 649.6)
880.11	Ignorance is the — destruction. (νόσου — ἀπαιδευσία)	= Ebr. 141 (= Mangey 649.7)
880.12	Every stratagem is — honourable. (οὐ πᾶς δόλος — ἴδιον)	= QG 4.228 (= Mangey 649.8)
881.1	It is as — with one another. (ἀμήχανον — σκότος)	= Fr. sp. 30 (= Mangey 649.9)
881.2	The happy — and expedient. (μακαρία — γινομένοις)	= QG 3.38 (b) (= Mangey 650.1)
881.3	The wise man — on divine matters. (ὁ σοφὸς — ἐντύχῃ)	= QG 4.47 (a) (= Mangey 650.2)
881.4	Foul speakers — character. (αἰσχροὶ — προχειρότατοι)	= Flacc. 34 (= Mangey 650.3)
881.5	Everything which — is beautiful. (τὰ μὴ σὺν — κόσμια)	= Leg. 3.158 (= Mangey 650.4)
881.6	Old age is an unruffled harbour. (ἀκύμαντος λιμὴν πολιά)	= Fr. sp. 47 (= Mangey 650.5)
881.7	Old age is the — be checked. (σώματος — παθῶν)	= unidentified 76 (= Mangey 650.6)
881.8a	Continued practice — ignorance. (ἡ συνεχὴς — ἀμελετησία)	= Sacr. 86 (= Mangey 650.7a)
881.8b	And, again — experience. (καὶ πάλιν — τριβή)	= unidentified 40 (= Mangey 650.7b)
881.9	Study is the nurse of knowledge. (μελέτη τροφὸς ἐπιστήμης)	= unidentified 47 (= Mangey 650.8)
881.10	Calumniators and — happiness. (διάβολοι — ἀλλότριοι)	= unidentified 15 (= Mangey 650.9)
881.11	What can be — undeniable proof. (τί ἂν γένοιτο — γένηται)	= unidentified 84 (= Mangey 650.10)
881.12	If any one — in a private station. (εἴ τις πάσας — τυγχάνοι)	= unidentified 21 (= Mangey 650.11)
881.13	As to sin — of righteousness. (ὡς τὸ ἑκουσίως — δικαιοσύνης)	= QG 4.64 (= Mangey 651.1)
881.14	It is not lawful — the uninitiated. (οὐ θέμις — ἀμυήτοις)	= unidentified 61 (= Mangey 651.2)
881.15	It is proper to — superfluity of. (ἄξιον — ἀναπέμπουσι)	= Legat. 47 (= Mangey 651.3)
881.16	To give equal — greatest injustice. (τὸ νέμειν — ἀδικίας)	= Anim. 100 (= Mangey 651.4)

881.17	A good physician — gentle degrees. (ἀγαθὸς — ἐμποιεῖ)	= *QE* 2.25 (d) (= Mangey 651.5)
881.18	Say what is right — is not right. (λάλει ἃ δεῖ — ἃ μὴ δεῖ)	= Fr. sp. 41 (= Mangey 651.6)
881.19	It is well to economise time. (χρόνου φείδεσθαι καλόν)	= *Contempl.* 16 (= Mangey 651.7)
881.20	Chatterers divulging — being heard. (οἱ λάλοι — οὐκ ἄξια)	= *QE* 2.118 (= Mangey 651.8)
882.1	To inquire and — instruction. (τὸ ζητεῖν — ἀνυσιμώτατον)	= *Anim.* 6 (= Mangey 651.9)
882.2	He who hungers and — of wise men. (ὁ πεινῶν — οἰκίας)	= *QE* 2.13 (b) (= Mangey 651.10)
882.3	For any one to — righteousness. (τὸ εἰδέναι — δικαιοσύνης)	= unidentified 94 (= Mangey 651.11)
882.4	Never reproach — conscience. (μηδενὶ συμφορὰν — εὑρεθῇς)	= unidentified 51 (= Mangey 652.1)
882.5	It is advantageous — one's betters. (τὸ ὑποτάσσεσθαι — ὠφέλιμον)	= *QG* 3.30 (a) (= Mangey 652.2)
882.6	A shameless — visible body. (ἀναιδὲς — σώματι)	= *QG* 4.99 (= Mangey 652.3)
882.7	A change of all — have lasted. (αἱ πάντων — δυνάμεις)	= unidentified 2 (= Mangey 652.4)
882.8	It is useful to be — of others. (χρήσιμον — σωφρονίζεσθαι)	= *Flacc.* 154 (= Mangey 652.5)
882.9	Punishment very — similar evils. (ἡ κόλασις — παθεῖν)	= *Legat.* 7 (= Mangey 652.6)
882.10	Associations with — associates. (βλαβεραὶ — εἴδωλα)	= *Fug.* 14 (= Mangey 652.7)
882.11	Every wise man is a friend of God. (πᾶς σοφὸς θεοῦ φίλος)	= *Her.* 21 (= Mangey 652.8)
882.12	Self-conceit, as — improvement. (οἴησις — ἀνέχεται)	= *QG* 3.48 (= Mangey 652.9)
882.13	Self-conceit is — unclean thing. (οἴησις ἀκάθαρτον φύσει)	= *Leg.* 1.52 (= Mangey 652.10)
882.14	As it is difficult to — against it. (ὥσπερ τὸ — πάντα)	= unidentified 123 (= Mangey 652.11)
882.15	What is the meaning — the earth. (τί ἐστιν — προσενεμήθη)	= *QG* 1.51 (= Mangey 653.1)
882.16a	"And God — of these things. (ἤγαγεν — προσέταττεν)	= *QG* 1.21 (= Mangey 653.2a)
882.16b	And this is an — glory of the elder. (ἀνδρὸς δὲ — εὐκλείας)	= *QG* 1.20 (= Mangey 653.2b)
882.16c	And when Adam — a second one, (καὶ θεασάμενος — γέννησιν)	= *QG* 1.28 (= Mangey 653.2c)
882.16d	on which account he — and joys.	= *QG* 1.29 (= Mangey 653.2d)

112 INSTRUMENTA

	(διό φησιν — ἥδεσθαι)	
883.1a	Truly the divine — as to touch it. (ἄβατος — ἐπιψαῦσαι)	= *QE* 2.45 (b) (= Mangey 654.1a)
883.1b	It is impossible — never saw before. (ἀμήχανον — ὄψεται)	= unidentified 6 (= Mangey 654.1b)
883.1c	All the different — be preserved. (αἱ φιλοσοφίαι — διώσασθαι)	= unidentified 4 (= Mangey 654.1c)
883.1d	Now he who desires — of his object, (δεῖ τὸν — προθέσεως)	= unidentified 14 (= Mangey 654.1d)
883.1e	and he will be — distils therefrom. (ἀδυνατήσει — μαρμαρυγῶν)	= unidentified 1 (= Mangey 654.1e)
883.1f	Do you not see that — destroy you. (οὐχ ὁρᾷς — ἀναλώσῃ)	= *QE* 2.28 (= Mangey 654.1f)
883.2	As pillars support — human race. (ὥσπερ κίονες — γένος)	= unidentified 122 (= Mangey 655.1)
883.3	If any one is — prepared store. (ἐάν τις — ὠφέλειαν)	= *Somn.* 1.177, 176 (= Mangey 655.2)
883.4	The influx of evils — be obscured. (ἡ φορὰ — τυφλουμένην)	= unidentified 38 (= Mangey 655.3)
884.1	There is nothing — as injustice. (οὐδὲν ἐναντίον — ἀδικία)	= *QG* 1.100 (a) (= Mangey 655.4)
884.2	Never to err in — say incurable. (τὸ μὴ ἁμαρτάνειν — ἔχοντες)	= *QG* 1.65 (= Mangey 655.5)
884.3	He contains — completed it. (περιέχει — πεπλήρωκεν)	= unidentified 71 (= Mangey 655.6)
884.4	By some lawgivers — by hearing. (παρ' ἐνίοις — ἀκοῇ)	= *QE* 2.9 (b) (= Mangey 655.7)
884.5	The wise man — heavenly things. (ὁ σοφὸς — ἐπιτύχῃ)	= *QG* 4.47 (a) (= Mangey 655.8)
884.6	For thus the lover — such men. (οὕτως γὰρ — λέγεται)	= *QG* 4.74 (= Mangey 656.1)
884.7	The wise man is — and happy men. (ὁ σοφὸς — ζωήν)	= *Ebr.* 100 (= Mangey 656.2)
884.8	But the — arise. (πνευματικὴ — μεταμορφούμενοι)	= *QG* 1.92 (= Mangey 656.3)
884.9	All the powers of — to the Father. (αἱ τοῦ θεοῦ — ἐφιέμεναι)	= *QE* 2.65 (= Mangey 656.4)
884.10	All those who — of the universe. (ὥσπερ οἱ — τελευτῶσα)	= *QE* 2.26 (= Mangey 656.5)
884.11	The contentious — knowledge. (αἱ περὶ τῶν — ἀλήθειαν)	= unidentified 3 (= Mangey 656.6)
884.12a	... not being — in their minds; (τὸ ἐμμελὲς — πειρωμένους)	= *QE* 2.38 (b) (= Mangey 656.7a)
884.12b	the eloquence of the — its words. (ὁ τοῦ σοφοῦ — κάλλος)	= *QE* 2.44 (= Mangey 656.7b)

YONGE'S COLLECTION OF FRAGMENTS OF PHILO 113

884.13	Those men — consistency. (τοὺς ἐντυγχάνοντας — συνᾴδουσιν)	= unidentified 107 (= Mangey 656.8)
884.14	Those men act — their union. (ἀτόπως — στερούμενα)	= QG 3.3 (a) (= Mangey 657.1)
885.1	Let there then — their blindness. (νόμος ἔστω — ἀορασίας)	= QG 4.40 (= Mangey 657.2)
885.2	There is nothing — servants of God. (οὐδὲν οὔτε — θεῷ)	= QE 2.105 (= Mangey 657.3)
885.3	No foolish — only king. (τῶν μὲν ἀφρόνων — ἐπιστήμονα)	= QG 4.76 (a), (b) (= Mangey 657.4)
885.4	A facility of — as enemies. (ἀνθρώποις — ἐχθρῶν)	= Deus 27 (= Mangey 657.5)
885.5a	Gaius [sic], as — of the decades, (ὁ μὲν Κάϊν — δεκάσιν)	= QG 1.77 (= Mangey 658.1a)
885.5b	such as now — against himself. (ἦν γνωσιμαχῶν — ἑαυτοῦ)	= gloss to QG 1.77 (= Mangey 658.1b)
885.6	To be aware of — of wicked men. (τὸ ἐπαισθάνεσθαι — ἀνδρός)	= unidentified 95 (= Mangey 658.2)
885.7	It is said — imperfect male. (λέγεται — ἄρσεν)	= QE 1.7 (a) (= Mangey 658.3)
885.8a	It is not lawful — the uninitiated (οὐ θέμις — ἀμυήτοις)	= unidentified 61 (= Mangey 658.4a)
885.8b	until they — not to be blamed. (ἄχρις ἂν — ἀμώμητα)	= unidentified 12 (= Mangey 658.4b)
885.8c	Now, to divulge — the priesthood. (τοῖς ἀμυήτοις — τελετῆς)	= QG 4.8 (c) (= Mangey 658.4c)
885.9a	It is absurd that — full of folly. (ἄτοπον ἐν μὲν — ἐκρίπτειν)	= unidentified 11 (= Mangey 658.5a)
885.9b	All men must — which is not lawful. (οὐ πάντων — θέμις)	= unidentified 62 (= Mangey 658.5b)
886.1	The man who lives — feared blows. (ἐντὸς φέρει — ψυχῇ)	= unidentified 27 (= Mangey 659.1)
886.2	The life of the — fear and grief. (τοῦ φαύλου — ἀνακέκραται)	= QG 1.49 (= Mangey 659.2)
886.3	The reasoning of — draw back. (ἐνίοις — παλινδρομοῦντες)	= QE 2.40 (= Mangey 659.3)
886.4	Before now, some — as before. (ἤδη τινὲς — νόσον)	= QG 1.85 (= Mangey 659.4)
886.5	To commit — mischievous. (τὸ ἐπιορκεῖν — ἀλυσιτελέστατον)	= unidentified 96 (= Mangey 659.5)
886.6	We ought to look — a second I." (φίλους — ἐγώ)	= QG 1.17 (a), (b) (= Mangey 659.6)
886.7	When the fruits — never ending. (ὅταν οἱ — ὦσιν)	= QE 1.1 (= Mangey 660.1)
886.8	The mercies — enjoyment of life.	= QE 2.71 (= Mangey 660.2)

(αἱ τοῦ θεοῦ — ἀπόλαυσιν)

886-92: "Fragments from a Monkish Manuscript" (= Mangey 660-70: "Johannes Monachus ineditus" [= Ber. gr. 46 and Coisl. 276])

886.9	It is said to you — to the soul. (σοὶ λέγεται — διαγγέλλῃ)	= *Her.* 105-6, 110 (= Mangey 660.3)
887.1	If you take away — the same time. (τῶν πολιτικῶν — φρονεῖν)	= unidentified 109 (= Mangey 661.1)
887.2	Good men — large houses. (ἄνδρες ἀγαθοὶ — πολιτείας)	= *QE* 1.21 (= Mangey 661.2)
887.3	If it depended — are near them. (ἕνεκα μὲν — ὠφελεῖσθαι)	= *QG* 3.8 (= Mangey 661.3)
887.4	There is no place — many stars. (τόπος — περιπολοῦσιν)	= unidentified 103 (= Mangey 661.4)
887.5	The comprehension — of man. (ἡ τῶν μελλόντων — ἀνθρώπῳ)	= *Her.* 261 (= Mangey 661.5)
887.6	All things are — the mortal race. (οὐ πάντα — γνώριμα)	= *Opif.* 61 (= Mangey 661.6)
887.7	God alone is — results of things. (τὸ τέλος — μόνος)	= unidentified 99 (= Mangey 661.7)
887.8	Quiet, which — give pleasure. (βελτίων — ἡσυχία)	= *Mos.* 1.285 (= Mangey 661.8)
887.9	The lawgiver — cause of benefit. (οὐ ποιήσετε — αἴτιον)	= unidentified 63 (= Mangey 661.9)
887.10	Those who do — beloved by God. (οἱ ἑαυτῶν — θεοφιλής)	= unidentified 56 (= Mangey 662.1)
887.11	There are — the human intellect. (μυρία γε — νοῦν)	= unidentified 53 (= Mangey 662.2)
887.12	No one — invisible God. (οὐδεὶς αὐχήσει — ἀλογιστίᾳ)	= *QE* 2.37 (= Mangey 662.3)
887.13	As pillars — race of mankind. (ὥσπερ κίονες — γένος)	= unidentified 122 (= Mangey 662.4)
887.14	I think it — perfect among men. (ἀδύνατον οἶμαι — δοκῇ)	= Fr. sp. 31 (= Mangey 662.5)
888.1	Slow counsel — is mischievous. (ἀκερδὴς — μετάμελος)	= unidentified 5 (= Mangey 662.6)
888.2	A teacher of a — of philosophy. (ὁ καλὸς — δόγμασιν)	= *QG* 2.41 (= Mangey 662.7)
888.3	If, when a — admitted advantage. (ἐὰν ἄρτι — αἴτιον)	= *QE* 2.25 (b), (c) (= Mangey 663.1)
888.4a	The ordinary — any perfect fruit; (ἡ τυχοῦσα — γέννημα)	= *Leg.* 3.89 (= Mangey 663.2a)
888.4b	for it is, as — continual exercise. (ἴσον — τεινόμενον)	= *QG* 2.54 (c), (d) (= Mangey 663.2b)

888.5	Those who are — to themselves. (οἱ ἄνανδροι — γίνονται)	= *Praem.* 5 (= Mangey 663.3)
888.6	Wickedness in — and death. (ἡ ἐν τῷ φαύλῳ — φονώντων)	= *QG* 2.12 (c) (= Mangey 663.4)
888.7	The thoughts of — life of enmity. (τοῦ φαύλου — πολέμιος)	= unidentified 105 (= Mangey 663.5)
888.8	That which is — the right way. (ἀνελεύθερον — ἔχον)	= unidentified 7 (= Mangey 664.1)
888.9	The servants of — servant of God. (οἱ ὑπηρέται — θεοῦ)	= unidentified 58 (= Mangey 664.2)
888.10	An irreconcileable — with slavery. (ἄσπονδος — ἀπειλεῖν)	= unidentified 10 (= Mangey 664.3)
888.11	Justice, above — and heaven. (σωτήριον — οὐρανοῦ)	= *QG* 1.98 (= Mangey 664.4)
889.1	It is good to begin — and leader. (καλόν ἐστιν — μνήμην)	= unidentified 42 (= Mangey 664.5)
889.2	Every soul which — season of joy. (ψυχὴ πᾶσα — εὐφροσύνης)	= *QE* 2.15 (b) (= Mangey 664.6)
889.3	The things of — of the Saviour. (μακρὰν — ἐπακολουθοῦντα)	= unidentified 44 (= Mangey 664.7)
889.4	It is a sign — a manly spirit. (ἀνδρείας ἐστὶ — θάρσος)	= Fr. sp. 6 (= Mangey 665.1)
889.5	As an equality — bond of equality. (ὥσπερ τῶν — ἰσότητος)	= unidentified 124 (= Mangey 665.2)
889.6	Inequality is — ends. (τὸ ἄνισον — ὠφέλειαν)	= unidentified 90 (= Mangey 665.3)
889.7	Obedience to the — existing things. (τὸ ἔννομον — ὄντων)	= *QE* 2.64 (= Mangey 665.4)
889.8	Those things — the second. (τὰ τῶν προτέρων — σωτήρια)	= unidentified 80 (= Mangey 665.5)
889.9	The outward — he has created. (αἱ αἰσθήσεις — σῴζει)	= *QG* 2.34 (a), (c) (= Mangey 665.6)
889.10	If you — absorbing quicksand. (ἐὰν πολὺς — τέλματος)	= unidentified 19 (= Mangey 666.1)
[— —	— — (ἡ αὐτάρκεια — καθαιρεῖν)	= *QE* 1.6 (b) (= Mangey 666.2; this fragment is also missing from Yonge, 4:265)]
890.1	One should — far from him. (ἀσκητέον — μακροτάτω)	= Fr. sp. 3 (= Mangey 666.3)
890.2	What can be a — the whole world. (ἡ ἀληθής — κόσμῳ)	= *Mos.* 2.108 (= Mangey 666.4)
890.3	The hopes — they are worthy. (ἀβέβαιοι — πάσχοντες)	= *Flacc.* 109 (= Mangey 666.5)
890.4	Who is there who — correct him? (τίς ἐξαμαρτών — ἐλέγχῃ)	= unidentified 88 (= Mangey 666.6)

890.5	Since the — for one's guides. (ἐπειδὴ πρὸς — ὁδηγίαν)	= unidentified 28 (= Mangey 666.7)
890.6	He who has — licentious tongue. (τῷ μὴ ἐφεδρεύει — λέλυται)	= unidentified 118 (= Mangey 666.8)
890.7	Perfection and — he has received. (ἐν θεῷ — μεμαθημένως)	= unidentified 24 (= Mangey 667.1)
890.8	These things — from arrogance. (φυσικώτατα — ὑπονόστησιν)	= *QG* 4.100 (= Mangey 667.2)
890.9	It is — illegitimate manner. (τῆς καρτερίας — ἀτυφίας)	= unidentified 102 (= Mangey 667.3)
890.10	If you — absurd conduct. (ἐὰν δόξαις — ἐκτραχηλισθῇς)	= unidentified 18 (= Mangey 667.4)
890.11	Sleep, according to — inactivity. (ὁ ὕπνος — ὑπεκλέλυνται)	= *QG* 1.24 (= Mangey 667.5)
890.12	Very naturally — back to it. (εἰκότως — ὁλοκλήρου)	= unidentified 22 (= Mangey 667.6)
890.13	It is better — line of conduct. (τοῦ προθύμως — αἰώνιος)	= unidentified 104 (= Mangey 667.7)
890.14	Some persons — the multitude. (φασί τινες — ἡττᾶσθαι)	= unidentified 111 (= Mangey 668.1)
891.1	Self-conceit is — thing by nature. (οἴησις ἀκάθαρτον φύσει)	= *Leg.* 1.52 (= Mangey 668.2)
891.2	To give thanks — of order. (τὸ εὐχαριστεῖν — εἰσηγουμένη)	= *QG* 1.64 (b), (c), (d) (= Mangey 668.3)
891.3	Envy naturally — is great. (πέφυκε τοῖς — φθόνος)	= *Fr. sp.* 25 (= Mangey 668.4)
891.4	The most — vigorous labour. (τὰ τέλεια — περιγίγνεσθαι)	= *Congr.* 162 (= Mangey 668.5)
891.5	It is absurd for — are acquired. (ἄτοπόν ἐστι — τιμαί)	= *Fr. sp.* 40 (= Mangey 668.6)
891.6	What is the — combined with blood. (τί ἐστιν — αἵματι)	= *QG* 2.59 (= Mangey 668.7)
891.7	The extremity of — gives his aid. (τῆς εὐδαιμονίας — θεοῦ)	= unidentified 83 (= Mangey 668.8)
891.8	It is impossible — has generated. (ἀμήχανον — σῴζει)	= *QG* 2.34 (b), (c) (= Mangey 669.1)
891.9	God wishing — church among us. (βουληθεὶς — βίον)	= *Her.* 112-13 (= Mangey 669.2)
891.10	The one most — and actions. (μία ἀνάπαυσις — πράξεων)	= unidentified 52 (= Mangey 669.3)
891.11	The extremity — alone. (πέρας εὐδαιμονίας — στῆναι)	= unidentified 70 (= Mangey 669.4)
891.12	The stars are turned — their own. (οἱ ἀστέρες — ἐξαιρέτοις)	= *QE* 2.55 (a) (= Mangey 669.5)
892.1	Some men think — upon the earth.	= *QG* 1.93 (= Mangey 669.6)

YONGE'S COLLECTION OF FRAGMENTS OF PHILO 117

	(ἔνιοι νομίζουσι— γῆς)	
892.2	There is no — and guides man. (οὔτε ἐνδυασμὸς — ἐστιν)	= *QG* 1.55 (a) (= Mangey 669.7)
892.3	He who — offers them. (ὁ μὴ ἐκ προαιρέσεως — ἀπαρχή)	= *QE* 2.50 (b) (= Mangey 670.1)
892.4	The mercies — happen first. (ἀεὶ φθάνουσι — προγενέσθαι)	= *QG* 1.89 (= Mangey 670.2)

892-94: "Fragments Preserved by Antonius" (= Mangey 670-74: "Ex Antonio")

892.5	The virtues — affairs of men. (ἀρεταὶ μόναι — ἐπίστανται)	= unidentified 8 (= Mangey 670.3a)
892.6	The contemplation of — all things. (ἡ θεωρία — περιμάχητος)	= *Leg.* 1.58 (= Mangey 670.3b)
892.7	If you wish to have — are doing ill. (εἰ βούλει — ἐπιτίμα)	= Fr. sp. 53 (= Mangey 670.4)
892.8	When you are — divine anger. (συγγνώμην — ἀπαλλαγή)	= Fr. sp. 56 (= Mangey 670.5)
892.9	The virtuous man — in injuring. (φιλάνθρωπος — βλάπτειν)	= *QG* 4.193 (= Mangey 670.6)
892.10	What is beautiful — as his own. (καλὸν τότε — γνωρίσματα)	= *Mos.* 1.59 (= Mangey 670.7)
892.11	It is well that — of improvement. (καλὸν ἀεὶ — ἐλπίδα)	= *Decal.* 113 (= Mangey 670.8)
892.12	One ought to — within them. (εὐδαιμονιστέον — τοιούτου)	= unidentified 34 (= Mangey 671.1)
892.13	Those who are — by treachery. (οἷς ἰσχὺς — κατορθοῦσι)	= *Flacc.* 1 (= Mangey 671.2)
892.14	The friendships of — insanity. (βλαβεραὶ — εἴδωλα)	= *Fug.* 14 (= Mangey 671.3a)
892.15	It is not the — such and such men. (οὐ ποιεῖ — συνδιατριβή)	= Fr. sp. 4 (= Mangey 671.3b)
892.16	One need not — threat of a fool. (οὔτε — εὐλαβεῖσθαι)	= Fr. sp. 14 (= Mangey 671.4a)
892.17	Light-minded men — by their ears. (οἱ ἐλαφροὶ — εἰσίν)	= Fr. sp. 15 (= Mangey 671.4b)
892.18a	Nothing that — contemplation, (χωρὶς θεωρίας — καλόν)	= *Praem.* 51 (= Mangey 671.5a)
892.18b	for knowledge — of all evils. (ἐπιστήμη — πάντων)	= unidentified 30 (= Mangey 671.5b)
892.19	Every argument — a bad object. (περισσὸς — ὁμόνοια ἦ)	= Fr. sp. 24 (= Mangey 671.5c)
893.1	The wicked man — with disdain. (ὁ φαῦλος — ἀτιμώτατον)	= *QG* 4.47 (b) (= Mangey 671.6a)

893.2	Excellence is — troubled life. (δυσεύρετον — καλόν)	= *Fug.* 153 (= Mangey 671.6b)
893.3	There is nothing — good actions. (οὐδὲν οὕτως — εὐφημία)	= *QE* 2.6 (b) (= Mangey 671.7)
893.4	It is sufficient not — to the mind. (τὸ μὴ — πίστιν)	= *Ebr.* 188 (= Mangey 671.8)
893.5	Reject with — all praise. (ἀποστρέφου — κρείττονα)	= *Fr. sp.* 50 (= Mangey 671.9)
893.6	Peace is the — a divine action. (τὸ μέγιστον — ἔργον)	= *Mos.* 1.304 (= Mangey 671.10)
893.7	Behave to your — mercy to them. (τοιοῦτος — ἀντιλάβωμεν)	= *Fr. sp.* 52 (= Mangey 672.1)
893.8	How great a — outward senses. (ὕπνος ἐστὶ — ἀργία)	= *Fr. sp.* 57 (= Mangey 672.2a)
893.9	Sleep is one — by means of sleep. (εἷς μὲν — βούλεται)	= *Fr. sp.* 58 (= Mangey 672.2b)
893.10	As much drinking — inveterate habit. (ὥσπερ — ἰάσασθαι)	= *Fr. sp.* 59 (= Mangey 672.2c)
893.11	Pardon is — engender repentance. (συγγνώμη — γεννᾶν)	= *QG* 1.82 (= Mangey 672.3)
893.12	Shamelessness — assent. (ἀναισχυντία — ἀσυγκαταθέτως)	= *Leg.* 2.65 (= Mangey 672.4)
893.13	Since God — some other abode. (ἐπειδήπερ — θεός)	= *Cher.* 98 (= Mangey 672.5a)
893.14	The mind of a — as in a palace. (οἶκος θεοῦ — βασιλείῳ)	= *Praem.* 123 (= Mangey 672.5b)
893.15	What is visible — and future. (ὀφθαλμοῖς — μέλλοντα)	= *Legat.* 2 (= Mangey 672.5c)
893.16	God who is — inflicted by men. (τὸν ὀμνύντα — τιμωρίας)	= *Spec.* 2.253 (= Mangey 672.6)
893.17	Those things — brought to light. (τὰ κἂν — ἀναλάμπει)	= *Mos.* 2.27 (= Mangey 672.7)
893.18	In his essential — towards all men. (τῇ μὲν — ἁπλότητα)	= *Fr. sp.* 51 (= Mangey 673.1)
893.19	A severe master — right by fear. (καὶ — νουθετοῦνται)	= *Deus* 64 (= Mangey 673.2)
893.20	It is the — without hesitation. (μέγιστον — κατορθοῦν)	= *Her.* 9 (= Mangey 673.3)
894.1	When once the wife — for his wife." (ἡ Φίλωνος — ἀρετή)	= *Fr. sp.* 18 (= Mangey 673.4)
894.2	The virtues of — of their fathers. (τέκνων — πατέρων)	= *Fr. sp.* 34 (= Mangey 673.5a)
894.3	Those who are — their children. (εὔπαιδες — ἐπιστήμονες)	= *QE* 2.19 (b) (= Mangey 673.5b)

YONGE'S COLLECTION OF FRAGMENTS OF PHILO 119

894.4	To drink poison — the same thing. (ἐκ χρυσοῦ — ἐστιν)	= Fr. sp. 8 (= Mangey 673.6a)
894.5	New vessels are — than new. (σκεύη μὲν — παλαιοτέρα)	= Fr. sp. 9 (= Mangey 673.6b)
894.6a	The fruits — on every occasion. (οἱ μὲν — φύονται)	= Fr. sp. 10 (= Mangey 673.6c)
894.6b	Many men select — who are rich. (πολλοὶ — πλουτοῦντας)	= Fr. sp. 11 (= Mangey 673.6d)
894.7	Many who appear — both classes. (πολλοὶ — ἕκαστον)	= Fr. sp. 12 (= Mangey 673.6e)
894.8	Youth which is — for old age. (νεότης — κακοπραγεῖ)	= Fr. sp. 19 (= Mangey 673.7)
894.9	What is — punishment hereafter. (οὐ τὸ — κολάσεως)	= Fr. sp. 26 (= Mangey 673.8)
894.10	God has — sorrows lightened. (ἐλπίδα — δράσαντες)	= *Praem.* 72 (= Mangey 673.9)
894.11	Pleasure appears — to be rough. (δοκεῖ μὲν — ἐστί)	= *QG* 1.41 (b) (= Mangey 674.1)

894: "The Following Fragments are from an Anonymous Collection in the Bodleian Library at Oxford: Extracts from Philo" (= Mangey 674: "Ex Anonymi Collectione Florilegâ. [*sic*] MS. Barocc. Nº 143. in Bibliotheca Bodleiana Oxonii")

894.12	A steadiness — guilty one. (ἡ πρὸς τοὺς — ποιεῖσθαι)	= unidentified 37 (= Mangey 674.2)
894.13	Of secret things — your friends. (τῶν ἀπορρήτων — ἀνατίθῃ)	= Fr. sp. 60 (= Mangey 674.3)
894.14	The life of — contrary winds. (ὁ τῶν ἀνθρώπων — πνευμάτων)	= *QE* 2.55 (b) (= Mangey 674.4)
894.15	Let us fear not— of the body. (φοβηθῶμεν — σώματος)	= Fr. sp. 28 (= Mangey 674.5)
894.16	Every foolish man — of motion. (στενοχωρεῖται — διαβαίνειν)	= *QG* 4.33 (a) (= Mangey 674.6)
894.17	The sons of the — injure the soul. (τὴν εὐταξίαν — γνωρίζομεν)	= unidentified 82 (= Mangey 674.7)
894.18	In [*sic*; Yonge, 4:277 has "An"] inveterate — a large size. (ἐγχρονίζον — αὐξάνοντα)	= *Decal.* 137 (= Mangey 674.8)

894-97: "The Following Fragments are from an Unpublished Manuscript in the Library of the French King" (= Mangey 675-80: "Ex Catenâ Ineditâ Cod. Reg. Nº 1825. in Bibliotheca Regis Christianissimi" [= Par. gr. 128])

894.19	Why is it that God — in existence.	= *QG* 1.94 (= Mangey 675.1)

	(διὰ τί ἄνθρωπον — γέγονε)	
895.1	The law does — violated the law. (οὐδὲν — τιμωρία)	= *QG* 3.52 (= Mangey 675.2a)
895.2	Not because — not made perfect. (οὐκ ἐπειδὴ — πληρουμένου)	= gloss to *QG* 3.52 (= Mangey 675.2b)
895.3	Why did — incurable wickedness. (διὰ τί ἐξῆλθεν — ἐχόντων)	= *QG* 4.51 (a) (= Mangey 675.3)
895.4	Having been — than themselves. (κατάσκοποι — αὐτῶν)	= *QG* 4.195.7* (= Mangey 675.4)
895.5	These are the — emigrated. (αὗται αἱ — μετῴκησαν)	= gloss to *QG* 4.195.7* (= Mangey 676.1)
895.6	Not on — their repentance. (οὐ διὰ τὸν — μετάνοιαν)	= *QG* 4.195.8* (= Mangey 676.2)
895.7	When he had two — of all men. (δυοῖν — κακοδαιμονέστατος)	= *QG* 4.198 (= Mangey 676.3)
895.8a	It is proper — a curse on myself. (ἄξιον καὶ — ἄξω)	= *QG* 4.202 (a) (= Mangey 676.4a)
895.8b	He had confidence — of God. (ἐθάρρει μὲν — θεοῦ)	= gloss to *QG* 4.202 (= Mangey 676.4b)
895.9	He is not so — O my father." (οὐκ ἐπὶ τῷ — πάτερ)	= *QG* 4.227 (= Mangey 676.5)
895.10	But if he — anything unskilfully. (ἀλλ' εἴ γε — σπουδαῖος)	= *QG* 4.228 (= Mangey 676.6)
896.1	What is the meaning — no addition. (τί ἐστι — δεόμενα)	= *QE* 2.1 (= Mangey 677.1)
896.2	He shows — both. (ἐμφανέστατα — ὑπογράφεται)	= *QE* 2.2 (= Mangey 677.2)
896.3	It is forbidden — of resources. (χήραν — ἀναπληροῦσθαι)	= *QE* 2.3 (a) (= Mangey 677.3)
896.4	He says that we — by hearing. (μάταιόν φησιν — ἀκοῇ)	= *QE* 2.9 (a), (b) (= Mangey 677.4)
896.5	Poverty by itself — God is just. (πενία — ἐστι)	= *QE* 2.10 (a), (b) (= Mangey 678.1)
896.6	Instead of saying — mother, deceit. (ἀντὶ τοῦ — ἔγγονα)	= *QE* 2.14 (= Mangey 678.2)
896.7	The blood of the — mingled together. (τὸ αἷμα — ὅσιον)	= *QE* 2.14 (= Mangey 678.3)
896.8	One must — seek to overthrow. (φωνὴν θεοῦ — καθαιρεῖν)	= *QE* 2.16 (= Mangey 678.4)
896.9	Pillars symbolically — beautiful. (στῆλαί εἰσι — καλοῖς)	= *QE* 2.17 (= Mangey 678.5)
897.1	And we ought — whatever itself. (σύμβολον — παράπαν)	= *QE* 2.24 (b) (= Mangey 679.1)
897.2	These things God — to Beersheba. (ταῦτα μὲν — Βηρσαβεέ)	= gloss to *QE* 2.25 (b) (= Mangey 679.2)

897.3	The express — good thing. (τὸ μὲν ῥητὸν — διαφωνεῖν)	= QE 2.38 (a) (= Mangey 679.3)
897.4	When he speaks — was left. (τοὺς ἑβδομήκοντα — ἀπελείφθη)	= gloss on Exod 24:11 (= Mangey 679.4)
897.5	He is — be given. (ἐναργέστατα — νομοθετεῖσθαι)	= QE 2.45 (a) (= Mangey 679.5)
897.6	But he says — the whole mind. (τὸ δὲ εἶδος — διάνοιαν)	= QE 2.47 (= Mangey 679.6)
897.7	Because the — countless instances. (ὅτι ἔμελλε — ἀχάριστον)	= QE 2.49 (a) (= Mangey 680.1)

San Francisco

BIBLIOGRAPHY SECTION

PHILO OF ALEXANDRIA
AN ANNOTATED BIBLIOGRAPHY 1993

D. T. Runia, A. C. Geljon, J. P. Martín,
R. Radice, K. G. Sandelin, D. Satran, D. Zeller

1993*

M. Alexandre jr, 'A Rhetorical Analysis of Philo's *De virtutibus*', *Euphrosune* 21 (1993) 9–28.

The author builds on earlier studies (cf. *SPhA* 6 (1994) 122, 7 (1995) 210) in which he has analysed the argumentative structure of parts of Philo's treatises. This time he deals with an entire treatise. He first notes that *Virt.* is divided into four parts which can each be treated as complete rhetorical units. This is followed by a more detailed analysis of the contents of *De humanitate* (§51–174) in which first the structural elements and then aspects of style are outlined. Philo combines technical rhetorical competence with literary and argumentative elegance. (DTR)

M. E. Allison, *The Motif of Parresia in Acts* (diss. Southern Baptist Theological Seminary 1993).

---

* This bibliography has been prepared by the members of International Philo Bibliography Project, under the leadership of D. T. Runia (Leiden). The principles on which the annotated bibliography is based have been outlined in *SPhA* 2 (1990) 141–142, and are largely based on those used to compile the 'mother work', R-R. One significant alteration is that all language restrictions have been abandoned. The division of the work this year has been as follows: material in English and Dutch by D. T. Runia (DTR) and A. C. Geljon (ACG); in French and Italian by R. Radice (RR); in German by D. Zeller (DZ); in Spanish and Portuguese by J. P. Martín (JPM); in Scandinavian languages by K. G. Sandelin (KGS); in Hebrew by D. Satran (DS). Other scholars who have given valuable assistance are R. M. van den Berg, P. Borgen, I. Croese, V. Guignard, P. W. van der Horst, H. J. de Jonge, A. Kamesar, J. Riaud. We also wish to thank M. Hofstede of the University Library in Leiden for efficiently performing diverse electronic searches. The bibliography is inevitably incomplete, because much work on Philo is tucked away in monographs and articles, the titles of which do not mention his name. Scholars are encouraged to get in touch with members of the team if they spot omissions (addresses below in 'Notes on contributors').

In chapter 3 various pagan and Jewish sources, including Philo and Josephus, are examined as background to a treatment of the motif of παρρησία in Acts. (DTR; based on summary in DA A54–04, p. 1416)

Y. AMIR, 'Monotheistische Korrekturen heidnischer Texte', in D.-A. KOCH and H. LICHTENBERGER (edd.), *Begegnungen zwischen Christentum und Judentum in Antike und Mittelalter: Festschrift für Heinz Schreckenberg*, Schriften des Institutum Judaicum Delitzschianum 1 (Göttingen 1993) 9–19.

How do Jewish authors use pagan texts referring to Greek gods? Aristobulus (in Eusebius *PE* 12.12.6) consciously replaces the name Zeus in Aratus by the term God. Philo, *Ebr.* 150 corrects Hesiod's plural gods with the singular number. In *Prob.* 116 he quotes Euripides with the plural form, but in *Prob.* 19 he has God instead of Zeus in a quotation from Sophocles. This text should not be emended, but one should follow the original mss. reading and Ambrose *Ep.* 37,28. In *Opif.* 104, however, the term God is already in Solon's poem, as is shown by the parallel quotation in Anatolius. Thus, it is concluded, Hellenistic Jews felt authorized to adjust words from pagan poets in a monotheistic sense. (DZ)

Y. DE ANDIA, *Henosis: l'union à Dieu chez Denys l'Aréopagite* (diss. Paris Sorbonne 1993), esp. Part IV Chapter I.

Some pages on Philo (and Gregory of Nyssa) are included as part of a massive thesis on the philosophical and religious theme of union with God in Dionysius the Areopagite. It will be published in definitive edition in the course of 1996. (DTR)

K. ARMSTRONG, *A History of God: From Abraham to the Present, the 4000 Year Quest for God* (London 1993), esp. 81–86.

In this 'biography of belief' Philo is briefly discussed as one of the first monotheists to fall in love with Greek philosophy. How can we only know of God's existence, and yet also be convinced that he speaks through the prophets? The answer for Philo involves the distinction between God's essence, which is wholly incomprehensible, and his activities in the world by means of his powers. Philo's transcendent theology is not as bleak as it sounds, but Jews have always found its contents somewhat inauthentic. (ACG)

J. N. BAILEY, *Repentance in Luke-Acts* (diss. Notre Dame 1993).

In the New Testament, the subject of repentance is most prominent in the Gospel of Luke and the Acts of the Apostles. Luke's view of repentance is unique in its religio-historical context and significant in his overall theology. This topic, however, has not been adequately investigated or explained. The author argues that Luke took over a theme that was present in Early Judaism and in Early Christianity and developed it in a way appropriate for a Christian community of Jews and Gentiles who were sensitive to literary and philosophical traditions of the Hellenistic world. Luke's treatment of the topic of repentance has important parallels in Jewish literature. For example, repentance was a characteristic feature of the community at Qumran. Even more significant parallels are found in the writings of Philo, who presented repentance in the most favourable light to an educated Hellenistic audience. (DTR; based on summary in DA A54–05, p. 1838)

G. H. BAUDRY, 'Le péché originel chez Philon d'Alexandrie', *Mélanges de Science Religieuse* 50 (1993) 99–115.

Philo does not have a united and coherent theory about original sin. The accounts of Genesis interest him only for their symbolic significance: the creation of Adam and Eve as an allegorical representation of human nature; their fall as a type for all sin. The origin of sin is found rather in the context of general reflections about evil. Evil follows on from existence in the changing sublunary world; evil and human sin are linked to man through his nature, which in accordance with Platonic anthropology is mixed. This is then combined with the pessimistic Jewish theory of a dominant inclination towards evil. The origin of sin is less protological than ontological. Philo has supplied the anthropological basis for the encratistic currents of thought out of which (but nor exclusively) the Christian theory of original sin will emerge. (RR, based on author's abstract)

L. BERK, 'Logos bij Johannes en Philo', *Interpretatie* 1.4 (1993) 17–19, 1.6 23–24.

According to the author it is important to notice that in the Johannine Prologue the Logos is called *a* God, and his Father *the* God. He regards Philo as a predecessor of John, because Philo too calls the Logos *a* god, next to *the* God. Attention is also drawn to parallels in phraseology concerning the Logos between the two authors. (ACG)

E. BIRNBAUM, 'The Place of Judaism in Philo's Thought: Israel, Jews, and Proselytes', *Society of Biblical Literature Seminar Papers* 32 (1993) 54–69.

The author discusses the distinction Philo makes between 'Israel' and the 'Jews'. 'Israel' signifies a rather loosely defined entity comprising those who can see God. To this class belong all respected philosophers, or philosophically-minded people, whether they are Jew or not. Philo calls 'Jews' those who are born as a Jew and those who have chosen to lead the Jewish way of life. They follow the Jewish laws and practices. When describing 'Israel' and the 'Jews' as collectivities, Philo uses different terms with different connotations. Moreover he speaks differently about the relationship between God and 'Israel' and that between God and the 'Jews'. It is not possible to reach firm conclusions on the question of whether Philo regards Jews and non-Jewish philosophers equally or that he regards Jews more highly. The article ends with some comments on the issue of universalism and particularism in Philo's thought. (ACG)

P. BORGEN, 'Heavenly Ascent in Philo: an Examination of Selected Passages', in J. H. CHARLESWORTH and C. A. EVANS (edd.), *The Pseudepigrapha and Early Biblical Interpretation*, Journal for the Study of the Pseudepigrapha Supplement Series 14 (Sheffield 1993) 246–268.

In the presentation of the research situation concerning the theme of heavenly ascent in antiquity Borgen notes that Philo is often neglected or, as was the case in the research of Goodenough, given too narrow an interpretation. In order to fill this gap Borgen shows that Philo has many references to the theme which reveal his indebtedness to Jewish tradition on for instance the figures of Enoch, Moses and Elijah. For Philo these figures serve as paradigms for others aiming at a heavenly goal. Also Greek ideas of Platonic, Stoic and astrological provenance have penetrated Philonic thought in this area. Borgen also discusses Philo's thoughts on the function of angels within the process of the heavenly ascent, comments upon the Alexandrian's individual experiences of it, and shows how the theme in his writings is contrasted to invasion into the heavenly realm by sinister forces of this world, for instance emperors, sophists and materialists. (KGS)

N. L. CALVERT, *Abraham Traditions in Middle Jewish Literature: Implications for the Interpretation of Galatians and Romans* (diss. Sheffield 1993).

For the chapter in this dissertation on Abraham traditions in Philo see the paper published in *SBLSPS* 33 (1994). Further details in Provisional bibliography below.

G. P. CARRAS, 'Dependence or Common Tradition in Philo *Hypothetica* viii 6.10 – 7.20 and Josephus *Contra Apionem* 2.190–219', *The Studia Philonica Annual* 5 (1993) 24–47.

The question of the relationship between Philo's summary of the Law in his *Hypothetica* and the similar passage in Josephus' *Contra Apionem* has long been debated. Carras first makes some background remarks about Philo's treatise and the problems of interpretation that surround it. In the main body of the article he discusses the main themes of its summary of the Law, relating them to the following categories of Jewish evidence: (1) biblical law; (2) OT non-legal material; (3) Jewish material from the close of the OT prior to the time of Philo; (4) material shared by Philo with his contemporaries; (5) ideas shared by the two works; (6) material unique to the *Hypoth.*; (7) ideas in the *Hypoth.* that were common in antiquity, among Jews as well as non-Jews. On the basis of his findings he concludes that the *Hypoth.* reveals a varied and complex collection of traditions and sources. What then is the relationship to Josephus' work? It is concluded that Josephus did not use Philo as a direct source. The common-source theory gains some support from the evidence, but it is necessary to qualify this conclusion by emphasizing that a body of shared traditions also played a significant role. (DTR)

G. CASADIO, 'Gnostische Wege zur Unsterblichkeit', in E. HORNUNG and T. SCHABERT (edd.), *Auferstehung und Unsterblichkeit*, Eranos N.F. 1 (München 1993) 203–254, esp. 214–218.

Philo's dualistic anthropology is to be counted as one of the premises of the Gnostic doctrine of immortality . For Philo the way to immortality is to get rid of the body and to surrender to the grace of a transcendent God. This God, however, is not consubstantial with the *pneuma* which he blows into man (Gen. 2:7). (DZ)

J. COHEN, *The Origins and Evolution of the Moses Nativity Story*, Numen Book series 58 (Leiden 1993), 40–46 and *passim*.

In his treatment of the Moses nativity story in post-biblical sources the author includes a discussion of Philo's description in *Mos*. He notes that Philo reveals parallels with the haggadic and midrashic traditions. In contrast to the biblical story Philo mentions God's leading role in the events. Philo not only enlarges on the biblical account, but also alters its structure: the description of the enslavement is placed at the end of the nativity story. Another difference is that he does not mention the basket. These alterations serve to remove difficulties inherent in the biblical text. (ACG)

N. G. COHEN, 'The Greek Virtues and the Mosaic Laws in Philo: an Elucidation of *De Specialibus Legibus* IV 133–135', *The Studia Philonica Annual* 5 (1993) 9–23.

The article shows how the 'philosophical' and the 'Jewish' components of Philo's thought are indissolubly entwined, as illustrated in a discussion of two detailed aspects of *Spec.* 4.133–135. Firstly, when Philo in this text speaks of the whole family of virtues, he is in fact talking about the practice of Judaism. In line with post-Platonic thought it is simply assumed that philosophy means knowledge that leads to the good life. The list of virtues that he gives also has to be read carefully. Like wisdom and justice, piety (θεοσέβεια) is a super-virtue that subsumes within it all the other virtues. Secondly, in §134 Philo alludes to the philosophical topos of the harmony of thoughts, words and actions, which he associates with the triad mouth, heart and hand in LXX Deut. 30:14. This homiletic association precedes Philo himself, as can be shown from an addition made in LXX text. Moreover vestiges of the same association are also discernible in later Rabbinic midrash, where 'philosophical' aspects are filtered out. (DTR)

J. DILLON, 'Philo and Middle Platonism: a Response to Runia and Sterling', *The Studia Philonica Annual* 5 (1993) 151–155.

Brief remarks in response to the papers of Runia and Sterling (see below) as part of a session of the Philo of Alexandria seminar held in San Francisco (on which see *SPhA* 5 (1993) 95, 246) devoted to the topic of Philo and Middle Platonism. The author agrees with Runia's characterization of Philo as a Platonizing expositor of scripture with a preference for Middle Platonist doctrines. He also finds himself in agreement with Sterling, who sees Philo as a 'pluralist'. He is less content, however, with Runia's positive statements on Goulet's monograph *La philosophie de Moïse* (cf. *SPhA* 2 (1990) 155). He doubts whether there was anything like Philo's enterprise before Philo, and thinks that Philo may well have invented the predecessors to whom he refers. (ACG)

P. ELLINGWORTH, *The Epistle to the Hebrews: A Commentary on the Greek Text*, New International Greek Testament Commentary (Grand Rapids 1993), esp. 45–48.

A short but judicious section is devoted to Philo as part of the discussion of the Epistle's background. 'The author is first and foremost a Christian; secondarily a Christian steeped in the OT; and no doubt in the third place a man affected by linguistic habits and intellectual traditions similar to those which contributed to Philo's development. On this basis both the similarities and the contrasts between Philo and Hebrews can be satisfactorily be explained. (47)' (DTR)

E. E. ELLIS, 'Χριστός in 1 Corinthians 10.4–9', in M. C. DE BOER (ed.) *From Jesus to John: Essays on Jesus and New Testament Christology in Honour of Marinus de Jonge*, Journal for the Study of the New Testament Supplement Series 84 (Sheffield 1993) 168–173.

It is argued that a wisdom Christology is present at 1 Cor. 10.4, 9, where Christ is given a predication and a function that were ascribed in the OT to Yahweh and in pre-Christian Judaism to the divine wisdom. Philo explains the rock in Deut. 8:15–16 as the wisdom of God, and Paul can identify the rock (and thus Christ) as the divine wisdom. He and Paul, though working in different hermeneutic traditions, may be drawing on a common Jewish tradition. (ACG)

C. A. EVANS, *Word and Glory: on the Exegetical and Theological Background of John's Prologue*, Journal for the Study of the New Testament Supplement Series 89 (Sheffield 1993), esp. 100–114.

There are many parallels between Philo's use of Logos and that in the Prologue of John. The idea of the Logos becoming a human being is not found in Philo. But his identification of the Logos with the 'heavenly man' of Gen. 1.27 may be regarded as a step towards the identification of the Logos with Jesus of Nazareth. Philo's notion of the Logos as intermediary and as angel of the Lord forms a bridge between Logos speculation and the Johannine Prologue. In short 'Philo's biblical exegesis makes explicit certain Wisdom features that constitute the important components in the bridge between Gen. 1–2 and John 1.1–18' (p. 112). (ACG)

D. FARIAS, *Studi sul pensiero sociale di Filone di Alessandria*, Pubblicazioni degli Istituti di Scienze giuridiche, economiche, politiche e sociali della facoltà di giurisprudenza della Università di Messina 180 (Milan 1993).

The fundamental theme of this book is the relationship between social ethics and creation, not so much in its theological or cosmological significance, but in its axiological value, that is to say in its value as gift (pp. 11 & 15). The character of grace attributed to creation is tied to the concept of measure (creation as what is well measured, i.e. in proportion to the capacity of man to accept it) and, more concretely, to the concepts of order and number. But the gift of creation entails two fundamental ideas: the idea of the disproportion between the Giver (God) and the beneficiary (man), and the idea of the reciprocity that exists between men (p. 42). To put the matter more clearly, whereas God alone gives without receiving anything in exchange, which makes Him alone the true Giver, mankind always gives in order to receive something back. Nevertheless on this score Philo does not reduce social relations to a kind of 'illumined utilitarianism' (p. 52), but refers it back to the initial absolutely unconditional gift of creation. In short, the debt that man has incurred to God should be repaid, not to God, who is wholly without needs, but to man's neighbour, thereby giving rise to a firm sense of fellowship both in the spiritual and the material sphere. In such a way, Farias goes on to argue, a solid foundation is given not only to the relationship between creationism and social thought, but also to the typically Philonic concept of natural law. Indeed, according to the Alexandrian a direct connection exists between the physical laws of the cosmos, the embodied laws as represented by the Patriarchs, the revealed laws, and—in the most attenuated form—the enacted legislation of society. All these laws have their foundation in the creative act of God, which is free and has a moral end. This means that in not a single case, not even in the physical world, can these laws be regarded as absolutely determined. The final chapter gives a more integrated treatment of themes which have been developed earlier in the monograph, and especially the theme of brotherhood, which is also conceived in terms of grace. The author emphasizes, however, that this solidarity cannot reach the deeper level of individual responsibility over against God. (RR)

L. H. FELDMAN, *Jew and Gentile in the Ancient World* (Princeton 1993).

There is no specific section on Philo in this massive treatment of the relation between Jew and Gentile in antiquity written from a firmly orthodox point of view, but he is continually used as a invaluable source of evidence, especially for the situation in the Diaspora and more particularly in Alexandria. See the list of references on pp. 629–30 and the index at p. 657. (DTR)

L. H. FELDMAN, 'Palestinian and Diaspora Judaism in the First Century', in H. SHANKS (ed.), *Christianity and Rabbinic Judaism: a Parallel History of their Origins and Early Development* (Washington 1993) 1–39, 327–336 (notes), esp. 28–39.

Philo is referred to extensively as a source for our knowledge of the religious and cultural background of the Diaspora and its success in the area of proselytism. A special box on 30–31 gives specific details on Philo and cites Smallwood's view that he is a more reliable recorder of events than Josephus. (DTR)

D. FERNANDEZ-GALIANO, 'Un monasterio pitagórico: los terapeutas de Alejandría', *Gerión* 22 (1993) 245–269.

Argues the thesis that the Monasterion which is described by Philo's *De vita contemplativa* is not a Christian monastery, as Eusebius believed, nor a Jewish one, as Philo presents it, but it is a pagan Pythagorean monastery, as may be concluded from a comparison with passages of Porphyry and Iamblichus. The article also includes a summary in Spanish of the contents of *Contempl.* The article makes no reference to other Philonic works and also not to the considerable bibliography on this question. (JPM)

J. FERNANDEZ LAGO, *La montaña en las Homilias de Origenes*, Collectanea Scientifica Compostellana 7 (Santiago de Compostela 1993).

Frequently adduces Philonic passages and concepts to explain the exegesis of mountains and others topographical termini given by Origen. Philo is considered an important antecedent for methods and contents of the Christian exegete. (JPM)

R. A. J. GAGNON, 'Heart of Wax and a Teaching that Stamps: τύπος διδαχῆς (Rom. 6:17b) once more', *Journal of Biblical Literature* 112 (1993) 667–687, esp. 681–687.

The author argues that Philo's extensive use of τύπος imagery can add our interpretation of the difficult τύπος διδαχῆς in Rom. 6.17b. He notes four points: (1) it is used specifically of the creation of man; (2) imprints are received on the soul when it thinks virtuous or evil thoughts; (3) teaching plays an important role in shaping the imprint and determining how deeply it is impressed; (4) the imprint is also affected by one's conduct. On the basis of these observations Gagnon argues that the genitive διδαχῆς should be taken as one of source, i.e. from teaching. Paul's phrase can be read as agreeing with a core meaning of the term τύπος. (ACG)

F. García Bazan, *Plotino sobre la trascendencia divina: sentido y origen*, Universidad Nacional de Cuyo (Mendoza 1993).

The author uses Philo frequently as a source for reconstructing the linguistic or philosophical background of Plotinus. García discusses the following themes: the terminology of mysteries (p.21), the distinction between the *nous* in movement and the nous in repose (pp. 92–93), the expression μόνος καὶ ἐρῆμος (p. 186), the language about God's nature (pp. 204–205), androgyny in the beginning by Gnostics and Philo (p. 247) the expression δεύτερος θεός (p. 262), and others. Philonic passages are adduced generally to illustrate a biblical philosophy against which the polemic of Plotinus is directed. (JPM).

A. C. Geljon, 'De goddelijke Logos bij Philo', *Interpretatie* 1.8 (1993) 28–29.

Response and critical remarks on the articles of Berk summarized above. In Philo the Logos has the function of a bridge between God in his transcendence and the created universe., but should not be seen as an independent entity. In the author's view Philo's role as a predecessor of John is rather questionable. (ACG)

J. Glucker, 'Piety, Dogs and a Platonic Reminiscence: Philo, *Quod deterius* 54–56 and Plato, *Euthyphro* 12e–15a', *Illinois Classical Studies* 18 (1993) [= *Studies in Honor of Miroslav Marcovich*] 131–138.

Glucker begins by citing the Philonic passage and marking all the allusions to the Platonic dialogue that it contains (15 in all). It is clear that Plato has passed through a serious transformation: the aporetic dialogue is converted into positive theology. After discussing various aspects of Philo's exploitation and alteration of Platonic themes, the author notes that use of this dialogue was rare in antiquity. Did Philo have Plato's text in front of him? Various considerations make this unlikely. It is more probable that he made use of notes that he himself had earlier compiled. The article ends with some interesting personal notes on reading Philo. (DTR)

G. Græsholt, 'Er Filon bare et sidespor? [In Danish, = Is Philo just a side-track?]', *Dansk Teologisk Tidskrift* 56 (1993) 19–34.

The article contains two parts, followed by a summary in English. Firstly the study *Judaism and Antiquity* (Sheffield 1990, Danish edition 1984) by B. Otzen is criticized for not taking Philo seriously as a representative of Diaspora Judaism. Secondly a picture of Alexandrian Judaism based on Philo is presented, making basically the same points as the author's article 'Philo of Alexandria: Some Typical Traits of his Jewish Identity' published in 1992 in *Classica et Medievalia* (see summary in *SPhA* 7 (1995) 196). Less emphasis is placed, however, on 'Philo's racism'. (KGS)

I. Gruenwald [א. גרינולד], לבעיית המחקר בעיסוקם של חכמים במיסטיקה ['Methodological Problems in Researching Rabbinic Mysticism'], in I. Gafni, A. Oppenheimer and M. Stern (edd.), *Jews and Judaism in the Second Temple, Mishna and Talmud Period. Studies in Honor of Shmuel Safrai* (Jerusalem 1993) 297–315.

This wide-ranging article addresses central questions in the determination of the nature and extent of early rabbinic mysticism: particularly, the complex nature of the relationship, historical and phenomenological, between mystical speculation and legal reasoning. By way of conclusion (313–314), the author distinguishes decisively between the mystical thought of Philo—whether understood in the extreme terms framed by Goodenough or according to the more controlled formulation of Winston—and the 'merkabah-mysticism' current among first and second century rabbinic figures. (DS)

V. GUIGNARD, *Le rapport d'Israel à l'histoire dans l'œuvre de Philon d'Alexandrie* (D.E.A. d'histoire ancienne, Poitiers 1993).

Philo's attitude towards history is tinged with scepticism, especially with regard to the prediction of the future, which explains his lack of interest in the messianic future. This means that there is no other source of earthly salvation in the immediate future than the protection of Rome. Philo's utter confidence in the particular solicitude of Providence for the Jews, as well as the certitude derived therefrom that the chosen people have a special place in history, are based on his faith and not in speculations about the future. (DTR, based on summary by author).

M. HARL, 'La Bible d'Alexandrie et les études sur la Septante: réflexions sur une première expérience', *Vigiliae Christianae* 47 (1993) 313–340, esp. 330–334.

Brief but important remarks about the place of Philonic exegesis in the context of the commentaries on the Septuagint published in the ambitious French research project 'The Alexandrian Bible'. (DTR)

M. HIMMELFARB, *Ascent to Heaven in Jewish and Christian Apocalypses* (Oxford 1993).

The main emphasis of this book is on Jewish and Christian apocalypses involving ascent to heaven, but it includes a number of important references to Philo, who plays an important comparative role; see pp. 43–44, 48–49, 70–71, 85. (DTR)

H. W. HOLLANDER and J. W. HOLLEMAN, 'The Relationship of Death, Sin and Law in 1 Cor. 15:56', *Novum Testamentum* 35 (1993) 270–291, esp. 275–8, 286.

In connecting mortality with the sin of the first man Adam, Paul shows familiarity with Jewish traditions, not only in apocalyptic authors, but also in Philo, as shown in quotations from *Opif.* and *QG* 1. (DTR)

P. W. VAN DER HORST, 'Philo van Alexandrinus over de toorn Gods', in A. DE JONG and A. DE JONG (edd.), *Kleine Encyclopedie van de toorn*, Utrechtse Theologische Reeks 21 (Utrecht 1993) 77–82.

God's anger is mentioned many times in the OT. The Greek philosophers, however, following Plato, are convinced that God is without passions and feelings, and so cannot feel anger. The author considers how Philo, as both an exegete and a philosopher, deals with the texts from the OT in which the divine anger is mentioned. Philo clearly states that God is not acquainted with any form of passion. He explains these texts by means of the principle later called *synkatabasis*. Moses adapts his writing to the level of his readers. To speak of God as a man is not in accordance with the truth, but has a didactic aim. There are people who cannot conceive of God in any other way. This idea of *synkatabasis* is also found in Clement and Origen. (ACG)

P. W. VAN DER HORST, 'Thou shalt not Revile the Gods': the LXX Translation of Ex. 22:28 (27), its Background and Influence', *The Studia Philonica Annual* 5 (1993) 1–8.

One of the many riddles of the LXX is the change from singular to plural in the text of Ex. 22:28. Philo is the first author where we can see the biblical passage at work. Three texts are discussed: *Spec.* 1.53, *Mos.* 2.203ff., *QE* 2.5. The general tendency of his interpretation is positive and apologetic in intent, e.g. that the commandment was given so that Jews would not revile other gods and God would not be reviled by non-Jews in return. This positive interpretation differs from later Patristic exegeses. (DTR)

A. KAMESAR, *Jerome, Greek Scholarship, and the Hebrew Bible: a Study of the* Quaestiones Hebraicae in Genesim, Oxford Classical Monographs (Oxford 1993).

This book contains frequent references to Philo and especially his *Quaestiones*, as is only to be expected in a study concentrating on Jerome's *Quaestiones Hebraicae in Genesim*, even though the author affirms (p. 93) that 'in contrast to the works of Philo..., it is not the commentary form that has intruded in *QHG*, but another form of exegesis, that is termed *excerpta* or scholia'. (DTR)

T. E. KNIGHT, 'The Use of Aletheia for the 'Truth of Unreason': Plato, the Septuagint, and Philo', *American Journal of Philology* 114 (1993) 581–609.

The author argues that Philo's notion of truth is not a natural semantic extension of Platonic usage, but is determined culturally. For Plato, truth is a property of the objects of knowledge. The grasping of this property takes place in a pluralistic, dialectical, and competitive context. Philo, on the other hand, regards truth as the content of belief, which comes about by conviction, rather than persuasion, as Plato. It is no longer the result of pluralistic discourse in an open society. This understanding of the notion of truth is determined by the way it is used in the LXX. (ACG)

C. KRAUS REGGIANI, 'L'uso della Scrittura in Filone di Alessandria', in H. MERKLEIN, K. MÜLLER and G. STEMBERGER (edd.), *Bibel in jüdischer und christlicher Tradition: Festschrift für Johann Maier zum 60. Geburtstag*, Bonner Biblische Beiträge (Bonn 1993) 177–191.

In order to deal with the subject indicated in her title, Kraus Reggiani dwells on three points: (1) the nature of the Septuagint text used by Philo (pp. 177ff.); (2) the choice of the Pentateuch as fundamental reference point for his thought (pp. 181ff.); the character and form of his allegorical practice (p. 183ff.). This last point is dealt with at slightly greater length and reaches the following conclusions: (a) Philo's thought is always developed with reference to the Bible; (b) his purpose is almost always exegetical in the allegorical-philosophical sense, even if (c) he does not do away with the literal meaning of the biblical text; finally (d) the philosophical results of the interpretation of the Sacred Text, which have substantially Platonic character, are of a metaphysical-ontological nature, but ultimately have an ethical-religious purpose (p. 190f.). (RR)

J.-Y. LELOUP, *Prendre soin de l'Être : Philon et les thérapeutes d'Alexandrie*, Spiritualités (Paris 1993).

The author presents a new translation of *De vita contemplativa*, inspired by the preceding translations of Geoltrain (Paris 1960, = RR 2253) and Miquel (PAPM vol. 29, Paris 1963, = RR 2210), but nevertheless novel because differing in intention. The aim of the work, in both translation and notes and also in the brief introduction (pp. 9–26) is to make the Philonic text more accessible by bringing it up to date or modernizing it, above all in relation to the centrality of the interpretation of scripture in the life of faith. See also the review by J. Riaud in *SPhA* 7 (1995) 226–227. (RR)

D. LINDSAY, *Josephus and Faith: 'Pistis' and 'Pisteuein' as Faith Terminology in the Writings of Flavius Josephus and the New Testament*, Arbeiten zur Literatur und Geschichte des hellenistischen Judentums 19 (Leiden 1993), esp. 53–73.

In spite of the title this study has an entire chapter devoted to Philo's use of the terminology of πίστις and πιστεύειν. Lindsay follows A. Schlatter in analysing the various usages of the term πίστις into four categories: (a) as pledge, security, proof; (b) as faithfulness in the execution of a charge; (c) as faith, trust (here Gen. 15:6 plays a crucial role); (d) conviction, belief. The verb πιστεύειν is used in credal formulas, but most of all in the expression πιστεύειν θεῷ. Because Philo is strongly influenced by Greek conceptuality and philosophical thought, his understanding of faith differs from that of the Bible, both in the LXX and in the NT. The author thus sees his use of faith terminology as an excellent example of his tendency to synthesize Jewish and Greek thought. At the same time it should be recognized that his expansion of the use of the two words, especially in the direction of credal faith, has opened the possibility of new developments in other directions. See further the review of the monograph by David M. Hay in *SPhA* 6 (1994) 216–219. (DTR)

H. E. LONA, *Über die Auferstehung des Fleisches: Studien zur frühchristlichen Eschatologie*, Beihefte zur Zeitschrift für die neutestamentliche Wissenschaft 66 (Berlin-New York 1993), esp. 99–103.

Retracing the use of the formula in Christian authors of the 2nd and 3rd cent. CE, Lona finds the philosophical background of Justinus, *Dial*. 5.4–6.2 in Philo; similarities in the interpretation of Plato's *Timaeus* and in the exegesis of Gen. 2:7 are pointed out. (DZ)

J. P. MARTÍN, 'Metáfora y metonimia para nombrar a Dios. Otra lectura de Filón', *Epimeleia* (Buenos Aires) 2.4 (1993) 153–167.

Allegory has been considered as an expansion of metaphor. But in many cases, Philonic allegory is in fact a reduction in the sense of metonymy, not of metaphor. From a linguistic point of view, the case of radical metonymy is the interpretation of the name of God as 'Who is'. The author concludes that the allegorical practice of Philo is a system that combines metaphorical and metonymical processes. (JPM)

J. P. MARTÍN, 'Metáfora y Alegoría', *Escritos de Filosofía* (Buenos Aires) 23–24 (1993) 149–167.

Attempts to develop a connection between two themes: on one hand, allegory has been considered generally as a type of metaphor; on the other hand, there is a large tradition that resorts to allegory as a method of knowledge. Philo is taken as a typical representative of this latter tradition. It is argued that the practice of allegory as a method of knowledge must be placed in an intermediate zone between poetics and speculative discourse, according to the distinction brought by P. Ricoeur, and that this zone is situated in the field of rhetoric. (JPM)

G. MAYER, 'Die herrscherliche Titulatur Gottes bei Philo von Alexandrien', in D.-A. KOCH and H. LICHTENBERGER (edd.), *Begegnungen zwischen Christentum und Judentum in Antike und Mittelalter: Festschrift für Heinz Schreckenberg*, Schriften des Institutum Judaicum Delitzschianum 1 (Göttingen 1993) 293–302.

Since in New Testament research on God's Kingdom Philonic evidence is often disregarded, Mayer inquires into the word group βασιλεύς and its equivalents. God's monarchy is manifested in the creation and preservation of the world. Nevertheless, in his intervention Philo distinguishes God's royal power from the preceding creative power (table 1 with the corresponding names κύριος and θεός). God descends into the soul, his palace. On the other hand, there is a 'royal way' from below to God, the King. Table 2 shows the competition between ἡγεμών and βασιλεύς. After a paragraph on the origin of these concepts, both in Hellenistic philosophy and in Jewish tradition (table 3), Mayer concludes with remarks on their symbolic meaning: in spite of God's unknowable essence, the language of his Kingship is required to confront him with man in demand and care. The result, that Philo places the emphasis on ethics, seems somewhat embarrassing, since the preceding proves only, that his use is not eschatological. Mayer was unable to take into consideration the essay of M. Umemoto (summarized in *SPhA* 6 (1994) 143f). (DZ)

A. M. MAZZANTI, 'Σωτήρ e σωτηρία nell'esegesi di Filone di Alessandria', *Annali di Storia dell'Esegesi* 10 (1993) 355–366.

Adhering faithfully to the texts, Mazzanti first considers the significance of the two terms σωτήρ and σωτηρία in relation to God, then examines them in the context of the divine reality (powers, angels etc.), and finally studies them in relation to human reality (ethics and anthropology). The salvific intervention of the divine—also in the context of sacrificial ritual—is rather well developed and involves both the psychic sphere (liberation from evil) and the bodily sphere (preservation of life). As far as the anthropological aspect is concerned the author emphasizes the prevalence of a dualistic conception that is not easily reconcilable with the biblical view. (RR)

W. B. McNeil, *Homeric Poetry in Philo of Alexandria* (M.A. thesis, Miami University 1993).

We have not been able to find an abstract for this American thesis. Its title speaks for itself and whets our appetite for more information. (DTR)

W. A. Meeks, *The Origins of Christian Morality* (New Haven 1993), esp. 29–31.

In the context of a chapter entitled 'Turning: moral consequences of conversion', the author discusses some passages from Philo's *Virt.* on conversion. These provide a useful point of comparison with early Christian texts. Various analogies are observed. In both, 'conversion is described as the transformation both of a way of thinking and of a form of life, as a change of allegiance from many false gods to the one true God, as a radical resocialization' (p. 30). (ACG)

F. Petit, *La Chaîne sur la Genèse: Édition intégrale II, chapitres 4 à 11*, Traditio Exegetica Graeca 2 (Louvain 1993), *passim*.

Philo's *Quaestiones in Genesim* are once again an important source used in the *Catena in Genesim* which is being reconstructed by the author. Of the 395 exegetical excerpts included in this volume, 20 can be attributed to Philo, as usefully listed on p. 248. For more information on this project see the review of vol. 1 in *SPhA* 5 (1993) 229–232. (DTR)

R. Radice, '*Didaskalikos* 164, 29–30 e la probabile influenze di Filone di Alessandria', *Archivio di Filosofia* 61 (1993) 45–63.

In the metaphysical doctrine of Plato expounded by Alcinous in the *Didaskalikos* it is possible to identify a contradiction between the doctrine of three principles (God, matter, Ideas) and the doctrine of the Ideas as thoughts of God. In effect if the Ideas are thought up by God, then there will not be three principles, but only two. The contradiction is resolved if the Ideas are meant not as created, but simply as placed in the mind of God. This position could be the fruit of the mediation between the current of Platonism influenced by Philo and the current which is properly Academic. (RR)

J. Rebolle Barrera, *La Biblia Judía y la Biblia Cristiana. Introducción a la historia de la Biblia* (Madrid 1993), esp. 240–244, 495–499.

Briefly adduces Philonic passages to show the reception of the Bible in the Diaspora and the Philo's influence on Christian exegesis. (JPM)

A. Reinhartz, 'Parents and Children: a Philonic Perspective', in S.J.D. Cohen (ed.), *The Jewish Family*, Brown Judaic Series 289 (Atlanta 1993) 61–88.

The author discusses the relationship between children and their parents as described in Philo's Exposition of the law. She deals with four aspects in particular: (1) The hierarchical structure of the parent-child relationship, which is an expression of the dualistic view of human society. (2) Parents' responsibilities towards their children, which consists of bringing children into the world and nurturing them. Moreover, parents should give their children financial support, and instruction or education. They are also obliged to exercise discipline over them. (3) Responsibilities of children towards their parents, as expressed in obedience, fear, courtesy and care for them in their old age. Here Philo bases himself mainly on the fifth commandment. (4) Family affection. In her conclusion the author notes three fundamental characteristics of the parent-child relationship: the presence of an indissoluble bound of love and kinship between parent and child; the inherent superiority of the parent to the child; the hierarchy of male and female. (ACG)

A. REINHARTZ, 'Philo's *Exposition of the Law* and Social History: Methodological Considerations', *Society of Biblical Literature Seminar Papers* 32 (1993) 6–21.

Philo's Exposition of the Law contains a great deal of socio-historical material pertaining to family life. Is it possible to exploit this material for our understanding of contemporary Alexandria? Reinhartz examines the methodological problems involved in this exercise. She identifies four exegetical moves that Philo generally makes in commenting on the biblical text: (a) providing a rationale for biblical law when none is given in the Bible itself; (b) extending the laws to other analogous situations; (c) reinterpreting laws that pertain to social conditions no longer operative in his milieu; (d) providing specific instructions when biblical has only a general formulation. The author concludes that it is easier to reconstruct Philo's own Jewish family values than the actual contours of Jewish family life. But if one moves with caution it is possible to derive information on the Jewish family in Alexandria, which then needs to be corroborated or corrected by information derived from elsewhere. This result is important for topics such as adultery, death of fathers of unmarried daughters, the exposure of infants and so on. (DTR)

G. P. RICHARDSON, 'Philo and Eusebius on Monasteries and Monasticism: the Therapeutae and Kellia', in B. MCLEAN (ed.), *Origins and Method: Towards a New Understanding of Judaism and Christianity. Essays in Honour of John C. Hurd*, Journal for the Study of the New Testament Supplement Series 86 (Sheffield 1993) 334–359.

Eusebius' identification of the Therapeutae with first-century Christians in his *Ecclesiastical History* provides valuable information about the state of Christian monasticism in his own day (end of the 3rd century). There are in fact striking resemblances between Philo's description of the buildings of the Therapeutae community and the extensive remains of Christian monasteries in the Kellia, a site about 60 km from Alexandria and only a short distance from the Jewish site. The author demonstrates these by means of analysis of Philo's text and drawings of archaeological remains. Eusebius, who had visited Egypt, may have observed these similarities and so developed his erroneous theory. This remains uncertain, but what is clear is 'that there is an unusually close similarity between a first-century form of Jewish monasticism and a fourth-century of form of Christian monasticism' (357). The author also notes that Philo's description of a wall dividing the sexes in the meeting-house is unique in ancient evidence, and speculates about possible influence on the design of later synagogues as well as Christian monasteries. (DTR)

C. RIEDWEG, *Jüdisch-hellenistische Imitation eines orphischen Hieros Logos: Beobachtungen zu OF 245 und 247 (sog. Testament des Orpheus)*, Classica Monacensia 7 (Tübingen 1993), *passim*.

Riedweg first establishes an new history of tradition of the so called 'Testament of Orpheus' with only two independent recensions (the original version accessible via Ps-Justin *De monarchia*, and the Jewish redaction of Aristobulus). The presentation of the corresponding texts with translation and critical notes is followed by an interpretation which settles the questions of genre, authorship, philosophical background and epic language. The Jewish redactor, probably Aristobulus himself, contributes Platonic-Aristotelian ideas on God. Relevant Philonic material is cited throughout. See further the review of this book by N. Walter below in the Review section. (DZ)

J. R. ROYSE, 'Reverse Indexes to Philonic texts in the Printed Florilegia and Collections of Fragments', *The Studia Philonica Annual* 5 (1993) 156–179.

In his monograph on the spurious texts of Philo of Alexandria (summarized in *SPhA* 6 (1994) 137) Royse provided lists of Philonic texts found in the printed Florilegia and in collections of fragments. This is now supplemented by a revised index which allows one to see which Philonic texts are found in these documents. The texts are sub-divided into four categories: (1) identified Philonic texts presented in the conventional order *Opif. Leg.* etc.; (2) fragmenta spuria; (3) other non-Philonic texts, e.g. glosses; (4) unidentified texts. The texts in the last three categories are indicated by the opening and final words. (DTR)

D. T. RUNIA, *Bios eudaimoon* (inaugural lecture, Leiden 1993), esp. 4–5.

The starting point of the oration is the fact that Philo ends his *De opificio mundi* and at least five other texts with the theme of *eudaimonia* (well-being). This turns out to be a characteristic of many Greek, Latin and Patristic works, going back at least as far as Plato, and has a protreptic origin. (DTR)

D. T. RUNIA, 'God of the Philosophers, God of the Patriarchs: Exegetical Backgrounds in Philo of Alexandria', in F. J. HOOGEWOUD and R. MUNK (edd.), *Joodse Filosofie tussen Rede en Traditie: Feestbundel ter ere van de tachtigste verjaardag van Prof. dr. H. J. Heering* (Kampen 1993) 13–23.

The antithesis between God of the philosophers and God of the patriarchs, made famous in the *Mémorial* of Pascal, is already found in a different form in Judah Halevi. The article shows that this theme has an anterior exegetical basis which goes all the way back to Philo. Three Philonic passages are discussed, *Mos.* 1.74–76, *Abr.* 50–52, *Mut.* 7–14, and some comments are given on his interpretation. In Philo's case a distinction is made based on Ex. 3:14–15, but there is no antithesis as we find in Pascal. If there is a connection between the two authors, Augustine may have been the intermediary. (DTR)

D. T. RUNIA, *Philo in Early Christian Literature: a Survey*, Compendia Rerum Iudaicarum ad Novum Testamentum III 3 (Assen–Minneapolis 1993).

This monograph contains the first comprehensive examination of the reception of Philo's writings and thought in Early Christian literature. The cut-off point is 400 AD (Isidore of Pelusium, Augustine), although some pointers to later developments are also given. The book is divided into four parts. The first part commences with a chapter on the legend of Philo Christianus, Philo's fate in the Jewish and pagan traditions and the fascinating story of the transmission of his writings. There follows a chapter stating the book's purpose and method and a chapter giving a status quaestionis. In the second part the Greek-speaking Christian authors are dealt with in chapters on Philo and the New Testament, the Apologists, Alexandria before Clement, Clement, Origen, the later Alexandrian tradition, Eusebius and the Cappadocians. The Latin fathers are treated in Part III, with chapters on Beginnings in the West, Ambrose, and Other Latin authors (including Jerome and Augustine). The fourth part is entitled Epilogue and reaches a number of conclusions, including suggestions for further research. In his treatment the author generally takes as his starting-point those passages in which Philo is named. This places the research on a sure footing. An appendix gives a complete list of such passages up to 1000 AD. Because of the vastness of the subject, the author makes extensive use of existing scholarship (hence the sub-title of the book), but also adds the results of his own research. See further the Special Section devoted to *SPhA* 6 (1994) 90–110, with comments by A. Terian, A. van den Hoek, R. L. Wilken, and D. Winston. (DTR)

D. T. RUNIA, 'Was Philo a Middle Platonist? a Difficult Question Revisited', *The Studia Philonica Annual* 5 (1993) 112–140.

This paper, part of the San Francisco seminar on Philo and Middle Platonism (see above under J. Dillon), is divided into two main parts. In the first the author looks back on his dissertation on Philo and Plato's *Timaeus*, considers developments since then and examines a number of questions that have been raised in critiques and reviews of the book. In the second part he returns to the question of whether Philo can and should be dubbed a Middle Platonist. First a typology of six different positions on the issue is presented. Then a number of clarificatory issues are discussed: (1) the question of loyalty; (2) scripture and the status of the scriptural commentary; (3) self-definition versus historical perspective; (4) the question of eclecticism. Runia then presents two case studies, one historical (the parallel figure Chaeremon the Egyptian and Stoic), one doctrinal (the question of God's relation to the Ideas). The upshot is that the author persists in his view that Philo should not be regarded as a Middle Platonist in the strict sense, even though Platonism patently exercised a strong influence on his thought. (DTR)

D. T. RUNIA and R. RADICE, 'Philo of Alexandria: an Annotated Bibliography 1990', *The Studia Philonica Annual* 5 (1993) 180–208.

Bibliography of Philonic studies primarily for the year 1990 (60 items), with addenda for the years 1986–89 (8 items). (DTR)

R. SORABJI, *Animal Minds and Human Morals: the Origins of the Western Debate* (Ithaca–London 1993), *passim*.

Frequent references to Philo's *De animalibus* in this wide-ranging and thought-provoking analysis of the history of philosophical debate on the status of animals. See esp. p. 161 and indices on p. 245, 262. (DTR)

G. E. STERLING, 'Platonizing Moses: Philo and Middle Platonism', *The Studia Philonica Annual* 5 (1993) 96–111.

Paper presented in the context of the SBL Philo Seminar (see above on J. Dillon). Argues that Philo's marriage of Jewish scripture and Greek philosophy through allegorical exegesis is an example of the effort to bridge East and West within the philosophical tradition. For Philo Platonism and Judaism are similar at the most essential point, namely the understanding of God. The author regards Philo's position as 'pluralistic', i.e. he is convinced of the validity of both Platonism and of Judaism. Comparable positions are taken up by Chaeremon of Alexandria, Plutarch, and Numenius, to each of whom brief discussions are devoted. The article concludes with some words on the question of Philo's Middle Platonism. 'Philo's Moses was not a Hebrew Moses; he was a Middle Platonist. It is from this perspective that I think *we* can speak of Philo as representative of Middle Platonism (p. 111).' (ACG)

H. TARRANT, *Thrasyllan Platonism*, (Ithaca-London 1993), esp. 109–117.

Argues that the epistemological passage in Porphyry *Harm*. 12–14 Düring goes back to Thrasyllus, and that its *logos* doctrine shows important resemblances to that of his contemporary Philo, which in turn suggests that much of Philo's *logos* theory 'will have evolved directly from his secular environment' (p. 116). (DTR)

A. TERIAN, 'Two Unusual Uses of *aṙn* in the Armenian Version of Philo's *Quaestiones*', *Annual of Armenian Linguistics* 14 (1993) 49–54.

An unusual derivation of a participial noun form, namely *aṙn*, is used at two places in the Armenian translation of Philo, at *QG* 1.27 and *QE* 1.1. According to Terian, at both places it is a derivation from *arnal*. In the case of the former passage the Armenian can be checked against the surviving Greek fragment. Marcus' emendation in the second passage cannot be maintained. (ACG)

T. H. TOBIN S.J., 'Was Philo a Middle Platonist? Some suggestions', *The Studia Philonica Annual* 5 (1993) 147–150.

Brief response to the papers of Sterling and Runia in the context of the SBL Philo Seminar (see above on J. Dillon). It is important to recognize, Tobin emphasizes, that Philo comes early in the history of Middle Platonism. The question of Philo's hairesis may be elucidated by the distinction between 'emic' and 'etic' analysis. (DTR)

P. J. TOMSON, '*Voor één dag genoeg*' (Matt 6:34): *het brood, het Woord en de wetenschap*, In Caritate 3 (inaugural address, Brussels 1993), esp. 11–18.

As part of general exploration of the Jewish background to the *logion* in the Sermon on the Mount a comparison is made between the Rabbinic Midrash and Philo. In both cases the motif of the gift of heavenly manna in Exodus is fundamental. The contrast between the spiritual realm and that of confused everyday experience is of course Platonic, but was also widespread in Jewish thought. Tomson prefers to speak of convergence between Platonism and Judaism rather than (in most cases) direct influence. He further notes important parallels between Philo and the Rabbis in relation to the theme of spiritual food and ends his section on Philo with some remarks on the translation of this theme into the ideal of scientific and philosophical knowledge, as espoused in our century by Albert Einstein. (DTR)

H. TRONIER, 'Virkeligheden som fortolkningsresultat: om hermeneutik hos Filon og Paulus [In Danish = Reality as a result of interpretation: on hermeneutics in Philo and Paul]', in M. MÜLLER and J. STRANGE (edd.), *Det gamle Testamente i jødedom og kristendom*, Forum for Bibelsk Eksegese 4 (Copenhagen 1993) 151–182, esp. 153–164.

Philo's and Paul's hermeneutical methods are compared and contrasted. Philo's allegories are based on a Platonic method consisting in a *diairesis* of concepts as exemplified by an analysis of *De migratione Abrahami*. In the Scriptures Philo by means of a deductive method looks for a hierarchy in which the concrete Scriptural concepts and events form manifestations of higher concepts in the transcendental sphere. The latter is not understood in spatial but in logical terms. According to Philo the rationality, i.e. real meaning of different events told in the Scriptures, is localized in those aspects which unite them as manifestations of transcendental concepts. The migration of Abraham from Haran to Canaan in reality means the migration from the body and its sense-perception to the noetic vision and thus conveys the same philosophical idea as for instance the Exodus of Israel from Egypt. The correct understanding of the rational structure of the Scriptural events corresponds to a transformation of the mind of the interpreter, who in the Scriptures will detect a reality which is familiar to him and is identical with his own noetic experience. (KGS)

W. C. VAN UNNIK, *Das Selbstverständnis der jüdischen Diaspora in der hellenistisch-römischen Zeit*, aus dem Nachlaß herausgegeben und bearbeitet von P. W. VAN DER HORST, Arbeiten zur Geschichte des antiken Judentums und des Urchristentums 17 (Leiden 1993), esp. 127–137.

The text of these lectures held in 1967 in Jerusalem is supplemented by P. W. van der Horst with notes, a biography of the author and list of his publications and two appendices. Van Unnik investigates the evaluation that Jews—especially Greek speaking Jews—connected with the term 'diaspora'. He contests the wide-spread optimistic interpretation of the term and makes it clear that from the use of the noun and the verb in ancient literature, in the LXX and in Jewish writings of Hellenistic and Roman times an unfavourable meaning prevails. The 'dispersion' does not in the first place signify a geographic fact, but is the result of divine anger which brings the nation close to dissolution. Philo, discussed on pp. 127–137, dissimulates this biblical interpretation somewhat, but in *Praem.* 164f he too echoes the Jewish hope for return and restoration. Like Josephus (pp. 137–147) he never uses the noun 'diaspora' to describe the situation of the Jewish people. The reason for this is apologetic. (DZ)

S.-K. WAN, 'Philo's *Quaestiones et Solutiones in Genesim*: a Synoptic Approach', *Society of Biblical Literature Seminar Papers* 32 (1993) 22–53.

The paper is divided into two halves. In the first Wan discusses the history of the zetematic genre, which is shown to have three general characteristics: it is apologetic, public, and popular or educative. Philo's *Quaestiones* appear to be the earliest extant example of this genre whose compositional principle was based on a continuous text. In the second half the relation of Philo's *Quaestiones* to his Allegorical Commentary is examined, taking the second creation of man (Gen. 2:7, *Leg.* 1.19–42, *QG* 1.1–5) as a case study. It is concluded that the *Quaestiones* should not be seen as a note-book or preliminary notes for the *Allegories*. On the other hand it cannot be denied that the consistently used question and answer technique gives a less sophisticated and more accessible interpretation, and so can be seen as 'preparatory' or 'preliminary' in the sense that they were intended as general introduction to the more advanced writings represented in the *Allegoriae*. (DTR)

R. McL WILSON, 'Philo and Gnosticism', *The Studia Philonica Annual* 5 (1993) 84–92.

In a general paper presented to the SNTS Philo seminar in 1992 the author summarizes the results of fifty years of research and reflection on the theme of Philo's relation to Gnosticism. It is necessary to be clear on what one understands Gnosticism to be before one can judge whether any ancient author belongs to it or has contributed to its development. In Wilson's view Philo is sometimes very close, but not so close that he can be said to have belonged, and it is also by no means certain that he contributed. What he certainly does do is provide us with evidence for the intellectual climate of the time. (DTR)

D. WINSTON, 'Philo and Middle Platonism: Response to Runia and Sterling', *The Studia Philonica Annual* 5 (1993) 141–146.

In his contribution to the session on Philo and Middle Platonism (see above on J. Dillon) Winston emphasizes that Philo did not regard his activity of Platonizing exegesis as subversive because he was convinced that his philosophical reading of scripture was entirely legitimate. A similar approach is shown by medieval kabbalists. Finally some comments are devoted to the parallel figures of Chaeremon and Numenius. (DTR)

C. D. YONGE, *The Works of Philo Complete and Unabridged*, with a Foreword by D. M. Scholer (Peabody Mass. 1993).

The publication of this first single-volume translation of Philo into a modern language is undeniably an important event in Philonic studies. It should be noted, however, that the translation dates to 1854–55 and could be published at an attractive price because it is in the public domain. The editor and his collaborators have added some missing sections and—most importantly—brought the divisions of the text up to date, taking the Loeb edition as their example. This makes the translation much more suitable for contemporary use. For a full description, analysis and evaluation of the venture the reader is referred to the Review article in *SPhA* 6 (1994) 171–182.

D. ZELLER, 'Notiz zu den 'immerfließenden Quellen der göttlichen Wohltaten'', *The Studia Philonica Annual* 5 (1993) 93–94.

In this note, an additional footnote to his book on Charis (see summary in *SPhA* 5 (1993) 195), the author continues his search for the origin of the Philonic poetic expression indicated in the title. No direct source is found, only a series of similar metaphors. The theological application, however, first occurs in Philo. (DZ)

Addenda 1990–1992

M. BARKER, 'Temple Imagery in Philo: An Indication of the Origin of the Logos?', in W. HORBURY (ed.), *Templum amicitiae. Essays on the Second Temple presented to Ernst Bammel*, Journal for the Study of the New Testament Supplement Series 48 (Sheffield 1991) 70–102.

The author argues that there existed in ancient Israel the belief that God, called Yahweh, was in fact an archangel, the chief of the sons of El. He was the second deity, and was believed to have been the human figure in the Hebrew Bible. This Great Angel, it is claimed, became Philo's Logos. Philo linked the Angel/Logos of his Judaism to the Reason/Logos of the philosophers. The Logos is also the High Priest, and most of Philo's description of the Logos is based on the imagery of the temple cult in Jerusalem. (ACG)

B. DECHARNEUX, 'Apparitions et miracles des anges et démons chez Philon d'Alexandrie et Plutarque', in A. DIERKENS, (ed.) *Apparitions et miracles*, Problèmes d'histoire des religions 2 (Brussels 1991) 61–68, esp. 62–64.

Lists and analyses those Philonic texts in which the appearance of angels is connected with miraculous events. The miracles fall into two categories: those that contravene the laws of nature and those that reveal to selected souls the course of future events. The link between the two is the role of the Logos. The remainder of the article discusses parallel texts in Plutarch. (DTR)

J. HAMMERSTAEDT, 'Zu einigen Philonfragmenten bei Euseb', *Jahrbuch für Antike und Christentum* 35 (1992) 12–18.

Complementary to a review (*ibid.* 203f) of a new edition of Eusebius' *Praeparatio Evangelica* the author re-examines the text, the construction and the significance of three Philonic fragments. The main infinitives in 8.6.1 are explained as a summary of a larger passage in Philo done by Eusebius in the same way as in 8.6.8f; in 8.6.1-4 the qualities of Moses are extolled in order to demonstrate the magnitude of his people as a whole; in 8.7.7 one should read δολοῦν instead of δουλοῦν and translate as 'falsify through crossbreeding'. (DZ)

M. LATTKE, *Hymnus: Materialien zu einer Geschichte der antiken Hymnologie*, Novum Testamentum et Orbis Antiquus 19 (Freiburg–Göttingen 1991), esp. 129–132.

Detailed terminological observations on Philo's references to hymns and liturgical songs. Philo scarcely uses ψάλλειν and ψαλμός, but his writings are rich in references to ὑμνεῖν, ὕμνος and related terms. Special attention is paid to the description of the liturgy of the Therapeutae. (DTR)

J. MANSFELD, 'Doxography and Dialectic: the Sitz im Leben of the 'Placita'', in W. HAASE and H. TEMPORINI (edd.), *Aufstieg und Niedergang der römischen Welt*, Teil II Principat Band 36.4 (Berlin-New York 1990) 3056–3229, esp. 3117–22.

Philo's passage in *Somn.* 1.21–32 about the unknowability of the heavens and the intellect is an extremely important document in the history of ancient doxography, as already demonstrated by Wendland in his neglected 1897 article. Mansfeld analyses the part of the text dealing with the mind and soul, as part of a comprehensive examination of the doxographical tradition on these subjects. Further references to Philo are listed in the index at 3225. (DTR)

S. M. POGOLOFF, *Logos and Sophia: the Rhetorical Situation of 1 Corinthians*, SBL Dissertation series 134 (Atlanta 1992), esp. 180–187.

The author interprets 1 Cor. 1–4 in terms of its rhetorical features. The fact that Apollos, who is named in 1 Cor., was a rhetor from Alexandria, induces the author to give a brief discussion of Philo as rhetor and the context of Alexandrian rhetoric. (ACG)

SUPPLEMENT

A Provisional Bibliography 1994–96

The user of this supplementary bibliography of very recent articles on Philo is once again reminded that it will doubtless contain inaccuracies and red herrings, because it is not in all cases based on autopsy. It is merely meant as a service to the reader. Scholars who are disturbed by omissions or keen to have their own work on Philo listed are strongly encouraged to take up contact with the bibliography's compilers (addresses in the section Notes on contributors).

1994

D. C. Aune, 'Mastery of the Passions: Philo, 4 Maccabees and Earliest Christianity', in W. Helleman (ed.), *Hellenization Revisited: Shaping a Christian Response within the Greco-Roman World* (Lanham 1994) 125–158.

G. H. Baudry, 'La theorie du penchant mauvais et la doctrine du peche originel', *Bulletin de litterature ecclesiastique* 95 (1994) 271–301.

A. P. Booth, 'The Voice of the Serpent: Philo's Epicureanism', in W. Helleman (ed.), *Hellenization Revisited: Shaping a Christian Response within the Greco-Roman World* (Lanham 1994) 159–172.

P. Borgen, 'Jesus Christ, the Reception of the Spirit, and a Cross-National Community', in J. B. Green and M. Turner (edd.), *Jesus of Nazareth: Lord and Christ. Essays on the Historical Jesus and New Testament Christology* (Grand Rapids-Carlisle 1994), esp. 226–228.

P. Borgen, '"Yes", "No", "How Far"?: The Participation of Jews and Christians in Pagan cults', in T. Engberg-Pedersen (ed.), *Paul in his Hellenistic Context* (Edinburgh 1994, Minneapolis 1995) 30–59, esp. 43–46.

N. L. Calvert, 'Philo's Use of Jewish Traditions about Abraham', *Society of Biblical Literature Seminar Papers* 33 (1994) 450–462.

S. Cheon, *An Investigation of Pseudo-Solomon's Interpretation of the Exodus Story in The Wisdom of Solomon 11–19* (diss. Graduate Theological Union, Berkeley 1994).

J. H. Corbett, 'Muddying the Water: Metaphors for Exegesis', in W. Helleman (ed.), *Hellenization Revisited: Shaping a Christian Response within the Greco-Roman World* (Lanham 1994) 205–221, esp. 214–215, 221.

K. L. Cukrowski, *Pagan Polemic and Lukan Apologetic: the Function of Acts 20:17–38 (Paul)* (diss. Yale University 1994), esp. chap. 2.

E. DASSMANN et al., *Reallexikon für Antike und Christentum*, Band XVI = Lieferungen 121–128 (Stuttgart 1994).
> F.-L. Hossfeld–G. Schöllgen, Art. 'Hohepriester' 4–58, esp. 19–23 (High priest); G. J. M. Bartelink, Art. 'Homer' 117–147, esp. 125–126 (Homer); K. Thraede, Art. 'Homonoia (Eintracht), 176–289, esp. 238–239 (concord); K. Hoheisel, Art. 'Homosexualität', 289–364, esp. 334–335 (homosexuality); J. Hammerstaedt, Art. 'Hypostasis', 986–1035, esp. 998–9 (hypostasis); K. Thraede, Art. 'Jacob und Esau', 1118–1217, esp. 1125–30 (Jacob and Esau).

E. DASSMANN et al., *Reallexikon für Antike und Christentum*, Lieferungen 129–130 (Stuttgart 1994).
> H. Thyen, Art. 'Ich-bin-Worte' 147–213, esp. 168–170 (I am sayings); M. Baltes, Art. 'Idee (Ideenlehre)' 213–246, esp. 235–238 (theory of Ideas).

R. E. DE MARIS, *The Colossians Controversy: Wisdom in Dispute at Colossae*, JSNTSup 96 (Sheffield 1994), esp. 114ff.

B. DECHARNEUX, *L'ange, le devin et le prophète: chemins de la parole dans l'œuvre de Philon d'Alexandrie dit "le Juif"*, Spiritualités et pensées libres (Brussels 1994)

B. DECHARNEUX, 'Philon d'Alexandrie, un philosophe témoin de la violence religieuse au premier siècle de notre ère', in *Violence et coexistence humaine: Actes du IIe Congrès mondial de l'ASEVICO* (Montréal 1994) 262–267.

J. DILLON, 'Philo and the Greek Tradition of Allegorical Exegesis', *Society of Biblical Literature Seminar Papers* 33 (1994) 69–80.

G. DORIVAL, *La Bible d'Alexandrie (LXX), Tome 4 Les Nombres* (Paris 1994).

N. A. EVANS, 'Diotima, Eros, Cherubim and the Sources of Divine Knowledge', *Society of Biblical Literature Seminar Papers* 33 (1994) 822–846, esp. 840ff.

J.J. FERNANDEZ SANGRADOR, *Los orígenes de la comunidad cristiana de Alejandría* (Salamanca 1994), esp. 47–50.

P. GARNSEY, 'Philo Judaeus and Slave Theory', *Scripta Classica Israelica* 13 (1994) 30–45.

M. GONZALEZ FERNANDEZ, 'Philon d'Alexandrie et Michel de Montaigne', *Bulletin de la Societe des amis de Montaigne* 37–38 (1994) 23–36.

M. GOODMAN, *Missionary Conversion: Proselytising in the Religious History of the Roman Empire* (Oxford 1994).

S. GORANSON, 'Posidonius, Strabo and Marcus Vipsanius Agrippa as Sources on Essenes', *Journal of Jewish Studies* 45 (1994) 295–298.

P. GRAFFIGNA, 'Tra il doppio e l'unita: parentela (συγγένεια) tra uomo e Dio in Filone d'Alessandria', *Koinonia* 19 (1994) 1–15.

P. HAJNAL, *Jewish Interpretations of the Creation of Man and Woman and the Fall in the Greco-Roman Period* (diss. Oxford 1994?).

D. M. HAY, 'Defining Allegory in Philo's Exegetical World', *Society of Biblical Literature Seminar Papers* 33 (1994) 55–68.

W. Helleman, 'Epilogue', in eadem (ed.), *Hellenization Revisited: Shaping a Christian Response within the Greco-Roman World* (Lanham 1994) 429–513, esp. 465–468.

R. J. V. Hiebert, 'Deuteronomy 22:28–29 and its Pre-mishnaic Interpretations', *Catholic Biblical Quarterly* 56 (1994) 203–220.

A. van den Hoek, 'Philo in the Alexandrian Tradition', *The Studia Philonica Annual* 6 (1994) 96–99.

W. Horbury, 'The Wisdom of Solomon in the Muratorian Fragment', *JThS* 45 (1994) 149–159.

P. W. van der Horst, 'Silent Prayer in Antiquity', *Numen* 41 (1994) 1–25, esp. 13.

D. N. Jastram, 'The "Praeparatio Evangelica" and "Spoliatio" Motifs as Patterns of Hellenistic Judaism in Philo of Alexandria', in W. Helleman (ed.), *Hellenization Revisited: Shaping a Christian Response within the Greco-Roman World* (Lanham 1994) 189–204.

J. G. Kahn, 'Libido sciendi: The Lust for Knowledge according to Philo Alexandrinus', in D. Assaf (ed.), *Proceedings of the 11th World Congress of Jewish Studies* (Jerusalem 1994) 103*–106*.

A. Kamesar, 'Philo, Grammatikē, and the Narrative Aggada', in J. C. Reeves and J. Kampen (edd.), *Purusing the Text: Studies in Honor of Ben Zion Wacholder* (Sheffield 1994) 216–242.

H.-J. Klauck, 'Ein Richter im eigenen Innern: das Gewissen bei Philo von Alexandrien', in idem, *Alter Welt und neuer Glaube: Beiträge zur Religionsgeschichte, Forschungsgeschichte und Theologie des Neuen Testaments*, Novum Testamentum et Orbis Antiquus 29 (Freiburg-Göttingen 1994) 33–58.

M. A. Kraus, 'Philosophical History in Philo's *In Flaccum*', *Society of Biblical Literature Seminar Papers* 33 (1994) 477–495.

J. R. Levison, 'Two Types of Ecstatic Prophecy according to Philo', *The Studia Philonica Annual* 6 (1994) 83–89.

M. Ludwig, *Wort als Gesetz: Eine Untersuchung zum Verständnis von 'Wort' und 'Gesetz' in israelitisch-frühjüdischen und neutestamentlichen Schriften: Gleichzeitig ein Beitrag zur Theologie des Jakobusbriefes*, Europäische Hochschulschriften 23.502 (Frankfurt etc. 1994).

J. M. Lieu, 'Circumcision, Women and Salvation', *New Testament Studies* 40 (1994) 358–370.

H. A. McKay, *Sabbath and Synagogue. The Question of Sabbath Worship in Ancient Judaism*, Religions in the Graeco-Roman World 122 (Leiden 1994), esp. 65–77.

J. Martens, '*Nomos Empsychos* in Philo and Clement of Alexandria', in W. Helleman (ed.), *Hellenization Revisited: Shaping a Christian Response within the Greco-Roman World* (Lanham 1994) 323–338.

J. P. MARTÍN, 'La cultura romana y la Prima Clementis', *Teologia: Revista de la Facultad de Teología de la pontificia Universidad Católica Argentina* 21 (1994) 55–71.

J. P. MARTÍN, 'Prima Clementis: ¿estoicismo o filonismo?', *Salmanticensis* 41 (1994) 5–36.

J. P. MARTÍN, 'Sobre Heráclito y la naturaleza que ama ocultarse', *Méthexis, Revista Argentina de filosofia Antigua* 7 (1994) 107–111.

A. MENDELSON, "Did Philo Say the Shema?' and Other Reflections on E. P. Sanders' *Judaism: Practice and Belief*', *The Studia Philonica Annual* 6 (1994) 160–170.

M. MORGEN, 'Le Fils de l'homme élève en vue de la vie eternelle (Jn 3, 14–15 éclairé par diverses traditions juives)', *Revue des Sciences Religieuses* 68 (1994) 5–17.

K. A. MORLAND, *The Rhetoric of Curse in Galatians: Paul Confronts another Gospel*, Emory Studies in Early Christianity (Atlanta 1994).

M. MÜLLER, *Kirkens første Bibel. [In Danish: The First Bible of the Church] Hebraica sive Graeca veritas?*(Copenhagen 1994), esp. 45–48.

R. NEUDECKER, 'Das 'Ehescheidungsgesetz' von Dtn 24,1–4 nach altjüdischer Auslegung. Ein Beitrag zum Verstandnis der neutestamentlichen Aussagen zur Ehescheidung', *Biblica* 75 (1994) 350–387.

G. S. OEGEMA, *Der Gesalbte und sein Volk: Untersuchungen zum konzeptualisierungsprozeß der messianische Erwartungen von den Makkabäern bis Bar Koziba* (Göttingen 1994), esp. 115–122.

J. P. PHANEUF, 'Philon d'Alexandrie', *Revue SCRIPTURA* 17 (1994) 79–87.

P.-H. POIRIER, 'Pour une histoire de la lecture pneumatologique de Gn 2, 7: quelques jalons jusqu'a Irenee de Lyon', *Revue des etudes augustiniennes* 40 (1994) 1–22.

R. RADICE, *La filosofia di Aristobulo e i suoi nessi con il De Mundo attribuito ad Aristotele*, Pubblicazioni del Centro di Ricerche di Metafisica: Collana Temi metafisici e problemi del pensiero antico. Studi e Testi 33 (Milan 1994).

R. RADICE, 'Il femminile come concetto allegorico in Filone di Alessandria', *Richerche Storico-Bibliche* 6 (1994) 167–177.

R. RADICE et al., *Filone di Alessandria: Tutti i trattati del Commentario Allegorico alla Bibbia*, I Classici del Pensiero: sezione I Filosofia classica e tardo-antica (Milan 1994).

G. REALE and R. RADICE, *Filone di Alessandria: L'erede delle cose divine*, Testi a fronte (Milan 1994).

G. J. REYDAMS-SCHILS, *Stoic and Platonist Readings of Plato's Timaeus* (diss. Berkeley 1994), esp. chap. 4 'Philo Judaeus, on a Cruise to Alexandria'.

G. J. REYDAMS-SCHILS, 'Stoicized Readings of Plato's *Timaeus* in Philo of Alexandria', *Society of Biblical Literature Seminar Papers* 33 (1994) 450–462.

C. RIEDWEG, Ps.-Justin (Markell von Ankyra?) Ad Graecos De vera religione (bisher "Cohortatio ad Graecos"): Einleitung und Kommentar, 2 vols., Schweizerische Beiträge zur Altertumswissenschaft 25 (Basel 1994), esp. 145–147 and passim.

D. T. RUNIA, 'Philonic Nomenclature', The Studia Philonica Annual 6 (1994) 1–27.

D. T. RUNIA, 'References to Philo from Josephus until 1000 AD', The Studia Philonica Annual 6 (1994) 111–121.

D. T. RUNIA, 'Philo in a Single Volume', The Studia Philonica Annual 6 (1994) 171–182.

D. T. RUNIA (ed.), The Studia Philonica Annual, volume VI, Brown Judaic Series 299 (Atlanta 1994).

D. T. RUNIA, R. M. VAN DEN BERG, R. RADICE, K.-G. SANDELIN AND D. SATRAN, 'Philo of Alexandria: an Annotated Bibliography 1991', The Studia Philonica Annual 6 (1994) 122–159.

B. SCHALLER, 'Philon, Josephus und das sonstige griechisch-sprachige Judentum in ANRW und weitere neueren Veröffentlichen', Theologische Rundschau 59 (1994) 186–214.

G. SCHIMANOWSKI, '"Abgrenzung und Identitätsfindung": Paulinische Paränese im 1 Thessalonischerbrief', in R. FELDMEIER and U. HECKEL (edd.), Die Heiden, Juden, Christen und das Problem des Fremden, WUNT 70 (Tübingen 1994) 296–316, esp. 306–309.

F. SIEGERT, 'Die Heiden in der pseudo-philonische Predigt De Jona', in R. FELDMEIER and U. HECKEL (edd.), Die Heiden, Juden, Christen und das Problem des Fremden, WUNT 70 (Tübingen 1994) 52–58.

M. SIMONETTI, Biblical Interpretation in the Early Church: an Historical Introduction to Patristic Exegesis, (Edinburgh 1994).

D. SLY, 'The Plight of Woman: Philo's Blind Spot?', in W. HELLEMAN (ed.), Hellenization Revisited: Shaping a Christian Response within the Greco-Roman World (Lanham 1994) 173–188.

H. J. SPIERENBURG, H. P. Blavatsky, On the Gnostics (San Diego 1994), esp. 40–50.

C. STEAD, Philosophy in Christian Antiquity (Cambridge 1994), esp. 56–62.

A. TERIAN, 'Had the Works of Philo been newly Discovered', The Biblical Archaeologist 57 (1994) 86–97.

A. TERIAN, 'Notes on the Transmission of the Philonic Corpus', The Studia Philonica Annual 6 (1994) 91–95.

H. TRONIER, Transcendens og Transformation i Første Korintherbrev (Copenhagen 1994), esp. 9–37.

H. TRONIER, 'Om engle og den sunde fornuft: angelus interpres og Logos [In Danish: On angels and common sense: the angelus interpres and the Logos]', in N. P. LEMCHE & M. MÜLLER (edd.) Fra dybet [In Danish:

Out of the Depths]. Festskrift til John Strange. Forum for Bibelsk Exegese 5 (Copenhagen 1994) 253–273.

N. UMEMOTO, 'Juden, "Heiden" und das Menschengeschlecht in der Sicht Philons von Alexandria', in R. FELDMEIER and U. HECKEL (edd.), *Die Heiden, Juden, Christen und das Problem des Fremden*, WUNT 70 (Tübingen 1994) 22–51.

S.-K. WAN, 'Charismatic Exegesis: Philo and Paul Compared', *The Studia Philonica Annual* 6 (1994) 54–82.

R. L. WILKEN, 'Philo in the Fourth Century', *The Studia Philonica Annual* 6 (1994) 100–102.

N. G. WILSON, *Photius The Bibliotheca* (London 1994), esp. 122–123.

D. WINSTON, 'Philo's Nachleben in Judaism', *The Studia Philonica Annual* 6 (1994) 103–110.

A. WOLTERS, '*Creatio ex Nihilo* in Philo', in W. Helleman (ed.), *Hellenization Revisited: Shaping a Christian Response within the Greco-Roman World* (Lanham 1994) 107–124.

1995

W. R. BAKER, *Personal Speech-ethics in the Epistle of James*, WUNT 2.68 (Tübingen 1995), esp. 69–74, 120–121, 168–170, 214–218, 271–274.

P. J. BEKKEN, 'Paul's Use of Deut. 30.12–14 in Jewish Context', in P. BORGEN and S. GIVERSEN (edd.), *The New Testament and Hellenistic Judaism* (Aarhus 1995) 183–204.

R. M. BERCHMANN, 'The Categories of Being in Middle Platonism: Philo, Clement, and Origen of Alexandria', in J. P. Kenney (ed.), *The School of Moses: Studies in Philo and Hellenistic Religion in Memory of Horst R. Moehring*, Brown Judaic Series 304 = Studia Philonica Monograph Series 1 (Atlanta 1995) 98–140.

E. BIRNBAUM, 'What Does Philo Mean by 'Seeing God'? some Methodological Considerations', *Society of Biblical Literature Seminar Papers* 34 (1995) 535–552.

M. BOCKMUEHL, 'Natural law in Second Temple Judaism', *Vetus Testamentum* 45 (1995) 17–44.

P. BORGEN, 'Man's Sovereignty over Animals and Nature according to Philo of Alexandria', in T. FORNBERG and D. HELLHOLM (edd.), *Texts and Contexts: Biblical Texts in their Textual and Situational Contexts: Essays in Honor of Lars Hartman* (Oslo etc. 1995) 369–389.

P. BORGEN, 'Some Hebrew and Pagan Features in Philo's and Paul's Interpretation of Hagar and Ishmael', in P. BORGEN and S. GIVERSEN (edd.), *The New Testament and Hellenistic Judaism* (Aarhus 1995) 151–164.

P. BORGEN and S. GIVERSEN (edd.), *The New Testament and Hellenistic Judaism* (Aarhus 1995).

D. CARABINE, *The Unknown God: Negative Theology in the Platonic Tradition: Plato to Eriugena*, Louvain Theological and Pastoral Monographs 19 (Leuven–Grand Rapids 1995), esp. 191–222.

J. CAZEAUX, "'Nul n'est prophète en son pays' — Contribution à l'étude de Joseph d'apres Philon', in J. P. KENNEY (ed.), *The School of Moses: Studies in Philo and Hellenistic Religion in Memory of Horst R. Moehring*, Brown Judaic Series 304 = Studia Philonica Monograph Series 1 (Atlanta 1995) 41–81.

N. G. COHEN, *Philo Judaeus: his Universe of Discourse*, Beiträge zur Erforschung des Alten Testaments und des Antiken Judentums 24 (Frankfurt etc. 1995).

N. G. COHEN, 'Philo and Midrash', *Judaism* 44 (1995) 196–207.

E. DASSMANN et al., *Reallexikon für Antike und Christentum*, Lieferungen 131–135 (Stuttgart 1995).

> E. Dassmann, Art. 'Jeremia' 543–626, esp. 554–555 (Jeremiah); P. Jay, Art. 'Jesaja' 764–821, esp. 778 (Isaiah); A. P. Bos, 'Art. Immanenz und Transzendenz' 1041–1092, esp. 1073–1076 (Immanence and Transcendence).

J. DILLON, 'Reclaiming the Heritage of Moses: Philo's Confrontation with Greek Philosophy', *The Studia Philonica Annual* 7 (1995) 108–123.

C. DOGNIEZ, *Bibliography of the Septuagint — Bibliographie de la Septante (1970–1993)*, Vetus Testamentum Supplements 60 (Leiden etc. 1995), esp. 82–83 and *passim*.

G. DORIVAL and O. MUNNICH, Κατὰ τοὺς ο'. *Selon les septante. Trente études sur la Bible greque des Septante. En hommage à Marguerite Harl* (Paris 1995).

K. G. EVANS, 'Alexander the Alabarch: Roman and Jew', *Society of Biblical Literature Seminar Papers* 34 (1995) 576–594.

F. FARRELL, 'Philo and the Fathers: the Letter and the Spirit', in *Scriptural Interpretation in the Fathers: Letter and Spirit*, The Patristic Symposium at Maynooth 2 (Dublin 1995).

T. FORNBERG and D. HELLHOLM, *Texts and Contexts: Biblical Texts in their Textual and Situational Contexts* (Oslo 1995).

A. C. GELJON and D. T. RUNIA, 'An *Index locorum* to Billings', *The Studia Philonica Annual* 7 (1995) 169–185.

P. VON GEMUNDEN, 'La culture des passions a l'epoque du Nouveau Testament: une contribution theologique et psychologique', *Etudes theologiques et religieuses* 70 (1995) 335–348.

K. M. GIRARDET, 'Naturrecht und Naturgesetz: eine gerade Linie von Cicero zu Augustinus?', *Rheinische Museum* 138 (1995) 266–298, esp. 292–298.

M. GOULDER, 'Colossians and Barbelo', *New Testament Studies* 41 (1995) 601–619, esp. 608–611.

G. GRÆSHOLT, 'Jødisk tradition i den hellenistisk-romerske verden: Filon', in P. BILDE, T. ENGBERG-PEDERSEN, L. HANNESTAD and J. ZAHLE (edd.), *Jødedommen og hellenismen*, Hellenismestudier 9 (Aarhus 1995) 13–25.

G. GRANATA, *Introduzione allo studio del De vita Mosis di Filone Alessandrino* (diss. Pisa 1995).

M. HEIL, 'Babrius und der erste Konsular des Germanicus', *Klio* 77 (1995) 224–231.

G. C. DEN HERTOG, 'Philo van Alexandrië', *Vrede over Israel* 39.6 (1995).

E. HILGERT, 'Philo Judaeus et Alexandrinus: The State of the Problem', in J. P. Kenney (ed.), *The School of Moses: Studies in Philo and Hellenistic Religion in Memory of Horst R. Moehring*, Brown Judaic Series 304 = Studia Philonica Monograph Series 1 (Atlanta 1995) 1–15.

C. R. HOLLADAY, *Fragments from Hellenistic Jewish Authors: volume III Aristobulus*, Texts and Translations 39, Pseudepigrapha Series 13 (Atlanta 1995)

N. HYLDAHL, 'Betragtninger vedrørende Filons antropolog', in P. BILDE, T. ENGBERG-PEDERSEN, L. HANNESTAD and J. ZAHLE (edd.), *Jødedommen og hellenismen*, Hellenismestudier 9 (Aarhus 1995) 26–42.

L. A. JERVIS, '1 Corinthians 14:34–35: A Reconsideration of Paul's Limitation of Free Speech of Some Corinthian Women', *JSNT* 58 (1995) 51–74, esp. 61–65.

A. KAMESAR, 'Philo and the Literary Quality of the Bible: a Theoretical Aspect of the Problem', *Journal of Jewish Studies* 46 (1995) 55–68.

A. KAMESAR, 'San Basilio, Filone, e la tradizione ebraica', *Henoch* 17 (1995) 129–139.

J. P. KENNEY, *The School of Moses: Studies in Philo and Hellenistic Religion in Memory of Horst R. Moehring*, Brown Judaic Series 304 = Studia Philonica Monograph Series 1 (Atlanta 1995).

K. L. KING, 'The Body and Society in Philo and the *Apocryphon of John*', in J. P. KENNEY (ed.), *The School of Moses: Studies in Philo and Hellenistic Religion in Memory of Horst R. Moehring*, Brown Judaic Series 304 = Studia Philonica Monograph Series 1 (Atlanta 1995) 82–97.

J. LAPORTE, *Théologie liturgique de Philon d'Alexandrie et d'Origène*, Liturgie 6 (Paris 1995).

J. R. LEVISON, 'Inspiration and the Divine Spirit in the Writings of Philo Judaeus', *JSJ* 26 (1995) 271–323.

J. R. LEVISON, 'The Prophetic Spirit as an Angel according to Philo', *HThR* 88 (1995) 189–207.

B. L. MACK, 'Moses on the Mountaintop: A Philonic View', in J. P.

KENNEY (ed.), *The School of Moses: Studies in Philo and Hellenistic Religion in Memory of Horst R. Moehring*, Brown Judaic Series 304 = Studia Philonica Monograph Series 1 (Atlanta 1995) 16–28.

H. MOEHRING, 'Arithmology as an Exegetical Tool in the Writings of Philo of Alexandria', in J. P. KENNEY (ed.), *The School of Moses: Studies in Philo and Hellenistic Religion in Memory of Horst R. Moehring*, Brown Judaic Series 304 = Studia Philonica Monograph Series 1 (Atlanta 1995) 141–176.

M. R. NIEHOFF, 'What's in a Name? Philo's Mystical Philosophy of Language', *Jewish Studies Quarterly* 2 (1995) 220–252.

E. F. OSBORN, 'Clement and the Bible', in G. DORIVAL and A. LE BOULLUEC (edd.), *Origeniana Sexta: Origen and the Bible* (Leuven 1995) 121–132, esp. 130–132.

G. REYDAM-SCHILS, 'Stoicized Readings of Plato's *Timaeus* in Philo of Alexandria', *The Studia Philonica Annual* 7 (1995) 85–102.

D. T. RUNIA, 'Why does Clement of Alexandria call Philo 'the Pythagorean'?,' *Vigiliae Christianae* 49 (1995) 1–22.

D. T. RUNIA, *Philo and Church Fathers: a Collection of Papers*, Supplements to Vigiliae Christianae 32 (Leiden 1995).

D. T. RUNIA, 'Art. 'Logos'', in K. VAN DER TOORN, P. VAN DER HORST and B. BECKING (edd.), *Dictionary of Deities and Demons in the Bible* (Leiden 1995) 983–994.

D. T. RUNIA (ed.), *The Studia Philonica Annual, volume VII*, Brown Judaic Series 305 (Atlanta 1995)

D. T. RUNIA, 'Philo of Alexandria and the Beginnings of Christian Thought', *The Studia Philonica Annual* 7 (1995) 143–160.

D. T. RUNIA, R. M. VAN DEN BERG, J. P. MARTÍN, R. RADICE and K.-G. SANDELIN, 'Philo of Alexandria: an Annotated Bibliography 1992', *The Studia Philonica Annual* 7 (1995) 186–222.

K.-G. SANDELIN, 'Does Paul argue against Sacramentalism and Overconfidence in 1 Cor 10.1–14?', in P. BORGEN and S. GIVERSEN (edd.), *The New Testament and Hellenistic Judaism* (Aarhus 1995) 165–182.

J. M. SCOTT, 'Philo and the Restoration of Israel', *Society of Biblical Literature Seminar Papers* 34 (1995) 553–575.

T. SELAND, 'The 'Common Priesthood' of Philo and 1 Peter: a Philonic Reading of 1 Peter 2:5, 9', *JSNT* 57 (1995) 87–119.

T. SELAND, *Establishment Violence in Philo and Luke: a Study of Nonconformity to the Torah and Jewish Vigilante Reactions*, Biblical Interpretations Series 15 (Leiden etc. 1995).

T. SELAND, 'Philo and the Clubs and Associations of Alexandria', electronic document accessible at ftp://ftp.lehigh.edu./pub/listserv/ioudaios-1/Articles/tsphilo (posted 1995).

D. I. SLY, *Philo's Alexandria* (London 1995).

R. SRIGLEY, 'Albert Camus on Philo and Gnosticism', *The Studia Philonica Annual* 7 (1995) 103–106.

G. E. STERLING, '"Thus are Israel': Jewish Self-Definition in Alexandria', *The Studia Philonica Annual* 7 (1995) 1–18.

G. E. STERLING, 'Philo of Alexandria Commentary Series', *The Studia Philonica Annual* 7 (1995) 161–167.

G. E. STERLING, 'Recluse or Representative? Philo and Greek-Speaking Judaism beyond Alexandria', *Society of Biblical Literature Seminar Papers* 34 (1995) 595–616.

G. E. STERLING, '"Wisdom Among the Perfect': Creation Traditions in Alexandrian Judaism and Corinthian Christianity', *Novum Testamentum* 37 (1995) 355–384.

A. TERIAN, 'The Armenian Translations of Philo', in C. ZUCKERMAN and M. E. STONE, *A Repertory of Published Armenian Translations of Classical Texts* (Jerusalem 1995) 36–44.

A. TERIAN, 'Inspiration and Originality: Philo's Distinctive Exclamations', *The Studia Philonica Annual* 7 (1995) 56–84.

R. TREVIJANO ETCHEVERRÍA, *Origenes del cristianismo. El trasfondo judío del cristianismo primitivo*, Plenitudo Temporis 3 (Salamanca 1995), esp. 134–146.

G. VELTRI, 'Philo and Azaria dei Rossi', *Jewish Studies Quarterly* 2 (1995) 372–395.

N. WALTER, 'Hellenistische Diaspora-Juden an der Wiege des Urchristentums', in P. BORGEN and S. GIVERSEN (edd.), *The New Testament and Hellenistic Judaism* (Aarhus 1995) 37–58.

S. K. WAN, 'Abraham and the Promise of the Spirit: Galatians and the Hellenistic-Jewish Mysticism of Philo', *Society of Biblical Literature Seminar Papers* 34 (1995) 6–22.

G. J. WARNE, *Hebrew Perspectives on the Human Person in the Hellenistic Era: Philo and Paul* (Lewiston N.Y. 1995).

D. WINSTON, 'Philo and the Hellenistic Jewish Encounter', *The Studia Philonica Annual* 7 (1995) 124–142.

D. WINSTON, 'Philo's Doctrine of Repentance', in J. P. KENNEY (ed.), *The School of Moses: Studies in Philo and Hellenistic Religion in Memory of Horst R. Moehring*, Brown Judaic Series 304 = Studia Philonica Monograph Series 1 (Atlanta 1995) 29–40.

D. WINSTON, 'Sage and Super-sage in Philo of Alexandria', in D. P. WRIGHT, D. N. FREEDMAN and A. HURVITZ (edd.), *Pomegranates and Golden Bells: Studies in Biblical, Jewish and Near Easter Ritual, Law and Literature in Honor of Jacob Milgrom* (Winona Lake, Indiana 1995) 815–824.

D. ZELLER, 'The Life and Death of the Soul in Philo of Alexandria: the Use and Origin of a Metaphor', *The Studia Philonica Annual* 7 (1995) 19–56.

1996

M. BALTES, *Die philosophische Lehre des Platonismus: einige grundlegende Axiome / Platonische Physik (in antiken Verständnis) I*, Der Platonismus in der Antike 4 (Stuttgart 1996), esp. 130–131, 409–413.

P. BORGEN, 'Moses, Jesus, and the Roman Emperor: Observations in Philo's Writings and the Revelation of John', *Novum Testamentum* 38 (1996) 145–159.

P. BORGEN, 'The Gospel of John and Hellenism: Some Observations', in R. A. CULPEPPER and C. C. BLACK (edd.), *Exploring the Gospel of John: In Honor of D. Moody Smith* (Louisville 1996) 98–123.

J. CAZEAUX, 'Etre juif et parler grec: l'allegorie de Philon', in C.-B. AMPHOUX and J.-P. BOUHOT (edd.), *Les premières traditions de la Bible*, Histoire du text biblique 2 (Lausanne 1996).

E. DASSMANN et al., *Reallexikon für Antike und Christentum*, Band XVII = Lieferungen 129–136 (Stuttgart 1996).
See above under 1994 and 1995.

J. DILLON, *The Middle Platonists: a Study of Platonism 80 B. C. to A.D. 220: Revised edition with a new afterword* (London 1996), esp. 436–441.

J. DILLON, 'The Formal Structure of Philo's Allegorical Exegesis', in J. GLUCKER and A. LAKS (edd.), *Jacob Bernays: un philologue juif*, Cahiers de Philologie 16 (Lille 1996) 123–131.

J. GLUCKER and A. LAKS (edd.), *Jacob Bernays: un philologue juif*, Cahiers de Philologie 16 (Lille 1996), esp. 21–23, 210–211.

R. KATZOFF [ר: קצוף], 'Philo and Hillel on Violation of Betrothal in Alexandria', in I. GAFNI, A. OPPENHEIMER and D. R. SCHWARTZ (edd.), *The Jews in the Hellenistic-Roman World. Studies in Memory of Menahem Stern* (Jerusalem 1996) 39*–57*.

I. G. KIDD, 'Theophrastus Fr. 184 FHS&G: Some Thoughts on his Arguments', in K. A. ALGRA, P. W. VAN DER HORST and D. T. RUNIA (edd.), *Polyhistor: Studies in the History and Historiography of Ancient Philosophy presented to Jaap Mansfeld on his Sixtieth Birthday*, Philosophia Antiqua (Leiden 1996) 135–144.

A. PIÑERO, J. MONTSERRAT TORRENTS and F. GARCÍA BAZÁN, *Escritos gósticos. Biblioteca de Nag Hammandi I: Textos filosofícos y cosmológicos* (Madrid 1996).

B. POUDERON, 'Apologetica (Suite et fin)', *Revue des Sciences Religieuses* 70 (1996) 224–239, esp. 233–236.

G. SELLIN, 'Die religionsgeschichtliche Hintergründe der platonischen 'Christusmystik'', *Theologische Quartalschrift* 176 (1996) 7–27.

Leiden, Buenos Aires, Luino,
Åbo, Jerusalem, Mainz

REVIEW ARTICLE

ARISTOBULUS: FROM WALTER TO HOLLADAY

Holladay's *Fragments From Hellenistic Jewish Authors Volume III: Aristobulus*

David Winston

Although only five brief fragments from Aristobulus' work survive, they constitute precious evidence for the sole philosophical precursor of Philo known to us by name. Yet, as Carl Holladay has noted in the introduction to his superbly annotated text and translation of the fragments of Aristobulus,[1] the testimony concerning him is sufficiently conflicting to have called his very existence into question, and spawn an unusually wide range of opinion regarding his date (from the 2nd century BCE to the 3rd century CE), provenance (Alexandria, Jerusalem, Cyprus), and religious identity (pagan, Jewish, Christian). The earliest testimony to a Jewish figure named Aristobulus occurs in the letter from Palestine to Egyptian Jews in 2 Macc 1:10–2:18, probably a forgery composed ca. 60 BCE (E. Bickerman, N. Walter, M. Hengel), though some argue for its authenticity and date it to ca. 164 BCE (B. Z. Wacholder, A. Momigliano, J. G. Bunge). The letter describes Aristobulus as a member of a priestly family, a teacher of king Ptolemy (probably in the literary sense, inasmuch as he had written a work addressed to the king), and connected with Egyptian Jewry. From the letter's context, the time-period envisioned is shortly after the Maccabean revolt, so that 'Ptolemy the king' must be assumed to be Ptolemy VI Philometor (181–145 BCE), as it was by Clement of Alexandria who is the first to identify the author Aristobulus with the figure mentioned in 2 Macc 1:10.

Doubts about the authenticity of the ancient testimony concerning Aristobulus were already raised in 1685 by Humphrey Hody, who later became Regius Professor of Greek at Oxford, and Richard Simon, who, under the influence of Spinoza and La Peyrère, launched the whole enterprise of Biblical higher criticism with his *Histoire Critique du Vieux Testament*. Their arguments were further bolstered by scholars like C. A.

---

[1] Carl R. Holladay, *Fragments From Hellenistic Jewish Authors, Vol. III: Aristobulus*, Text and Translations 39, Pseudepigrapha Series 13 (Atlanta: Scholars Press, 1995).

Lobeck, A. Elter, P. Wendland and H. Willrich, so that by the end of the nineteenth century, Leopold Cohen confidently concluded that Aristobulus can be eliminated from the list of Hellenistic Jewish authors. In the twentieth century, the great French historian of philosophy, Émile Bréhier, similarly insisted on the inauthenticity of the Aristobulan fragments, which he felt reflected a clumsy dependence on Philo.

In spite of this chorus of opposition, there were some who continued to maintain the genuineness of the fragments. The chief champion for authenticity in the nineteenth century was the Dutch classicist Lodewijk Kaspar Valckenaer, in his *Diatribe de Aristobulo Judaeo* (published posthumously in 1806). His detailed defense was considerably reinforced by the authoritative voice of the great German historian of Greek philosophy, Eduard Zeller, and the influential work of Emil Schürer, whose *Geschichte des Jüdischen Volkes im Zeitalter Jesu Christi* (3rd–4th ed. 1901–09) began its career in 1874 as *Lehrbuch der neutestamentlicher Zeitgeschichte*. But the most definitive case by far was made in Nikolaus Walter's *Der Thoraausleger Aristobulos* (1964).

Holladay provides us with a clear and succinct account of the scholarly debate.[2] The chief arguments against the authenticity of the fragments revolve around (1) the silence of the tradition prior to Clement concerning Aristobulus, (2) the latter's apparent dependence on the *Epistle of Aristeas* and Philo of Alexandria, and (3) indications of historical anachronism in Aristobulus' account of the Septuagint, in his citation of the pseudo-Orphic poem, and in his pseudonymous verses on the 'sevens'.

To Hugo Willrich it seemed especially unlikely that Josephus would pass over Aristobulus in silence, given that historian's strong apologetic intent, and the testimony of 2 Macc 1:10 could easily be downplayed either by denying that the addressee is the Jewish philosopher Aristobulus, or by noting that no writings are there attributed to him. Arguments from silence, however, are rarely decisive, and as for Josephus, it is well known that he neglects to quote the Hellenistic Jewish historians preserved in Alexander Polyhistor's Περὶ Ἰουδαίων. From another source he mentions Demetrius the Chronographer, Philo Epicus, and Eupolemus, but oddly considers them to be Greek authors, and nowhere does he quote their writings. Moreover, only once does Josephus

---

[2] In summarizing Holladay's account (43–75), I have occasionally added further detail from N. Walter's comprehensive analysis in *Der Thoraausleger Aristobulos: Untersuchungen zu seinen Fragmenten und zu pseudepigraphischen Resten der jüdisch-hellenistischen Literatur*, TU 86 (Berlin 1964). Detailed references to scholarly work referred to in the text by the authors' names only can be found in both publications.

mention his predecessor Philo (*Ant.* 18.259), and then only in connection with his embassy to Rome. All this is in accord with his tendency not to mention the Jewish sources on which he relies. As for Philo's failure to mention Aristobulus, this too is fully in line with his general policy of referring to his predecessors anonymously.

One of the earliest arguments against the authenticity of the fragments was Aristobulus' supposed dependence on the *Epistle of Aristeas*, an argument that was based on his assertion that the Septuagint was a product of the period of Ptolemy II and Demetrius of Phalerum (fr. 3), and his assumption that there already existed a partial Greek translation of the Hebrew Bible before the time of Alexander, from which Plato and Pythagoras could have drawn. (*Ep. Arist.* 30 is ambiguous and could be interpreted to mean that before the making of the Septuagint there already existed an earlier, though imperfect, translation of the Torah). Since the *Epistle of Aristeas* was generally seen as the source of the tradition concerning the origin of the Septuagint, it was concluded that Aristobulus was dependent on the Epistle. Walter has pointed out, however, that it seems more likely that the special form of the Septuagint legend as presented by pseudo-Aristeas was not yet known by Aristobulus. Not once does he mention the number of the translators. Moreover, it is certain that pseudo-Aristeas was not the inventor of this legend, since it only served him as a framework for dealing with the issue of the superiority of Judaism over Hellenism. This is further supported by his spiritualized interpretation of the dietary rules and the section on the seven banquets, which forms the largest single unit of the book. William W. Tarn had already noted that the endings of each answer of the seventy two sages to the king's queries referring everything to God was a tag that was added by pseudo-Aristeas, who in this section was clearly dependent on a source that discussed kingly virtue, though his view that this source was Jewish is unconvincing. Thus acquaintance with the Septuagint legend is no sure indication of Aristobulus' dependence on pseudo-Aristeas, if that legend already existed earlier independently of the latter. Manuel Joël argued that Philo knew nothing of a Greek Torah translation dating before the Septuagint. To this Walter counters that Philo's account is not a historical investigation of old Torah translations, but only an attempt to demonstrate the high worth of the Septuagint, and on other occasions, he does indeed speak of the dependence of older Greek writers on the Torah (e.g., Heraclitus at *Her.* 214, *QG* 4.152). One cannot, therefore, be certain that Philo was unacquainted with the passage in Aristobulus. Moreover, Clement and Eusebius, who knew and cited the Aristobulan passage, nonetheless never made use of his assumption of an earlier translation, although they too held the theory of the literary dependence of Greek writers on Moses (Walter 88–103).

Other similarities between Aristobulus and the *Epistle of Aristeas* involve the common theme of philosophical instruction addressed to a king dealing with questions generated by the Biblical text, the allegorizing of scriptural passages, the use of similar terminology, and reference to the pervasiveness of the divine δύναμις throughout the natural world. But once again, according to Walter, it is more likely that the direction of the influence runs from Aristobulus to the *Epistle of Aristeas* than vice-versa, inasmuch as the form of the tradition in Aristobulus is less developed than its counterpart in the Epistle. It is particularly clear that the allegoresis practiced by pseudo-Aristeas is considerably more sophisticated than that of Aristobulus. Moreover, as to Aristobulus' description of Demetrius of Phalerum (fr. 3.2), he does not mistakenly identify Demetrius as the chief librarian at Alexandria as *Ep. Arist.* 9 does.

As for the relationship between Aristobulus and Philo, Paul Wendland concluded that it was the former who was dependent on the latter. Edmund Stein, however, convincingly refuted this position, pointing out that Aristobulus' allegoresis is rudimentary, hardly advancing beyond Palestinian anti-anthropomorphic allegorizing. Moreover, Aristobulus made no attempt to provide a rationale for the anthropomorphisms of Scripture, whereas Philo is the first to argue for their pedagogical value. Finally, Philo's sophisticated Logos concept with its two polar 'Powers' is entirely lacking in Aristobulus. In addition, Walter pointedly faulted Wendland's tendency to read Aristobulus in terms of the ways in which he seems to have misconstrued Philo's thought, and also noted the absence in Aristobulus of Philo's reading of Scripture on two different levels, and the ethical-psychological form of Philonic allegoresis with its highly distinctive technical terminology.

As to the arguments based on historical anachronism, it has been noted that in referring to the origin of the Septuagint, Aristobulus spoke of the zeal of Ptolemy Philadelphus in that undertaking and its execution under the direction of Demetrius of Phalerum. This is highly dubious, however, in view of the well-known traditon, reported by Hermippus, that Demetrius had been exiled to Upper Egypt by Philadelphus after he had advised Ptolemy I to appoint a different successor (Diogenes Laertius 5.78). Thus, not only was Aristobulus' reference in error, but it was also rather unlikely that such an error could have been committed in a work composed only a century later. Valckenaer (52–55) assumed that in the first two years of Philadelphus' reign Demetrius was still in his good graces, and that only after the discovery of his earlier intrigues was he displaced, while F. Bleek, following several earlier writers, suggested that Demetrius might have played an influential role during the last two years of the reign of Ptolemy I, when Philadelphus was co-regent (Walter 96, n. 1). Such explanations, however, as Holladay has observed, 'are predicated on the assumption that Aristobulus intended to give a historical report. At the level of popular tradition, a connection between Philadelphus[3] and Demetrius is certainly conceivable in the middle of the second century BCE' (p. 68).

As early as Johann Eichhorn, Aristobulus' citation of the pseudo-Orphic poem was seen as an indication of his late date, but it was Anton Elter's detailed treatment that brought this issue into prominence. The problem lies in the fact that the Eusebian recension (C) of the poem includes a section on Moses that is missing in the Clementine recension (B), an omission difficult to explain in light of Clement's apologetic purposes which would have been well served by its inclusion. It was therefore concluded that Aristobulus' version, as quoted by Eusebius, and by implication Aristobulus himself, must have postdated Clement. Although Elter's elaborate sixteen-stage theory to account for the redactional history of the poem failed to convince, his notion of an evolutionary development found favor with many. Walter has suggested that the Eusebian version does not date to the time of Aristobulus but rather originated after the time of Clement, since it was cited in order to illustrate God's creation and sustenance of the world, though in fact other themes, such as God's oneness, transcendence, and inscrutability, are dominant. Moreover, Aristobulus claims to have removed the name of Zeus throughout, but in the quoted poem there is no clear evidence of this. Walter therefore postulates another, stoicising, pseudo-Orphic poem (X) as the one that was originally quoted by Aristobulus. Thus the recensions of pseudo-Justin (A), Clement, and the postulated version are dated by him early, whereas the Eusebian recension was composed between the time of Clement and Eusebius. In this way, he could explain Clement's omission of the Moses verses. This has turned out to be the most controversial element in Walter's interpretation of Aristobulus, for it has been challenged by Clara Kraus Reggiani, Christoph Riedweg, and Roberto Radice.

The final segment of the historical anachronism argument is in reference to Aristobulus' use of forged Greek verses. The set of pseudonymous verses related to the number seven that are attributed by him to Hesiod, Homer, and Linus, was also thought to require a late date, since it seemed very unlikely that in a work addressed to Ptolemy Philometor, Aristobulus would have used quotations attributed to well-known

---

[3] I assume 'Philometor' in Holladay's text is a typographical error for Philadelphus.

Greek poets, whose pseudonymous character could so readily have been detected. Walter has pointed out, however, that among the verses cited by Aristobulus, some may well be genuine (new finds of Homeric papyri have confirmed that the pre-Alexandrian Homeric text was considerably richer than what has been transmitted to us through medieval manuscripts), while others are Pythagorizing verses of either pagan or Jewish origin. It is best to assume a Pythagorean or, as the case may be, a Pythagorizing florilegium, in which various verses from old Epic poets that were suited to number speculation were strung together. Out of these an Alexandrian Jew selected such verses as were related to the number seven, not hesitating in the process to change the 'four' in the genuine Homeric verse to 'seven' (*Od.* 5.262: 'Now the fourth day came and all his work was done'), and also to rework other verses. If the underlying arithmological florilegium had already set forth certain relationships between numbers and the cosmos, these could then readily be adapted to Jewish concerns. In short, concludes Walter, the pseudonymous verses cited by Aristobulus derive partly from Pythagorean circles, and only to a much lesser extent from Pythagorizing Jews (Walter 150–71).

Assessing Walter's overall contribution to the history of scholarship on Aristobulus, Holladay notes the thoroughness with which he examined previous scholarship on the question, his methodical analysis of previous objections to authenticity accompanied by a convincing refutation, and his informed treatment of the various philosophical traditions that had left their imprint on Aristobulus' work. The result has been a sharp reversal of the earlier skepticism with regard to the authenticity of Aristobulus' fragments, and the establishment of a virtual consensus for their genuineness (M. Hengel, A.-M. Denis, P. M. Fraser, J. J. Collins, A. Y. Collins, M. Goodman). It is thus quite conceivable that Aristobulus in the period ca. 176–170, when Ptolemy Philometor was sole ruler yet was still a young boy, composed an exegetical work on the Bible dedicated to the young king. Such addresses to royalty were conventional and it is therefore in no way anomalous that Aristobulus could consider himself as the king's tutor, especially in view of the latter's youth.

Holladay notes that the description of Aristobulus as a 'Peripatetic' appears for the first time in Clement of Alexandria, but that it is not certain whether or not it originated with him. He may have received this designation, as well as the designation of Philo as a Pythagorean, from a tradition developed earlier in Alexandria, and probably deriving from Aristobulus' own reference to the 'Peripatetic school' in fr. 5 as the source for the 'wisdom as a lamp' metaphor. 'The designation is now recognized', says Holladay, 'as an inappropriate designation for Aristobulus, if taken strictly to refer to his membership in the Aristotelian school in Alexandria. Clement's use of the label appears to be quite loose: Aristobulus is a Peripatetic in the same sense that Philo is a Pythagorean'.

In his recent monograph on the pseudo-Orphic poem[4] Christoph Riedweg concludes that either the author of the Aristobulan version and the author of the *De Mundo* drew their theological views from the same Peripatetic source, or what is more likely, the Jewish reviser of pseudo-Orpheus already knew the *De Mundo*, which means that the latter was written at the latest in the first half of the second century BCE (not impossible in view of H. Strohm's demonstration that Theophrastus was the source of much of his physical theory). Furthermore, the fact that the author of the *De Mundo*, whose philosophical views are as much Platonist as they are Aristotelian, attributed his work to Aristotle makes it evident that he considered himself a Peripatetic. Since the views of the reviser of the pseudo-Orphic poem are similar to those of the *De Mundo*, he too could analogously be designated as a Platonizing Peripatetic. It is therefore no argument against Aristobulus' designation as a Peripatetic that his writing contains many Stoic and Pythagorean components.[5]

In his monograph[6] Roberto Radice reaches conclusions similar to those of Riedweg, though, unlike the latter, following in the footsteps of his teacher Giovanni Reale,[7] he considers the *De Mundo* to be a

---

[4] *Jüdisch-hellenistischer Imitation eines orphischen Hieros Logos*, Classica Monacensia 7 (Tübingen 1993). See also the review by N. Walter in the Book Review section.
[5] According to Riedweg, the Jewish reviser is probably Aristobulus himself. The most important indication of this, he thinks, is Aristobulus' statement (fr. 4.7, Holladay 173) that he has exchanged the names for Zeus with the word θεός, thus presenting the contents of the verses 'as was necessary'. 'This makes one sit up and take notice: Was it not also necessary for a Platonizing Peripatetic to correct the statement that God bestows upon mortals not only the good but also the bad, and to modify the assertion concerning God's absolute invisibility by adding that he can be grasped by the intellect and that his effects can be traced in Nature? Aristobulus was all the more prepared to make such changes inasmuch as, in accordance with all the philosophers, he believed that one must have 'pious conceptions of God' (fr. 4.8, Holladay 175)'. It should also be noted that Riedweg, unlike Kraus Reggiani and Radice, denies not only the existence of Walter's 'X' recension, but also that of a separate Clementine (B) recension. See Riedweg 73–101 and H. Strohm, 'Studien zur Schrift von der Welt', *Museum Helveticum* 9 (1952) 137–75.
[6] *La filosofia di Aristobulo e i suoi nessi con il 'De mundo' attribuito ad Aristotele*, Pubblicazioni del Centro di Ricerche di Metafisica: Collana Temi metafisici e problemi del pensiero antico. Studi e Testi 33 (Milan 1994). Although this title is found in Holladay's bibliography, it undoubtedly appeared too late for him to be able to take full account of it in his own study. See also the review by N. Walter in the Book Review section.
[7] See now G. Reale, and A. P. Bos, *Il trattato Sul cosmo per Alessandro attribuito ad Aristotele*, Pubblicazioni del Centro di Ricerche di Metafisica: Collana Temi metafisici e

genuine work of Aristotle. Like Riedweg he believes that the evidence demonstrates that the pseudo-Orphic poem cited by Aristobulus and transmitted by Eusebius, is a revision that was made by Aristobulus himself, and reveals very close correspondences with the *De Mundo*.[8] Moreover, in view of the fact that Aristobulus lived at a time when the esoteric works of Aristotle were still unavailable (Andronicus' edition of the Aristotelian corpus dates from the first century BCE), his reading of the *De Mundo* was shaped only within the context of the exoteric works, in which there was a strong Platonic element.[9]

It should be pointed out, however, that one can account for Clement's designation of Aristobulus as a Peripatetic without having to assume either that the *De Mundo* is a genuine work of Aristotle, or that it had been composed at the latest in the first half of the second century BCE. There is no record of any doubts as to the authenticity of the *De Mundo* until the fifth century CE, when Proclus, citing the work as evidence of Aristotle's views, added the proviso 'if the book *De Mundo* is by him'.[10] Moreover, (Pseudo-) Justin Martyr, in his *Cohortatio ad Graecos*, ch. 5 (PG 6.252), referred to an Aristotelian work 'addressed to Alexander of Macedon', which may be a reference to the *De Mundo*. Clement, who like most Jews and Christians, would have found the *De Mundo* theologically attractive, was most likely aware of this book and undoubtedly took it to be a genuine work of Aristotle, as Apuleius did in the preface to his paraphrase of this Greek treatise, and John Philoponus, who cited it twice as a work of Aristotle.[11] He would certainly have noticed the striking correspondences between the *De Mundo* and Aristobulus, and

---

problemi del pensiero antico. Studi e Testi 42 (Milan 1995).

[8] Riedweg and Radice have undoubtedly arrived at these conclusions independently, since Riedweg's work appeared too late for it to have been used by Radice. P. Moraux, *Der Aristotelismus bei den Griechen*, vol. 2 (Berlin 1984) 42, had already pointed out that, in an introductory sentence, Aristobulus says that Orpheus 'also expounds in this way about everything being governed by the power of God' (fr. 4.4, Holloday 165), and that in the Orpheus citation itself several motifs are echoed that likewise occur in the *De Mundo*, namely that God is unique, perfect, and all things are his work, and that he is invisible, has his abode in the heaven, and wanders about in all things. The δύναμις θεοῦ, however, says Moraux, is not mentioned *expressis verbis*, and nothing points to the antithesis θεός–θεοῦ δύναμις. Radice (127, n. 27) refers to Moraux, but then goes on to offer a much more detailed attempt to demonstrate the very close connections between the pseudo-Orphic poem cited by Aristobulus and the *De Mundo*.

[9] See Radice 11–41.

[10] Proclus, *In Platonis Timaeum commentaria*, ed. E. Diehl (Leipzig 1903–06) 3.272. See J. Kraye, 'Aristotle's God and the Authenticity of *De mundo*: An Early Modern Controversy', *Journal of the History of Philosophy* 28 (1990) 339–58.

[11] Philoponus, *De aeternitate mundi contra Proclum*, ed. H. Rabe (Leipzig, 1899) 174 and 179. See Kraye *art. cit.* (n. 10).

on this basis would have referred to the latter as a Peripatetic. If, then, the *De Mundo* is to be dated either to the first century BCE or to the first century CE, as most scholars believe, the similarities between it and Aristobulus could be attributed to their use of common sources.

We turn now to a closer look at Radice's monograph, in which he seeks to show that the Aristotelian phase of Alexandrian Jewish thought attested by Aristobulus is structurally dependent on the *De Mundo*, whose theory of the divine δύναμις grounded the theoretical foundations of the philosophical exegesis of the Bible. Issues such as the nature of God and the concept of creation were particularly problematic for the Hellenistic Jewish effort to reconcile Scripture with Greek philosophy. Yet in these matters the *De Mundo* either said very little or was content with broad generalities, thus easing the task of the Jewish exegete considerably. Above all, through its distinction between God's οὐσία and his δύναμις, the *De Mundo* provided a valuable philosophical key for unraveling the complex relationship between God and the world and thereby harmonizing the divine transcendence with its world-wide immanence.[12]

Radice discerns three components in *De Mundo*'s theory of the θεῖα δύναμις. The distinction between the divine essence and its power is aimed at removing the anthropomorphic conception of God, allowing

---

[12] That the author of the *De Mundo* did not go into the difficult problem of the relationship between the divine δύναμις and οὐσία, should not surprise us, for, as Moraux has pointed out (*op. cit.* (n. 8) 40), he was not a profound metaphysician or theologian: 'Whether the δύναμις is some sort of emanation from the οὐσία, whether it represents some kind of subordinate hypostasis, whether it is distinguished from the οὐσία *realiter* or is actually identical with it and can be considered a separate aspect of God's essence only from the human point of view, he says not a word and was clearly unconcerned about such matters'. The same, I think, could probably be said of Aristobulus. Moraux has also noted that it is difficult to determine the origin of the distinction between God's οὐσία and his δύναμις, a motif that first appears in Aristobulus and the *Epistle of Aristeas* (132, 143, 157, 236, 248, 252, 268). (For Philo's use of the 'Powers' and its possible sources, see D. Winston, *Logos and Mystical Theology* (Cincinnati 1985) 19). From various testimonies, we see that the δύναμις theory became in the first centuries of the Imperial age the common property of Platonists, Peripatetics, and even Pythagoreans. Pseudo-Onatas knows the contrast between God himself and his δυνάμεις (*De Deo* 139, 5–8), and pseudo-Ecphantus held the view that the θεία δύναμις, which he designated as intellect and soul, was the true cause of the movement of all bodies (Hipp. *Haer.* 1.15). In a doxographical report we hear that Plato considered God the first cause, but that he accepted as the second cause the δυνάμεις that proceed from God (Epiph. *Haer.* 1.6 = *Doxographi Graeci* 588.24–27, cf. Moraux 41–47). On the *De Mundo*, see also H. B. Gottschalk, 'Aristotelian Philosophy in the Roman World from the Time of Cicero to the End of the Second Century AD', in *ANRW* 2.36.2 (1987) 1132–39; J. Mansfeld, '*Peri Kosmou*: A Note on the History of a Title', *VC* 46 (1992) 391–411. In Mansfeld's view, a Peripatetic philosopher of Platonic leanings using a Stoic book-title can hardly be dated earlier than the late first century BCE.

him to 'rule without pain or toil, free from all bodily weakness' (400b6–10). In addition, the author also removes that which is not πρέπον or suitable to the divine dignity, 'for it is more noble, more becoming, for him to reside in the highest place, while his power, penetrating the whole of the cosmos, moves the sun and moon and turns the whole of the heavens' (398b6–10). The latter component orients the entire discourse towards divine transcendence and to a celestial religiosity that severs God from the world. Were this element lacking, the God concept of the *De Mundo* would probably, as in the Stoa, have taken a conspicuously immanentist turn. In the Stoic schema, where the divine power is always connected with God's immanence, the distinction between essence and power and the motif of divine dignity that is tied to it, not only does not appear but has no *raison d'être* in the first place, since it would contradict the presuppositions of Stoic thought. In their system God's essence and his power end up coinciding with the *pneuma* that is diffused throughout the cosmos. Although one might thus be tempted to conclude that *De Mundo* stands in direct opposition to the Stoic view, it would be more correct to say, in view of the fact that the *De Mundo*'s notion of divine transcendence is not absolute, but is based instead on a heaven-earth duality, that it simply differs from it. Aristobulus, on the other hand, holds that God's exalted state (μεγαλεῖον) requires the ascription of all his physical attributes to his δύναμις rather than to God himself. We thus find in Aristobulus all three elements that characterize the position of the *De Mundo* (οὐσία, δύναμις, τὸ πρέπον).

Radice next examines Aristobulus' somewhat obscure interpretation of God's descent on Sinai. While insisting on the facticity of the descent, he asserts that it was not local (μὴ τοπικὴν εἶναι), since God is everywhere (fr. 2.15, Holladay 145). Against this position, Philo contended that there could not be any descent without change of place, and God is beyond all spatiality. Yet, argues Radice, inasmuch as Aristobulus cannot be so incoherent within the short space of a few lines, it is likely that he held a concept of God that permitted a descent without involving any spatial displacement. In light of the *De Mundo*'s δύναμις theory, however, the apparent incoherence dissolves, inasmuch as the descent is to be considered only as a diffusion of the all-penetrating divine power. But if God's power is thus eternally diffused, how can one explain God's special descent on Sinai? The answer is that God is everywhere by natural necessity, and exceptionally, in contravention of natural law, he is able directly to reveal his own majesty (μεγαλεῖον), which in this case corresponds to his essence. For Philo, on the other hand, admitting a real descent is implausible, since for him the concept of μεγαλεῖον has changed, inasmuch as his God is ontologically transcendent and therefore absolutely alien to any local connotation. For him, the divine δύναμις assumes the role of an hypostasis, the Logos with its Powers, a reality that is independent of God.

In short, both the *De Mundo* and Aristobulus have employed the notions of the divine οὐσία and δύναμις and also that of the πρέπον/μεγαλεῖον of God in their efforts to demythologize the deity. But when it comes to the theme of creation, says Radice, we find that Aristobulus, harking back to Scripture, veers from the course taken by the *De Mundo*. According to Aristobulus, it is God who imposes order (τάξις) on the world, maintains it, and activates it (fr. 5.12, Holladay 185). In the *De Mundo* we find that the question of order in the world is treated in a chapter other than the one that treats of God. In chapter 5 (396b29) the author speaks of a single force or harmony that organizes the universe through the mixture of opposite elements. From diverse unmixed elements (air, earth, fire, and water) it has fashioned the entire cosmos, embracing it in a single sphere, thus forcing the opposing elements to come to terms. Here, according to Radice, the author is referring to the static, synchronic order, which is a product of the cosmos itself. In chapter 6 (399a12) the single harmony that is produced by all the heavenly bodies as they sing and dance in concert has one beginning and end, thus converting ἀκοσμία into κόσμος. By a single inclination all things are spurred to action and perform their peculiar functions. This single agent is unseen, but is perceived through its deeds. God thus preserves an order that already exists, yet he may also be considered the creator of an order that can be called dynamic, since it is related to the harmonious development of beings in their respective species, or species in their genera. It is God's function to set the world in motion through his δύναμις.

For Aristobulus, on the other hand, it is God who has established the structural order of all things, heaven and earth and all that is in it, which once having been established remains so fixed for all time: 'For once he arranged all things, he thus holds them together (συνέχει) and presides over their movements (καὶ μεταποιεῖ, lit. refashions or remodels them; Radice translates: 'and makes them evolve') (fr. 5.12, Holladay 185). This final establishment of the order is sealed on the seventh day. Hence the perfection of the number seven, and the fact that all of created reality carries in it the hebdomad as the seal of completed actuality (cf. Philo *Spec.* 2.59). Thus, for Aristobulus, God is both the author of the static order of the cosmos, and also its activating force (Radice, 97–107).

Finally, Radice compares the attempts of both Aristobulus and Philo to justify the value of the Sabbath theologically and exegetically. In *Leg.* 1

Philo describes a model of creation in which the seventh day marks the start of the production of immortal and divine realities, the intellect and the virtues. Man, too, must on the seventh day do what his Creator has done, that is, set aside sensible reality and cultivate the spiritual. Aristobulus, however, follows a different plan. For him, God's activity on the seventh day has no connection with the genesis of virtue. It consists simply, as we have already seen, in the fixing of order, a sort of seal of perfection immanent in all mundane things, and corresponding to their hebdomaticity. There is a relationship between the light of the seventh day in which all things are comprehended and the ἕβδομος λόγος, through which we have knowledge of things human and divine.

In Scripture, the formula 'And God saw that this was good' is missing on the seventh day, since it is a day of God's rest. Aristobulus, however, attributes to God a form of action on the seventh day, and therefore finds himself constrained to tie to this action a corresponding divine reflection as on the other days. This reflection is even more significant than the others, inasmuch as it deals not with a single act of creation, but with all of creation (not simply θεωρεῖν but συνθεωρεῖν). There are traces of such an interpretation also in Philo, in *Opif.* 129, where Gen. 2:4–5 is said to refer to the incorporeal Ideas, by which, as by seals, the sensible objects were molded. Thus both Aristobulus and Philo arrive at the same conclusion: the Sabbath is tied to contemplation and meditation. Yet they follow different paths. In effect, Philo speaks not of God's reflection but of that of Moses on God's work. This is so because Philo had already placed God's noetic activity on day one.

Although one may take issue with some of Radice's positions, such as his assertion that the *De Mundo* is a genuine work of Aristotle, or his conception of Philo's Logos as a reality that is independent of God, he has nonetheless shed new light on the thought of Aristobulus. Indeed, the recent spate of new studies on the Jewish pseudo-Orphic poem and the *De Mundo* and their interrelationships with Aristobulus, have now considerably extended the impact of Walter's decisive contribution to the restoration of one who was formerly a very shadowy figure at best. In this context, Holloday's splendid new edition of the Aristobulan fragments with its exemplary commentary, which now makes them more accessible than ever before, takes on a heightened significance. It provides the scholarly community with precisely the tools that it needs in order to illuminate the Alexandrian Jewish background of the thought of one who ultimately brought Aristobulus' first uncertain and halting exegetical efforts to so brilliant a conclusion.

The Graduate Theological Union, Berkeley

BOOK REVIEW SECTION

Gilles DORIVAL avec la collaboration de Bernard Barc, Geneviève Favrelle, Madeleine Petit, Joëlle Tolila, *La Bible d'Alexandrie. Les Nombres, Traduction du texte grec de la Septante, Introduction et Notes*, Les Éditions du Cerf, Paris 1994. 604 pages. ISBN 2-204-05014-8. 240FF.

This publication is the fifth and most recent in the French series on the LXX under the direction of Marguerite Harl at the Centre Lenain de Tillemont of the Sorbonne. It concludes the first part of a collaborative project on the LXX, which deals with the five Books of Moses or the Pentateuch. All volumes are set up in a similar way with an introduction, a translation of the Greek text, a commentary, and a multitude of scholarly notes. In order of their appearance, the previous volumes are: volume one, *La Genèse* by Marguerite Harl (1986); volume three, *Le Lévitique* by Paul Harlé and Didier Pralon (1988); volume two, *L'Exode* by Alain Le Boulluec and Pierre Sandevoir (1989); volume five, *Le Deutéronome* by Cécile Dogniez and Marguerite Harl (1992). Subsequent volumes will deal with the remaining parts of the LXX: the historical, prophetic and sapiential books.

Eight years ago, three members of the group published a complementary study that outlined preliminary questions connected with the project, gave background information, and provided a substantial bibliography for each step along the way.[1] The study outlined the main incentive for starting the series on the 'Alexandrian Bible': a working tool was much needed not only on the LXX as a Greek translation of the Hebrew scriptures, but on the LXX as a work in its own right. A new approach would not only be beneficial for those interested in the history of post-classical Greek, but also for Hebrew and Greek textual studies, Jewish and Christian exegesis, and Greek Patristic studies. Working tools on the LXX did exist, but were mostly outdated, like the edition of H. B. Swete which was published over ninety years ago.[2] More recent studies on the LXX were not always satisfactory to the authors, either

---

[1] M. Harl, G. Dorival and O. Munnich, *La Bible Grecque des Septante. Du judaïsme hellénistique au christianisme ancien*, Initiations au Christianisme ancien (Paris 1988). See also the article by M. Harl, 'La Bible d'Alexandrie et les études sur la Septante: réflexions sur une première expérience', *VC* 47 (1993) 313–340.

[2] H. B. Swete, *An Introduction to the Old Testament in Greek* (Cambridge 1902), which was revised by R. R. Ottley (New York, 1914; reprinted 1968).

because they primarily offered bibliographic information or else because they left relevant questions unaddressed. Moreoever, important recent discoveries, in particular the Dead Sea scrolls, had changed the map of scholarship considerably. In addition, Jewish non-canonical writings and Aramaic Targumim have received more scholarly recognition over the last thirty years and provided the LXX with an additional and more congenial context.[1]

In the vision of the group, the new tool would not only deal with the history and problems of the LXX text itself, but also with the history of its reception, its exegesis, and its theology. The reception of the Jewish-Hellenistic scriptures is, of course, a major issue, because the LXX as a collection was mainly handed down through its Christian recipients. As is well known, this fate was shared by other Jewish Hellenistic writings like the works of Philo and Josephus. The abandonment of the Greek scriptures by their Jewish audiences may have had multiple causes, but among them certainly was their appropriation by Christian readers. The old and venerable codices of the fourth and fifth centuries—Vaticanus, Sinaiticus, and Alexandrinus—bear clear witness to the success of the tradition in and on Christian terms.

Traditionally in LXX studies, much effort goes into the comparison of the Greek text with its Hebrew model. The problem is which Hebrew model was involved? In addition, comparisons are often made for the sake not of the Greek but of the Hebrew text. This process can go divergent ways: on the one hand, the Greek can be called on to restore obscure parts of the Hebrew; on the other hand, the Greek with its reportedly numerous flaws and even corruptions is there to show the superiority of the Hebrew.[2] One way or another, this line of thinking falls short in a fundamental sense, since the Hebrew text as established by the Jewish Masoretes dates from a later period than the LXX.[3] The Masoretic text began to be established from the second century CE onwards and only reached its normative value towards the end of the ninth century. The discovery of the Dead Sea scrolls, therefore, was an important turning point, because it gave more insight into pre-Masoretic versions of the Hebrew Bible.[4] It has become clear that both the Greek and Hebrew texts evolved in rather complex ways, and that, in comparing the two, simple presuppositions or solutions are no longer tenable. Every book

---

[1] Harl, Dorival, and Munnich, *La Bible Grecque des Septante* 10–12
[2] *Ibid.*, 11
[3] The name stems from the the activities of Jewish scholars, the Masoretes, who intended to give a most accurate biblical text. The term is possibly related to *masar*, to deliver up, but the Hebrew root is uncertain.
[4] Harl, Dorival, and Munnich, *La Bible Grecque des Septante* 10–11

has to be taken on its own merits and with its own characteristics, for these texts, whether Greek or Hebrew did not develop in a monolithic but rather in a fluid way, being the work of constant recopying, revising and re-editing.[1]

The latest volume by Gilles Dorival is the most extensive of the series so far, both in terms of number of pages and detail of analysis.[2] Its lengthy introduction (188 pages) starts with discussions of the unity of the book of Numbers and of its varying subdivisions in modern and in ancient times.[3] The major editions of the Greek text, even the more recent ones, do not offer a justification for their chapter divisions, which do not seem to be based on the manuscript traditions themselves. The divisions of the Hebrew are determined on a practical basis by the cycles of reading.[4] These could be made on the basis of a year-long cycle as in the Babylonian tradition in which the five books of the Torah contained 54 sections, 10 of which (9 in the Samaritan tradition) were taken up by the book of Numbers. A three-year cycle could also be used, as in the Palestinian traditions. In that case there were more or less three times the number of sections.

A discussion of the title of the book provides interesting insights.[5] As is well known, the Greek title, ΑΡΙΘΜΟΙ,[6] is not paralleled in the Masoretic text, since this takes the first word or words of the various books as its titles.[7] In Rabbinic Judaism, however, titles exist that do reflect the contents in a broader sense and that parallel the Greek better. Thus Genesis is *Seper yesirat ha'olam*, 'Book of the Creation of the World'; Exodus is *Seper yesi'at Misrayim*, 'Book of the Departure from

---

[1] *Ibid.,* 11.
[2] Marguerite Harl's first volume on Genesis was 336 pages long, of which 75 were taken up by the introduction. This fourth volume has grown to almost double the length, some 604 pages, of which 188 form the introduction. *Biblia Patristica* (vol.1), on the other hand, shows that the Book of Numbers is the least frequently quoted among early Patristic authors, while the Book of Genesis is predictably the most popular: more than half the quotations of the Pentateuch derive from Genesis. These figures are similar for the Jewish Hellenistic author Philo: more than half the quotations from the Torah stem from Genesis, while the book of Numbers is the least represented.
[3] Dorival, *Les Nombres* 19–35
[4] The unity of a reading is called *parasja* or *sidra* (or in plural *parasjôt* and *sidarim*).
[5] Dorival, *Les Nombres* 32–35.
[6] Under the influence of the Vulgate this title has continued to be used among Christians up to the present. The Vulgate gives both the Hebrew and the Greek titles in its headings; for Numbers it reads: *Incipit liber Vaiedabber, id est Numeri.*
[7] Perhaps appropriately, the titles and subtitles of Dorival's book themselves do not always exactly correspond with what they contain either. These sections are entitled: 'The Unity of the *Greek* (Book of) Numbers', and 'The *Greek* Title and Its Significance', but the Hebrew and Aramaic counterparts are given equal attention, and justly so.

Egypt';[1] Leviticus is *Seper torat hakohannim*, 'Book of the Law of the Priests'; and Deuteronomy is *Seper mishneh torah*, 'Book of the Second Law'. The title of Numbers, however, stands apart from this pattern and does not seem to parallel the LXX title: *homesh happiqqudim*, 'Fifth of the Census (of Soldiers)', since every fifth of the Torah consists of one book.[2] The second word of the title, which has to do with mustering soldiers, is harder to explain as a parallel to 'Numbers', although Dorival does mention that the result is the same, since the counting of soldiers results in numbers.

Subsequent chapters deal with questions involving the Greek text of Numbers, with the scholarly editions of the LXX, and with papyrus 4QLXXNum of cave 4 of Qumran, which contains parts of chapters 3 and 4. The discussion goes on to the relationship between the LXX and the Masoretic text, the Samaritan Bible, and the Peshitta, the Syriac translation of the Hebrew Bible.[3] As a model for the Greek translation, Dorival hypothesizes an independant proto-Masoretic Hebrew text, but he remains uncertain of its geographical associations: was this text brought by Palestinian Jews to Alexandria or was it used in Alexandria to begin with?[4]

In the section on the LXX as translation, important issues of correspondances and divergences from the Hebrew are raised by comparing the terminology in the other books of the Pentateuch, in particular Genesis, Exodus and Leviticus.[5] Dorival comes to a remarkable conclusion that sounds contradictory at first: the translation is both literal and free. On the basis of syntactical comparison, it is literal; on the basis of lexicological criteria, it is free. He notices a tendency in the Greek text to historicize; namely, to embed episodes from the history of Israel into Numbers. He explains this as a exegetical device which is present not

---

[1] It would have been helpful if the sources where these titles can be found had been indicated, in particular in connection with the first two books of the Torah.

[2] As J. Levenson points out to me (personal communication), another indication for a close relationship between the title of the LXX and rabbinic traditions may exist in the prophetic reading (*haftarah*) that accompanies the first *parasjah* from Numbers, *Bemidbar* 1–4. The reading is from Hosea 2:1–22 (MT) and starts with: 'But one day the number of the sons of Israel will be like the sand of the sea, which can neither be measured nor numbered ...'

[3] Dorival, *Les Nombres* 36–47

[4] As the author formulates it, the problem is not clear: 'Ce modèle hébreu original était-il le texte protomassorétique en usage à Jérusalem au IIIè siècle avant notre ère et que les traducteurs venus de Palestine auraient apporté à Alexandrie? Ou bien était-il le texte utilisée par les Juifs d'Égypte' (47). The first statement, it should be noted, does not exclude the second.

[5] *Ibid.*, 48–65

only in the LXX but also in Targum literature. There is a tendency to insert clarifications from other books of the Pentateuch, thus the Bible is explained by the Bible.[1] Dorival describes this as the phenomenon of intertextuality.[2]

Comparisons are made not only with the Hebrew, but also with the Greek. In a section written by E. Lévinas, the lexical connotations and innovations of the Greek of Numbers are discussed. Lévinas points out connections with the language and vocabulary of the political and social realms and of the militairy and judicial systems. A survey of the religious terms conclude this very informative chapter.[3]

A large part of the introduction is filled with a description and analysis of the exegetical tendencies of the Greek text that differentiates it from the Masoretic version.[4] Dorival stresses the originality and independence of this exegesis, although occasionally correspondences reveal themselves with rabbinic traditions, whether Targum, Mishnah, Talmud, or Midrash. He points out that the LXX seems to be the oldest source of the Jewish hermeneutical tradition that has survived. Most of the exegetical features, emerging in topics such as leading personalities, the Levites, and cult language, are presented in a catalogue-like fashion, which does not encourage continuous reading. The specialist who is interested in the Book of Numbers itself or the reader who wants to probe into its linguistic depths will, however, find a treasure trove. For readers with a more general background who are interested in some of the details (but not in all), or users who are interested in one specific problem, a very useful index of Greek words accompanies the volume[5]; their occurrence in the introduction and the commentary proper is effectively distinguished.

It is impossible in this context to discuss the commentary in detail (and the readers should have something left to discover for themselves). Whenever this user was dealing with a passage in a Patristic context quoted from Numbers, she derived great benefit from consulting Dorival's translation and complementary notes. A multitude of passages are discussed both from Hellenistic Jewish and from Early Christian sources—no minor achievement in itself given the vast

---

[1] See also G. Dorival, 'Les Phénomènes d'intertextualité dans le livre grec des *Nombres*', in G. Dorival and O. Munnich (edd.), *Selon les Septante. Hommage à Marguerite Harl* (Paris 1995).
[2] Dorival, *Les Nombres* 66–72
[3] *Ibid.*, 158–74. This author does not appear to be mentioned as a collaborator either on the title page or in the preface, where it certainly would have been appropriate.
[4] *Ibid.*, 78–157
[5] *Ibid*, 581–93

amount of literature in the field. Obviously Origen is preponderant, but Philo and Josephus are also well represented.

One critical note to the publisher and binder: the books should have been bound in a more solid way, since the leaves detach rather easily. Part of the reason may be that the harsh North American climate is too much for French glues, but a valuable working tool should endure in spite of weather and time. This does not detract from the great appreciation felt for Dorival's diligent work and for that of the Parisian group as a whole, whose subsequent volumes are eagerly anticipated. We all benefit very much from their remarkable work!

Annewies van den Hoek
Harvard Divinity School

C. DOGNIEZ, *Bibliography of the Septuagint — Bibliographie de la Septante (1970–1993)*. Supplements to Vetus Testamentum 60. E. J. Brill, Leiden etc. 1995. xxxii + 329 pages. ISBN 90-04-10192-6. NLG189, $122.50.

The predecessor of this volume, compiled by S. P. Brock, C. T. Frisch and S. Jellicoe and published in 1973 (= R-R 1010), essentially covered the period 1900–69 and consisted of 200 pages. This volume covers the much shorter period of 1970–93 and contains no less than 310 pages. It is an indication of the explosion of scholarship on the Septuagint and related studies, not least in France where this work was compiled (see also the previous review on *La Bible d'Alexandrie*). It is also an indication of the difficulty of the task that confronted Madame Dogniez, a task of which she has acquitted herself extremely well. The bibliography continues the method of its predecessor. The items are listed by title only, i.e. without annotations. They are organized systematically in 31 sections, some of which are further sub-divided. These commence with general studies, then deal with editions and translations, the language of the LXX, and the LXX in relation to other writings such as the Hebrew text, Qumran, the New Testament, Philo, Josephus. Then follow sections on the witnesses to the Greek text, the transmission of the text, revisions and new translations, the LXX in relation to the Church Fathers. The longest section lists all the scholarly items focusing on particular books, from the Pentateuch and Genesis to Bel and the Dragon. Finally there are sections on the versions of the LXX in other languages and on illustrations of LXX themes, whether in the mss. or elsewhere.

The compiler of the bibliography emphasizes in her introduction (published in both French and English) that she constantly had to make category distinctions and make judgments on borderline cases. For example it was quite impossible to include all material on biblical epigraphy in Greek and iconography. When items focused on particular books or verses of the LXX she made every effort to include them under the particular book involved. Often this meant including items under more than one section.

There is only one index at the end of the book, namely to authors of scholarly items (including names of editors of composite volumes). This is the work's major weakness. The only access the reader has to the wealth of information which it contains is via the table of contents and the index of authors' names. Obviously an electronic version would allow more detailed searching. An index of names and of biblical passages would certainly also have been a help. But this is much easier said than done, as the reviewer knows from his own experience. In my view this bibliography should be accepted on its own merits with all its limitations. But the future clearly lies elsewhere. Only by means of electronically accessible, fully annotated bibliographies will it be possible for scholars to remain effectively abreast of the vast amount of scholarship being published at the present time. The foreseeable future will bring no relief. Moreover the advent of electronic publishing which is taking place at this very moment will, I fear, complicate the task of the bibliographer enormously.

On pages 82–83 21 studies are cited on the subject of Philo and the LXX. This selection is, I think, a little on the thin side. For example the important French monographs of Nikiprowetzky (1977) and Goulet (1987) should have been included. Nevertheless it is striking how little fundamental work has been done on Philo's use of the LXX during the period of the bibliography. It is a pity that the compiler seems to be unaware of the existence of this Annual. Otherwise she would not have missed three important contributions: M. B. Dick's article on the Ethics of the Old Greek Book of Proverbs in vol. 2, J. R. Royse's contribution on Philo, Κύριος and the Tetragrammaton in vol. 3, and P. W. van der Horst's article on the LXX translation of Ex. 22:28 in vol. 5 (the Dutch version is cited on p. 139). Another important item on Philo's Bible which was not included was the chapter on Philo's Bible in the *De gigantibus* and the *Quod Deus sit immutabilis* by D. Gooding and V. Nikiprowetzky, which is hidden away in the Commentary on these treatises edited by David Winston and John Dillon (= R-R 8358).

It would, however, be most discourteous to end on this critical note. The *per definitionem* never-ending work of the bibliographer is done selflessly in the service of scholarship. I am sure that all scholars working in the field will be immensely grateful to Madame Dogniez for her untiring and meticulous labour. She has supplied us with a truly valuable and lasting instrument of research.

> David T. Runia
> Leiden University

Jan Willem van HENTEN and Pieter van der HORST (edd), *Studies in Early Jewish Epigraphy*, Arbeiten zur Geschichte des antiken Judentums und Urchristentums 21. E. J. Brill, Leiden, 1994. x + 290 pages. ISBN 90-04-09916-6, NLG 130, $74.50.

One of the most important recent advances in the study of Second Temple Judaism has been the work on Jewish inscriptions. Since Baruch Lifshitz' extensive prolegomenon to the reprinting of Jean-Baptiste Frey's first volume, major strides have occurred.[1] This attractive volume makes a significant contribution to the discussion by offering nine interpretative essays exploring a range of epigraphic issues. The articles are selections from among the papers delivered at a conference in Utrecht, 18–19 May 1992. The participants included members of the Cambridge Divinity Faculty Jewish Inscriptions Project, the Tübinger Atlas des Vorderen Orients project, and a number of Dutch scholars. Unfortunately, there were no North American representatives, even though a good deal of work has been done here, e.g., by B. Brooten, L. Kant, and J. H. Kroll.[2] The editors' introduction situates the essays within the framework of advances made within the last twenty years. I should mention that since the publication of their work, D. Noy's edition of Jewish inscriptions from western Europe—including the city of Rome—has appeared.[3]

The essays address three major areas within Jewish epigraphy: the relationship between literary evidence and inscriptions (chapters one

---

[1] J.-B. Frey, *Corpus of Jewish Inscriptions: Jewish Inscriptions from the Third Century B.C. to the Seventh Century A.D.*, volume one: *Europe*, with prolegomenon by B. Lifshitz (New York 1975) 21–107.
[2] B. Brooten, *Women Leaders in the Ancient Synagogue*, BJS 36 (Chico, CA 1982), whose views on Yael in the Aphrodisias inscription are critiqued by G. Mussies (pp. 261–69); L. H. Kant, 'Jewish Inscriptions in Greek and Latin', *Religion (Hellenistisches Judentum in römischer Zeit, ausgenommen Philon und Josephus)*, ANRW 2.20.2 (Berlin/New York 1987) 671–713; and J.H. Kroll, 'The Greek Inscriptions', *The Synagogue at Sardis: Archaeological Exploration of Sardis Report* (Cambridge, MA forthcoming).
[3] D. Noy (ed.), *Jewish Inscriptions of Western Europe*, 2 vols. (Cambridge 1993–95). Volume two is devoted to Rome.

and two), subgenres within inscriptions (chapters three through five), and various historical issues (chapters six through nine). While some of these deal with matters peripheral to Philonic studies, others explore matters of significant concern to Philonists.

The essays of William Horbury, 'Jewish Inscriptions and Jewish Literature in Egypt, with Special Reference to Ecclesiasticus', and Jan Willem van Henten, 'A Jewish Epitaph in a Literary Context: 4 Macc 17:8–10', discuss the relationship between epigraphic and literary evidence. After identifying the extant literary and epigraphic evidence from Egypt, Horbury addresses the thorny issue of the linguistic circumstances of Egyptian Jews. He concludes that there was an Aramaic-speaking segment, but that knowledge of Hebrew was restricted to a limited reading circle. The literary Greek of the metrical inscriptions suggests that the Hellenistic literature of Egyptian Jews was much larger than what is now extant (pp. 20–21, 42). Using Ecclesiasticus and the 114 extant epitaphs of Egyptian Jews as his data base, he argues that there is a surprising degree of similarity between the literature and inscriptions of Egyptian Jews, especially in their 'nihilistic' assessment of death. If he is correct, then Philo's acceptance of the immortality of the soul would be a minority position advocated over against a more common nihilism. Van Henten compares the literary epitaph in 4 Macc 17:8–10 with epigraphic epitaphs. The most interesting aspect of his essay is his identification of the formula ἐνθαῦτα ... ἐγκεκήδευνται (v. 9) with parallel conventions attested almost exclusively in Asia Minor. He cautiously suggests that 4 Macc may have its *Sitz im Leben* in the region, although he does not exclude Antioch of Syria (p. 68).

The next three essays address specific subgenres. Johan H. M. Strubbe, 'Curses Against Violation of the Grave in Jewish Epitaphs of Asia Minor', explores thirteen funerary maledictions from Asia Minor and one from Rome (a Phrygian's epitaph). He challenges Paul Trebilco's argument that pagans had some knowledge and respect for Jewish traditions in Asia Minor by arguing that pagans did not understand Jewish curses.[1] He provides a critical edition of all fourteen curse epitaphs in an appendix (pp. 106–28). Similarly, Pieter van der Horst, 'Jewish Poetical Tomb Inscriptions', not only analyzes the major features of seven metrical inscriptions, but provides the extant twenty metrical texts in an appendix (pp. 142–47). Unfortunately, he does not provide any critical apparatus, although he modifies the texts he cites in several instances.[2]

---

[1] P. R. Trebilco, *Jewish Communities in Asia Minor*, SNTSMS 69 (Cambridge 1991).
[2] He cautions the reader that he has made minor modifications (p. 142 n. 41). I would have preferred explanations for these, e.g., although his basic text for the Leontopolis

Alice Bij de Vaate analyzes the alphabetic inscriptions found in Palestinian graves, 'Alphabet Inscriptions from Jewish Graves'. She persuasively argues that these unusual inscriptions were not abecedaria, but apotropaic formulae designed to ward off either grave offenders or evil demons.

The final four essays wrestle with historical problems. David Noy analyzes the epigraphic evidence for the important Jewish communities of Leontopolis and Venosa.[1] He maintains that neither betrays evidence of the acculturation commonly attributed to them, i.e., Tell el Yehoudiyeh does not hellenize and Venosa does not hebraize. They do, however, have different postures towards the larger culture: whereas the Egyptian community is unconcerned with differentiating itself, the Italian community draws clear lines. One of the most important contributions for Philonists is that of Gert Lüderitz who asks 'What is a Politeuma?' After carefully canvassing the usage of πολίτευμα in pagan contexts, he comes to the organization of three Jewish communities: Alexandria, Leontopolis, and Berenice. He suggests that the problematic phrase τῶν ἀπὸ τοῦ πολιτεύματος of *Pseudo-Aristeas* 310 refers to the Alexandrian (rather than Jewish) civic government. I find his interpretation unpersuasive. The function of the groups mentioned is to certify the accuracy of the translation. While it is *possible* that Pseudo-Aristeas wants us to think that the Alexandrians lent their approval to the translation, I find this far less probable than that the official Jewish civic body placed their *imprimatur* on it. He rightly raises questions about the structure in Leontopolis. This leads him to conclude that the attested Jewish πολίτευμα in Berenice was probably unique—a logical conclusion if he is correct about Alexandria and Leontopolis. Tessa Rajak moves the discussion to the evidence from Rome by raising a number of methodological issues illustrating the problems confronting interpretations of the epigraphic evidence. Gerard Mussies concludes the volume with an article on Jewish onomastics. After surveying the issues peculiar to onomastics, he traces the Goliath family from the Masada evidence and then analyzes the Aphrodisias list. Two of his conclusions are worth special mention. He argues that Ἰαηλ the προστάτης, was not a woman (*contra* B. Brooten) but a man; otherwise she would have been labelled a προστάτις. He also points out that Σαβ(β)άθιος or Εὐσαβ(β)άθιος (both derived from Sabbath) are not necessarily Jewish since Σαμβαθαῖος and

---

inscriptions is W. Horbury and D. Noy, *Jewish Inscriptions of Graeco-Roman Egypt* (Cambridge 1992), his text of *CPJ* 1489=*JIGRE* 114 agrees with neither in places and *CPJ* 1508=*JIGRE* 31 follows *CPJ* rather than *JIGRE* in l. 9.

[1] A subsequent item of note is G. Bohak, '*Joseph and Aseneth* and the Jewish Temple in Heliopolis' (Ph.D. dissertation, Princeton 1994).

Σαββαθαῖος were popular names among Egyptians who probably understood 'brother of the man of honor' by them.[1]

The consistent quality of the essays make this an exceptionally valuable collection. The reference value of the monograph is appreciably enhanced by the two collections of texts by Strubbe and van der Horst. We are indebted to Van Henten and Van der Horst for providing a serviceable work for a field which is in transition from the stage of editions and interpretations of limited ranges of material to larger syntheses with far-ranging implications for our understanding of Judaism. As such it is a worthy companion to Van der Horst's earlier *Ancient Jewish Epitaphs*.[2] While the work does contain an index of passages, it would have been helpful to have an author and subject index as well.

Gregory E. Sterling
University of Notre Dame

Christoph RIEDWEG, Jüdisch-hellenistische Imitation eines orphischen Hieros Logos. Beobachtungen zu OF 245 und 247 (sog. Testament des Orpheus). Classica Monacensia 7. Gunter Narr Verlag Tübingen 1993. X + 136 Seiten.

Roberto RADICE, *La filosofia di Aristobulo e i suoi nessi con il «De mundo» attribuito ad Aristotele*. Con due Appendici contenenti i frammenti di Aristobulo, traduzione a fronte e presentazione delle varianti. Prefazione di Abraham P. Bos. Pubblicazioni del Centro di ricerche di metafisica. Collana–Temi metafisici e problemi del pensiero antico. Studi e testi, 33. Vita e Pensiero, Milano 1994. 240 Seiten. ISBN 88-343-0558-2.

Ch. Riedweg legt hier die Nebenfrucht einer Arbeit über den pseudojustinischen Traktat *'Cohortatio ad Graecos'* (von R. jetzt *'Ad Graecos de vera religione'* betitelt und vermutungsweise dem Markell von Ankyra zugeschrieben) vor, die 1992 von der Philosophischen Fakultät I in Zürich als Habilitationsschrift angenommen wurde. Dieser Traktat, der—wenn die Zuschreibung an Markell richtig ist—aus dem 4. Jh. n. Chr. stammt, enthält eine stattliche Zahl von Gedichten bzw. poetischen Fragmenten unter den Namen berühmter Griechen, die aber seit fast 200 Jahren allgemein als jüdische Fälschungen angesehen werden.[3]

---

[1] He derives -θαῖο- from Coptic *taio*, 'honor' (p. 272).
[2] P. W. van der Horst, *Ancient Jewish Epitaphs An Introductory Survey of a Millenium of Jewish Funerary Epigraphy (300 BCE–700 CE)* (Kampen 1991).
[3] Vgl. N. Walter, Der Thoraausleger Aristobulos. Untersuchungen zu seinen Fragmenten

Unter diesen Texten befindet sich auch ein dem mythischen Sänger Orpheus zugeschriebenes Gedicht, das zwar dieses Namens wegen auch in den Ausgaben der Orphiker-Fragmente abgedruckt wird,[1] aber ebenfalls nach einhelliger Meinung als jüdische Fälschung gilt (ohne daß damit ein Zeugnis für einen jüdisch-orphischen Mysterienkult gegeben wäre, wie einzelne Forscher meinten).

Nach einer 'Bestandsaufnahme' der recht zerstreuten Überlieferung der zum Gedicht gehörigen Hexameter und einer Zuordnung aller Einzelzitate zu den beiden Hauptfassungen[2] (S. 6-24, mit einem übersichtlichen Stemma auf S. 24) bietet Riedweg zunächst den Text und eine deutsche Übersetzung der beiden Hauptfassungen, die er als 'Urfassung' und 'Aristobulische Überarbeitung' bezeichnet, was in etwa den von Otto Kern gedruckten beiden 'Redactiones' entspricht.[3] Über die Zuordnung der fragmentarischen Zitate vor allem bei Clemens von Alexandrien zu den beiden Hauptfassungen hatte Riedweg schon auf S. 14-19 Rechenschaft gegeben. So ergibt sich für ihn, daß die 'Aristobulische Überarbeitung'—da sie bei dem jüdischen Autor Aristobulos (um 150 v. Chr.) zitiert wird—schon um 150 v.Chr. existiert hat, was zugleich bedeutet, daß die 'Urfassung' noch älter sein muß. Sie wird—außer in der pseudojustinischen *Coh. ad Graecos*—auch in einer, ebenfalls dem Justin zugeschriebenen, kleinen Schrift *De monarchia* zitiert, die man früher allgemein als frühchristlich, aber nicht näher datierbar einstufe, für die nun Riedweg aber den recht plausiblen Vorschlag macht, sie als jüdisch-hellenistisch (und aus dem 1. vor- oder nach-christlichen Jh. stammend) anzusehen. Dennoch bleibt es auch für R. dabei, daß Aristobulos (um 150 v. Chr.), die älteste Quelle für eine Fassung unseres 'Orpheus', schon die 'Aristobulische Überarbeitung' bringt, während die (ältere) 'Urfassung' erst viel später belegt wäre.

---

und zu pseudepigraphischen Resten der jüdisch-hellenistischen Literatur, Berlin 1964 (TU 86), Teile II und III.

[1] So bei O. Kern, Orphicorum fragmenta, Berlin 1922 (Riedweg scheint eine in 'Dublin—Zürich' erschienene Ausgabe mit gleicher Jahreszahl zu kennen: S. 113); zwei Fassungen dieses jüdischen Gedichts, die kürzere *'Redactio Iustiniana'* mit 21 Hexametern und die längere *'Redactio Aristobuliana'* mit 41 Hexametern, stehen dort unter den Nummern 245 und 247; unter Nr. 246 wird Material zu einer mittleren *'Redactio Clementina'* zusammengestellt, deren Text aber nicht rekonstruiert wird.

[2] Vgl. die vorige Anm.—Dazu kommt als jüngste Fassung eine frühbyzantische, christliche Bearbeitung, die sämtliche ansonsten bekannten Verse des Gedichts in *einer* Fassung zusammenbringt, was nicht ohne sachliche Spannungen abgeht; diese Sammelrezension steht in der sog. 'Tübinger Theosophie', die aus der Zeit um 500 stammt. Da sie anerkanntermaßen für das Verständnis des jüdisch-hellenistischen Textes als eines solchen nichts Eigenes austrägt, wird sie auch von R. nur im Rahmen der 'Bestandsaufnahme' registriert (S. 19-23), aber dann nicht mehr eigens behandelt.

[3] Vgl. oben Anmerkung 2.

Das ist natürlich theoretisch nicht auszuschließen (S. 3 u.ö.). Problematisch wird die Sache aber angesichts des unleugbaren Sachverhalts, daß Clemens von Alexandrien an verschiedenen Stellen aus beiden Fassungen des Gedichts zitiert, aber dennoch die 'Spitzensätze' der 'Aristobulischen Überarbeitung', die sicher auf Mose zu deuten sind, nicht kennt (während er die Schrift des Aristobulos mehrfach zitiert). Natürlich hat Riedweg recht mit der Meinung, daß wir Clemens nicht postum zwingen können, etwas zu tun, was wir gerne hätten (S. 4)—eben die von ihm zitierten Verse wirklich komplett wiederzugeben. Clemens zitiert in Strom. V 123-124 eine ganze Passage aus der überarbeiteten Fassung; aber es fehlen in diesem Zitat jene zwei Zeilen, die die auf Abraham gemünzte Fassung (wie Clemens ganz richtig versteht, der sagt, Orpheus rede hier 'von Abraham oder seinem Sohn' [Isaak]) nun auf Mose übertragen. Clemens markiert sonst ganz deutlich, wo er beim Zitieren abkürzt oder etwas überspringt; aber an der genannten Stelle weist er nicht auf dergleichen hin, so daß aller Grund zu der Annahme besteht, daß sein 'Orpheus'-Exemplar der überarbeiteten Fassung die Mose-Verse nicht enthielt.[1] Das ist gewiß ein *argumentum e silentio*, aber meiner Meinung nach ein solide begründetes. Das bedeutet jedoch, daß man mit einer dem Clemens vorliegenden 'Abraham-Überarbeitung' rechnen muß, von der die 'Mose-Überarbeitung' zu trennen ist; die letztere ist uns erst durch Euseb innerhalb eines Aristobulos-Zitats (Praep. Ev. XIII 12,5) bekannt. Riedweg meint hingegen, daß Clemens die zwei Verse übersprungen habe, 'weil ihm die Anspielung auf Moses zu direkt war' (S. 17). Aber warum sollte er in Bezug auf Mose als einen, dem sich Gott selbst zu erkennen gegeben habe, heikler sein als bei Abraham? Stattdessen erkennt Riedweg in den vom 'aristobulischen' Bearbeiter hinzugefügten Zeilen Anspielungen *sowohl* auf Abraham *als auch* auf Mose (S. 52. 55 usw.); damit würde dann die Frage unbeantwortbar, ob das Gedicht in der überarbeiteten Fassung Abraham *oder* Mose als den 'Einzigen' (!), dem sich Gott zu erkennen gegeben habe, meint. Daß auf diese Weise eine geschlossene Interpretation dieser Fassung erreicht werden kann, scheint mir doch sehr fraglich zu sein. Doch will ich die Auseinandersetzung um die Anzahl von anzunehmenden Rezensionen des jüdischen Pseudo-Orpheus hier nicht weiterführen;

---

[1] Diese Erwägung hat Carl R. Holladay in einem Manuskript 'The Textual Tradition of Pseudo-Orpheus: Walter or Riedweg?', das er mir Ende 1955 freundlicherweise zusandte, noch einmal nachdrücklich unterstrichen (p. 17-20; der Titel des Aufsatzes meint übrigens nicht, daß H. einem der beiden Genannten einseitig beistimmt). Übrigens wird Volume IV von Carl R. Holladay's 'Fragments from Hellenistic Jewish Authors', der dem jüdisch-orphischen Gedicht in seinen vier Rezensionen in subtiler Analyse gewidmet ist, demnächst erscheinen.

Riedweg stellt meine Auffassung auf S. 73-79 dar[1] und setzt sich mit meiner Argumentation auseinander, freilich mehr mit Einzelheiten dieser Argumentation als mit den für meine Sicht grundlegenden und übergreifenden Erwägungen, da er die grundsätzliche Möglichkeit, die Geschichte des Gedichts als eine Folge von vier (oder unter Einrechnung der jüngsten, christlichen Bearbeitung in der Tübinger Theosophie: fünf) Fassungen zu sehen, schon zu Anfang, bei der 'Bestandsaufnahme' (S. 6-24), abgeblockt hatte. Eine Feststellung Riedwegs sei hier erwähnt, die aber wohl nicht nur mich betrifft, sondern—*mutatis mutandis*—auch ihn selbst: er meint, ich hätte mich von der (stark analytischen) 'Denkweise Anton Elters ... bei aller Kritik im einzelnen noch nicht genügend freigemacht' (S. 78). Das ist wohl ganz richtig; ich hatte es mir tatsächlich als 'Verdienst' angerechnet, die 'erstaunliche Vielzahl von Rezensionen unseres Gedichts' nach Elter (so R., ebd.) auf (nur!) vier bzw. fünf Fassungen reduziert zu haben. Umgekehrt steht es so, daß Riedweg eben bei der Darbietung der beiden Hauptfassungen durch Otto Kern (s. oben) einsetzt und an diesem Modell (aus dem er die von Kern selbst schon stiefmütterlich behandelte *'Redactio Clementina'* ganz ausblendet)—'bei aller Kritik im einzelnen'—festhält, ohne daß eine andere Gesamtsicht noch viel Chancen hätte.

Überhaupt fragt Riedweg weniger danach, *wer* in der 'Aristobulischen Überarbeitung' gemeint sei, als danach, *was* in ihr ausgesagt wird. Und das ist natürlich weit wichtiger, ebenso wie auch die von Riedweg mit Nachdruck gestellte Frage nach der 'Gattung' des vorliegenden Textes. Hier hat er wohl recht mit der Meinung, daß man sich bisher mit der Bestimmung als 'Testament' (in der ältesten Quelle für die Urfassung, der Schrift *De monarchia*) zu schnell zufriedengegeben hat. Er sieht das Gedicht in Analogie zu anderen orphischen Texten, zumal solchen, die unter dem Titel *'Hieros Logos'* gehen, als Imitation eines Mysterientextes an, der nach der Einleitung (V. 1-2) nur dem Musaios als 'Geheimlehre' übergeben wird, aber vor 'Ungeweihten' nicht publiziert werden soll (S. 44-55). Ob damit nicht auch die Vorstellung verbunden werden kann, daß es sich um eine letztgültige, Früheres revidierende und insofern 'vermächtnishafte' Äußerung des 'Orpheus' handelt, will ich hier nicht weiter erörtern. Schade ist es aber, daß Riedweg genauso wenig wie seinerzeit ich auf den Gedanken gekommen ist, das Gedicht mit dem

---

[1] Nachdem er schon gleich auf S. 2 seiner Arbeit meine Argumentation pauschal als 'wenig stichhaltig' eingestuft hatte.—Meine Auffassung hatte ich in der oben (Anm. 1) genannten Arbeit entwickelt (S. 225-241); noch einmal habe ich sie, leichter zugänglich, dargestellt in: Jüdische Schriften aus hellenistisch-römischer Zeit, hrsg. v. W. G. Kümmel [= JSHRZ], Bd. IV, Lfg. 3, Gütersloh 1983, S. 217-226. Eine Art 'mittlerer Lösung' wird C. R. Holladay bieten (s. vorige Anm.).

Corpus der 'Orphischen Hymnen'[1] zu konfrontieren. Sie werden schon in der überlieferten Überschrift der Sammlung 'an Musaios' adressiert und beginnen mit einem Gebet, einer 'Art Mustergebet von 44 V[ersen], das O[rpheus] dem angeredeten Freunde oder Schüler empfiehlt' und das sich an etwa 80 Gottheiten bzw. Mächte oder Hypostasen (wie 'Nomoi' oder 'Physis') richtet und spürbar von stoischer Philosophie, aber kaum von spezifisch 'orphischen' Elementen beeinflußt ist.[2] Einem solchen 'polytheistischen' Orpheus würde in unserem Gedicht ein 'monotheistischer' gegenübergestellt, unter Adressierung an den gleichen 'Freund oder Schüler' Musaios (daß 'Kind' in der Anrede an ihn [Zeile 2] nicht unbedingt 'Sohn' heißen muß, sagt Riedweg auf S. 48, gewiß mit Recht). Freilich entstand die Sammlung (nach K. Ziegler) frühestens im 2. Jh. n. Chr. Was das für einen Zusammenhang mit unserem jüdisch-orphischen Gedicht und eventuell auch für das Alter des (nach R. deutlich älteren) Zeugen des jüdischen Orpheus (die Schrift *De monarchia*) bedeutet, müßte man überlegen; aber die Adressierung an den gleichen Musaios und die antithetische Bezugnahme auf seinen horrenden Polytheismus (die Einleitung in *De monarchia* spricht freilich von 360, Theophilos gar von 365 Göttern) können doch wohl kaum Zufall sein. Und die Annahme einer bewußten Imitation von orphischen *Hieroi Logoi* einerseits und andererseits die Feststellung, es handele sich um ein quasi 'letztgültiges Vermächtnis', mit dem 'Orpheus' alles zuvor von ihm Gelehrte außer Kraft setzt (so in *De monarchia*, *Cohortatio ad Graecos* und bei Theophilos), widersprechen einander durchaus nicht; mit der Elle einer präzisen Gattungsbestimmung muß man den Ausdruck 'Testament' ja nicht unbedingt messen.

Wichtiger aber scheint mir an der anzuzeigenden Arbeit zu sein, daß sich Riedweg stärker als andere (den Rez. voll eingeschlossen) um eine genauere Analyse des 'philosophischen' oder 'theologischen' Inhalts bemüht.[3] Riedweg identifiziert den Autor der Urfassung als einen hellenistischen Juden (S. 55-62) und den philosophischen Hintergrund der Urfassung als stoisch (S. 62-64), den des Überarbeiters der 'aristobulischen' Fassung aber als platonisch-aristotelisch (S. 79-95). Hier spielt vor allem der Vergleich mit der (pseudo-aristotelischen) Schrift *De mundo* eine wichtige Rolle (S. 89ff), und es ist sehr dankenswert, daß

---

[1] W. Quandt (Hrsg.), Orphei Hymni, Berlin 1941; ³1962. Diese an 87 Götter bzw. ihnen zugeordnete Mächte gerichteten Hymnen werden nicht unter die Orphischen Fragmente gerechnet, sind also auch in der Ausgabe Kerns (s. oben Anm. 2) nicht enthalten.
[2] K. Ziegler, im Art. Orphische Dichtung, Kl. Pauly IV, 1972, 356-362, spez. 357.
[3] Übrigens ist auch auf die umfangreiche Nachweisung der Benutzung 'epischen Formelguts' bei Pseudo-Orpheus (Riedweg S. 64-73) besonders aufmerksam zu machen.

Riedweg diesen Beziehungen genauer nachgeht[1] und außerdem auch Bezüge auf platonische Dialoge (bes. Timaios, aber auch Phaidros; S. 82ff) feststellt. Man wird Riedweg darin zustimmen, daß dieser Aufweis des Hintergrunds für alle Zusätze der einen (oder—nach meiner Ansicht—drei) Überarbeitung(en) ein gemeinsamer ist, der besser als 'aristotelisch' (mit stoischen Anteilen) zu kennzeichnen ist, nicht einfach als 'stoisch', wie ich es tat. Das entspricht eben der geistigen Nähe zur Schrift *De mundo*.

Freilich möchte R. nun das Alter dieses pseudo-aristotelischen Traktats ziemlich weit hinaufrücken, nämlich 'im Lichte der Parallelen mit der aristobulischen Überarbeitung' des Pseudo-Orpheus in das 2. Jh. vor Chr. (S. 90), während üblicherweise der Traktat etwa um 100–150 n.Chr. oder wenigstens in der Zeit Philons angesetzt wird. Das ist eine neue Sicht, bei der Riedweg—wie gleich zu zeigen sein wird—auch von anderer Seite Unterstützung bekommt. Zu meiner Sicht von der Entstehung der Überarbeitung(en) (im 1. Jh. n. Chr. oder kurz danach) paßt die geläufige Ansetzung von *De mundo* natürlich besser, und insofern hängt sehr viel an der Frage, ob die 'aristobulische' Redaktion des Gedichts tatsächlich schon ins 2. Jh. vor Chr. gehört. Wenn freilich sich auch besondere Beziehungen zwischen *De mundo* und dem *Kontext* bei Aristobulos aufzeigen ließen, wäre die Lage allerdings anders; dann würde sich auch die Ansetzung der 'aristobulischen Überarbeitung' des Orpheus-Gedichts in das 2. Jh. vor Chr., also in die Zeit des jüdischen Autors Aristobulos selbst (wobei Riedweg dahin tendiert, den Überarbeiter mit Aristobulos selbst gleichzusetzen: S. 95-101) tatsächlich nahelegen. Es hängt hier eben eins am anderen (so sieht es auch Riedweg am Schluß seiner Arbeit, S.105f.).

Aber wichtiger als die Frage der zeitlichen Ansetzung sind die geistes- bzw. philosophiegeschichtlichen Zusammenhänge, die Riedweg aufzeigt und die zum besseren Verständnis des Gedichts wesentlich beitragen. Vor allem bietet sich in *De mundo* ein Vergleichstext an, der einen strikten Monotheismus vertritt, und zwar im Unterschied zur Stoa nicht als Deismus, der Gott und Physis (bzw. Kosmos) letztlich identifiziert, sondern strikt zwischen Gott und Kosmos scheidet, was der (hellenistisch-)jüdischen Sicht von der Welt als Schöpfung Gottes stark entgegenkommt. Und so wird man die Arbeit Riedwegs auf jeden Fall hinsichtlich der durch sie ermöglichten genaueren Interpretation

---

[1] Ich hatte auf die auffällige Nähe beider Texte (vor allem zu der von mir hypothetisch rekonstruierten 'stoisierenden Rezension X') nur erst hingewiesen (JSHRZ IV [s. oben Anm. 6] S, 224 mit Anm. 43), was Riedweg (S. 89 Anm. 270) durchaus anerkennt. Doch lag hier in meinen Augen nach dem damaligen Forschungsstand kein Argument für eine so frühe Ansetzung beider Texte vor.

dieses merkwürdigen, aber jedenfalls bemerkenswerten hellenistisch-jüdischen Pseudepigraphons dankbar begrüßen.

Die andere zu besprechende Arbeit von Roberto Radice rückt nun den Vergleich zwischen Aristobulos und *De mundo* noch stärker in den Mittelpunkt und vergrößert damit die Bezugsbasis für diesen Vergleich über das pseudo-orphische Gedicht hinaus. Radice kennt und nennt die Arbeit Riedwegs noch nicht, und schon insofern ist die gleichzeitige Bearbeitung der gleichen Fragestellung bemerkenswert genug. Auch Radice möchte *De mundo* einer erheblich früheren Zeit zuordnen, als es bisher üblich ist, nämlich der Zeit vor der Mitte des 2. Jh., ja gar dem Ende des 3. Jh. v. Chr. Damit geht er nicht ganz so weit wie D. M. Schenkelveld (Elenchos 12, 1991, 221-255), der mit einer sprachlich-stilistischen Untersuchung zu dem Ergebnis kommt, daß die Möglichkeit bestehe, die Schrift doch dem Aristoteles selbst oder wenigstens seinem direkten Umfeld zuzuweisen. Immerhin meint auch Radice, daß die Argumente, mit denen *De mundo* dem Aristoteles abgesprochen wird, schwächer seien, als üblicherweise angenommen wird.

Radice möchte zeigen, daß (a) Aristobulos insgesamt (einschließlich des Pseudo-Orpheus-Gedichts) von *De mundo* abhängig ist (Kap. I; daher die oben genannte zeitliche Ansetzung), daß (b) das pseudo-orphische Fragment in der überarbeiteten 'aristobulischen' Fassung zum Text des Aristobulos gehört (Kap. II, in Auseinandersetzung mit meiner Auffassung) und auch seinerseits von *De mundo* abhängig ist (die Beziehungen beider Texte zueinander werden gesondert untersucht in Kap. V), daß (c) die gelegentlich erwogene Zuweisung dieser Schrift an einen hellen-istisch-*jüdischen* Autor nicht in Frage kommt (diesem Nachweis ist eine Untersuchung des Begriffs δύναμις [θεοῦ] gewidmet: Kap. III); dazu dient auch eine Untersuchung des Themas 'Ordnung und Geschöpflichkeit der Welt' in Kap. IV.

Dies alles steht aber im Dienste einer noch weiter ausgreifenden These: daß nämlich hinsichtlich der 'Philosophie' des Aristobulos und der Philons von Alexandrien ein Unterschied in der gedanklichen Entwicklung festzustellen sei, der so m. W. bisher noch nicht gesehen worden ist. Ich hatte meinerseits aufgezeigt, daß die Methode der allegorischen Auslegung bei Aristobulos erst in den Anfängen steckt im Gegenüber zu ihrer viel weiter entwickelten Anwendung bei Philon.[1]

---

[1] Vgl. meine in Anm. 1 genannte Arbeit, S. 124-149. Zur Entwicklung der jüdisch-alexandrinischen Allegoristik vgl. inzwischen die Darstellung von F. Siegert, Drei hellenistisch-jüdische Predigten, Bd. II, Tübingen 1992 (WUNT 61), S. 55-91; darin (S. 75-79) auch ein Exkurs 'Der sichtbare Zeus und der unsichtbare Gott der Bibel'.

Radices Sicht führt weit darüber hinaus und untersucht in diesem Sinne auch die philosophischen Ansichten, vor allem zur Kosmologie. An sich ist die Annahme einer Entwicklung von Aristobulos hin zu Philon bei dem Zeitabstand zwischen diesen beiden 'Eckpunkten' jüdisch-alexandrinischer Philosophie bzw. Theologie (ca. 2 Jahrhunderte) ja gar nicht verwunderlich, sondern a priori einleuchtend. Schwierig ist nur der Umstand, daß der Bestand an erhaltenen Texten (Aristobulos: wenige Fragmente—gegenüber mehreren Bänden an erhaltenen Schriften Philons) sehr ungleich ist. Dessen ist sich Radice voll bewußt; er spricht von einer Brücke (über die zwei Jahrhunderte hinweg), die auf der einen Seite einen sehr soliden, auf der anderen Seite aber einen recht wackeligen Pfeiler hat. Aber das schließt ja nicht aus, daß man die Frage des philosophiegeschichtlichen Unterschieds stellt und sinnvoll zu bearbeiten versucht. Das Ergebnis geht bei Radice dahin, daß Aristobulos unter dem Einfluß von (Pseudo-)Aristoteles' *De mundo* tatsächlich eher als Aristoteliker eingeordnet werden kann, wie das auch der Bezeichnung als 'Peripatetiker' durch die Kirchenväter Clemens und Eusebios entspricht,[1] während bei Philon eine stärkere Hinwendung zu Platon deutlich erkennbar ist. Voraussetzung dafür ist auch eine andere philosophiegeschichtliche Einordnung der Schrift *De mundo*, die man früher eher der Stoa als dem Peripatos zuordnete, die nun aber sowohl von Riedweg wie auch—noch stärker—von Radice als wesentlich aristotelisch angesehen wird. Man muß sich zwar insoweit, als bei dieser Zuordnung das pseudo-orphische Gedicht als originaler Bestandteil des Aristobulos-Fragments 4 eine ziemlich große Rolle spielt, des Risikos bewußt bleiben, das in dieser Hinsicht meiner Meinung nach immer noch besteht; aber auch, wenn man die 'aristobulische' Rezension des jüdischen 'Orpheus' erst in der Zeit zwischen Clemens und Eusebios entstanden denkt, muß deswegen die von Radice vertretene Sicht von der Entwicklung der alexandrinisch-jüdischen Theologie bzw. ihrer griechisch-philosophischen Beimengungen keineswegs hinfällig sein. Freilich müßte bei dieser Sicht wohl die Frage nach den stoischen Einflüssen noch genauer bearbeitet werden, als das jetzt bei Radice geschah.

Es ist bemerkenswert, welch starke Beachtung die vorphilonische Epoche der jüdisch-alexandrinischen Literatur in letzter Zeit gerade auch in der italienischen Philologie seit den Arbeiten von C. Kraus Reggiani (1973 und 1982) und C. Angelino u. a. (1983) findet. Radice gibt seiner Arbeit Text und Übersetzung der Fragmente des Aristobulos bei

---

[1] Ich hatte den Wert dieser Charakterisierung seinerzeit (s. oben Anm. 1, S. 10-13) wohl zu gering veranschlagt.

und erleichtert damit dem Leser den Zugang zum Originaltext. Seine Arbeit scheint mir für eine neue Gesamtsicht des alexandrinisch-jüdischen Hellenismus so bedeutsam zu sein, daß ich eine (englische oder deutsche) Übersetzung des Buches gern anregen möchte. Jedenfalls gebührt Radice ebenso wie Riedweg Dank für das neue Licht, das mit ihren Arbeiten auf das hellenistische Judentum vor und bei Philon geworfen wird und das die weitere Forschung ganz gewiß befruchten wird.

Nikolaus Walter
Jena/Naumburg (Saale)

David I. BREWER, *Techniques and Assumptions in Jewish Exegesis before 70 CE*, Texte und Studien zum antike Judentum 30, Tübingen, J.C.B. Mohr (Paul Siebeck), 1992. xiii + 209 pages. ISBN 3-16-145803-6. $155.

A basic assumption of this book is that it is somehow possible to speak of a difference between exegesis before and after 70 CE. Obviously, this is a somewhat arbitrary distinction, but 70 is such a significant date that we can use it to mark the diversification of the types of exegesis. The four main modes of interpretation which Brewer considers are: *peshat*, nomological, ultra-literal, and *derash*. The exegetical techniques discussed in the book are the *middoth* named in the lists of Hillel, Ishmael, Eliezer, and others.

In the first part of the book Brewer considers the exegesis of the scribes, meaning by scribes the rabbis before 70 CE. In the second part many kinds of exegetes of the bible are grouped under the sobriquet 'non-scribes'. These include Josephus, Philo, the *Dorshe Reshumot* ('Interpreters of Signs/Symbols') and the *Dorshe Hamurot* ('Interpreters of Difficulties'), Qumran texts, apocalyptic and wisdom literature.

According to Brewer the scribes have a nomological approach to scripture so that all the bible is considered as a law written by God. This approach is based on five main assumptions:

(1)   scripture is totally self-consistent;
(2)   every detail in scripture is significant;
(3a) scripture is understood according to its context;
(4a) scripture does not have a secondary meaning;
(5a) there is only one valid text form of scripture.

Non-scribes on the other hand have an inspired approach as they consider all scripture, translations, and exegesis as inspired. Their first two assumptions are the same as those of the nomological approach; however, the other three are different:

(3b) scripture may be interpreted contrary to or without regard to context;
(4b) scripture has secondary meanings;
(5b) variant texts and translations are valid forms of scripture.

Philo of Alexandria is one of the authors studied among the 'non-scribes'. Brewer devotes a chapter to him (198–212), in which he cites with approval those scholars who read Philo's work as an attempt to provide a systematic exposition of the Pentateuch. The author analyzes the main problems that Philonic scholarship has debated (and is still debating). Did Philo know Hebrew? Did he know Palestinian halakhic traditions? What are the Hellenistic influences on his thought? Is it possible to uncover his sources? Is there any evidence of Philo using techniques similar to the *middoth* of the later rabbis, in particular *gezerah shavah*, reversal of text order, and *notariqon*? A large part of the analysis deals with allegory and with Philo's attempt to find philosophical truths behind the primary meaning of the text. Philo distinguishes between the extreme allegorists who deny the validity of the Law and those allegorists, like himself, who look for hidden meanings, try to clarify symbols, and study textual details for the sake of finding the true meaning of the Torah. Besides the extreme allegorists, Philo also criticises the literalists who reject allegorical interpretations. To identify these literalists is not easy. According to some scholars they could be Palestine rabbis, Pharisees, in particular, or conservative Jews in Alexandria. They could also be exegetes from whom Philo learnt the techniques of minute analysis of the text, similar to later *middoth*. In any case, Philo is critical of them and of those who do not look for the true meaning hidden in the words, attaining only γλισχρολογία ('petty quibbling'). At the same time he probably learned from all these exegetes; his sources are various and cannot all be specified. We cannot be certain whether he learned his methods of interpretation from Greek sources as Daube and Lieberman maintain, or whether exegetical techniques were brought to Alexandria from Palestine or vice versa. We can only point to Philo's basic approach with certitude: scripture is inspired; exegesis must be inspired too, since exegesis also comes directly from God. Brewer points out that according to Philo the whole Bible, including the Law, is prophecy. Scripture is self-consistent and apparent contradictions must be explained. 'Whenever unacceptable nonsense such as mythological elements, anthropomorphisms, contradictions, grammatical difficulties such as spelling errors, strange sentence constructions, or even poor style such as needless repetition occur in scripture, they indicate—

according to Philo—that prophetic irrationality was involved at this point and therefore that allegory had to be used in order to extract the inspired but obscured message' (p. 209).

Francesca Calabi
University of Pavia

Jonathan COHEN, *The Origins and Evolution of the Moses Nativity Story*, Studies in the History of Religion 58. E. J. Brill, Leiden 1993. viii + 205 pages. ISBN 90-04-09652-3. NLG132.50, $86.

Reactions to the limitations of historical-critical methodology have taken various turns. One of the most important is the replacement of source criticism with literary analyses. Jonathan Cohen has consciously moved in this direction by following the hermeneutical lead of Samuel Loewenstamm who has developed a form of *Traditionsgeschichte* based on the form critical work of H. Gunkel and the comparative work of scholars like U. M. D. Cassuto. The task as Cohen practices it is to explore the evolution of a narrative through the analysis of its 'story patterns'. A story pattern refers to a cluster of motifs as they can be recovered from a wide range of sources, for example, the story of a foundling which is attested in both Ancient Near Eastern and Greco-Roman sources in antiquity. Authors of larger narratives often interweave multiple story patterns. How they deal with the interaction of these story patterns varies: some authors leave tensions, others attempt to unify the narrative by omitting a problematic aspect of a particular pattern, still others drop one pattern altogether if it presents severe difficulties. Since the story patterns are common property which undergo mutations, it is sometimes possible to reconstruct early story patterns from later texts.

In this monograph Cohen has elected to work through the evolution of the Moses nativity narrative. He begins by examining the biblical account (chapter one). He argues that there were two originally independent birth patterns: the ark pattern which finds a parallel in the Sargon legend and the murder pattern which has a parallel in the Matthean infancy narrative in the New Testament. The Exodus story also incorporates the tradition of enslavement. He proceeds to trace the role of these patterns and their interactions in the retellings of the story. He begins with a survey of a wide range of post-biblical sources including Jubilees, Ezekiel's *Exagoge*, Pseudo-Philo's *Biblical Antiquities*, Philo's *Life of Moses*, Josephus' *Jewish Antiquities*, the speech of Stephen in Acts 7, and the fresco at Dura-Europa (chapter two). He then turns to the *midrashim* (chapter three). Since there are a large number of texts from a wide chronological spectrum, he organizes his analysis around motifs based on the biblical story and those which are external to the biblical story. The final three chapters extend the scope much further. They cover the *Asatir*, a Samaritan work (chapter four); Rashi's commentary (chapter five); and Christian sources such as Matthew and the *Protevangelium of James* (chapter six). He also provides three appendices which address the tidings to the shepherds in Luke, some observations on Ibn Ezra's commentaries, and an English translation of the relevant section of the *Asatir*. He includes a bibliography as well as reference and modern author indices.

I will use his analysis of Philo as an illustration of Cohen's procedure. He begins by noting Philo's sources: the biblical text, the elders, and his own creativity (cf. *Mos.* 1.4). While he notes the similarities between Philo's account and numerous other versions, he does not posit any specific sources. This is short-sighted since Philo certainly knew the *Exagoge* of Ezekiel. I count at least twenty-one examples of common departures from the LXX between the two authors including a significant number of verbal echoes. Cohen's failure to take this into consideration is unfortunate since Philo's dependence raises the question whether sources such as Ezekiel might have influenced Philo's decisions to include or exclude a specific motif or even a larger pattern, e.g., the common exclusion of the ark. Cohen is much more helpful when he analyzes Philo's story in light of the biblical text. He points out, for example, that Philo rearranges the order of the enslavement of the people by placing it at the end of the story (Exod 1:11-14//*Mos.* 1.33-39) rather than before the murder decrees (Exod 1:15-16//*Mos.* 1.8). This move avoids problems in the biblical text such as how to relate the enslavement with the fear of multiplication of the people. It also means that the birth of Moses is only associated with the murder plot. In these ways Philo has removed some of the problems with the biblical text, although according to Cohen with much less of a sense of the aesthetic than the biblical narrators (p. 43). He concludes his analysis with some observations on the influence of Philo's story on Clement of Alexandria and Gregory of Nyssa. He has clearly read the primary texts carefully, but he has not engaged the arguments in standard secondary works such as A. van den Hoek's exemplary study of the relationship between Philo and Clement (*Clement of Alexandria and his Use of Philo in the* Stromateis, VCSup 3 [Leiden 1987] esp. 48-68) or the editions of Gregory's *Life of Moses* which point out the similarities between Philo and the Cappodocian (Daniélou, Musurillo, Malherbe and Ferguson). I should also point out that D. T. Runia has subsequently published a very helpful summary of scholarly analyzes of Philo's reception by Christians including these authors (*Philo in Early Christian Literature: A Survey*, CRINT 3.3 [Assen/Minneapolis 1993] 132-56, 243-61, esp. 256-61). While Cohen's task is not source criticism, these works would inform his analysis.

While there are shortcomings in the work, I also want to register a sense of appreciation. Cohen has covered an enormous body of literature. It would be easy for anyone with expertise in a particular author (especially the earlier authors) to point out limitations. It is, however, important to realize what he has done. He has shown how the use of patterns in subsequent versions of the story often illuminate the patterns and tensions within the biblical text. It is an effective argument for the need to take the interpretations of authors such as Philo seriously when assessing the biblical text.

Gregory E. Sterling
University of Notre Dame

Naomi G. COHEN, *Philo Judaeus: His Universe of Discourse*. Beiträge zur Erforschung des Alten Testaments und des Antiken Judentums 24. Peter Lang, Frankfurt am Main 1995. xx + 381 pages. ISBN 3-820-41650-1. DM 98.

In her foreword to this book, Naomi Cohen speaks of her effort to 'bring Philo back into the library of committed Jews', by translating one of his works into Hebrew (p. xiii). The book presently under review seems in many ways to be motivated by the same goal. Indeed, Cohen declares that the 'major thrust' of her book is 'to show how thoroughly Jewish (in the traditional sense) this highly sophisticated, and highly cultured man was' (p. xv).

In his own day, Philo was indisputably a committed Jew, devoting most of his writings to commentaries on Jewish scriptures, presenting proud expositions of Jewish history, beliefs, and practices, and bravely leading a delegation to the Emperor Caligula to plead on behalf of his fellow Jews. Over nineteen centuries later, then, why should such a clearly devoted Jew as Philo need to be 'brought back' to his descendant co-religionists?

First, of course, we can point to the transmission of his works. Written in Greek and preserved by the Church, his writings survived by dint of Christian, not Jewish, efforts. Though Philonic themes or interpretations may be detected on occasion in some Jewish works, any direct influence has yet to be established. Significantly, the first Jewish writer to mention Philo by name was Azariah dei Rossi, a Jew living in Renaissance Italy in the sixteenth century.

Perhaps more relevant, however—now that his works have been known to Jews for over four hundred years at least—is that Philo often does not sound very Jewish. His allegorical interpretations of the Bible —abstract and philosophical as they are—seem far removed from the legal and halakhic concerns of Rabbinic Judaism. To my knowledge, few scholars if any have argued that Philo did not observe Jewish laws. Nonetheless, his emphasis upon and preference for the internal, spiritual aspects of Jewish beliefs and customs overshadow any image of him as a Jew preoccupied with outward observance of the commandments.

To highlight Philo's Jewishness, Cohen focuses upon one Philonic passage, *Spec.* 4.132–50, allotting several chapters to topics suggested to her by this text. These topics encompass the following: the Decalogue as framework for Mosaic Law; Greek virtues and Mosaic laws; Philo's Shema, including such issues as phylacteries and the *mezuzah*; and ancestral traditions, including Philo's understanding of the term ἄγραφος νόμος or unwritten law.

These chapters are interspersed with others on related matters. Two introductory chapters set forth the author's views on Philo and his works and on the existence of a common 'Palestinian/Diaspora Midrashic Tradition'. Another chapter examines certain terms in Philo's vocabulary—some of which appear in the *Spec.* IV passage under investigation—showing that they carry significant Jewish nuances beside their generally recognized meanings. Yet another chapter examines Philo's curriculum of study as discussed in his treatise *Congr.* Finally, over a dozen endnotes extend chapter discussions, covering such broad-ranging subjects as the practice of healing by spitting, and the Passover Haggadah and Philo.

Within this framework, one can discern two lines of argumentation in Cohen's attempt to establish Philo's essential Jewishness. First, she contends that he drew from an ancient midrashic pool of oral traditions —both aggadic or non-legal and halakhic or legal—shared in common by Palestine and the Diaspora. Sidestepping (wisely, in my view) the questions of whether Philo knew Hebrew and whether Palestine or the Diaspora was the original source of the traditions, Cohen maintains that knowledge of Hebrew was not a prerequisite for access to these traditions (since they circulated widely through oral transmission and were probably translated—at least orally), nor is it necessary to posit direct influence of one source upon another. The very occurrence in Philo's work of traditions from this common treasury shows him to be conversant with the mainstream of Jewish communal life of his day, regardless of where the traditions originated.

Cohen's second line of argumentation pertains to Philo's use of a special 'Judeo-Greek vocabulary', consisting of over a dozen individual words and some words used in combination. While these terms denote commonly accepted meanings and some may have philosophical nuances, they also carry Jewish connotations—which are more often than not related to Jewish laws and their observance. Δικαιοσύνη, for example, can mean justice or righteousness, in a general sense, and observance of the commandments, in a Jewish sense. Presumably, the more it can be shown that Philo uses these words with their Jewish nuances, the more he can be seen as a practitioner of what Cohen calls 'normative Judaism'. This term encompasses 'the traditional 'rules' and 'ordinances' recognized by the rank-and file of the community to be binding upon Jews committed to the proper fulfillment of the Mosaic code' (p. 9 n. 7).

Before turning to the contribution of Cohen's book to our understanding of Philo's 'universe of discourse', I shall first evaluate how well she uses these two lines of argumentation. Lest any details obscure my position, let me state at the outset my overall sympathy with the author's aims and general conclusions.

Among the parallel interpretations Cohen adduces to illustrate the existence of a joint Palestinian/Diaspora midrashic tradition, I found some to be convincing, some to be weak, and many to be suggestive, but certainly not conclusive. A particularly convincing example can be found in *Spec.* 4.149–50, in which Philo comments on Deut 19:14. Ostensibly an injunction about honoring physical boundaries set by those who lived earlier, this verse is construed metaphorically, here and in an impressive number of sources, as pertaining to the observance of ancestral customs. The very fact that this interpretation is not dictated by the plain sense of the verse and is found in works both earlier than Philo and from provenances other than his offers strong evidence that it came from an ongoing tradition.

Much less convincing is Cohen's argument that Philo uses water as a metaphor for the Torah as a source of wisdom and that this too reflects a Palestinian/Diaspora tradition. Philo does not use the word Torah. Moreover, his words in Cohen's examples–such as 'the principles and lore of wisdom (τὰ σοφίας δόγματα καὶ θεωρήματα)'—are not clearly equivalent to 'Torah' as understood in the rabbinic passages she provides, especially since Torah can have a number of meanings. In addition, Philo uses the water metaphor in expounding verses different from those mentioned in the other sources presented. It is possible that Philo drew this metaphor from a shared midrashic tradition, but Cohen has not demonstrated this. Instead, the water image would seem to be a commonplace metaphor which various sources used independently of each other.

Among the merely suggestive but not conclusive illustrations, I would place Cohen's discussion of 'Philo's Shema'. The Shema, of course, consists of three Biblical passages: Deut 6:4-9, 11:13-21, and Num 15:37-41, twenty verses in all. In *Spec.* 4.137-42, Philo discusses seven of these verses, Deut 6:6-9 and 11:18-20, two passages whose contents overlap but appear in different order.[1] Cohen notes that the *Spec.* IV passage she has selected follows Philo's explication of the Ten Commandments and the particular laws associated with each commandment. She also observes that in Jewish liturgy, the Ten Commandments and the Shema were recited together, as evidenced by various sources from antiquity. In Philo's discussion of the overlapping contents of seven verses from the Shema, Cohen sees an echo of this liturgical practice. Strikingly, neither here nor anywhere else does Philo cite the opening verse of the prayer. In Hebrew, this verse begins with the words *Shema Yisrael*, which give the prayer its very name. Philo also omits twelve other verses: Deut 6:5; 11:13-17, 21; and Num 15:37-41.[2] Cohen makes much of the absence of the Numbers passage, claiming it was not yet part of the Shema in Philo's day. She is silent, however, about the other missing verses. While it is certainly worthwhile to mention the appearance of certain verses from the Shema here and the link between the Ten Commandments and the Shema in other Jewish sources, to speak of 'Philo's Shema' and declare this passage to reflect the contemporary 'Jewish theory and practice of his day' (p. 109) goes beyond the available evidence. This is but one example where the evidence presented calls for conclusions more tentative than those given.

As for Cohen's second line of argumentation, since the notion of Philo's Judeo-Greek vocabulary is central to her thesis about his essential Jewishness, discussion of it probably would have been more effective in an introductory chapter instead of where it stands now in

---

[1] These contents pertain to what came to be known as *tefillin*, or phylacteries (Deut 6:8; 11:18), study of Torah (Deut 6:6-7; 11:19), and the *mezuzah*, a fixture attached to doorposts of Jewish homes containing parchment upon which certain biblical verses are written (Deut 6:9; 11:20).

[2] He may allude to Deut 6:5 in *Decal.* 64 and he mentions Deut 11:13-14 in *Praem.* 101, but the contexts are completely separate from each other and from the *Spec.* IV passage examined in this book. Also, though it is tangential to our present concerns, we might note that as the Shema evolved, a statement in praise of God, recited quietly, was added after the opening verse (Deut 6:4).

the middle of the book. Though I agree in principle with Cohen's assessment, I was not always persuaded by her definitions and examples of usage. In addition, some words are given thorough consideration, replete with Philonic references and sample passages, but others are accorded barely a page with perhaps one or two Philonic citations.

For reasons well known, situating Philo in relation to other Jewish traditions of interpretation and practice is a challenge.[1] To her credit, Cohen acknowledges problems with drawing distinctions too sharply between such terms as Jewish and Hellenistic, Palestine and the Diaspora, and rabbinic and non-rabbinic. Despite this recognition, Cohen sometimes uses terms that can be misleading. Besides her frequent mention of Torah and Philo's Shema, for example, she also speaks of Philo's *tefillin* (pp. 149, 155) and description of the *mezuzah* (p. 177). When Philo interprets the biblical verses relevant to these two ritual objects, however, he does not clearly speak of such objects but instead focuses upon the symbolic meaning and purpose of the biblical injunctions.[2] In addition, when applied to the first century, the term 'normative Judaism' suggests a uniformity or consensus not supported by the evidence. If Cohen means that Philo observed Jewish laws and customs as they were understood in his contemporary community, it would have been better to state this without characterizing him as 'normative'.

Cohen asserts clearly and often that the significant point about the Palestinian/Diaspora tradition is that material was shared in common, regardless of where it originated. She also recognizes the importance of locating parallels to Philo in pre-rabbinic and non-rabbinic sources. Nonetheless one detects a bias toward rabbinic traditions, especially those that can be traced to Palestine, as a point of reference for understanding Philo. Moreover, if the origin of a tradition is truly beside the point, perhaps it is enough to speak of a common treasury of Jewish interpretations without reference to Palestine or the Diaspora.

We must now consider how well the book as a whole succeeds in depicting Philo's 'universe of discourse'. With her focus upon certain elements in Philo's *œuvre*, Cohen sometimes loses sight of the broader picture. Below are three illustrations.

The first pertains to Philonic discussions which were *not* part of the common midrashic tradition. While many interpretations circulated

---

[1] The difficulties posed by this endeavor are sharply drawn in B. J. Bamberger, 'Philo and the Aggadah', *HUCA* 48 (1977) 153–85 and L. L. Grabbe, 'Philo and the Aggada: a Response to B. J. Bamberger', *SPhA* 3 (1991) 153–66.
[2] In fact Philo does not use even use the words *tefillin* or *mezuzah*, and he has no Greek equivalent for *tefillin*, as Cohen herself points out (pp. 153–54). He follows the Septuagint understanding of *mezuzot* in Deut 6:9 and 11:20 as φιλιαί, 'doorposts'.

widely, surely some—whether from Palestine, Alexandria, or elsewhere—remained unique to their place of origin and were not shared beyond it. In Philo's writings, we find evidence of traditions held in common with other communities as well as those that were likely specific to Alexandria. To be sure, examination of such independent Philonic traditions is clearly beyond the purview of Cohen's book. Ultimately, however, we could best evaluate the significance of Philo's interpretations from the common treasury if we had some idea of their proportion to interpretations independent of this treasury. When examining Philo's Judeo-Greek vocabulary, Cohen is often careful to note the generally accepted meanings of certain words alongside the Jewish meanings. Her discussion of Philo's shared traditions would benefit as well from acknowledgment, when appropriate, of interpretations that probably derive just from his Alexandrian Jewish heritage. In looking, for example, at 'Philo's Curriculum of Study' in *Congr.*, Cohen focuses upon his vocabulary, paying little attention to the allegorical interpretation in which the words are set. This interpretation, in which Sarah and Hagar symbolize different realms of study, probably derives from a Greek allegorization of Homer in which Penelope and her handmaidens represent philosophy and the preliminary studies respectively.[1] Recognition that this is probably evidence of a separate Alexandrian Jewish tradition might help to keep in perspective her own focus on the interpretations shared in common.

Second, although Cohen concentrates on the many instances in which Philo speaks ambiguously about Jewish laws and practices, he also speaks about these subjects in explicit terms. To assess Philo's attitude fairly, we must ask what he says expressly about these laws and practices and why he often refers to them obliquely. Regardless of his high regard for and devotion to the particular laws, Philo explicitly places them at the bottom of a hierarchy. First in this hierarchy are 'laws endowed with life and reason'—embodied in the patriarchs Abraham, Isaac, and Jacob. These are followed by the Ten Commandments. In *Abr.* 3–5, Philo explains that the particular laws are *copies* of archetypal laws exemplified by the patriarchs.[2] Philo also tells us (*Decal.* 175; *Spec.* 1.1;

---

[1] J. Dillon, 'Ganymede as the Logos: Traces of a Forgotten Allegorization in Philo', *SPh* 6 (1979–80) 37–40, esp. 37; and Y. Amir, 'The Transference of Greek Allegories to Biblical Motifs in Philo', in F. E. Greenspahn, E. Hilgert, and B. L. Mack (edd.), *Nourished With Peace: Studies in Hellenistic Judaism in Memory of Samuel Sandmel*, Scholars Press Homage Series 9 (Chico, CA 1984) 15–25, esp. 15–18.

[2] *Pace* Cohen (p. 267 n. 12), this is not the same as claiming that they followed the particular laws, but rather that the patriarchs represent a higher principle of law, whose details are later spelled out in the particular laws.

4.132) that God proclaimed the Ten Commandments or general headings (τὰ γενή) under which the particular laws (οἱ ἐν εἴδει νόμοι) are organized. As Philo reveals elsewhere, he considers the εἶδος, or species, inferior to the γένος, or genus (*Cher.* 5–8; *Post.* 105, *et al.*). If Philo had specific terms for Jewish laws, why does he so often allude to them ambiguously? By using words with general and Jewish meanings, Philo was able to present Judaism as a particular expression of universal values and ideals. Ironically, whereas he emphasized the universal aspects of the particular, Cohen emphasizes the particular dimensions of the universal. No doubt such a corrective may be necessary nineteen centuries after Philo, when many may have lost sight of his commitment to Jewish practices. Still, one should bear in mind the probable impulse behind Philo's ambiguity.

Third and finally, how representative is *Spec.* 4.132–50 of what Cohen calls Philo's 'universe of discourse'? To answer this requires that we situate the passage within the context of all Philo's works. According to Cohen, this passage falls at the culmination of Philo's *magnum opus*, written for readers like himself, thoroughly at home in both Jewish and classical Greek culture. She 'categorically' asserts that *Opif.* and *Praem.* are the beginning and end of this *magnum opus*. Leaving open whether Philo himself developed in this way, she maintains that his work progresses from a philosophical to a more traditional Jewish stance and 'culminates in a virtually normative Jewish frame of reference' (p. 31). Viewed thus, *Spec.* 4.132–50 has an enhanced significance. Not only does it follow Philo's discussion of the particular laws, it also comes near the end of his *magnum opus* and, as Cohen's words strongly suggest, may well represent the epitome of his lifetime's intellectual work.

This account of Philo's writings is incomplete in several respects. Besides the different philosophical and Jewish emphases in the treatises between *Opif.* and *Praem.*, one also finds different literary forms of biblical commentary, different vocabulary patterns, and different traditions. Moreover, some treatises toward the end take up biblical material covered earlier. Surprisingly Cohen does not mention that many—perhaps most—scholars view these treatises not as one *magnum opus*, but as *two* exegetical series, known as the Allegory and the Exposition. While this position may not solve every difficulty, it provides a more satisfactory answer about why one set of treatises differs so markedly from the other and why, to some extent, Philo covers the same biblical ground in both sets. In addition, Philo's different philosophical and Jewish emphases are explained much more persuasively, in my view, by the argument that he composed these series for different though perhaps overlapping audiences: one, familiar with Jewish history, beliefs, and practices and more interested in the deeper, spiritual meaning of scripture; and the other, less familiar with Jewish history, beliefs, and practices and in need of instruction. Besides these Philonic works, however, we also have much of his biblical commentary *Questions and Answers on Genesis and Exodus* and miscellaneous treatises devoted to philosophical, political, and other topics. Cohen uses a passage from *QG* to illustrate the common midrashic tradition, but she says nothing about how this series might be connected to Philo's so-called *magnum opus*. Nor does she comment about his non-exegetical works even though they contain material relevant to her concerns, especially about Jewish laws and customs (see, e.g., *Legat*. 115–18, 209–12; *Hypoth*. 6.9; 7.6).

When viewed in light of these considerations, the *Spec*. IV passage upon which Cohen focuses takes on a somewhat different significance. True, the passage offers some fine examples of Philo's multivalent Judeo-Greek vocabulary, his familiarity with certain Jewish traditions, and his attitude toward observing Jewish laws and customs. In assessing Philo's universe of discourse, however, we must keep in mind the relationship between parts and the whole of his thought.

In this book, then, Naomi Cohen calls attention to a crucial part of Philo's universe of discourse. It would be gratifying were Philo to find his way back into the library of committed Jews after centuries of neglect. Whether he does or not, however, his fundamental commitment as a Jew is worth remembering by all students of Philo, regardless of their own religious convictions and scholarly interests.

Ellen Birnbaum
Cambridge, Massachusetts

Jean LAPORTE, *Théologie Liturgique de Philon d'Alexandrie et d'Origène*, Liturgie 6. Editions de Cerf, Paris 1995. 278 pages. ISBN 2-204-05130-6.

Jean Laporte who previously published his thesis on Philo of Alexandria (*La Doctrine eucharistique chez Philon d'Alexandrie*, Paris 1972), broadens his scope with the present study on the liturgical theology in the Alexandrian context to include the writings of Origen. Laporte's principal thesis aims to prove the dependency of Origen upon Philo, especially under the rubric of eucharist as sacrifice which he organizes around the biblical concept of Levitical priesthood. This volume represents the mature work of the author as it draws together papers delivered at professional meetings over the past fifteen years in both North America and Europe.

Each of the seven chapters focuses on complementary and diverse dimensions of liturgical theology. In some cases sacramental theology is reflected through the lens of other doctrinal questions, such as original sin, the fall and redemption. In other cases, he examines biblical typology as a key for understanding the sacraments, especially the eucharist. Biblical themes such as the Passover and the high priest as mediator of prayer and sacrifice are hinges around which he explores the liturgical theology of both Philo and Origen. The fifth chapter traces the Alexandrian doctrine on original sin through the 'ages of life'. Here the author attempts a synthesis by examining a dozen Philonic passages which treat virtue and vice. Steeped in the classical Greek philosophy of Plato and Aristotle, Philo prescribes—like the Stoics—that education and purification of reason are the best remedy for vice, the precocious malady of the soul. The sixth chapter continues the development of the concept of original sin through biblical exegesis. Origen's prologue on the *Commentary on the Song of Songs* and his *Commentary on the Epistle to the Romans* provide the vocabulary to address such topics as sinful flesh, the old and new Adams and the seed of Abraham. In the Gnostic context of the Alexandrian school, the sacrament of baptism is anomalous. Instead of redressing the fall as described in Genesis, the typology of baptism refers more explicitly to Exodus. In baptism a person is purified of his or her passions and passes over to a type of moral and religious conversion. Allegory serves to speak of this conversion in terms of Egypt which is the attachment to carnal vices, dependence upon demons and slavery in the bodily life according to the image of earthly humanity. In typical Alexandrian exegesis, elements can be interpreted according to several meanings in different contexts. For example, the serpent in reference to Eve represents pleasure, while the serpent lifted by Moses is the mastering of oneself. The final chapter ends where he began by examining the theme of the high priesthood which is important for the doctrine of the Word and christology in the Alexandrian school.

Alexandrian biblical exegesis according to the various senses of scripture uses the typology of the Old Adam, the author of original sin, and the new Adam who is the Christ, the redeemer. The Gnostic context favors the inherent dualism of spirit and flesh. Within this biblical commentary Laporte explores the manifestations of rigorous asceticism as a means for growing in the Spirit and dominating the flesh. Typically one associates the school of Alexandria with the Gnostic split between the spirit and the flesh, between the spiritual and the material worlds. The author takes a different approach to dualism in treating the divorce between the soul and the spirit in the writings of Philo and Origen. Alexandrian writers such as Clement and Origen responded less directly to the tenets of Gnosticism as a popular manifestation of religion; rather, they appealed to philosophical currents to express the unique character of the truths of revelation. Participation in the eucharist remained in the realm of contemplative communion with the Logos. Origen avoids the Gnostic body/soul split by concentrating much more on the life of the spirit and less on the things of the creative order.

Liturgical theology is intimately connected to one's thought on sacred scripture. The Word of God is like the bread of life. According to Philo, God is adapted to each person according to his or her situation, capacity, and needs. The Logos is the archetype of the rational soul and a divine source of light in the soul. On the human plane, Philo considered the Logos—as it expressed in the scriptures—as the food of the soul. Origen draws upon Philo but insists that the Logos is personal. The divine Word has spoken through the prophets and is the true author of the words of the scriptures. In the incarnation the Word becomes flesh in order to sacrifice his blood for the remission of sins and to help humanity through example, teaching, and the care that Christ gives to heal souls. As faith deepens, human understanding enters into a relationship with the divine Word and is transformed. Both the bread of the Word and the bread of the eucharist, therefore, are complementary modes of participation in the divine Logos. Origen even warns the faithful against obscuring the Word through excessive reverence for the eucharistic elements. The eucharistic celebration is a kind of *ascesis*, a way of liberating the spirit from the things of the flesh. Consequently Origen argues against any simple identification of bread and body. The mystery of eucharistic presence is inherent to the mystery of the manifestation of the Word in the scripture, and what it means cannot be considered except in the light of the word spoken and proclaimed. What is given in the sacrament cannot be different from that which is given in the Word.

Laporte's style is very direct and accessible. He strives effectively to write clearly, not allowing himself to get side-tracked with endless excursuses on related subjects. This readability in conjunction with the vast documentation makes this book a valuable tool for anyone interested in the Alexandrian school of theology and liturgy.

Michael S. Driscoll
University of Notre Dame

Baudouin DECHARNEUX, *L'ange, le devin et le prophète: chemins de la parole dans l'œuvre de Philon d'Alexandrie dit 'le Juif'*. Spiritualités et pensées libres. Editions de l'Université de Bruxelles, Brussels 1994. 160 pages. ISBN 2-8004-1094-9. BFr 650, FFr 120.

In the introduction to his important work on the development of Jewish belief in angels in the pre-rabbinic period, Michael Mach informs his reader that Philo's writings will be bracketed in his study because they cannot be fitted into the general line of development.[1] The decision to exclude Philo was all the more regrettable—if perfectly understandable—because to my knowledge no monograph devoted to Philo's angelology was available. This lacuna has now at least partly been filled by the study under review. The author, who teaches Early Christian Literature at the Free University of Brussels, draws together various strands of his research that he has previously published in a large number of articles. The result is a compact book that requires concentrated reading, but has much to offer the patient Philonist.

The title of the work indicates that the author takes a broad approach. The main subject is Philo's views on angels, but these cannot be understood without relating them to the human figures of the diviner and the prophet. Moreover, as the subtitle of the work indicates, the theme of angels leads the interpreter into the very heart of Philo's religious and philosophical thought. Angels are intermediary beings who mediate the divine word to human beings. For this reason they are often called λόγοι as well as ἄγγελοι. Decharneux emphasizes the strong connections that bind Philo's conceptions to central themes in Greek philosophy, especially in the Platonic tradition. At the same time he is very sympathetic to the method of the history of religions, which is contrasted with the claims of rationality made by the philosophical tradition. It will thus not surprise students of Philo that he frequently cites Bréhier's book on Philo, but is very critical of the more systematic approach of Wolfson. The chief entry into Philo's thought, however, is—quite rightly—via the texts, especially the numerous allegorical passages in which angels and divine *logoi* play a prominent role. Finally we should note that he is strongly aware of Philo's concrete historical and social location, drawing on the final page the important conclusion that Philo's reconciliation of Jewish faith and contemporary philosophy bears a strongly ideologized stamp which allows too little room for doubt and critical reflection.

---

[1] M. Mach, *Entwicklungsstadien des jüdische Engelglaubens in vorrabbinischer Zeit*, TSAJ 34 (Tübingen 1992) 8.

The main contents of the book consists of twelve mostly rather short chapters. A list of their titles indicates very clearly the book's broad scope: I Philonic definition of angels and difficulties of interpretation; II Functions of angels; III Angels as saviours of human beings; IV Angels as *logoi* of God; V Influences of the *Phaedrus* and the *Epinomis*; VI Chaldeanism or the limits of cosmological piety; VII The chariot of the Great King, a founding myth of angelology; VIII The ark and the Cherubim; IX Balaam, symbol of the professional diviner; X Joseph the inspired diviner; XI The figure of the Prophet and the High Priest; XII The Logos High Priest and Levitic spirituality.

On the basis of these analyses Decharneux reaches the unsurprising conclusion that Philo's angelology is a complex affair with many strands that are very difficult to disentangle, indeed seemingly 'un labyrinthe sans issue' (138). Yet the chief role of angels is clear enough. They have the task of binding together the invisible (and divine) and the visible (and mortal). Philo's thought shows a strong henological tendency, aspiring to a vision of the divine unity. Angels operate at three levels at the same time: in theology, cosmology and anthropology. By perceiving angels as cosmic *logoi* of God, Philo is able to achieve a 'double tour de force' (142): he is able to demonstrate the complementarity of revealed religion and philosophy as roads to the same knowledge; moreover he can embark on a rereading of scripture that will impose on it a unificatory philosophical conception. On this subject, the relation between religion (or faith) and philosophy, Decharneux's own views become somewhat labyrinthine (and not always very clearly expressed). Sometimes these two are presented as reciprocating each other like set of infinite mirrors (92, a lovely image). At other times religion continues where philosophy decides to withdraw into ἐποχή (84). But is it not the claim of the kind of Platonism to which Philo is attracted that it can furnish a return to the source of unity, a rational procedure which Philo places at the heart of his thought, even if he is ever aware of the limitations that necessarily accompany this manner of enquiry when it draws close to its goal?

The study under review is clearly not the last word on the subject (nor does its author present it as such). Its method is impressionistic rather than systematic. Especially the biblical and Jewish background of Philo's angelology requires further investigation (precisely the subject that Mach declined to take on). Coverage of the secondary literature is extensive, but primarily focused on material written in French. It was therefore most surprising not to see any reference to A. Méasson's important work *Du char ailé de Zeus à l'Arche d'Alliance* (reviewed in this journal (1 (1989) 153–55). It was also a pity that David Winston's important studies on Philo's views on prophecy were not taken into account. But in the case of a thinker as elusive and complex as Philo, an impressionistic method has much to recommend it. Moreover not every work has to cover every detail of the scholarship on its subject. The reader who takes the time to study this elegantly produced book will find the effort generously rewarded.

David T. Runia
Leiden University

David T. RUNIA, *Philo and the Church Fathers: A Collection of Papers.* Supplements to Vigiliae Christianae 32, E.J. Brill, Leiden 1995. xii + 275 pages. ISBN 90-04-10355-4. NLG 155, $100.

This handsomely produced volume contains fourteen previously published articles by Professor Runia, collected as a companion to his 1993 *Philo in Early Christian Literature: a Survey,* CRINT 3.3 (Assen/Minneapolis). Only the first article, Runia's inaugural address upon acceptance of the C.J. de Vogel Extraordinary Chair of Ancient Philosophy at the University of Utrecht, has never before appeared in English. Six articles will be familiar to readers of *The Studia Philonica Annual,* having originally appeared in its pages. Nevertheless, it is handy to have all of them in one place, for these are articles one will want to consult often, for both research and teaching.

Researchers will appreciate especially the last two chapters, invaluable tools for work on 'Philo and the Church Fathers': an exhaustive listing of references to Philo from Josephus to 1000 CE, including many indirect references (chapter thirteen); and an index to the *Apparatus Testimoniorum* of the great *editio maior* of Philo's works by Cohn and Wendland (chapter fourteen). The latter is useful not only for researchers interested in the sources Philo used, but especially for those (like myself) interested in what passages in Philo were used by later authors. In addition, chapter two, 'Philonic Nomenclature', is a treasure trove for anyone studying how the ancients thought of Philo, for it provides an exhaustive list, with extensive analyses, of titles and descriptions given to Philo in sources, both Greek and Latin, to the year 1000.

Many of the articles strike that happy (and difficult to achieve!) balance of introductory focus and scholarly contribution that will make them irresistible for use in class. Chapter six, 'Philo and Origen: Preliminary Survey', presents a succinct summary of the state of a question which many erroneously consider to have been settled long ago—the extent of, and especially the character of, Origen's indebtedness to Philo. As Runia reminds us, 'Origen does not merely cite Philo, but always adapts him' (p. 126), and yet these adaptations may mean that Origen has taken Philo more deeply into his system than most scholars have been willing to entertain (e.g., extending to the doctrine, familiar to all scholars of patristic exegesis, of the creation of humanity according to, and not directly as, the image of God). Chapter ten, on 'Philo and the Neoplatonist Tradition', is another essay which simultaneously lays out the *status quaestionis* and by judicious analysis also advances it, again the sort of essay perfect for class (especially the 'detour' on the fate of Philo's writings, handily schematized on p. 192). The essay will be of interest to students of the history of theology as well as of the history of philosophy, for, as Runia points out, to ask the question of Philo's relation to the Neoplatonist tradition is to ask to what degree Philo is the 'father of negative theology' (p. 184). Runia ultimately decides that the evidence is too fragmentary to permit firm judgment—an answer typical of the gentle scholarly hand wielded throughout these essays, resolutely refusing to force the evidence, yet always turning it to clarifying use:

> The contacts between philosophers and other religious traditions in the second and third centuries were more extensive than has often been thought. If any interest was shown in writings of Philo, then I would argue that it will have occurred on his own terms, i.e. as an expositor of ancient and venerable scriptures ... (p. 202).

Chapter nine presents texts and translations (with commentary) of five letters of Isidore of Pelusium (c. 370–c. 435) which discuss Philo. Isidore is a long-neglected figure now coming into increasing prominence in Late Antique studies, and there is virtually nothing else of his immense *œuvre* of 2000 letters to give to students in translation. The commentaries on the text continue the line of thought developed in chapter seven ("'Where, Tell Me, is the Jew ...?': Basil, Philo, and Isidore of Pelusium'), which showed how useful Philo became to 4th and 5th century apologetic directed at the Jews:

> Philo [is] ... regarded as a proto-Christian, but at the same time he is and remains a Jew. As such he can be used as valuable apologetic ammunition in the contest—dialogue one can hardly call it—against the Judaism of Isidore's own time (143).

The programmatic essay in chapter one, 'Philonism and Christian Thought', provides an excellent introduction to anyone, scholar or student, who might ask why patrologists and other students of Late Antiquity should study Philo. Runia uses the notion of 'Philonism' to refer to a first and second century BCE movement in which the biblical tradition was first brought into direct contact with Greek philosophical thought. Philo is its 'most important and most vital representative' (p. 12). The utility of the concept is proved as the reader watches Runia deftly using it to demonstrate the influence of Philonic themes and initiatives on seemingly unlikely figures (such as Augustine, pp. 19-21) as well as to characterize that influence more precisely in figures where it has long been acknowledged (e.g., 'Gregory of Nyssa ... retain[s] the central thesis of Philonism that God is Being, and is not *beyond* being, as promulgated in ... Neoplatonism', p. 18, original emphasis). At the heart of 'Philonism' is Philo's decision to use Platonist, as opposed to other, philosophical paradigms, and Runia does not shrink from exploring the reasons why Philo made this choice, managing to steer a sturdy middle course between those who see a fundamental affinity between the Bible's theism and Plato's idealism, and those who regard the combination as essentially an adventitious and destructive Hellenization (summary at p. 15). Chapter eleven continues the examination of the influence of 'Philonism', showing in more detail how the 'philosophical theology' (p. 218) which it represents surfaces in patristic, and especially Augustinian, interpretations of God's self-naming at Exod 3:14-15. When Pascal later contrasts the 'God of the philosophers' with the 'God of Abraham, Isaac, and Jacob' we see the radical undermining of the age old Philonic tradition (and thus by contrast see that tradition more clearly, although in my view Augustine lays more of the groundwork for Pascal's undermining than Runia gives him credit for).

In the remainder of the essays, Runia explores other, more specialized topics: Clement of Alexandria's description of Philo as 'the Pythagorean', chapter three; the text of Philo's *De virtutibus*, chapter four; the authenticity of the *De resurrectione* of Athenagoras, chapter five (with the conclusion, based on the treatise's use of Philonic vocabulary, that it is spuriously attributed); the extent to which early Christian writers held Philo responsible for Arianism, chapter nine (only to a very limited extent, Runia concludes); and a review essay on J. Royse's *The Spurious Texts of Philo of Alexandria* (Leiden 1991). There is also a section of 'Addenda et Corrigenda' (pp. 250-61), updating the essays as necessary, to bring this volume of first-rate and eminently serviceable scholarship to its close, leaving the reader very much in Runia's debt.

John C. Cavadini
University of Notre Dame

Romano SGARBI, *Analisi linguistico-filologica dell'interpretazione armena della trattazione greca filoniana intorno all'altare.* Memorie, Instituto Lombardo—Classe Lettere, vol. 39 fasc. 3. Instituto Lombardo, Milan 1989. 132 pages (97-228). L. 18.000.

Romano SGARBI, *Problemi linguistici e di critica del testo nel De vita contemplativa di Filone alla luce della versione armena.* Memorie, Instituto Lombardo—Classe Lettere, vol. 40 fasc. 1. Instituto Lombardo, Milan 1992. 44 pages (5-48). L. 10.000.

Each of the two studies is limited to a work within the Armenian corpus of Philo, a work of which the Greek is extant and which therefore provides a valuable control to assess the *modus operandi* of the ancient Armenian translators. The first is a linguistic-philological analysis of *Yałags bagnin irac'* (Τὰ ἄλλα περὶ τὸ θυσιαστήριον = *Spec.* 1.285-345), and the second a textual commentary on *Yałags varuc' kenac' tesakani* (Περὶ θεωρητικοῦ βίου = *De vita contemplativa*). In the first study Sgarbi establishes the close syntactical affinities between the Greek and the Armenian versions, typical of the translations of the so-called Hellenizing or Hellenophile School of early Armenian translators who produced several such interlinear translations of Greek philosophical and patristic works— including several of the works of Philo. The author begins by inviting attention to the various editions of the Greek text and to the special place of the Armenian text in verifying the Greek readings of the much later manuscripts. In the second study he utilizes the critical edition of *Contempl.* prepared by Conybeare and pays much more attention to textual criticism.

Although in the first study Sgarbi occasionally points out corruptions in the Greek and the helpfulness of the Armenian in making necessary emendations (at times he even points out how the Armenian text supports certain conjectural emendations made in the published edition[s] of the Greek text), his focus is not so much on text-critical issues as it is on pointing out the Armenian translators' handling of the Greek at every instance. Sometimes the philological minutiae into which the author delves appear to be of far greater concern to someone interested in linguistic technicalities and comparative grammar, and this is quite justifiable since Armenian and Greek are early siblings within the family of Indo-European languages. However, a word of caution here is necessary since the Armenian syntax in all such translations by the above mentioned school is quite artificial and full of anomalies.

Every now and then, in both studies, Sgarbi points out parallels in other translations by the same school where the Greek is handled similarly by the translators (in some of his previous publications he analyzes certain other translations by the school). Many of his observations are indeed well demonstrated tendencies on the part of the Armenian translators. Such tendencies include using verbal or participial forms to render a noun, an adjective, or even an adverb; and sometimes using nominal forms for the various verbal or participial forms. Of special interest are the translators' renderings of Greek compounds. These and other tendencies of the translators appear among the conclusions made by the author, in the ten-point summary at the end of the first study. The ten points made as conclusions at the end of the second study are more of textual significance and point out some of Conybeare's oversights in his critical edition of *De vita contemplativa*.

The author is certainly well in command of the languages involved and his method—given the nature of the Armenian documents at hand—is both valid and commendable, especially in the second study where he shows greater methodological restraint (his apparent unfamiliarity with recent English publications on the 'Scuola Ellenistica' by this reviewer and occasional misprints in the Armenian are non-consequential, e.g., pp. 98 n. 3, 122 (*bis*), in the first study; pp. 6 n. 6, 21, 30, 37, in the second study). It is precisely from such comparative studies on Philonic treatises which exist in both languages that one gathers essential information before attempting to tackle any of Philo's works which survives in Armenian only. In this respect, Sgarbi's work is of great help and makes a special and rare contribution to Philonica. The more we know about the *modus operandi* of the Armenian translators of Philo, the better we are equipped in our approach to the rest of their work.

Abraham Terian
Sterling College

Graham J. WARNE, *Hebrew Perspectives on the Human Person in the Hellenistic Era: Philo and Paul*. Mellen Biblical Press, Lewiston 1995. xi +291 pages. ISBN 0-7734-2420-2. $99.95.

This important study is the fruit of research done under the supervision of Michael Lattke and Francis I. Andersen at the University of Queensland. The author teaches at Kenmore Christian College in Brisbane.

The concise introductory and concluding chapters suggest that Warne has reflected on broad issues of human existence and the differences between ancient Greek and Hebrew cultural and religious traditions.

Philo, he contends, was dominated by the Greek conceptuality of the human as 'a bi-partite body and soul'. The dominant perspective of the Apostle Paul, by contrast was 'clearly Hebraic, presenting a view of the human person as a single complete entity, even into the post-mortem state' (252). Both perspectives can be useful to us today, Paul's emphasizing a holistic approach, Philo's stressing 'the eternal nature and worth of the higher self or soul, which demands care' (252). Both writers assume human dependence on the God of Moses; of course Paul's anthropology is also influenced by christology. Later church writers combined the two perspectives of Philo and Paul. Nevertheless, their anthropological perspectives *were* different and reflected 'each exegete's particular *evangelistic* purpose' (254, emphasis mine).

The author's primary concern seems clearly to provide a fuller understanding of Pauline thought and especially of 1 Corinthians, but the book offers extensive discussion of some of Philo's anthropological terms and ideas as well (especially terms related to ψυχή). Warne's opening chapter sketches the Hellenistic and Jewish backgrounds of both men. The second chapter traces the uses of *nephesh* in the Hebrew Bible, concluding that there is a consistent pattern of stressing the unity of human personality. Chapter three surveys the history of Greek uses of ψυχή from Homer to Aristotle. The most ancient uses resemble the Hebrew holistic pattern, but from the Orphics to Plato a strong tradition develops of contrasting the soul (immortal) and the body (perishable). Socrates introduced the concept of caring for one's soul, by which he meant 'the self-consciousness of the human individual' (108).

Chapter four discusses 'the soul in Philonic conceptuality'. Philo's starting point is Platonic dualism. His statements about human creation in Genesis 1–2 point up the sovereignty of the human νοῦς, intrinsically related to the Creator through the divine Logos (125–32). Philo often portrays the soul as tri-partite, but sometimes simply divides it into rational and irrational elements. All human beings have to make a fundamental choice, making either love of God or love of self their guiding principle. The former choice leads toward a perfection best symbolized by Moses, one attained after death when the soul returns to God (144–47).

Chapter five focuses on 'the soul in the Pauline Corpus' (mainly the undisputed epistles). The Pauline letters use ψυχή only 13 times, but all of these uses emphasize a Hebraic orientation to the unity of human personality. The climax of the book, however, is reached in chapter six, where Warne argues that 1 Corinthians 2 and 15 reflect a 'confrontation' between Paul and his correspondents in Corinth, Christians who had some kind of connection with Philo. His analysis of this letter's relation to Philonic texts builds on studies by Birger Pearson and R. A. Horsley. Though there is no proof that either Philo or Paul knew of the other's existence, Warne thinks it probable that Apollos brought to Corinth an Alexandrian view of human nature that was rooted in 'a form of hellenized Judaism of the Philonic type'. 1 Cor 2 draws sharp contrasts between 'those who are mature' and 'spiritual', on the one hand, and those who are 'babes' or 'unspiritual' (ψυχικός) on the other. 1 Cor 15 teaches that the 'man from heaven', with a σῶμα πνευματικόν, appears after the 'man of dust', with his σῶμα ψυχικόν. Warne argues that the Corinthians had developed an elitist spirituality which involved a distortion of Philonic ideas, but he thinks that Paul sought to correct it in a non-Philonic direction. For the apostle, the human body must undergo 'a radical death' before it can experience spiritual transformation. Philo, by contrast thinks that those who properly care for the soul experience death as only 'another stage in the soul's onward progress' (241).

The author has approached his questions and data with care and a quite open-minded appreciation of the perspectives of both Paul and Philo. His methodology stresses extended word studies, and the assumption of a sharp and rather easily defined dichotomy of 'Hebraic' and 'Greek' modes of thought runs through the book. The general argument and conclusions offer no major surprises, although Warne adds support to the theory that 1 Corinthians responds to Christians attracted to an anthropology akin to Philo's. The bibliography of works consulted is fairly comprehensive, but it effectively ends around the mid-1980s and does not include such items as Thomas Tobin's *The Creation of Man* and David Runia's *Philo of Alexandria and the Timaeus of Plato*. Warne's chief interest is clearly in Paul, and the interpretations of his epistles is generally well-reasoned (though the 'tri-partite' terminology in 1 Thess 5:23 is dismissed too quickly on the ground that 'one must interpret this text in the light of other Pauline anthropological statements', p. 199). Like other recent studies, this one pays good attention to the different audiences and aims reflected in Paul's different letters. More consideration of the nuances of Philo's statements and of the audience(s) and purposes of his different treatises would have been helpful, not least in regard to the Alexandrian's references to the soul's immortality. Finally, while the scholarly objective of explaining these two first-century writers in their own historical period is essential, this reader wishes the author had said more about the permanent value of Philo's concept of 'care for the higher self'.

David M. Hay
Coe College

Torrey SELAND, *Establishment Violence in Philo and Luke: A Study of Non-Conformity to the Torah and Jewish Vigilante Reactions*. Biblical Interpretation Series 15, E.J. Brill, Leiden 1995. xvi + 353 pages. ISBN 90-04-10252-3. NLG 184, $119.

Did the urbane and erudite Philo of Alexandria authorize the practice of lynching? Erudite and urbane scholars are likely to flinch at this question, not least those in the U.S., where lynching is a veritable synecdoche for racial injustice. Seland is sensitive to such concerns, but he does not view avoidance as the proper solution to unpleasant questions. *Establishment Violence* has two foci. One is a careful examination and refinement of the proposals of J. Juster and E. R. Goodenough regarding Philo's views of 'mob justice'. The other looks at two possible examples of such justice in Jerusalem: Acts 6–8 (Stephen) and 21–23 (Paul). I am not certain whether the stories from Acts serve to illustrate the findings about Philo, or if Philo is used as 'background' to elucidate some incidents from the period of Christian origins. If this is a defect, it nonetheless means that those with interest in either subject may profit from Seland's monograph.

The heart of this work is an exploration of 'establishment violence', which is not slangy speech but a technical expression for vigilantism, '... violence performed by persons identifying themselves with the established order and defending that order by means in violation of the formal and regular orders of the society' (256). Seland deftly draws upon recent social-scientific exegesis and study to lend profile to what seems an ugly business. After an explanatory introduction and a chapter dealing with previous research on Philo, he devotes two parallel chapters to each of his subjects, one sketching the general context and the second addressing specific texts.

The issue that drives this study is whether Philo's legal discussions—especially those in *Spec*. 1.54–57, 1.315–318, 2.252–254—reflect actual life and practices, as Goodenough proposed decades ago, or are more or less purely hypothetical discussions oriented toward (elite) ethics. Seland challenges the latter view with detailed and careful argumentation. One example of his scope is an illuminating survey of the interpretation of the Phineas-episode of Num 25 through the rabbinic period. Related to this is a study of 'zeal' (ζῆλος) and zealots. The illumination supplied by social-scientific categories helps dispel some of the quandaries produced by purely historical research about 'the Zealots'. It is revealing that, when he considers social conditions, Seland focuses mainly upon Palestine. He does not, for example, scrutinize riots in Alexandria, although

J. H. Charlesworth, 'The Son of David: Solomon and Jesus' (72–87); A. Yarbro Collins, 'Apotheosis and Resurrection' (88–100); A. Pilgaard, 'The Hellenistic *Theios Aner*—a Model for Early Christian Christology? (101–22); J. Nissen, 'The Distinctive Character of the New Testament Love Command in Relation to Hellenistic Judaism' (123–50); P. Borgen, 'Some Hebrew and Pagan Features in Philo's and Paul's Interpretation of Hagar and Ishmael' (151–64); K. G. Sandelin, 'Does Paul argue against Sacramentalism and Over-confidence in 1 Cor 10.1–14?' (165–82); P. J. Bekken, 'Paul's Use of Deut 30.12–14 in Jewish Context' (183–203); N. Hyldahl, 'Paul and Hellenistic Judaism in Corinth' (204–16); N. Willert, 'The Catalogues of Hardships in the Pauline Correspondence: Background and Function' (217–43); O. Davidsen, 'The Structural Typology of Christ: Some Modal-Semiotic Comments on the Basic Narrative of the Letter to the Romans' (244–62).

As these titles show, the main thrust of the conference was to show, by means of concrete and often quite detailed examples, how knowledge of the Jewish Diaspora background of the New Testament can help us understand it better. Three contributions focus on aspects of Philo. Peder Borgen searches for Jewish expository patterns behind Paul's celebrated allegory of Sarah and Hagar and finds himself disagreeing with C. K. Barrett's conclusion that Philo's allegories offer little assistance for its interpretation. They offer a vital clue because they show that Hagar and Ishmael are regarded as proselytes. Karl-Gustav Sandelin appeals to parallel passages in Philo to show that in 1 Cor. 10:1–14 Paul is not remonstrating against over-confidence on the part of the Corinthians, but rather warning them against idolatry and participation in pagan cults. Similarly Per Jarle Bekken looks at Paul's use of the well-known verses in Deut. 30:12–14. Parallels in Philo suggest that Paul is developing Jewish exegetical techniques, both in terms of form (interweaving of quotation and comment) and content (eschatology).

Among the remaining papers two may be specially recommended for readers of this Annual. Lars Hartmann develops some very interesting ideas in his examination of forms of biblical usage in the Alexandrian Judaic tradition prior to Philo. The Bible provided these Jews, he claims, with a frame of reference within which they could operate in their social and political lives. Nikolaus Walter asks how Hellenistic Judaism contributed to the crucial decision of early Christianity to direct its message to Gentiles as well as Jews. He takes his cue from the mention of the Hellenists in Acts 6, but argues that the position of these re-immigrants has to be seen against the broad backdrop of Diaspora Judaism in all its various facets (including Philo, who represents no more than a minority view). Walter's position can be instructively compared with the argument developed by Gregory Sterling in the previous volume (VII) of this Annual. Finally I would like to mention a Postscript to the article, in which he gives a nuanced answer to the controversial issue of possible Hellenization in the translation of the Septuaginta.

David T. Runia
Leiden University

Mireille HADAS-LEBEL, *Flavius Josephus: Eyewitness to Rome's First-Century Conquest of Judea*, Translated by Richard Miller, Macmillan, New York 1993. ISBN 0-02-541619. $20.

The two most important witnesses to Greek-speaking Judaism in the Second Temple period are Philo and Josephus. General assessments of the latter fall into distinct literary categories: some introduce a reader to scholarly appraisals of a broad range of Josephan studies,[1] others concentrate on a particular aspect,[2] and still others concentrate on the man.[3] Mireille Hadas-Lebel's *Flavius Josèphe*, now translated into English, falls into the last category. While it is impossible for a contemporary scholar to write a biography of an ancient figure by modern standards, Professor Hadas-Lebel succeeds in offering a well-rounded sketch by interweaving the exceptionally large amount of autobiographical material Josephus provides with mostly literary—rabbinic and classical—and partly archaeological information.

Professor Hadas-Lebel works through Josephus' life using his own accounts as her basis. She appropriately devotes half of the work to the events of 66-70 (chapters four-seven). The first three chapters present the young Jerusalem priest and the final chapter the historian in Rome. She includes two epilogues: the first presents his extant works except *Against Apion* which is never given adequate treatment (pp. 207-21 [cf. pp. 202-03 for her brief comments on *Against Apion*]); the second sets out the *Nachleben* of his works (pp. 223-38). The volume is designed as an introduction, not as a full-scale critical analysis. It is exceptionally well written

---

[1] H. St. J. Thackeray, *Josephus: The Man and the Historian* (1929; reprint, New York 1967) and P. Bilde, *Flavius Josephus between Jerusalem and Rome: His Life, his Works, and their Importance*, JSPSup 2 (Sheffield 1988).

[2] T. Rajak, *Josephus: The Historian and his Society* (Philadelphia 1983), which concentrates on the war; and S. Mason, *Josephus and the New Testament* (Peabody, MA 1992), which explores the importance of Josephus for the NT.

[3] R. Laquer, *Der jüdische Historiker Flavius Josphus* (Giessen 1920; reprint, Darmstadt 1970); G.A. Williamson, *The World of Josephus: The Life, Times and Works of the First Century Historian* (Toronto 1964); and S. Schwartz, *Josephus and Judean Politics*, Columbia Studies in the Classical Tradition 18 (Leiden 1990). Cf. also the novel by L. Feuchtwanger, *Josephus* (New York 1932).

and translated.¹ There are numerous helps for the beginning reader such as a résumé of Josephus (p. xi), a listing of *dramatis personae* (pp. xiii-xvi), a chronology (pp. 239-41), and five maps (pp. 243-47).

Philo appears at numerous points in the work both as an author and as a historical figure from an important Alexandrian family. One of the most interesting possibilities she raises is that Josephus' fascination with Philo's works may have led to his planned multi-volume *Customs and Causes*, to which he alluded in *Ant.* 1.25; 4.198; 20.268 (pp. 217-18).

There are some general limitations of the work which should be noted. First, the author sometimes takes controversial positions without defending them, e.g., she prefers Josephus' account of his activities in *The Jewish War* to that of the *Life* (p. 69)² and places the *Life* before *Contra Apionem* (p. 218).³ While extensive argumentation would have been out of place, she should provide some justification in the notes. Second, she accords Josephus' account of his activities more weight than many Josephan scholars would at times, e.g., she takes seriously his claim to be a child prodigy (pp. 16-18) even though this was a common literary topos.⁴ Third, there is no bibliographical aid for the novice. I assume this was the decision of the publisher since the French edition has a brief bibliography (pp. 287-88). It would have been very easy to include this and expand it with a few more English titles. Finally there are a couple of errors, e.g., James did not die in 57 (p. 27) but in 62 (as Hadas-Lebel's chronology requires [p. 239]) and the Pharisees were not part of the priestly aristocracy (p. 45 l. 8 vs. *Ant.* 20.191).

Such limitations do not, however, negate the basic contribution of the work. While a reader may not agree with all of her positions, they are defensible. Further, the work strikes a healthy stance of critical judgment of one of Judaism's most controversial figures: she is not apologetic, yet she admires Josephus for his talents and contributions. Her

---

¹ There are a couple of slips in the English, e.g., p. 132 l. 2 from bottom, 'deeply restored' = deeply respected; p. 136 l. 5 from bottom, 'Herodian'=Herodium or Herodion; p. 252 n. 3 'II Maccabeans' = 2 Maccabees.
² I presume she is following the lead of A. Pelletier, *Flavius Josèphe: Autobiographie* (Paris 1959) xvi-xviii, over against Laquer, *Der jüdische Historiker Flavius Josephus* and S. Cohen, *Josephus in Galilee and Rome: His* Vita *and Development as a Historian*, Columbia Studies in the Classical Tradition 8 (Leiden 1979).
³ The *Life* must have followed the death of Agrippa II (*Life* 354-60). The problem is that the date of Agrippa's death is disputed: Photius places it in 100 CE, but numismatic evidence ceases in 94 CE. If the former is correct, then the *Life* probably followed *Against Apion*; however, if the latter accurately attests the end of his reign and life, then *Against Apion* probably followed the *Life* which was an appendix to the *Antiquities*.
⁴ For a wide range of parallels see R. Bultmann, *The History of the Synoptic Tradition* (New York 1976) 300-01.

assessment is refreshing. It helps to make the 'biography' a work that scholars can read with pleasure and students with profit.

Gregory E. Sterling
University of Notre Dame

NEWS AND NOTES

Paris Colloque

A Colloque International on 'Philon d'Alexandrie et le langage de la philosophie' was held in Paris from 26 to 28 October 1995. The conference was organized by Prof. Carlos Lévy, Professor of Ancient Philosophy at the Université de Paris XII – Val de Marne and Director of the Centre d'études sur la philosophie hellénistique et romaine at that institution. The main theme of the conference focused on how Philo makes use of philosophical themes and terminology and whether we can agree with Nikiprowetzky's thesis that philosophy for Philo was an instrument in the service of exegesis. As the following programme of the conference makes quite clear, a busy and profitable time was had by all participants.

First day, held at the Université de Paris – Val de Marne, Créteil

C. Lévy (Paris): Ouverture du colloque
J. Riaud (Angers): Présentation des Etudes Philoniennes de V. Nikiprowetzky
M. Alexandre (Paris): Le lexique des vertus: vertus philosophiques et vertus religieuses chez Philon
R. Arnaldez (Paris): De quelques mots-clés dans la pensée de Philon*
J. Bouffartigue (Paris): La structure de l'âme chez Philon: terminologie scolastique et métaphores
M. G. Crepaldi (Padua): Admiration philosophique et admiration théologique: la valeur du θαυμάζειν dans la pensée de Philon
F. Deutsch (Angers): La 'philautie' dans l'œuvre de Philon
J. Dillon (Dublin): Ἀσώματος: aspects of incorporeality in Philo's thought
J. G. Kahn (Jerusalem): Terminologie hebraïque, terminologie grecque, à propos de quelques traités de Philon
A. Le Boulluec (Paris): La place des concepts philosophiques dans la réflexion de Philon sur le plaisir

Second day, held at the École Normale Superieure, Fontenay

C. Lévy (Paris), Ethique de la transcendance et éthique de l'immanence: le problème de l'οἰκείωσις chez Philon
J. P. Martín (Buenos Aires): Le réseau sémantique θεός-νοῦς-ἀρχή*
F. Siegert (Neuchâtel): Les métaphores ontologiques, cosmologiques et politiques dans le fragment philonien *De deo*
J. Whittaker (Newfoundland, Canada): Comment définir l'âme rationnelle?
B. Lévy (Paris): Dieu et la création du mal
C. Aslanoff (Jerusalem): Exégèse philonienne et herméneutique rabbinique
B. Besnier (Paris): A propos de la fin du *De migratione Abrahami*
J. Cazeaux (Lyon): Philon ou la tapisserie de Pénélope
B. Decharneux (Brussels): Le cheminement philonien de la parole*

Third day, held at École Normale Superieure, Rue Jourdan (Paris)

D. T. Runia (Leiden): L'exégèse philosophique et la réception de la pensée philonienne dans la tradition chrétienne
G. E. Sterling (Notre Dame): Demonology in popular religion and Colossian Christianity
G. Baechtle (Oxford): A propos de Philon et du moyen platonisme
B. Desbordes (Münster): Un exemple d'utilisation de la philosophie: la stratégie du recours à la thèse des lieux naturels
P. Graffigna (Genoa): La presence d'Héraclite dans le traité philonien *De vita Moysis**
V. Guignard (Angers): Le rapport de Philon à la philosophie grecque dans le portrait des empereurs
A. Petit (Clermont-Ferrard): Philon et la pythagorisme
C. Imbert (Paris): Philon et la logique des stoïciens
R. Radice (Milan): Le judaïsme alexandrin et la philosophie grecque: influences probables et points de contacts*
A. Michel (Paris): Philon et l'Académie.

*Professors Arnaldez, Martín and Decharneux were prevented by sickness from presenting their papers. The paper of Prof. Crepaldi was read out by Prof. F. Calabi (Pavia), that of Prof. Radice by Prof. Lévy.

The papers of the conference will be edited by Carlos Lévy and published by Brepols.

David T. Runia

Philo of Alexandria Seminar

The Philo of Alexandria Seminar of the Society of Biblical Literature met for two sessions on November 19th and 20th, 1995, in Philadelphia. The first session was devoted to 'The Influence of Philo's Mysticism on Christianity and Judaism'. The session was organized as a panel with Gregory E. Sterling presiding. There were three papers: David Winston, 'Philo's Mysticism', Brian E. Daley, S.J., 'Ecstacy and Transformation: Gregory of Nyssa on the Dynamics of Mystical Union'; and Elliot R. Wolfson, 'Traces of Philonic Doctrine in Medieval Jewish Mysticism'. Bernard McGinn responded to all three papers. The papers appear in revised form in a Special section of this Annual. David T. Runia presided over the second session, which was devoted to Philo's relationship to Judaism. There were four papers: Ellen Birnbaum, 'What Does Philo Mean by "Seeing God"? Some Methodological Considerations'; James M. Scott, 'Philo and the Restoration of Israel'; Katherine G. Evans, 'Alexander the Alabarch: Roman and Jew'; and Gregory E. Sterling, 'Recluse or Representative? Philo and Greek-Speaking Judaism Beyond Alexandria'. All four papers appeared in the *SBLSP* 34 (1995) 535-52, 553-75, 576-94, and 595-616 respectively. There was a business meeting after the second session in which reports from the editors of three major publications were presented: David T. Runia, *The Studia Philonica Annual*;

David Hay, The Studia Philonica Monograph Series; and Gregory E. Sterling, The Philo of Alexandria Commentary Series. 1995 was the final year of the Philo of Alexandria Seminar. It was most pleasing to be able to report, however, that the Society of Biblical Literature has granted the group a new three year term as the Philo of Alexandria Working Group (1996-98).

Gregory E. Sterling

Philo of Alexandria on the World Wide Web.

Among the ever increasing amount of information available on the Internet there is now also a Web page on Philo of Alexandria. Those who are interested may try out the following address:

http:/www.hivolda.no/asf/kkf/philopag.html

The purpose of the page is to present scholarly material on the web which is of relevance to the study of Philo of Alexandria in the form of a resource page for scholarly studies. The page is set up and maintained by Torrey Seland, Associate Professor in Biblical Studies at Volda College, Volda, Norway. At present it contains lists of electronically available resources for the study of Philo and a number of electronically published articles and reviews. A click on the appropriate title and these documents are called up on the screen. Prof. Seland hopes that this page may prove useful for studies of Philo and his world and be followed by other initiatives on the new electronic medium. Those interested in setting up Philo related links or presenting articles on the World Wide Web may contact him by email at ts@hivolda.no.

Prof. Seland also maintains a more general set of resource pages for Biblical studies; see http://www.hivolda.no/asf/kkf/rel-stud.html.

Another address on the World Wide Web of interest to Philo scholars is the following:

http://proffen.avh.unit.no/rel/Filon.htm

This page gives information on progress on the Philo of Alexandria Concordance project, which after many years—it was first reported in the pages of *Studia Philonica* 2 (1973) 75-76, and was discussed in depth in this journal in 2 (1990) 112-114—is now reaching completion. This reference tool differs from what is available elsewhere, for example on the TLG, in that it will be fully lemmatized, with each record referring not only to the form of the word itself, but also the dictionary form of that word. Moreover it will allow the user to see the use of the word in its context far better than other indices. More information on this project can be requested from the publisher E. J. Brill, P.O. Box 9000, 2300 PA Leiden, The Netherlands (fax 31 71 5317532) or from Kaare Fuglseth at kaafu@alfa.avh.unit.no.

David T. Runia

Adamantius: an Origenian newsletter

Philo scholars will be interested in the new initiative taken by the Italian Research Group on Origen and the Alexandrian Tradition. This group intends to publish annually a newsletter recording the activities of the group and also reporting on more general developments in Origenian studies. The newsletter has the most appropriate name of *Adamantius*, in honour of the great Church father of course, but perhaps also with a hint that the modern scholar has to be rather determined to keep abreast of the numerous developments in this area of study. The first volume of *Adamantius* was published in October 1995. It contains a limited amount of bibliographical material, including some Philonica on pp. 18–19 and valuable summaries of books and articles on Alexandrian thought on pp. 20–27. Further information on this publication can be gained from Prof. Lorenzo Perrone, Dipartimento di Filologia Classica, Via Galvani 1, 56100 Pisa, ITALY (email anchy@mbox.vol.it).

David T. Runia

NOTES ON CONTRIBUTORS

Ellen BIRNBAUM is an administrator at Harvard University, where she has also taught about the Bible and its interpreters. Her postal address is 78 Porter Road, Cambridge, MA 02140, U.S.A.; her electronic address is ellen_birnbaum@harvard.edu.

Francesca CALABI is Lecturer in the History of Ancient Philosophy at the University of Ferrara and Assistant Professor of the History of Ancient Philosophy at the University of Pavia. Her postal address is Via Marchiondi 7, 20122 Milano, ITALY (fax 39 2 58314911); her electronic address is fcalabi@imiucca.csi.unimi.it.

Caroline CARLIER is preparing a doctoral disseration at Paris-Sorbonne IV under the supervision of Monique Alexandre. Her postal address is 8 Rashba Street, Jerusalem 92265, ISRAEL; her electronic address is Caroline@www-mail.huji.ac.il.

John CAVADINI is Associate professor of Early Church and the History of Christianity at the University of Notre Dame in Indiana. His postal address is Department of Theology, University of Notre Dame, IN 46556, U.S.A.

Brian DALEY, S.J., is the Huisking Professor of Theology at the University of Notre Dame in Indiana. His postal address is Department of Theology, University of Notre Dame, Notre Dame, IN 46556, U.S.A.

Michael S. DRISCOLL is Assistant professor of Theology at the University of Notre Dame in Indiana. His postal address is Department of Theology, University of Notre Dame, Notre Dame, IN 46556, U.S.A.; his electronic address is Driscoll.7@nd.edu.

Kathy L. GACA is currently the Hannah Seeger Davis Post-doctoral Fellow in Hellenic Studies at Princeton University. Her postal address is Princeton University, Program in Hellenic Studies, Joseph Henry House, Princeton, NJ, 08544-1014, U.S.A.

Albert-Cees GELJON teaches classical languages at the Christelijke Scholengemeenschap Oude Hoven, Gorinchem, and is a Junior Researcher for the Netherlands Organization for the Advancement of Research

(N.W.O.). His postal address is Ijsbaan 175, 4206 VD Gorinchem, THE NETHERLANDS; his electronic address is geljon@rulcri.leidenuniv.nl.

David M. HAY is McCabe Professor of Religion, Coe College, Cedar Rapids, Iowa. His postal address is Department of Religion and Philosophy, Coe College, Cedar Rapids IA 52402, U.S.A.; his electronic address is dhay@coe.edu.

Annewies VAN DEN HOEK is Lecturer in Greek and Latin at the Harvard Divinity School, Harvard University, and also Fellow for Research at the Boston Museum of Fine Arts. Her postal address is 26 Common Street, Dedham, MA 02026, U.S.A.; her electronic address is ahoek @div.harvard.edu.

Jose Pablo MARTÍN is Professor of History of Philosophy in the Universidad del Salvador, Buenos Aires. His postal address is Azcuenaga 1090, 1663 San Miguel, ARGENTINA; his electronic address is: martin@ unisar.edu.ar.

Richard I. PERVO is Professor of New Testament and Patristics at Seabury-Western Theological Seminary in Illinois. His postal address is Seabury-Western Theological Seminary, 2122 Sheridan Rd., Evanston, IL 60201, U.S.A.

Roberto RADICE is Lecturer in Ancient Philosophy at the Sacred Heart University, Milan. His postal address is Via XXV Aprile 4, 21016 Luino, ITALY; his electronic address is rradice@galactica.it.

James R. ROYSE is a software engineer specializing in real-time financial applications. His postal address is 2200 31st Avenue, San Francisco CA 94116, U.S.A. A current email address can be obtained from the editor.

David T. RUNIA is Professor of Ancient and Medieval Philosophy at Leiden University, and also C. J. de Vogel Professor Extraordinarius in Ancient Philosophy at Utrecht University. His postal address is Rijnsburgerweg 116, 2333 AE Leiden, THE NETHERLANDS; his electronic address is runia@rulcri.leidenuniv.nl.

Karl-Gustav SANDELIN is Professor of New Testament Exegetics, Åbo Akademi University, FINLAND. His postal address is Teologiska fakulteten vid Åbo Akademi, Biskopsg. 16, 20500 Åbo, FINLAND; his electronic address is Karl-Gustav.Sandelin@abo.fi.

NOTES ON CONTRIBUTORS

David SATRAN is Senior Lecturer in the Department of Comparative Religion, Hebrew University, Jerusalem. His postal address is Department of Comparative Religion, Hebrew University, Mt. Scopus, Jerusalem 91905, ISRAEL; his electronic address is Satran@hum.huji.ac.il.

Gregory E. STERLING is Associate Professor in New Testament, Department of Theology, University of Notre Dame. His postal address is Department of Theology, University of Notre Dame, Notre Dame IN 46556, U.S.A.; his electronic address is gregory.e.sterling.1@nd.edu.

Fred STRICKERT is Associate Professor of Religion at Wartburg College, Waverly, Iowa. His postal address is Department of Religion and Philosophy, Wartburg College, Waverly, IA 50677, U.S.A; his electronic address is Strickert@Wartburg.edu.

Abraham TERIAN is Professor of Religion and Philosophy at Sterling College. His postal address is Department of Religion and Philosophy, Sterling College, Sterling, Kansas 67579, U. S. A.

Nikolaus WALTER is Professor of New Testament, Faculty of Theology, Friedrich-Schiller University of Jena, Germany. His postal address is Wilhelm-Wagner-Straße 7, 06618 Naumburg (S), DEUTSCHLAND.

John WHITTAKER is Professor of Classics at the Memorial University of Newfoundland, St. Johns, CANADA. His postal address is Department of Classics, Memorial University of Newfoundland, St. Johns, CANADA A1C 5S7 (fax 709 737-4569).

David WINSTON is Emeritus Professor of Hellenistic and Jewish Studies, Graduate Theological Union, Berkeley. His postal address is 1220 Grizzly Peak, Berkeley CA 94708, U.S.A.

Elliot R. WOLFSON is Professor of Hebrew and Judaic Studies and Director of Religious Studies, New York University. His postal address is Skirball Department, New York University, 51 Washington Square South, New York, N.Y. 10003, U.S.A; his electronic address is wolfsn@is2.nyu.edu.

Dieter ZELLER is Professor für Religionswissenschaft des Hellenismus at the Johannes-Gutenberg University of Mainz and Honorar-Professor at the Ruprecht-Karls University of Heidelberg. His postal address is Schillerweg 4, 6228 Eltville (Erbach), DEUTSCHLAND.

INSTRUCTIONS TO CONTRIBUTORS

Authors of articles and book reviews in *The Studia Philonica Annual* are asked to conform to the following guidelines.

1. *The Studia Philonica Annual* accepts articles for publication in the area of Hellenistic Judaism, with special emphasis on Philo and his *Umwelt*. Articles on Josephus will be given consideration if they focus on his relation to Judaism and classical culture (and not on primarily historical subjects). The languages in which the articles may be published are English, French and German. Translations from Italian or Dutch into English can be arranged at a modest cost to the author.

2. Since the Annual is being produced with a minimum of secretarial assistance, the editors request with some insistence that all articles and reviews be submitted on microdiskette. In the case of longer articles, contributions submitted as typescript will only be accepted by way of exception. For the formatting of submitted material the editors have the following order of preference:

(a) Apple Macintosh, formatted preferably in MS-Word, using SMK Greek (or SuperGreek) and SuperHebrew;

(b) MS-DOS on formatted in MS-Word or Word Perfect. Users of Nota Bene are requested to submit a copy exported to DCA format.

In all cases it is **imperative** that a hard copy accompany the text on diskette, and that authors gives full details of the word processor used. No handwritten Greek or Hebrew can be accepted. Authors are requested not to vocalize their Hebrew (except when necessary) and to keep their use of this language to a reasonable minimum. It should always be borne in mind that not all readers of the Annual can be expected to read Greek or Hebrew. Transliteration is permissible for incidental terms.

3. With regard to the citation of scholarly references the Annual will henceforth subscribe to the conventions embodied in the following examples (note (i) that no publishers' names are given, (ii) for articles single quotation marks are used, and (iii) that books and journals are italicized, series are not):

A. Mendelson, *Secular Education in Philo of Alexandria,* Monographs of the Hebrew Union College 7 (Cincinnati 1982) 15–27.

Y. Amir, 'The Transference of Greek Allegories to Biblical Motifs in Philo', in F. E. Greenspahn, E. Hilgert, B. L. Mack (edd.), *Nourished with Peace: Studies in Hellenistic Judaism in Memory of Samuel Sandmel,* Scholars Press Homage Series 9 (Chico, California 1984) 15–25.

J. P. Martín, 'El encuentro de exégesis y filosofia en Filón Alejandrino', *Revista Biblica* 46 (1984) 199–211.
Mendelson *op. cit.* (n. 0) 23ff.
Amir, *art. cit.* (n.0) 16–18 **or** Martín 'El encuentro' 199–201.

It is also possible to give references by author and date in the footnotes only, with full details presented in a bibliography at the end of the article (see the example on pp. 295–319 of volume 3). Contributors are asked to follow these guidelines very closely, since mss. that deviate significantly cannot be accepted.

For the abbreviations to be used, see further below. A sound guide to the way that Philonic scholarship should be cited will be found in R. Radice and D. T. Runia, *Philo of Alexandria: an Annotated Bibliography 1937–1986*, VCSup 8 (Leiden 1988). Note that with regard to the use of capitals in citing English references, both English-American and continental European conventions are permissible.

4. It is suggested that the following abbreviations be used (this **replaces** the guidelines set out in *SPh* 1 (1971) 92–96, 2 (1972) 77–80).

(a) Philonic treatises are to be abbreviated according to the following list. Numeration is according to Cohn and Wendland's edition, using Arabic numbers only (e.g. *Spec.* 4.123). Note that *De Providentia* should be cited according to Aucher's edition, and not the LCL translation of the fragments by F. H. Colson.

Abr.	*De Abrahamo*
Aet.	*De aeternitate mundi*
Agr.	*De agricultura*
Anim.	*De animalibus*
Cher.	*De Cherubim*
Contempl.	*De vita contemplativa*
Conf.	*De confusione linguarum*
Congr.	*De congressu eruditionis gratia*
Decal.	*De Decalogo*
Deo	*De Deo*
Det.	*Quod deterius potiori insidiari soleat*
Deus	*Quod Deus sit immutabilis*
Ebr.	*De ebrietate*
Flacc.	*In Flaccum*
Fug.	*De fuga et inventione*
Gig.	*De gigantibus*
Her.	*Quis rerum divinarum heres sit*
Hypoth.	*Hypothetica*
Ios.	*De Iosepho*
Leg. 1–3	*Legum allegoriae* I, II, III
Legat.	*Legatio ad Gaium*
Migr.	*De migratione Abrahami*

Mos. 1–2	De vita Moysis I, II
Mut.	De mutatione nominum
Opif.	De opificio mundi
Plant.	De plantatione
Post.	De posteritate Caini
Praem.	De praemiis et poenis, De exsecrationibus
Prob.	Quod omnis probus liber sit
Prov. 1–2	De Providentia I, II
QE 1–2	Quaestiones et solutiones in Exodum I, II
QG 1–4	Quaestiones et solutiones in Genesim I, II, III, IV
Sacr.	De sacrificiis Abelis et Caini
Sobr.	De sobrietate
Somn. 1–2	De somniis I, II
Spec. 1–4	De specialibus legibus I, II, III, IV
Virt.	De virtutibus

(b) Standard works of Philonic scholarship are abbreviated:

Aucher	*Philonis Judaei sermones tres hactenus inediti* (Venice 1822), *Philonis Judaei paralipomena* (Venice 1826)
G-G	H. L. Goodhart and E. R. Goodenough, 'A General Bibliography of Philo Judaeus', in E. R. Goodenough, *The Politics of Philo Judaeus: Practice and Theory* (New Haven 1938, reprinted Hildesheim 1967²) 125–321
PCH	*Philo von Alexandria: die Werke in deutscher Übersetzung*, edited by L. Cohn, I. Heinemann et al., 7 vols. (Breslau, Berlin 1909–64)
PCW	*Philonis Alexandrini opera quae supersunt*, ediderunt L. Cohn, P. Wendland, S. Reiter, 6 vols. (Berlin 1896–1915)
PLCL	*Philo in Ten Volumes (and Two Supplementary Volumes)*, English translation by F. H. Colson, G. H. Whitaker (and R. Marcus), 12 vols., Loeb Classical Library (London 1929–62)
PAPM	*Les œuvres de Philon d'Alexandrie*, French translation under the general editorship of R. Arnaldez, J. Pouilloux, C. Mondésert (Paris 1961–)
R-R	R. Radice and D. T. Runia, *Philo of Alexandria: an Annotated Bibliography 1937–1986*, VCSup 8 (Leiden 1988)
SPh	*Studia Philonica*
SPhA	*The Studia Philonica Annual*

(c) Biblical books, Pseudepigraphical, Qumran, Rabbinic and Gnostic literature are to be abbreviated as recommended in the 'Instructions to Contributors' in the *Society of Biblical Literature Membership Directory and Handbook 1994*, pp. 223–240 (copies available on request). Note that biblical books are not italicized and that between chapter and verse a colon is placed (placement of a full stop after the abbreviation is optional, provided the author is consistent). Authors writing in German or French should follow their own conventions for biblical citations.

(d) Classical and Patristic authors should be cited in the manner recommended by the three Oxford lexica:

H. G. Liddell, R. Scott , H. S. Jones (edd.), *A Greek-English Lexicon* (Oxford 1940^9);
P. G. W. Glare (ed.), *The Oxford Latin Dictionary* (Oxford 1982);
G. W. H. Lampe (ed.), *A Patristic Greek Lexicon* (Oxford 1961).

Preferred abbreviations for Josephus, however, are *AJ*, *BJ*, *c. Ap.*, and *Vita*, but English abbreviations (*Antiquities*, *War*, etc.) are permitted. Once again consistency is the first requirement.

(e) Journals, monograph series, source collections and standard reference works are to be be abbreviated in accordance with the recommendation listed in the 'Instructions to Contributors' in the *Society of Biblical Literature Membership Directory and Handbook 1994*, pp. 223–240. The following list contains a selection of the more important abbreviations (adding a few abbreviations of Classical and philosophical journals and standard reference books not furnished in the list mentioned above.

ABD	*The Anchor Bible Dictionary* , 6 vols. (New York etc. 1992)
AC	*L'Antiquité Classique*
ACW	Ancient Christian Writers
AGJU	Arbeiten zur Geschichte des antiken Judentums und des Urchristentums
AJPh	*American Journal of Philology*
AJSL	*American Journal of Semitic Languages*
ALGHJ	Arbeiten zur Literatur und Geschichte des hellenistischen Judentums
ANRW	*Aufstieg und Niedergang der römischen Welt*
AP	*L'Année Philologique (founded by Marouzeau)*
BAGD	*A Greek-English Lexicon of the New Testament and other Early Christian literature*, edited by W. Bauer, W. F. Arndt, F. W. Gingrich, F. W. Danker (Chicago 1979^2)
BDB	*Hebrew and English lexicon of the Old Testament*, edited by F. Brown, S. R. Driver, C. A. Briggs (Oxford 1952)
BibOr	Bibliotheca Orientalis
BJRL	*Bulletin of the John Rylands Library*
BJS	Brown Judaic Studies
BZAW	Beihefte zur Zeitschrift für die alttestamentliche Wissenschaft
BZNW	Beihefte zur Zeitschrift für die neutestamentliche Wissenschaft
BZRGG	Beihefte zur Zeitschrift für Religions- und Geistesgeschichte
CAH	*The Cambridge Ancient History*, edited by J. B. Bury *et al.*, 16 vols. (Cambridge 1923–)
CBQ	*The Catholic Biblical Quarterly*
CBQMS	The Catholic Biblical Quarterly. Monograph Series
CChr	Corpus Christianorum, Turnhout

CIG	*Corpus Inscriptionum Graecarum*, edited by A. Boeckh, 4 vols. in 8 (Berlin 1828–77)
CIJ	*Corpus Inscriptionum Judaicarum*, edited by J. B. Frey, 2 vols. (Rome 1936–52)
CIL	*Corpus Inscriptionum Latinarum* (Berlin 1862–)
CIS	*Corpus Inscriptionum Semiticarum* (Paris 1881–1962)
CP	*Classical Philology*
CPJ	*Corpus Papyrorum Judaicarum*, ed. by V. Tcherikover and A. Fuks, 3 vols. (Cambrige Mass. 1957–64)
CQ	*The Classical Quarterly*
CR	*The Classical Review*
CRINT	Compendia Rerum Iudaicarum ad Novum Testamentum
CPG	*Clavis Patrum Graecorum*, edited by M. Geerard, 5 vols. (Turnhout 1974–87)
CPL	*Clavis Patrum Latinorum*, edited by E. Dekkers (Turnhout 1954)
CSCO	Corpus Scriptorum Christianorum Orientalium
DA	Dissertation Abstracts
DBSup	*Dictionnaire de la Bible*, Supplément (Paris 1928–)
DSpir	*Dictionnaire de Spiritualité*
EncJud	*Encyclopaedia Judaica*, 16 vols. (Jerusalem 1972)
EPRO	Études préliminaires aux religions orientales dans l'Empire romain
FrGH	*Fragmente der Griechische Historiker*, edited by F. Jacoby
GCS	Die griechischen christlichen Schriftsteller, Leipzig
GLAJJ	M. Stern, *Greek and Latin authors on Jews and Judaism*, 3 vols. (Jerusalem 1974–1984)
GRBS	*Greek, Roman and Byzantine Studies*
HKNT	Handkommentar zum Neuen Testament, Tübingen
HNT	Handbuch zum Neuen Testament, Tübingen
HR	*History of Religions*
HThR	*Harvard Theological Review*
HUCA	*Hebrew Union College Annual*
JAAR	*Journal of the American Academy of Religion*
JAOS	*Journal of the American Oriental Society*
JbAC	*Jahrbuch für Antike und Christentum*
JBL	*Journal of Biblical Literature*
JHI	*Journal of the History of Ideas*
JHS	*The Journal of Hellenic Studies*
JJS	*The Journal of Jewish Studies*
JQR	*The Jewish Quarterly Review*
JR	*The Journal of Religion*
JRS	*The Journal of Roman Studies*
JSHRZ	*Jüdische Schriften aus hellenistisch-römischer Zeit*
JSJ	*Journal for the Study of Judaism (in the Persian, Hellenistic and Roman Period)*
JSNT	*Journal for the Study of the New Testament*
JSNTSup	Journal for the Study of the New Testament. Supplement Series
JSOT	*Journal for the Study of the Old Testament*
JSP	*Journal for the Study of the Pseudepigrapha and Related Literature*
JSS	*Journal of Semitic Studies*
JThS	*The Journal of Theological Studies*

KB	L. Koehler and W. Baumgartner, *Lexicon in Veteris Testamenti libros*, 3 vols. (Leiden 1967–83³)
KJ	*Kirjath Sepher*
LCL	Loeb Classical Library
LSJ	*A Greek-English lexicon*, edited by H. G. Liddell, R. Scott, H. S. Jones (Oxford 1940⁹)
MGWJ	*Monatsschrift für Geschichte und Wissenschaft des Judentums*
Mnem	*Mnemosyne*
NCE	*New Catholic Encyclopedia*, 15 vols (New York 1967)
NHS	Nag Hammadi Studies
NovT	*Novum Testamentum*
NTA	*New Testament Abstracts*
NTOA	Novum Testamentum et Orbis Antiquus
NTS	*New Testament Studies*
OLD	*The Oxford Latin dictionary*, edited by P. G. W. Glare (Oxford 1982)
OTP	J. H. Charlesworth (ed.), *The Old Testament Pseudepigrapha*, 2 vols. (New York-London 1983–85)
PAAJR	*Proceedings of the American Academy for Jewish Research*
PAL	*Philon d'Alexandrie: Lyon 11–15 Septembre 1966* (Paris 1967)
PG	Patrologiae cursus completus: series Graeca, edited by J. P. Migne, 162 vols. (Paris 1857–1912)
PGL	*A Patristic Greek lexicon*, ed. by G. W. H. Lampe (Oxford 1961)
PhilAnt	Philosophia Antiqua
PL	Patrologiae cursus completus: series Latina, edited by J. P. Migne, 221 vols. (Paris 1844–64)
PW	Pauly-Wissowa-Kroll, *Real-Encyclopaedie der classischen Altertumswissenschaft*, Stuttgart
PWSup	Supplement to PW
RAC	*Reallexikon für Antike und Christentum*
RB	*Revue Biblique*
REA	*Revue des Études Anciennes*
REArm	*Revue des Études Arméniennes*
REAug	*Revue des Études Augustiniennes*
REG	*Revue des Études Grecques*
REJ	*Revue des Études Juives*
REL	*Revue des Études Latines*
RGG	*Die Religion in Geschichte und Gegenwart*, 7 vols. (Tübingen 1957–65³)
RhM	*Rheinisches Museum für Philologie*
RQ	*Revue de Qumran*
RSR	*Revue des Sciences Religieuses*
SB	H. L. Strack and P. Billerbeck, *Kommentar zum Neuen Testament aus Talmud und Midrasch*, 6 vols. in 7 (Munich 1922–61)
SBLDS	Society of Biblical Literature. Dissertation Series
SBLMS	Society of Biblical Literature. Monograph Series
SBLSPS	Society of Biblical Literature. Seminar Papers Series
SC	Sources Chrétiennes
Sem	*Semitica*
SHJP	E. Schürer, *The history of the Jewish people in the age of Jesus Christ*, revised edition, 3 vols. in 4 (Edinburgh 1973–87)
SJLA	Studies in Judaism in Late Antiquity

SNTSMS	Society for New Testament Studies. Monograph Series
SR	*Studies in Religion*
StUNT	Studien zur Umwelt des Neuen Testaments
SVF	Stoicorum veterum fragmenta, edited by J. von Arnim
TDNT	*Theological Dictionary of the New Testament*, 10 vols. (Grand Rapids 1964–76)
THKNT	Theologischer Handkommentar zum Neuen Testament, Berlin
TRE	*Theologische Realenzyklopädie*, Berlin
TSAJ	Texte und Studien zum Antike Judentum
TU	Texte und Untersuchungen zur Geschichte der altchristlichen Literatur, Berlin
TWNT	*Theologisches Wörterbuch zum Neuen Testament*, 10 vols. (Stuttgart 1933–79)
VC	*Vigiliae Christianae*
VCSup	Supplements to Vigiliae Christianae
VT	*Vetus Testamentum*
WUNT	Wissenschaftliche Untersuchungen zum Neuen Testament
ZAW	*Zeitschrift für die alttestamentliche Wissenschaft*
ZKG	*Zeitschrift für Kirchengeschichte*
ZKTh	*Zeitschrift für Katholische Theologie*
ZNW	*Zeitschrift für die neutestamentliche Wissenschaft*
ZRGG	*Zeitschrift für Religions- und Geistesgeschichte*

www.ingramcontent.com/pod-product-compliance
Lightning Source LLC
Chambersburg PA
CBHW031709230426
43668CB00006B/165